BEGINNING MANDARIN CHINESE CHARACTERS

Learn 300 Characters and 1200 Chinese Words Through Interactive Activities and Exercises

Haohsiang Liao and Kang Zhou

TUTTLE Publishing

Tokyo | Rutland, Vermont | Singapore

ABOUT TUTTLE
"Books to Span the East and West"

Our core mission at Tuttle Publishing is to create books which bring people together one page at a time. Tuttle was founded in 1832 in the small New England town of Rutland, Vermont (USA). Our fundamental values remain as strong today as they were then—to publish best-in-class books informing the English-speaking world about the countries and peoples of Asia. The world has become a smaller place today and Asia's economic, cultural and political influence has expanded, yet the need for meaningful dialogue and information about this diverse region has never been greater. Since 1948, Tuttle has been a leader in publishing books on the cultures, arts, cuisines, languages and literatures of Asia. Our authors and photographers have won numerous awards and Tuttle has published thousands of books on subjects ranging from martial arts to paper crafts. We welcome you to explore the wealth of information available on Asia at **www.tuttlepublishing.com**.

Published by Tuttle Publishing, an imprint of
Periplus Editions (HK) Ltd

www.tuttlepublishing.com

PHOTOS Front cover Jacob Lund/Shutterstock.com; **Pp14** maoyunping/Shutterstock.com; **22** Stuart Jenner/Shutterstock.com; **30** Rainer Lesniewski/Shutterstock.com; **38** imtmphoto/Shutterstock.com; **45** Featureflash Photo Agency/Shutterstock.com; **46** Kit8.net/Shutterstock.com; **56** photastic/Shutterstock.com; **64** Chayasit Fangem/Shutterstock.com; **72** tomertu/Shutterstock.com; **80** miwa-in-oz/Shutterstock.com; **81** TungCheung/Shutterstock.com; **89** Freer/Shutterstock.com; **99** makiwang/Shutterstock.com; **107** Tomasz Bidermann/Shutterstock.com; **114** Katerina Davidenko/Shutterstock.com; **115** By LEE SNIDER PHOTO IMAGES/Shutterstock.com; **123** Artem Shadrin/Shutterstock.com; **124** aphotostory/Shutterstock.com; **132** dolphfyn/Shutterstock.com; **140** Photobank/Shutterstock.com; **143** Artwell/Shutterstock.com; **152** michaeljung/Shutterstock.com; **161** Rawpixel.com/Shutterstock.com; **170** Lorelyn Medina/Shutterstock.com; **179** Iakov Filimonov/Shutterstock.com

ISBN: 978-0-8048-4507-6

Distributed by

North America, Latin America & Europe
Tuttle Publishing
364 Innovation Drive
North Clarendon, VT 05759-9436 U.S.A.
Tel: 1 (802) 773-8930; Fax: 1 (802) 773-6993
info@tuttlepublishing.com; www.tuttlepublishing.com

Japan
Tuttle Publishing
Yaekari Building 3rd Floor
5-4-12 Osaki
Shinagawa-ku
Tokyo 141 0032
Tel: (81) 3 5437-0171; Fax: (81) 3 5437-0755
sales@tuttle.co.jp; www.tuttle.co.jp

Asia Pacific
Berkeley Books Pte. Ltd.
61 Tai Seng Avenue, #02-12
Singapore 534167
Tel: (65) 6280-1330; Fax: (65) 6280-6290
inquiries@periplus.com.sg; www.periplus.com

20 19 18 10 9 8 7 6 5 4 3 2 1
Printed in Singapore 1809MP

How to Download the Audio and Printable Flashcards.

1. Make sure you have an Internet connection.
2. Type the URL below into your web browser.

http://www.tuttlepublishing.com/beginning-mandarin-chinese-characters-downloadable-content

For support, you can email us at info@tuttlepublishing.com.

Contents

LESSON 15

Weather and climate (II)

LESSON 16

Chinese language learning

LESSON 17

My Chinese class

LESSON 18

A typical day

LESSON 19

Visiting a friend's home (I)

LESSON 20

Visiting a friend's home (II)

Introduction

A brief history of Chinese characters

The official writing system of Chinese language comprises characters. A character is called **zì** 字 in Chinese, so Chinese characters are called **Zhōngguó zì** 中国字 or **Hànzì** 汉字. Each character corresponds to one syllable. For example, the term **Zhōngguó** (China) has two syllables (**Zhōng** and **guó**), so it contains two characters. **Zhōng** is written as 中, **guó** is written as 国, so **Zhōngguó** is written as 中国.

The history of the earliest set of Chinese characters in comparatively full forms dates back to 1200–1500 BC, when they were used on oracle bones. These characters are called **Jiăgŭwén** 甲骨文 (oracle bone inscriptions). Since then, Chinese characters have gone through a few significant evolutions in forms, and the characters used today are based on **Kăishū** 楷书 (Regular Script), the script that has served as the standard for writing since the end of Han Dynasty (206 BC–220 AD).

Scholars have not come to a conclusion about the total number of Chinese characters, but the most authoritative dictionaries include about 50,000. This number may seem intimidating to learners of the Chinese language, but the good news is that less than 4000 among these 50,000 are in common use. As a matter of fact, if you know 1000 to 1500 characters, you can already read simple Chinese stories. Being able to recognize 2500 to 3000 characters will enable you to read Chinese newspapers and most books.

In modern times, a romanization system has been developed to teach school children and foreigners how to pronounce the characters. This system was mainly developed by the Mainland Chinese government in late 1950s and is called **Hànyŭ Pīnyīn** 汉语拼音 (often referred to as **Pīnyīn** 拼音). While other systems of romanization exist, **Pīnyīn** has become the standard method of writing Mandarin Chinese phonetically in Mainland China and to some extent in Taiwan. **Pīnyīn** has also been widely adopted not only for educational purposes, but for inputting Chinese characters into computers and mobile phones.

In this book we introduced 15 characters in each lesson, 300 characters in total and an additional 25 characters in the Appendix. These are the most important basic Chinese characters you need to know if you travel or live in China, along with 1,200 closely-related vocabulary and phrases. It presents the characters in a series of 20 easy lessons—giving clear pronunciations and English definitions for each character along with a writing guide showing you how the character is written.

Formation of Chinese characters

Chinese characters are formed in six ways:

	Formation	English	Examples and Explanations
1.	**Xiàngxíngzì** 象形字	Pictographs	日 **rì** (sun) 川 **chuān** (river) The shape of the character 日 resembles the sun. Similarly, 川 resembles a river.
2.	**Zhǐshìzì** 指事字	Simple Ideographs	二 **èr** (two)—two lines represent "two." 中 **zhōng** (middle)—the line passing through the middle of the box reveals the meaning of the character.
3.	**Huìyìzì** 会意字	Compound Ideographs	休 **xiū** (rest) 森 **sēn** (forest) The left component 亻 of 休 means "person" and the right component 木 means "tree." So 休 can be understood as "a person leaning on a tree," namely, "to rest." Three trees 木 together form a forest: 森.
4.	**Xíngshēngzì** 形声字	Semantic-Phonetic Compounds	饭 **fàn** (food) 请 **qǐng** (invite) These consist of a semantic component and a phonetic component. The semantic component, usually on the left-hand side, reveals the meaning or category of the character. The phonetic component, usually on the right-hand side, gives you a hint of the sound of the character. The left component 饣 of 饭 is a semantic component meaning "food-related." The right component 反 is pronounced as **fǎn**, which sounds similar to the character 饭 **fàn**. Similarly, the left component 讠 of 请 is a semantic component meaning "speech-related." The right component 青 is pronounced as **qǐng**, which sounds similar to the character 请 **qǐng**.
5.	**Zhuǎnzhùzì** 转注字	Mutually Explanatory Characters	考 **kǎo** (test; investigate) 老 **lǎo** (old; aged) These two characters were once the same character, but have diverged over the centuries to have slightly different forms and pronunciations, and different meanings.. **Zhuǎnzhùzì** are smallest in percentage of Chinese characters.
6.	**Jiǎjièzì** 假借字	Borrowed Characters	令 **lìng** (command) 长 **zhǎng** (elder) The original meaning of 令 is "command." Later it was used to form compounds such as 县令 (**xiànlìng**: county magistrate), thus giving it the added meaning of "magistrate." Similarly, the original meaning of 长 is "elder." Later it was used to form compounds such as 县长 (**xiànzhǎng**: county's head commissioner).

Some learners of Chinese will be surprised to find that the majority of Chinese characters are **Xíngshēngzì** 形声字, and not **Xiàngxíngzì** 象形字. That means most Chinese characters are not pictures; instead, they are composed of one semantic component and one phonetic component. The semantic component refers to the meaning or category of the character, while the phonetic component reveals what the character may sound like.

Simplified characters vs. traditional characters

The history of simplification of Chinese characters has been a long one. As mentioned above, Chinese characters have gone through a few significant evolutions in forms from **Jiǎgǔwén** 甲骨文 (oracle bone inscriptions) to **Kǎishū** 楷书 (Regular Script) and those significant evolutions for the most part involved simplification in form. For instance, the key difference between **Kǎishū** 楷书 (Regular Script) and its predecessor **Lìshū** 隶书 (Clerical script) is that **Kǎishū** 楷书 are thinner and simpler than **Lìshū** 隶书. Compare the character **jù** 懼 (to fear) in both scripts:

Lìshū 隶书 **Kǎishū** 楷书

Two forms of Chinese characters are in use in contemporary Chinese-speaking societies: Mainland China has adopted simplified characters (**Jiǎntǐzì** 简体字), while Taiwan and Hong Kong use traditional characters (**Fántǐzì** 繁体字). Traditional characters inherit the long history of the Chinese writing system whereas simplified characters promulgated and standardized by the Chinese government beginning in the 1950s in an effort to increase literacy.

The character simplification movements by the Chinese government in the 1950s and 1960s have affected a significant number of traditional characters, but the majority of novice-level characters remain intact. Take a look at the following commonly used 25 characters:

Traditional Character	Simplified Character	Pinyin	English
一	一	**yī**	one
二	二	**èr**	two
三	三	**sān**	three
四	四	**sì**	four
五	五	**wǔ**	five
六	六	**liù**	six
七	七	**qī**	seven
八	八	**bā**	eight
九	九	**jiǔ**	nine
十	十	**shí**	ten
百	百	**bǎi**	hundred
千	千	**qiān**	thousand
元	元	**yuán**	Chinese dollars
你	你	**nǐ**	you
我	我	**wǒ**	I; me
他	他	**tā**	he; him
她	她	**tā**	she; her
是	是	**shì**	be
謝	谢	**xiè**	thank
中	中	**zhōng**	middle
美	美	**měi**	pretty; beautiful
國	国	**guó**	nation; country
人	人	**rén**	people
歲	岁	**suì**	years of age
好	好	**hǎo**	good

Among these 25 characters, only three are simplified: 謝 = 谢, 國 = 国, and 歲 = 岁.

These simplifications come with rules. For instance, 謝 is simplified by having its left semantic component 言 being replaced with 讠, which resembles its cursive form in calligraphy.

Since the simplified characters did not gain official recognition until the 1950s in Mainland China, most original signs at historical sites, famous restaurants, and leading newspapers were still written in traditional characters. In Hong Kong and Taiwan, due to increasing interactions with Mainland China or simply for the sake of saving time, you will also encounter simplified characters. As learners of Chinese, you should aim to be able to read both versions of the characters, but choose one version in writing, as most Chinese intellectuals do.

In this volume, *Beginning Mandarin Chinese Characters*, all characters are introduced in their simplified forms. Systematic exposure to traditional characters will be conducted in the next volume, *Intermediate Mandarin Chinese Characters*.

Basic concepts of Chinese written texts

Space

Unlike English, words in a Chinese sentence do not have a space between them. For example, a sentence such as "I am American" is written without a space between the words "I" (我), "am" (是), and "American" (美国人). Instead of being written "我 是 美 国 人" it is written "我是美国人." However, you can use a comma (,) to separate sentence elements, and end a sentence with a small circle (。) or a question mark (?) depending on the nature of the sentence.

Layout

Chinese texts can be presented in three ways: (1) horizontally from left to right, (2) horizontally from right to left and (3) vertically from top to down.

Take a look at how the name of the book **Táiběirén** 台北人 (Taipei people) is presented in three different covers. The picture on the left represents the majority of how Chinese texts are written today: horizontally, from left to right (i.e. 台北人). In books or newspapers, you will likely encounter texts presented vertically, such as the picture in the middle. Occasionally, you will also see texts written horizontally from right to left, as they would do traditionally, as in the picture on the right (臺 is the traditional form for the character 台).

In the same vein, the author's name, **Bái Xiānyǒng** 白先勇, is written from left to right in the picture on the left, from top to down in the middle, and from right to left in the picture on the right.

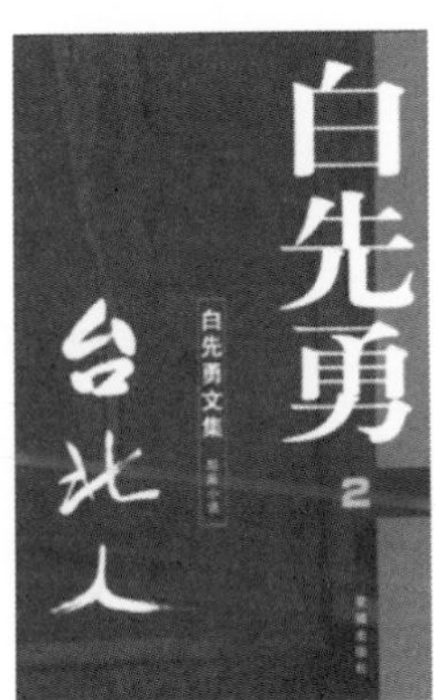

Nowadays, due to the standardization of electronic devices, Chinese texts in the emails, text messages, or MS Word documents are all typed horizontally from left to right.

Learner's Guide

Learning objectives

In this book, you are going to learn 300 useful Chinese characters by theme, spread out in 20 lessons. With these 300 characters, you will:

- master the core Chinese characters needed for basic conversations and authentic language situations.
- become familiar with the characters required for the HSK (**Hànyǔ Shuǐpíng Kǎoshì** 汉语水平考试 *Chinese Proficiency Test*) Levels 1 and 2.

To help you achieve these goals, this book provides a systematic introduction to the basic Chinese characters. Each lesson includes:

- a warm-up narrative to show you how these characters are grouped together under the theme.
- each character's pronunciation, meaning, radical, stroke order, and number of strokes.
- example sentences to show how each Chinese character is used in context.
- helpful writing practice guides to teach you how to write each character.
- useful review exercises to enhance your ability to use these characters.
- review exercises to give you opportunities to practice character recognition, vocabulary usage, and language production.

Moreover, after five lessons there are section reviews which solidify your learning by providing a variety of exercises.

How to use the materials

Each lesson contains the following components:

- Introduction
- Warm up
- Vocabulary
- New Characters
- Individual Character Explanation
- Exercises

Below are the step-to-step explanations for each component with illustrations.

Introduction provides useful background information to orient learners to the topic of the lesson.

LESSON 12

Where is the bank? 这儿有银行吗?

1. Introduction

There is a Chinese joke that goes that an international student arrived in China after one year of Chinese language study in his home country. One day, he asked his Chinese friend what the characters 很行 (**hěn xíng**: capable) meant, as he frequently saw the sign 中国很行 (**Zhōngguó hěn xíng**: China is capable) on the street. It turned out that what he actually saw was the sign for the Bank of China 中国银行 (**Zhōngguó yínháng**); he misinterpreted 银行 (**yínháng**: bank) as 很行 (**hěn xíng**: capable).

The more Chinese characters you learn, the more similarities you will find between some of them. You will also discover that, a number of Chinese characters have more than one pronunciations, such as 行 (**xíng** or **háng**). Do attend to this along your course of Chinese studies.

Warm up provides a narrative to show how the new characters introduced in the lesson are grouped together under the theme, followed by two or three reading comprehension questions.

2. Warm up

Read the passage below and answer the questions using Chinese characters.

钱小姐：请问，去中国银行怎么走？远不远？
王小姐：很近，过了路口往前走是一个公园，银行在公园的旁边。
钱小姐：谢谢您。
王小姐：今天是星期天，银行不开门。
钱小姐：是啊，今天是星期天，不是星期一。谢谢您！
王小姐：不客气。再见！

1. Where does Ms Qian want to go?

____

2. How to go to the bank?

____

3. Is the bank open today?

____

Vocabulary lists the new words and characters covered in the lesson. Each Chinese word is written in simplified characters, accompanied by its pinyin and English equivalent.

3. Vocabulary

	Word	Pinyin	English equivant
1.	银行	**yínháng**	bank
2.	远	**yuǎn**	far
3.	近	**jìn**	close
4.	过	**guò**	pass; go past
5.	路口	**lùkǒu**	intersection
6.	公园	**gōngyuán**	park
7.	在	**zài**	in; at
8.	旁边	**pángbiān**	on the side; beside

New Characters provides a full list of the new fifteen characters introduced in the lesson.

4. New Characters

Fifteen characters are introduced in this lesson. Use the following explanations to help you understand and remember the characters.

对 起 里 银 行 过 街 路 在 公 园 旁 边 远 近

Individual Character Explanations provides the following information of each character: (1) the character number for reference, (2) its standard form, (3) its pinyin, (4) its English equivalent, (5) its semantic radical, (6) some useful phrases and sentences in pinyin, characters, and English translations, and (7) its stroke order.

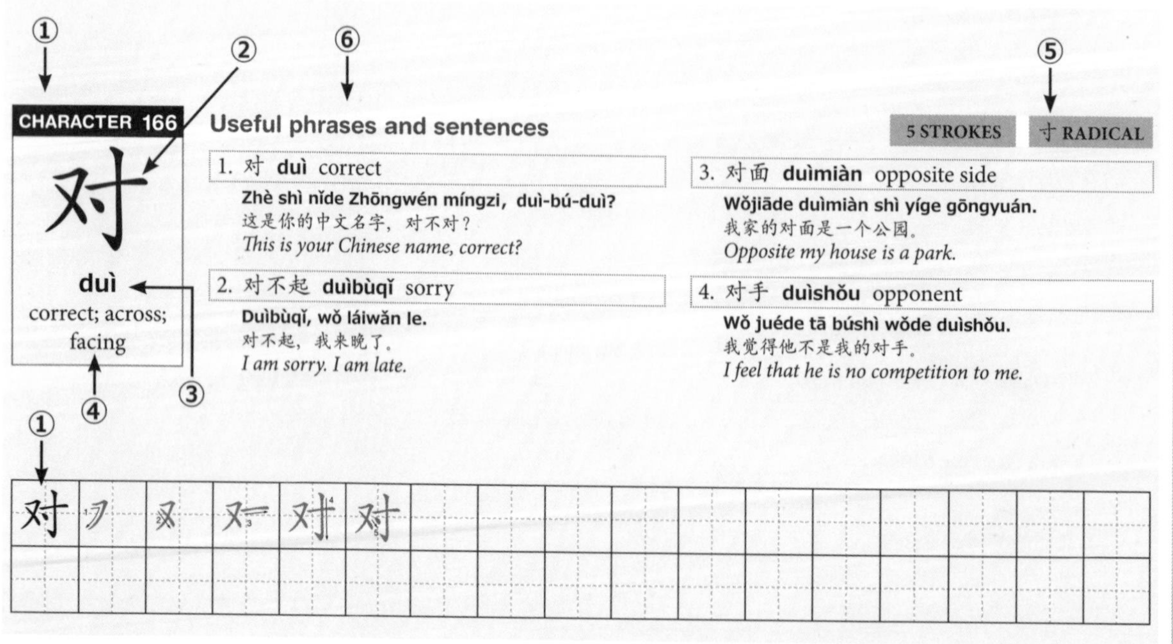

Exercises provides various types of exercises to enhance your ability to use these characters, including (1) fill in the blanks, (2) questions, and (3) improvisation assignments.

Lesson 12 Exercises

Part 1 Choose from the following words to fill in the blanks.

过、在、旁边、远

1. 请问，中国银行在公园的（　　　　）吗？
2. 你（　　　　）街的时候不要打电话。

LESSON 1

How much is this? 这个多少钱？

1. Introduction

Have you ever gone shopping in China? Were things expensive or not? Did you bargain? People who have never been to China often misunderstand the shopping culture there. First, they think that everything in China is inexpensive, which is untrue. Imported goods are outrageously pricey. Second, they think that bargain is allowed everywhere in China, which again is wrong. You can practice your bargaining skills only with smaller vendors, but not when you shop at the supermarkets or shopping malls. Recently, online shopping has been made easy and has become one of the most popular ways of shopping among the younger generations.

2. Warm up

Write the prices of the following goods using Chinese characters.

1. How much are the shoes?

____

2. How much is the bag?

____

3. How much are the T-shirts?

____

3. Vocabulary

	Word	Pinyin	English equivalent
1.	十一	**shíyī**	eleven
2.	二十	**èrshí**	twenty
3.	三十四	**sānshísì**	thirty four
4.	五元	**wǔyuán**	five yuan (Chinese dollars, formal)
5.	两块/元	**liǎngkuài/yuán**	two Chinese dollars; (kuai is used informally to mean yuan)
6.	六块七	**liùkuàiqī**	six Chinese dollars and seventy cents
7.	八百	**bābǎi**	eight hundred
8.	九百零六	**jiǔbǎilíngliù**	nine hundred and six

4. New Characters

Fifteen characters are introduced in this lesson. Use the following explanations to help you understand and remember the characters.

一　二　三　四　五　六　七　八　九　十　零　两　百　元　块

CHARACTER 1

一

yī

one

Note: Yī, with the first tone, refers to the number and digit *one*. When **yī** is followed by a syllable using tones 1, 2, or 3, its tone will become **yì**, for example **yìqǐ** (together). When **yī** is followed by a syllable using a neutral tone or tone 4, it needs to be changed to **yí**, for example **yíge**.

1 STROKE　一 RADICAL

Useful phrases and sentences

1. 一 **yī** one

yī èr sān
一二三
one two three

2. 一个 **yíge** one (for general objects)

Wǒ chīle yíge píngguo.
我吃了一个苹果。
I ate an apple.

3. 一次 **yícì** once (one time)

Wǒ qùguo Táiwān yícì.
我去过台湾一次。
I have been to Taiwan once.

4. 一起 **yìqǐ** together

Wǒmen yìqǐ qù, hǎo ma?
我们一起去，好吗？
Let's go together, shall we?

CHARACTER 2

二

èr
two

Useful phrases and sentences

2 STROKES　二 RADICAL

1. 二 **èr** two

Yī jiā yī děngyú èr.
一加一等于二。
One plus one equals two.

2. 二月 **èryuè** February

Wǒ èryuè bú shàngkè.
我二月不上课。
I don't have school in February.

3. 二十 **èrshí** twenty

Tā xiěle èrshíge Hànzì.
他写了二十个汉字。
He wrote twenty characters.

4. 十二 **shí'èr** twelve

Yīnián yǒu shí'èrge yuè.
一年有十二个月。
There are twelve months in a year.

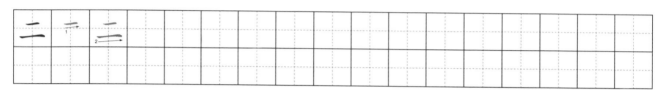

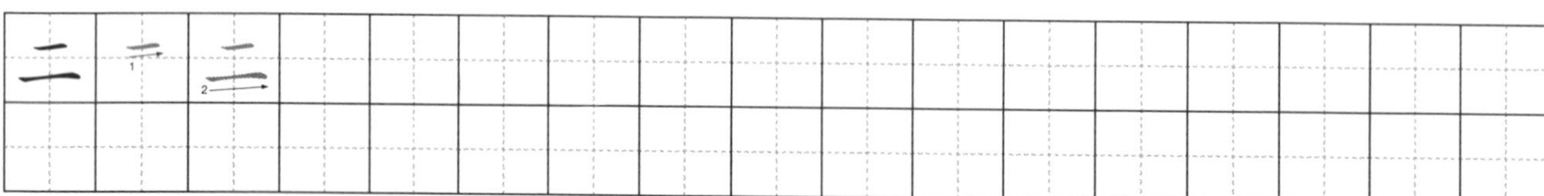

CHARACTER 3

三

sān
three

Useful phrases and sentences

3 STROKES　一 RADICAL

1. 三本 **sānběn** three (for books)

Wǒ yǒu sānběn Yīngwén shū.
我有三本英文书。
I have three English books.

2. 三个月 **sānge yuè** three months

Wǒ xué Zhōngwén xuéle sānge yuèle.
我学中文学了三个月了。
I have been learning Chinese for three months.

3. 三天 **sāntiān** three days

Zhècì wǒ huì zaì Bōshìdùn zhù sāntiān.
这次我会在波士顿住三天。
I will be staying in Boston for three days this time.

4. 星期三 **xīngqīsān** Wednesday

Jīntiān shì xīngqīsān.
今天是星期三。
Today is Wednesday.

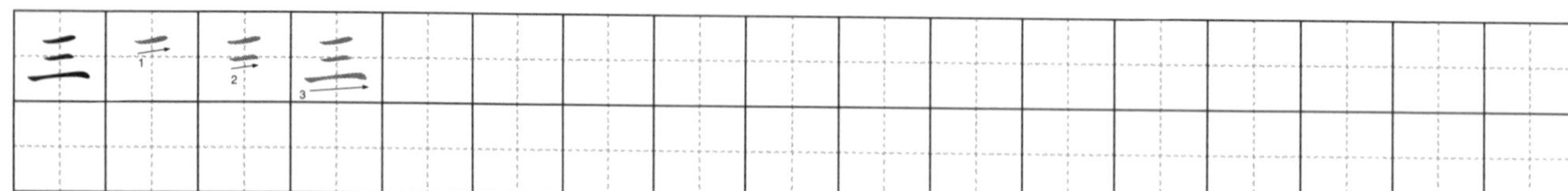

CHARACTER 4

sì
four

Useful phrases and sentences

5 STROKES　口 RADICAL

1. 四张 **sìzhāng** four (for papers or tables)

Wǒde fángjiān yǒu sìzhāng zhuōzi.
我的房间有四张桌子。
There are four desks in my room.

2. 大四 **dàsì** senior in college

Wǒ shì dàsìde xuésheng.
我是大四的学生。
I am a senior in college.

3. 四川 **Sìchuān** Sichuan (place name)

Wǒ hěn xǐhuan chī Sìchuān cài.
我很喜欢吃四川菜。
I like Sichuan food very much.

4. 四点 **sìdiǎn** four o'clock

Xiànzài xiàwǔ sìdiǎn.
现在下午四点。
It's four o'clock in the afternoon now.

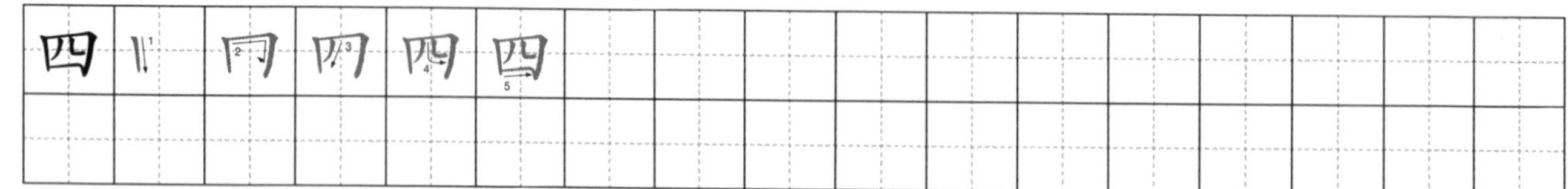

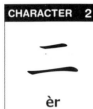

CHARACTER 5

wǔ
five

4 STROKES | 一 RADICAL

Useful phrases and sentences

1. 五月 **wǔyuè** May

Zhège chéngshì wǔyuè zuì piàoliang.
这个城市五月最漂亮。
This city is most beautiful in May.

2. 五个月 **wǔge yuè** five months

Wǒ rènshi tā yǐjīng wǔge yuè le.
我认识他已经五个月了。
I've known him for five months.

3. 星期五 **xīngqīwǔ** Friday

Xīngqīwǔ wǎnshang wǒ cháng qù tiàowu.
星期五晚上我常去跳舞。
I often go dancing on Friday night.

4. 五只 **wǔzhī** five (for animals such as cats and puppies)

Tā jiā yǒu wǔzhī māo.
他家有五只猫。
He keeps five cats at home.

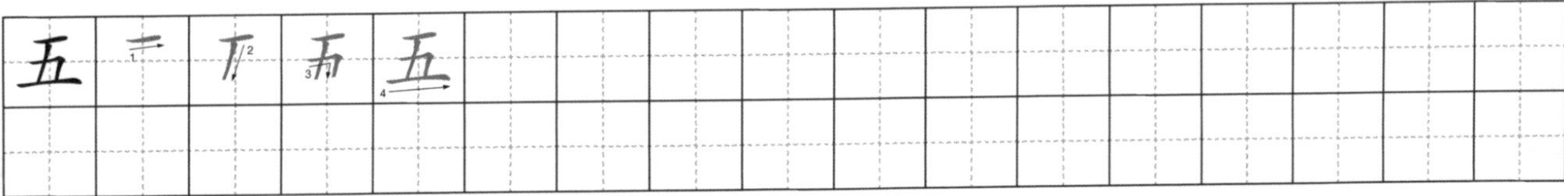

CHARACTER 6

liù
six

4 STROKES | 亠 RADICAL

Useful phrases and sentences

1. 六把 **liùbǎ** six (for chairs)

Tā zuótiān mǎile liùbǎ yǐzi.
他昨天买了六把椅子。
He bought six chairs yesterday.

2. 星期六 **xīngqīliù** Saturday

Wǒ xīngqīliù huì qù kāfēiguǎn kànshū。
我星期六会去咖啡馆看书。
I am going to a coffee shop to read books on Saturday.

3. 六月 **liùyuè** June

Wǒ liùyuè yào qù Běijīng.
我六月要去北京。
I am going to Beijing in June.

4. 六个月 **liùgeyuè** six months

Wǒ lái Zhōngguó liùgeyuè le.
我来中国六个月了。
I have been in China for six months.

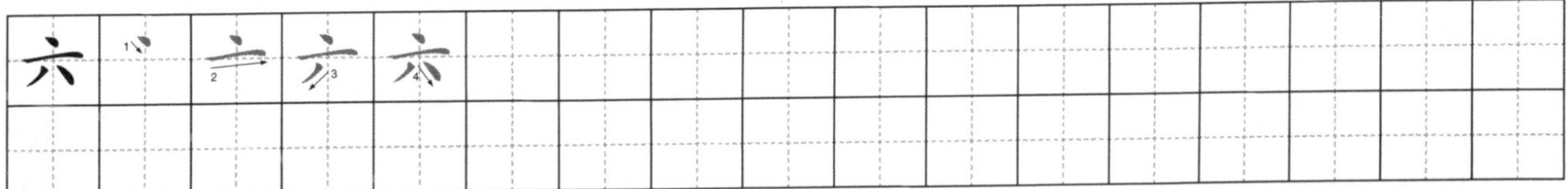

CHARACTER 7

qī
seven

2 STROKES | 一 RADICAL

Useful phrases and sentences

1. 七天 **qītiān** seven days

Yíge xīngqī yǒu qītiān.
一个星期有七天。
There are seven days a week.

2. 七月 **qīyuè** July

Běijīng qīyuè tài rè le.
北京七月太热了。
It is too hot in July in Beijing.

3. 乱七八糟 **luànqībāzāo** mess

Tāde fángjiān luànqībāzāo de.
他的房间乱七八糟的。
His room is a mess.

4. 七岁 **qīsuì** seven years old

Wǒ jīnnián qīsuì.
我今年七岁。
I am seven years old this year.

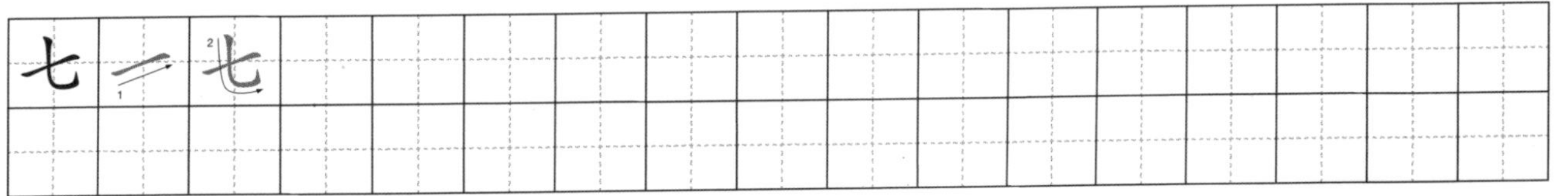

CHARACTER 8

bā
eight

Useful phrases and sentences

2 STROKES | 八 RADICAL

1. 八个小时 **bāge xiǎoshí** eight hours
Kāichē qù Huáshèngdùn yào bāge xiǎoshí.
开车去华盛顿要八个小时。
It takes eight hours to drive to Washington DC.

2. 八分钟 **bāfēn zhōng** eight minutes
Hái yǒu bāfēn zhōng jiù shàngkè le。
还有八分钟就上课了。
There are eight minutes until the class begins.

3. 八折 **bāzhé** twenty percent discount
Zhège shāngdiàn jīntiān dǎ bāzhé.
这个商店今天打八折。
This store has everything 20% off today.

4. 八月 **bāyuè** August
Wǒde shēngrì shì bāyuè bāhào.
我的生日是八月八号。
My birthday is August 8th.

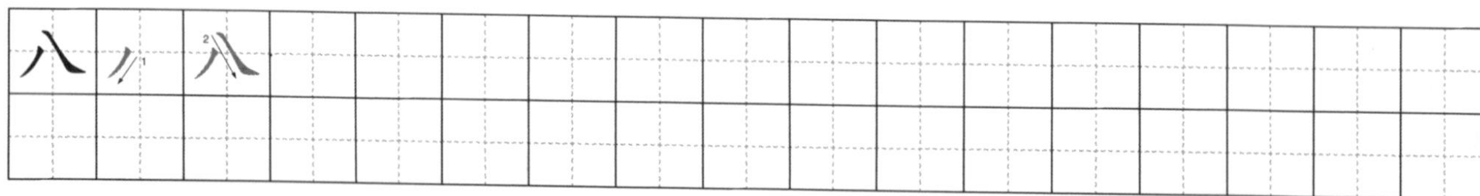

CHARACTER 9

jiǔ
nine

Useful phrases and sentences

2 STROKES | 丿 RADICAL

1. 九点 **jiǔdiǎn** nine o'clock
Wǒ zǎoshang jiǔdiǎn shàngkè.
我早上九点上课。
I have class at 9 a.m.

2. 九百 **jiǔbǎi** nine hundred
Zhège shǒujī jiǔbǎi kuài, hěn piányi.
这个手机九百块，很便宜。
This cell phone is 900 kuai. It's cheap.

3. 九十 **jiǔshí** ninety
Zhège jiǔshí kuài.
这个九十块。
This costs ninety kuai.

4. 十九 **shíjiǔ** nineteen
Tā jīnnián shíjiǔsuì, búshì èrshísuì.
他今年十九岁，不是二十岁。
He is nineteen years old, not twenty.

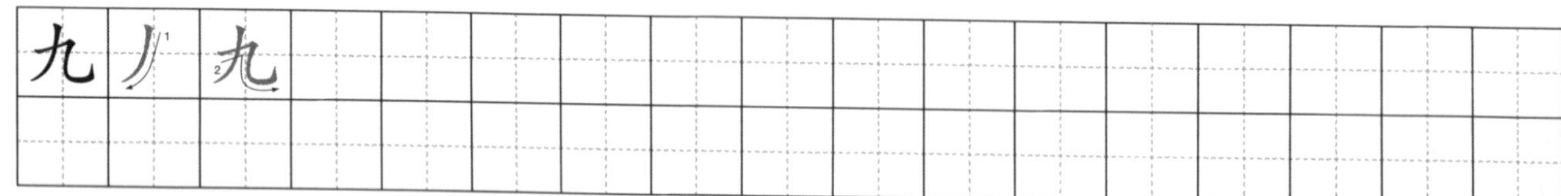

CHARACTER 10

shí
ten

Useful phrases and sentences

2 STROKES | 十 RADICAL

1. 十分 **shífēn** fully; very
Zhè běn shū shífēn yǒu yìsi, nǐ yě mǎi ba.
这本书十分有意思，你也买吧。
This book is very interesting. Why don't you buy one too?

2. 十字路口 **shízìlùkǒu** intersection
Nǐ zài xiàyíge shízìlùkǒu zuǒzhuǎn.
你在下一个十字路口左转。
Turn left at the next intersection.

3. 十月 **shíyuè** October
Wǒ shíyuè xiǎng qù Rìběn.
我十月想去日本。
I am thinking about going to Japan in October.

4. 十点 **shídiǎn** ten o'clock
Wǒ měitiān shídiǎn shàng Zhōngwén kè.
我每天十点上中文课。
I have Chinese class at ten o'clock every day.

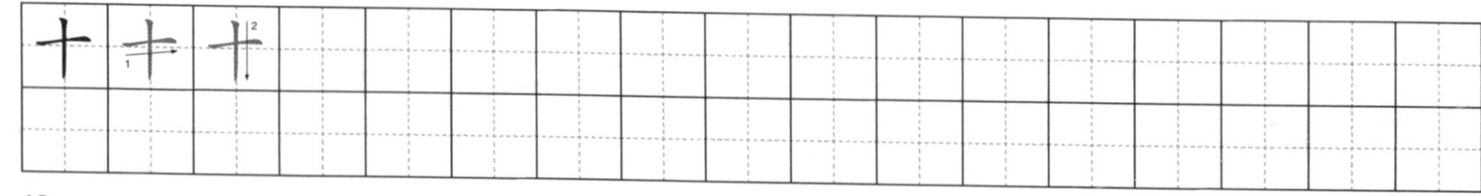

CHARACTER 11

líng
zero

Useful phrases and sentences

13 STROKES | 雨 RADICAL

1. 零 **líng** zero

Xiànzài zǎoshang sìdiǎn língwǔ.
现在早上四点零五。
It is 4:05 a.m.

2. 零下 **língxià** below zero (temperature)

Xiànzài cái shíyuè, yǐjīng língxià liùdù le.
现在才十月，已经零下六度了。
It's only October, but it's already minus six degrees.

3. 二零一七年 **èr-líng-yī-qī-nián** year of 2017

Jīnnián shì èr-líng-yī-qī-nián.
今年是二零一七年。
It's 2017 this year.

4. 零钱 **língqián** small change

Kěyǐ jièwǒ liǎngkuài qián ma? Wǒ méiyǒu língqián.
可以借我两块钱吗？我没有零钱。
Can I borrow two kuai? I don't have any small change.

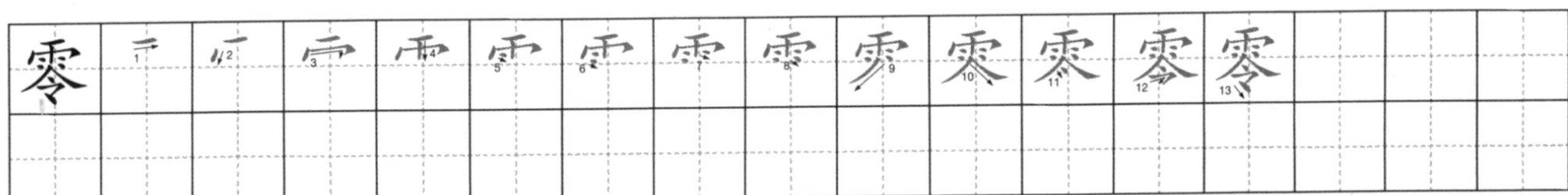

CHARACTER 12

liǎng
two (for pairs)

Useful phrases and sentences

7 STROKES | 一 RADICAL

1. 两个 **liǎngge** two (for pairs)

Nǐ tīngshuōguo zhè liǎngge rén ma?
你听说过这两个人吗？
Have you heard about these two people?

2. 两次 **liǎngcì** twice

Zhège bówùguǎn hěn hǎo, wǒ qùnián qùle liǎngcì.
这个博物馆很好，我去年去了两次。
This museum is good. I went there twice last year.

3. 两岁 **liǎngsuì** two years old

Tāde érzi liǎngsuì le.
她的儿子两岁了。
Her son is two years old.

4. 两块(儿) **liǎngkuài(r)** two pieces (for block-shaped things)

Wǒ zǎoshang chīle liǎngkuài(r) dàngāo.
我早上吃了两块(儿)蛋糕。
I ate two pieces of cake this morning.

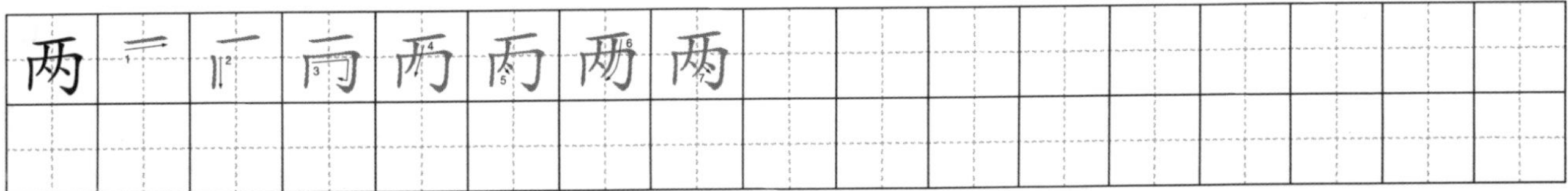

CHARACTER 13

bǎi
hundred

Useful phrases and sentences

6 STROKES | 一 RADICAL

1. 百 **bǎi** hundred

Wǒ jīnnián xuéle liǎngbǎige Hànzì.
我今年学了两百个汉字。
I've learned two hundred characters this year.

2. 一百年 **yìbǎinián** one hundred years

Zhège xuéxiào yǒu yìbǎiniánde lìshǐ le.
这个学校有一百年的历史了。
This school has a history of one hundred years.

3. 六百 **liùbǎi** six hundred

Zhèige liùbǎi kuài.
这个六百块。
This costs six hundred kuai.

4. 百事可乐 **Bǎishì kělè** Pepsi-Cola

Nǐ xǐhuan Bǎishì kělè ma?
你喜欢百事可乐吗？
Do you like Pepsi-Cola?

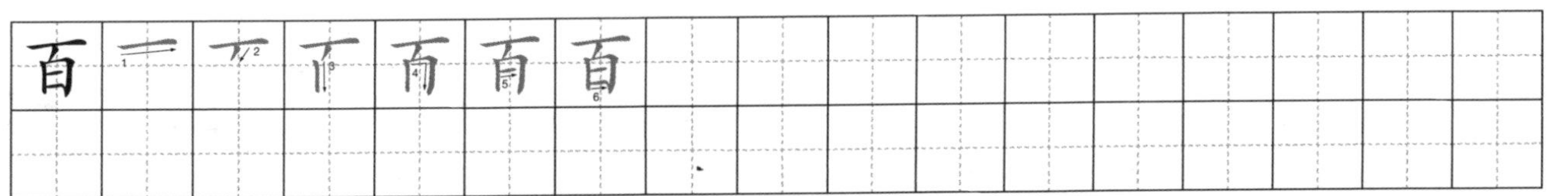

CHARACTER 14

元

yuán
Chinese dollar

Useful phrases and sentences

4 STROKES | 二 RADICAL

1. 元 **yuán** Chinese dollar
   Mǎi yíge píngguo shǒuji yào huā sìqiān yuán.
   买一个苹果手机要花四千元。
   An iPhone costs four thousand Chinese yuan.

2. 美元 **Měiyuán** U.S. dollar
   Zài Měiguó, yìbǎi Měiyuán néng mǎi hěnduō dōngxi.
   在美国，一百美元能买很多东西。
   In U.S.A., you can buy many things with one hundred U.S. dollars.

3. 日元 **Rìyuán** Japanese yen
   Zài Rìběn yòng Rìyuán.
   在日本用日元。
   They use Japanese yen in Japan.

4. 两百元 **liǎngbǎi yuán** two hundred dollars
   Nèige yào liǎngbǎi yuán.
   那个要两百元。
   That costs two hundred yuan.

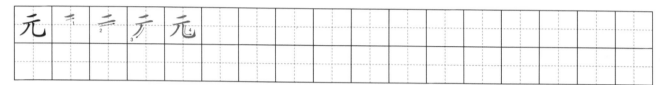

CHARACTER 15

块

kuài
a measure word (used for money, slices, or block-shaped items)

Useful phrases and sentences

7 STROKES | 土 RADICAL

1. 块 **kuài** a piece, slice or lump
   Wǒ zǎoshang zhǐ chīle wǔkuài bǐnggān.
   我早上只吃了五块饼干。
   I only ate five cookies this morning.

2. 一块儿 **yíkuàir** together as a group
   Wǒmen yíkuàir qù kàn diànyǐng ba.
   我们一块儿去看电影吧。
   Let's go to see a movie together.

3. 五十块钱 **wǔshíkuài qián** fifty *kuai*
   Wǒ zuótiān chīfàn huāle wǔshíkuài qián.
   我昨天吃饭花了五十块钱。
   I spent fifty kuai.

4. 五百块钱 **wǔbǎikuài qián** five hundred *kuai*
   Wǒ yǒu wǔbǎikuài qián.
   我有五百块钱。
   I have five hundred kuai.

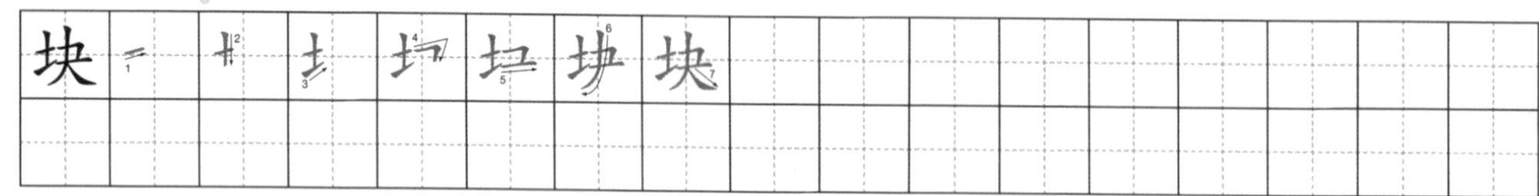

Lesson 1 Exercises

Part 1 Write the number for the following characters.

1. 九 (　　　　)
2. 四十八 (　　　　)
3. 七十六 (　　　　)
4. 六十三 (　　　　)
5. 七十一 (　　　　)
6. 九十九 (　　　　)
7. 两百零二 (　　　　)
8. 八百五十九 (　　　　)

Part 2 Write the characters for the following numbers.

1.	67	(　　　)	5.	987	(　　　)
2.	23	(　　　)	6.	476	(　　　)
3.	92	(　　　)	7.	520	(　　　)
4.	108	(　　　)	8.	914	(　　　)

Part 3 Answer the following questions using Chinese characters.

1. Q: What is your phone number?

   A: ____。

2. Q: What is the phone number of your best friend?

   A: ____。

3. Q: What is your room number?

   A: ____。

4. Q: What is your teacher's office number?

   A: ____。

Part 4 Search online how much these items are in China and in your country. Write down the prices using Chinese characters.

Item	Price in China	Price in your country
A cup of Starbucks coffee		
A pair of Nike shoes		
A bottle of orange juice		
A movie ticket		

LESSON 2

What is your name? 你叫什么名字？

1. Introduction

Personal names are important to Chinese people, as in every culture. A typical Chinese name consists of two or three characters. The first character is the family name, while the second and third characters are the given name. There are a few Chinese family names that have two characters, but they are uncommon. Chinese given names often reveal parents' hopes and wishes for their children. Do you have a Chinese name? If so, what is your family name? What is your given name? Do you know what your Chinese name means?

2. Warm up

Read the passage below and answer the questions using Chinese characters.

A: 你好！我姓李，我叫李元。你叫什么名字？
B: 你好！我姓王，我叫王美。那个 (**nàge**: that) 男生 (**nánshēng**: male student) 叫什么名字？
A: 他叫李友，是我的好朋友 (**péngyou**: friend)。

1. What is A's name? ____________________

2. Who is A speaking with? ____________________

3. Who is that male student? ____________________

3. Vocabulary

	Word	Pinyin	English equivalent
1.	我	**wǒ**	I; me
2.	你	**nǐ**	you
3.	他	**tā**	he; him
4.	她	**tā**	she; her
5.	叫	**jiào**	be named; call
6.	什么	**shénme**	what
7.	名字	**míngzi**	name; given name
8.	你好	**nǐ hǎo**	hello; hi

4. New Characters

Fifteen characters are introduced in this lesson. Use the following explanations to help you understand and remember the characters.

我 你 他 她 叫 姓 什 么 名 字 好 李 王 男 美

CHARACTER 16

我

wǒ
I; me

7 STROKES | 戈 RADICAL

Useful phrases and sentences

1. 我姓... **Wǒxìng...** My surname ...

Wǒ xìng Zhāng, bú xìng Lǐ.
我姓张，不姓李。
My surname is Zhang, not Lǐ.

2. 我的 **wǒde** my; mine

Wǒde shū zài nǎr?
我的书在哪儿？
Where is my book?

3. 我有 **wǒ yǒu** I have

Wǒ yǒu hěnduō shū.
我有很多书。
I have many books.

4. 我在 **wǒ zài** I am in/at

Wǒ zài jiā.
我在家。
I am at home.

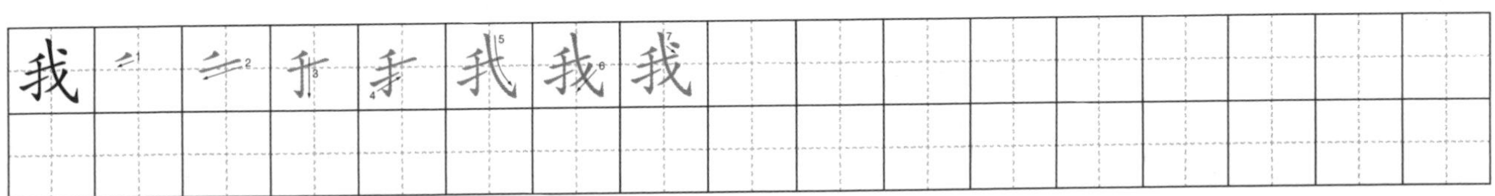

CHARACTER 17

你

nǐ
you

7 STROKES | 亻 RADICAL

Useful phrases and sentences

1. 你是 **nǐ shì** you are

Nǐ shì xuésheng ma?
你是学生吗？
Are you a student?

2. 你的 **nǐde** your; yours

Zhè shì nǐde shū ma?
这是你的书吗？
Is this your book?

3. 你有 **nǐ yǒu** you have

Nǐ yǒu kèběn ma?
你有课本吗？
Do you have the textbook?

4. 你在 **nǐ zài** you are at/in

Nǐ zài nǎr?
你在哪儿？
Where are you?

CHARACTER 18

tā
he; him

Useful phrases and sentences

5 STROKES | 亻 RADICAL

1. 他不是 **tā bú shì** he is not

Tā bú shì xuésheng.
他不是学生。
He is not a student.

2. 他的 **tāde** his

Tāde Hànyǔ hěn hǎo.
他的汉语很好。
His Chinese is good.

3. 他有 **tā yǒu** he has

Tā yǒu sānběn shū.
他有三本书。
He has three books.

4. 他在 **tā zài** he is at/in

Tā zài shítáng.
他在食堂。
He is in the dining hall.

CHARACTER 19

tā
she; her

Useful phrases and sentences

6 STROKES | 女 RADICAL

1. 她是 **tā shì** she is

Tā shì wǒde lǎoshī.
她是我的老师。
She is my teacher.

2. 她的 **tāde** her

Tāde xuésheng hěn hǎo.
她的学生很好。
Her students are good.

3. 她有 **tā yǒu** she has

Tā yǒu èrshíge xuésheng.
她有二十个学生。
She has twenty students.

4. 她在 **tā zài** she is at/in

Tā zài Měiguó gōngzuò.
她在美国工作。
She is working in U.S.A.

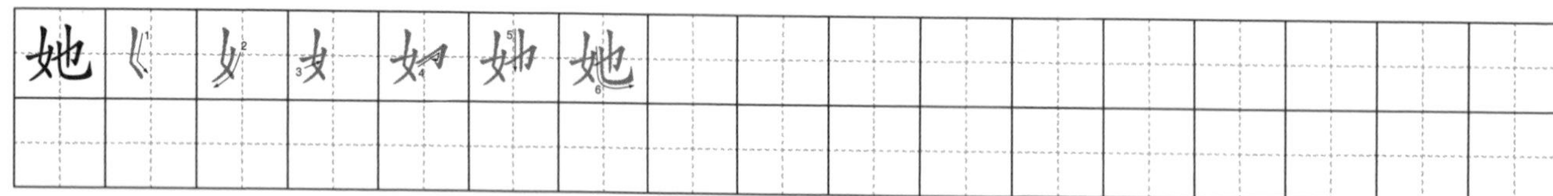

CHARACTER 20

jiào
be named; call

Useful phrases and sentences

5 STROKES | 口 RADICAL

1. 叫 **jiào** be named; call

Wǒ jiào Lǐ Dàzhōng.
我叫李大中。
My name is Li Dazhong.

2. 叫他 **jiào tā** call him

Wǒmen jiào tā "Lǐ Lǎoshī."
我们叫他 "李老师"。
We call him Teacher Li.

3. 叫一下 **jiào yíxià** call (a directive)

Qǐng jiào yíxià tā.
请叫一下他。
Please call him.

4. 吼叫 **hǒujiào** howl; roar

Zhèlǐ bù-kěyǐ hǒujiào.
这里不可以吼叫。
Howling is not permitted here.

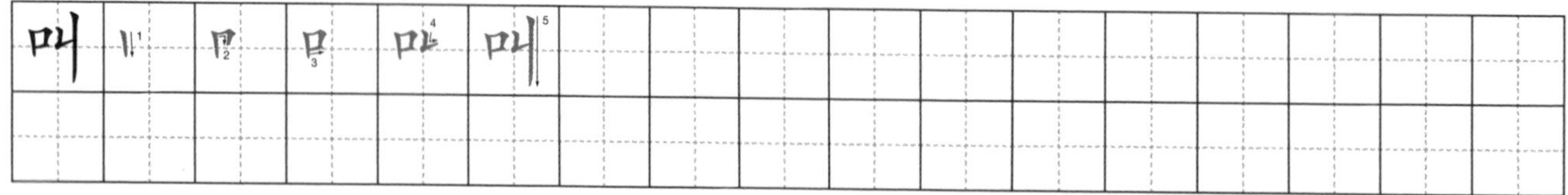

CHARACTER 21

姓

xìng
family name; be surnamed

8 STROKES | 女 RADICAL

Useful phrases and sentences

1. 姓什么 **xìng shénme** be surnamed what

Nǐ xìng shénme?
你姓什么?
What is your family name?

2. 姓高 **xìng Gāo** surnamed Gao

Wǒ xìng Gāo.
我姓高。
My family name is Gao.

3. 他的姓 **tāde xìng** his family name

Tāde xìng hé tāde xìng dōu shì Lǐ.
他的姓和她的姓都是李。
His and her family names are both Li.

4. 您贵姓 **nín guìxìng** what is your honorable family name (polite)

Qǐng wèn, nín guìxìng?
请问，您贵姓?
Excuse me, what is your honorable family name?

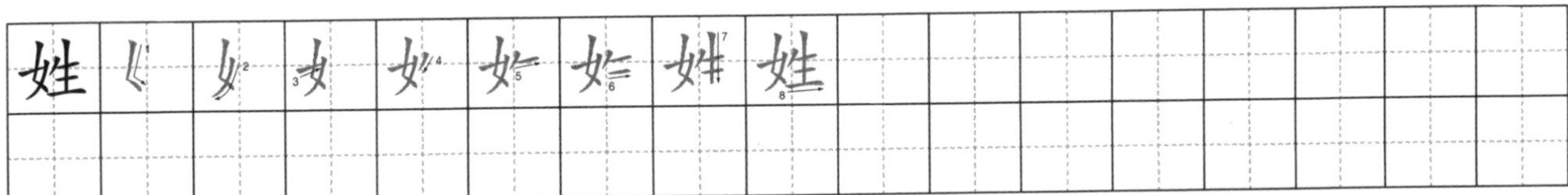

CHARACTER 22

什

shén
what

4 STROKES | 亻 RADICAL

Useful phrases and sentences

1. 什么 **shénme** what

Nǐ jiào shénme?
你叫什么?
What is your name?

2. 什么是 **shénme shì** what is/are

Shénme shì "bāozi"?
什么是"包子"?
What are "steamed buns"?

3. 是什么 **shì shénme** is/are what

Zhè shì shénme?
这是什么?
What is this?

4. 有什么 **yǒu shénme** have what

Nǐ yǒu shénme xiǎngfǎ?
你有什么想法?
What thoughts do you have?

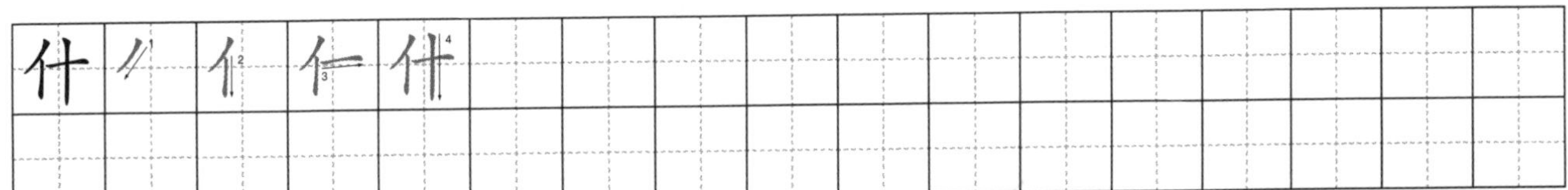

CHARACTER 23

么

me
a suffix (used to form a question word or an indefinite pronoun)

3 STROKES | 丿 RADICAL

Useful phrases and sentences

1. 那么... **nàme...** like that ...

Bié nàme shuō!
别那么说!
Don't say it that way!

2. 什么字 **shénme zì** what character

Zhè shì shénme zì?
这是什么字?
What is this character?

3. 多么 **duōme** how (much) [used in exclamations]

Tā duōme cōngming a!
他多么聪明啊!
He is so clever!

4. 这么 **zhème** so

Zhèběn shū zhème guì.
这本书这么贵。
This book is so expensive.

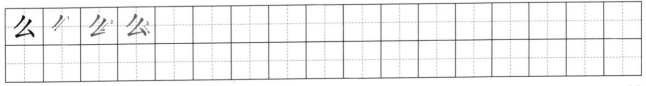

CHARACTER 24

míng
name

Useful phrases and sentences

6 STROKES | 口 RADICAL

1. 名字 **míngzi** name
Tāde míngzi shì Lǐ Yǒu.
他的名字是李友。
His name is Li You.

2. 有名 **yǒumíng** famous
Tā hěn yǒumíng.
她很有名。
She is famous.

3. 名人 **míngrén** celebrity
Zhèlǐ yǒu hěnduō míngrén.
这里有很多名人。
There are many celebrities here.

4. 名画 **mínghuà** famous painting
Zhè shì Zhōngguó mínghuà.
这是中国名画。
This is a famous Chinese painting.

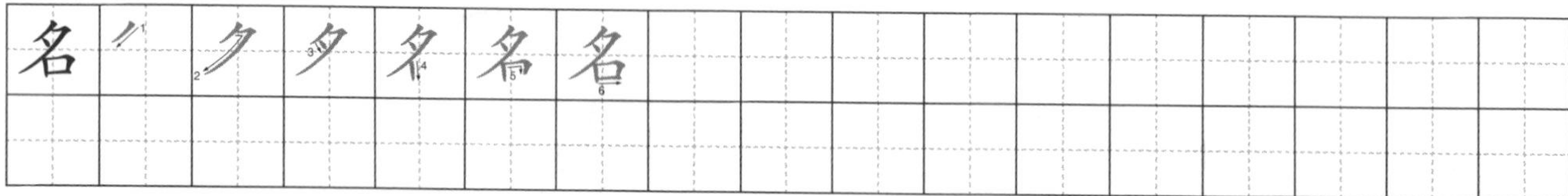

CHARACTER 25

zì
character; letter (of alphabet)

Note: zì loses its tone in the compound **míngzi** (name).

Useful phrases and sentences

6 STROKES | 宀 RADICAL

1. 字典 **zìdiǎn** dictionary (of characters)
Zhè shì nǐde zìdiǎn ma?
这是你的字典吗？
Is this your dictionary?

2. 认字 **rènzì** recognize words
Tā huìshuō Zhōngwén, kěshì bú rènzì.
他会说中文，可是不认字。
He speaks Chinese, but he cannot read Chinese.

3. 写字 **xiězì** write characters
Wǒ měitiān xiězì.
我每天写字。
I write characters every day.

4. 字母 **zìmǔ** letter (of alphabet)
Yīngwén yǒu èrshíliùge zìmǔ.
英文有二十六个字母。
There are twenty-six letters in English.

字 1 2 3 4 5 6 字

CHARACTER 26

hǎo
good

Useful phrases and sentences

6 STROKES | 女 RADICAL

1. 你好 **nǐ hǎo** hello; hi
Nǐ hǎo ! Wǒ jiào Wáng Míng.
你好！我叫王明。
Hello! My name is Wang Ming.

2. 很好 **hěn hǎo** very good
Wǒde lǎoshī hěn hǎo.
我的老师很好。
My teacher is very good.

3. 好人 **hǎo rén** good person
Tā shì hǎo rén.
他是好人。
He is a good man.

4. 好看 **hǎokàn** good looking
Nǐ xiěde Hànzì hěn hǎokàn.
你写的汉字很好看。
The characters you wrote look good.

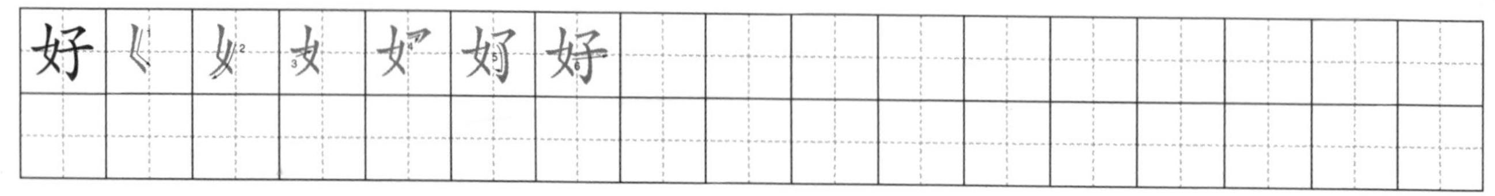

CHARACTER 27

李

Lǐ
family name; plum

7 STROKES | 木 RADICAL

Useful phrases and sentences

1. 姓李 **xìng Lǐ** surnamed Li

Wǒ xìng Lǐ.
我姓李。
My family name is Li.

2. 李先生 **Lǐ Xiānsheng** Mr. Li

Lǐ Xiānsheng jiào shénme míngzi, nǐ zhīdao ma?
李先生叫什么名字，你知道吗？
Do you know what Mr. Li's given name is?

3. 李小姐 **Lǐ Xiǎojie** Ms Li

Lǐ Xiǎojie jīnnián èrshíbāsuì.
李小姐今年二十八岁。
Ms Li is twenty-eight years old.

4. 李小龙 **Lǐ Xiǎolóng** Bruce Lee

Nǐ zhīdao Lǐ Xiǎolóng ma?
你知道李小龙吗？
Do you know of Bruce Lee?

CHARACTER 28

王

Wáng
family name; king

4 STROKES | 一 RADICAL

Useful phrases and sentences

1. 姓王 **xìng Wáng** surnamed Wang

Tā xìng Wáng ma?
她姓王吗？
Is her family name Wang?

2. 王小姐 **Wáng Xiǎojie** Ms Wang

Wáng Xiǎojie shi Zhōngguó rén, tāde Yīngwén hěn hǎo.
王小姐是中国人，她的英文很好。
Ms Wang is Chinese. Her English is very good.

3. 王先生 **Wáng Xiānsheng** Mr. Wang

Wáng Xiānsheng shì lǎoshī.
王先生是老师。
Mr. Wang is a teacher.

4. 国王 **guówáng** king

Měiguó yǒu guówáng ma?
美国有国王吗？
Does U.S.A. have a king?

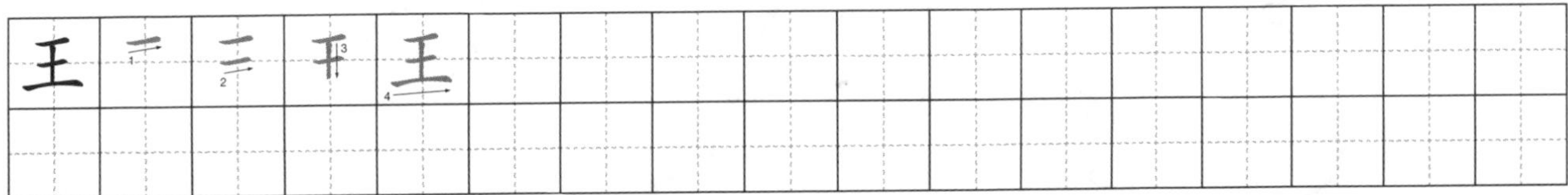

CHARACTER 29

男

nán
male

7 STROKES | 田 RADICAL

Useful phrases and sentences

1. 男生 **nánshēng** male student

Wǒmen bān yǒu shíge nánshēng.
我们班有十个男生。
There are ten male students in our class.

2. 男人 **nánrén** man

Nàge nánrén shì nǐde péngyou ma?
那个男人是你的朋友吗？
Is that man your friend?

3. 男孩(儿) **nánhái(r)** boy

Zhège nánhái(r) hěn hǎokàn.
这个男孩(儿)很好看。
This boy is good looking.

4. 男装 **nánzhuāng** men's clothing

Nǐ xǐhuan zhèjiā shāngdiànde nánzhuāng ma?
你喜欢这家商店的男装吗？
Do you like the men's clothing in this store?

CHARACTER 30

美

měi
beautiful

Useful phrases and sentences

9 STROKES 羊 RADICAL

1. 美丽 **měilì** beautiful
   Tā shìge měilìde nǚrén.
   她是个美丽的女人。
   She is a beautiful woman.

2. 很美 **hěn měi** very beautiful; very pretty
   Zhèlǐde fēngjǐng hěn měi.
   这里的风景很美。
   The scenery here is very pretty.

3. 美女 **měinǚ** pretty girl
   Nàge měinǚ jiào shénme míngzi?
   那个美女叫什么名字？
   What is the pretty girl's name?

4. 美好 **měihǎo** wonderful
   Shēnghuó hěn měihǎo.
   生活很美好。
   Life is wonderful.

美	1	2	3	4	5	6	7	8	9							

Lesson 2 Exercises

Part 1 Choose from the following words to fill in the blanks.

名字、好、姓、什么、你、她

1. 你（　　　　）！我是学生，（　　　　）呢？
2. 我叫李友，你叫（　　　　）（　　　　）？
3. 他（　　　　）王，他叫王男。
4. （　　　　）是你的 (**nǐde**: your) 朋友吗？

Part 2 Complete the following dialogues using Chinese characters.

1. A: 你叫什么名字？

   B: ____。

2. A: 你姓什么？

   B: ____。

3. A: 你的朋友姓什么？

B: ____。

4. A: 你的朋友叫什么名字？

B: ____。

Part 3 Use the following prompts to give a one-minute speech.

你好！我姓 __________，我叫 ______________________。我有 _______ 个朋友,

他们的 (**tāmende**: their) 名字是 ____。

我们是 ____。

LESSON 3

Where are you from? 你是哪国人？

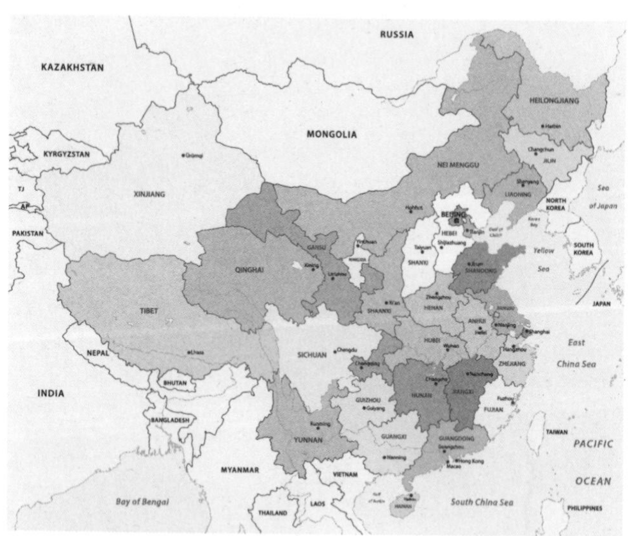

1. Introduction

When Chinese people first meet, they often ask each other where in China they are from. There are two reasons for this. First, if they are from the same place, they easily feel affinity towards one another. The other reason is that you can predict their dining preferences. For example, Cantonese people tend to eat lightly while people in Sichuan love spicy food.

Nothing opens more doors for conversation in China than cuisine. Where have you been to in China? What's your impression on these places? Did you try any local signature dishes?

2. Warm up

Read the passage below and answer the questions using Chinese characters.

> Wang: 请问，你是中国人吗？
> Kevin: 我不是中国人，我是英国人。
> Wang: 你是英国人？
> Kevin: 是，我是英国人。我爸 (**bà**: father) 妈 (**mā**: mother) 是中国人。

1. Is Kevin Chinese?

   ____

2. What is Kevin's nationality?

   ____

3. What is Kevin's parents' nationality?

   ____

3. Vocabulary

	Word	Pinyin	English equivalent
1.	请问	**qǐng wèn**	Excuse me/ Can I ask?
2.	哪(儿)	**nǎ(r)**	where
3.	中国	**Zhōngguó**	China
4.	中国人	**Zhōngguó rén**	Chinese people
5.	英国	**Yīngguó**	Britain
6.	英国人	**Yīngguó rén**	British people
7.	美国	**Měiguó**	U.S.A.
8.	美国人	**Měiguó rén**	American
9.	不是	**bú shì**	not be; is not
10.	朋友	**péngyou**	friend
11.	好朋友	**hǎo péngyou**	good friend

4. New Characters

Fifteen characters are introduced in this lesson. Use the following explanations to help you understand and remember the characters.

请 问 您 是 不 哪 儿 国 人 中 英 们 的 朋 友

CHARACTER 31

请

qǐng
please; invite

10 STROKES | 讠 RADICAL

Useful phrases and sentences

1. 请问 **qǐng wèn** excuse me; may I ask
   Qǐng wèn nǐ jiào shénme míngzi?
   请问你叫什么名字？
   Excuse me, what's your name?

2. 请坐 **qǐng zùo** please have a seat
   Huānyíng! Qǐng zuò.
   欢迎！请坐。
   Welcome. Please have a seat!

3. 请客 **qǐngkè** treat; invite
   Jīntiān wǒ qǐngkè.
   今天我请客。
   It's my treat today.

4. 请假 **qǐngjià** ask for leave
   Wǒ míngtiān kěyǐ qǐngjià ma?
   我明天可以请假吗？
   Can I ask for leave tomorrow?

请 1 2 3 4 5 6 7 8 9 10

CHARACTER 32

wèn
ask

Useful phrases and sentences

6 STROKES | 门 RADICAL

1. 问 **wèn** ask

Wǒ xiǎng wèn lǎoshī yíge wèntí.
我想问老师一个问题。
I'd like to ask my teacher a question.

2. 问题 **wèntí** question

Wǒ yǒu yíge wèntí.
我有一个问题。
I have a question.

3. 问候 **wènhou** greet; greetings

Zhōngguó rén zěnme wènhou biérén?
中国人怎么问候别人？
How do Chinese people greet each other?

4. 学问 **xuéwèn** knowledge

Tā hěn yǒu xuéwèn.
他很有学问。
He is knowledgeable.

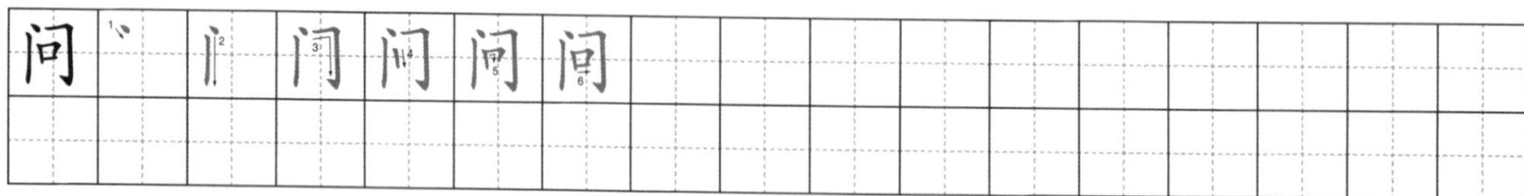

CHARACTER 33

您

nín
you (honorific use)

Useful phrases and sentences

11 STROKES | 心 RADICAL

1. 您好 **nín hǎo** hello; hi

Xiānsheng, nín hǎo.
先生，您好。
Hello Sir.

2. 谢谢您 **xièxie nín** thank you

Wǒ yīnggāi xièxie nín.
我应该谢谢您。
I should thank you.

3. 您是... **nín shì...** you are ...

Qǐng wèn, nín shì ...?
请问，您是...？
Excuse me, you are ...?

4. 祝您 **zhù nín** I wish you ...

Zhù nín shēngrì kuàilè.
祝您生日快乐。
I wish you a happy birthday! (Happy Birthday to you!)

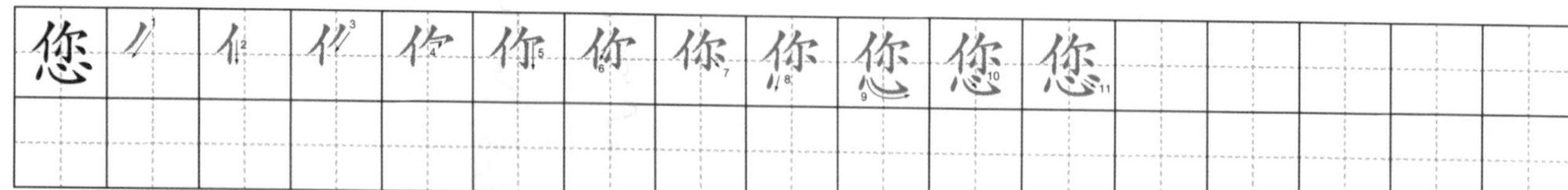

CHARACTER 34

shì
yes; be

Useful phrases and sentences

9 STROKES | 日 RADICAL

1. 是 **shì** be; is; yes

Tā shì Zhōngguó rén.
他是中国人。
He is Chinese.

2. 是 **shì** yes; OK (in the sense of "I agree")

Shì, wǒ míngtiān jiùqù.
是，我明天就去。
OK, I will go tomorrow.

3. 我是... **wǒ shì...** I am ...

Nǐ hǎo, wǒ shì Wáng Dàzhōng.
你好，我是王大中。
Hi, I am Wang Dazhong.

4. 是不是 **shì-bú-shì** be-not-be (used for asking yes-no questions)

Wáng Xiānsheng shì-bú-shì Yīngguó rén?
王先生是不是英国人？
Is Mr. Wang British?

是 | 1 | 2 | 3 | 4 | 5 | 6 | 7 | 8 | 9

CHARACTER 35

bù
not

Note: When the syllable following **bù** uses tone 1, 2, or 3, **bù** is tone 4, for example **bù hǎo**. When **bù** is followed by a syllable using tone 4, it needs to be changed to **bú**, for example **bú huì**.

Useful phrases and sentences

4 STROKES | 一 RADICAL

1. 不是 **bú shì** not be; no
   Tā bú shì wǒde péngyou.
   他不是我的朋友。
   He is not my friend.

2. 不好 **bù hǎo** not good
   Wǒ zuìjìn shēntǐ bù hǎo.
   我最近身体不好。
   I am not feeling well recently.

3. 不会 **bú huì** don't know how
   Wǒ bú huì zuòfàn, nǐ huì ma?
   我不会做饭，你会吗？
   I don't know how to cook, do you?

4. 不错 **bú cuò** not bad
   Zhège wénzhāng hěn bú cuò.
   这个文章很不错。
   This article is quite good.

不 1 2 3 4

CHARACTER 36

nǎ
where

Useful phrases and sentences

9 STROKES | 口 RADICAL

1. 哪儿 **nǎr** where
   Nǐ qù nǎr?
   你去哪儿？
   Where are you going?

2. 哪国人 **nǎguó rén** people of which nationality
   Nǐ shì nǎguó rén?
   你是哪国人？
   What nationality are you?

3. 哪个 **nǎge** which
   Nǐ xiǎng mǎi nǎge bāo?
   你想买哪个包？
   Which bag do you want to buy?

4. 哪些 **nǎxiē** which ones
   Nǐ xiǎng qù Shànghǎi nǎxiē dìfang?
   你想去上海哪些地方？
   Which places do you want to go in Shanghai?

哪 1 2 3 4 5 6 7 8 9

CHARACTER 37

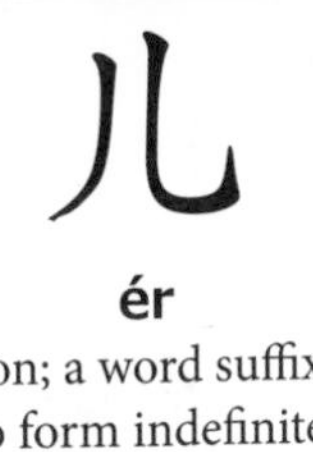

ér
son; a word suffix to form indefinite pronouns of location

Useful phrases and sentences

2 STROKES | 儿 RADICAL

1. 儿 **ér** (word suffix usually indicating northern accent)
   Tāmen qù nǎr?
   他们去哪儿？
   Where are they going?

2. 儿子 **érzi** son
   Wǒ yǒu liǎngge érzi.
   我有两个儿子。
   I have two sons.

3. 儿童 **értóng** child
   Zài Zhōngguó, měinián liùyuè yīrì shì Értóngjié.
   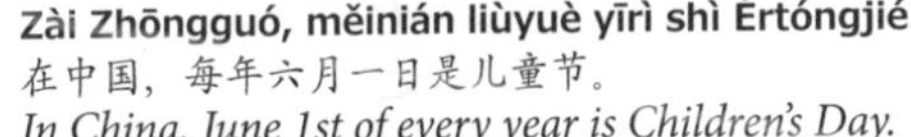
   在中国，每年六月一日是儿童节。
   In China, June 1st of every year is Children's Day.

4. 儿歌 **érgē** children's song
   Zhōngguó zuì yǒumíngde érgē shì něige?
   中国最有名的儿歌是哪个？
   What is the most famous Chinese children's song?

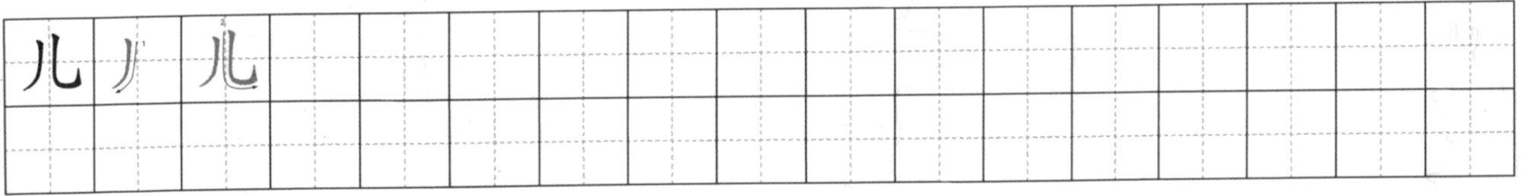

CHARACTER 38

guó
nation; country

Useful phrases and sentences

8 STROKES | 口 RADICAL

1. 美国 **Měiguó** U.S.A.

Nǐ xiǎng qù Měiguó shàng dàxué ma?
你想去美国上大学吗？
Do you want to go to college in U.S.A.?

2. 国家 **guójiā** country

Nǐ qùguo nǎxiē guójiā?
你去过哪些国家？
What countries have you visited?

3. 国籍 **guójí** nationality

Nǐde guójí shì Jiānádà ma?
你的国籍是加拿大吗？
Are you of Canadian nationality?

4. 外国人 **wàiguó rén** foreigner

Běijīng yǒu hěnduō wàiguó rén.
北京有很多外国人。
There are many foreigners in Beijing.

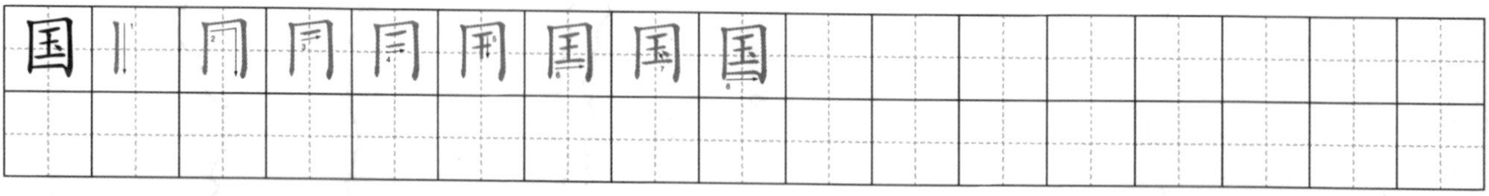

CHARACTER 39

rén
person; people

Useful phrases and sentences

2 STROKES | 人 RADICAL

1. 人 **rén** person; people

Jīntiān shāngchǎng yǒu hěnduō rén.
今天商场有很多人。
There are many people in the shopping mall today.

2. 人口 **rénkǒu** population

Xiānggǎng hěn xiǎo, kěshì yǒu qībǎi duō wàn rénkǒu.
香港很小，可是有七百多万人口。
Hong Kong is small, but it has about seven million people.

3. 人们 **rénmen** people

Zài Sìchuān, rénmen dōu xǐhuan chī hǔoguō.
在四川，人们都喜欢吃火锅。
In Sichuan, the people like to eat hot-pot.

4. 中国人 **Zhōngguó rén** Chinese people; ethnic Chinese

Zài Jiāzhōu yǒu hěnduō Zhōngguó rén.
在加州有很多中国人。
There are many Chinese people in California.

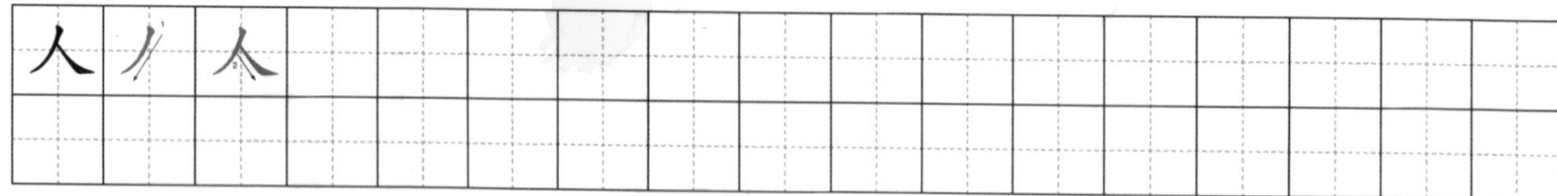

CHARACTER 40

zhōng
middle; center; China

Useful phrases and sentences

4 STROKES | 丨 RADICAL

1. 中文 **Zhōngwén** Chinese language (usually written language)

Nǐde Zhōngwén míngzi hěn hǎotīng.
你的中文名字很好听。
Your Chinese name sounds pleasant.

2. 中国 **Zhōngguó** China

Zhōngguóde rénkǒu yǒu shísānyì.
中国的人口有十三亿。
China's population is 1.3 billion.

3. 中级 **zhōngjí** mid-level

Zhèxuéqī wǒ shàng zhōngjíbān Zhōngwénkè.
这学期我上中级班中文课。
I take mid-level Chinese class this semester.

4. 中餐 **Zhōngcān** Chinese food; noon meal

Tā shì Měiguó rén, tā hěn xǐhuan chī Zhōngcān.
他是美国人，他很喜欢吃中餐。
He is American and he likes to eat Chinese food.

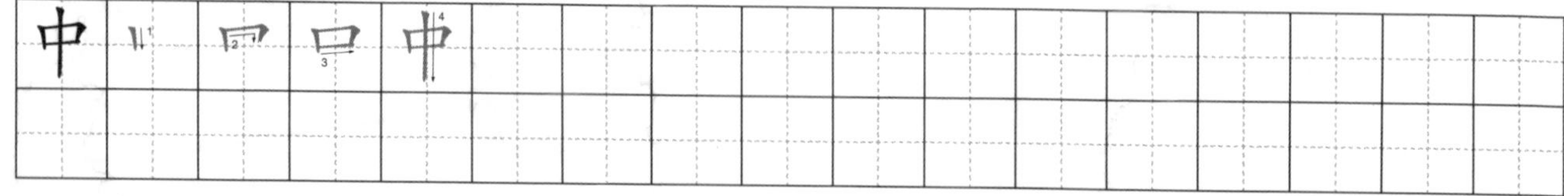

CHARACTER 41

英

yīng
English; British; brave

8 STROKES | 艹 RADICAL

Useful phrases and sentences

1. 英文 **Yīngwén** English language (usually written language)

Zài Zhōngguó, měige xuésheng dōu děi xué Yīngwén.
在中国，每个学生都得学英文。
In China, every student has to learn English.

2. 英国 **Yīngguó** England

Wǒ bù xǐhuan Yīngguóde tiānqì.
我不喜欢英国的天气。
I don't like the weather in England.

3. 英里 **yīnglǐ** mile

Bōshìdùn dào Niǔyuē liǎngbǎi duō Yīnglǐ.
波士顿到纽约两百多英里。
The distance between Boston and New York is about two hundred miles.

4. 英雄 **yīngxióng** hero

Shéi shì nǐ xīnzhōngde yīngxióng?
谁是你心中的英雄？
Who is the hero of your heart?

英

CHARACTER 42

men
(plural suffix for people)

5 STROKES | 亻 RADICAL

Useful phrases and sentences

1. 你们 **nǐmen** you (plural)

Nǐmen dōu huì shuō Yīngwén ma?
你们都会说英文吗？
Do you all speak English?

2. 我们 **wǒmen** we; us

Nǐ zuò wǒmen zhōngjiān ba.
你坐我们中间吧。
Please sit between us.

3. 他们 **tāmen** they; them (male)

Tāmen juéde Zhōngcān tài yóu le.
他们觉得中餐太油了。
They think that Chinese food is too greasy.

4. 她们 **tāmen** they; them (female)

Tāmen jīntiān dōu qǐngjià le.
她们今天都请假了。
All of them asked for leave today.

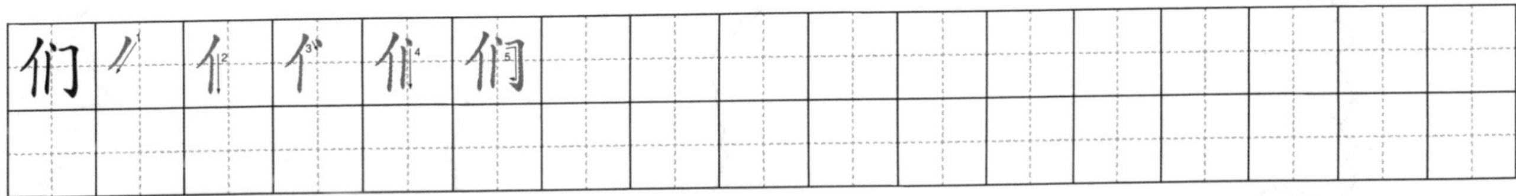

CHARACTER 43

de
(possessive marker)

8 STROKES | 白 RADICAL

Useful phrases and sentences

1. 你们的 **nǐmende** your (plural)

Nǐmende érzi jǐsuì le?
你们的儿子几岁了？
How old is your son?

2. 您的... **Nínde...** your ...

Nínde lǎoshī shì Zhōngguó rén ma?
您的老师是中国人吗？
Is your teacher Chinese?

3. 他们的... **tāmende...** their ...

Tāmende gōngzuò hěn máng.
他们的工作很忙。
Their work is very busy.

4. 我们的 **wǒmende** ours

Wǒmende xiǎngfǎ hěn bù yíyàng.
我们的想法很不一样。
Our thoughts are quite different.

的

CHARACTER 44

朋

péng
friend

Useful phrases and sentences

8 STROKES | 月 RADICAL

1. 朋友 **péngyou** friend

Nǐde wàiguo péngyou duō ma?
你的外国朋友多吗？
Do you have a lot of foreign friends?

2. 男朋友 **nánpéngyou** boyfriend

Nǐde nánpéngyou gāo ma?
你的男朋友高吗？
Is your boyfriend tall?

3. 女朋友 **nǚpéngyou** girlfriend

Tāde nǚpéngyou hěn hǎokàn.
他的女朋友很好看。
His girlfriend is pretty.

4. 好朋友 **hǎo péngyou** good friend

Wǒde hǎo péngyou shì Měiguó rén.
我的好朋友是美国人。
My good friend is American.

CHARACTER 45

yǒu
friend

Note: **yǒu** loses its tone in the compounds **péngyou** *(friend)* and **shìyou** *(roommate).*

Useful phrases and sentences

4 STROKES | 又 RADICAL

1. 友好 **yǒuhǎo** friendly

Nǐ juéde Niǔyuē rén bù yǒuhǎo ma?
你觉得纽约人不友好吗？
Do you think that New Yorkers are not friendly?

2. 友谊 **yǒuyì** friendship

Yǒuyì dìyī, bǐsài dì'èr.
友谊第一，比赛第二。
Friendship comes before competition.

3. 室友 **shìyou** roommate

Wǒde shìyou bù xǐhuan shuōhuà.
我的室友不喜欢说话。
My roommate does not like to talk.

4. 网友 **wǎngyǒu** netizen

Hěnduō Zhōngguó wǎngyǒu shuō Yīngguó hěn piàoliang.
很多中国网友说英国很漂亮。
Many Chinese netizens say that England is pretty.

Lesson 3 Exercises

Part 1 Choose one character from the left row and one from the right row to make a meaningful compound words.

朋	文
英	儿
请	们
哪	国
人	友
中	问

Part 2 Ask your friends for the following information. Write down the information in the chart below.

	姓	名	他/她是哪国人？
1.			
2.			
3.			

Part 3 Use the following prompts to give a one-minute speech.

1. Q: 请问，你是中国人吗？

   A: ____。

2. Q: ____？

   A: 我是英国人。

3. Q: 你的好朋友是哪国人？

   A: ____。

4. Q: 你的男／女朋友是哪国人？

   A: ____。

5. Q: 你的<u>老师</u> (**lǎoshī**: teacher) 是哪国人？

   A: ____。

LESSON 4

How many people are there in your family?

你家有几口人？

1. Introduction

To control the rapid growth of population, the Chinese government implemented the "one child policy" in the 1970s nationwide, especially in major cities. Under this policy only one child was allowed in most families. This policy ended in 2015 as China faced the challenge of an aging population. Each family now is allowed to have two children.

In this lesson, you will learn how to introduce your family members and their age. In traditional Chinese culture, it is not impolite to ask about someone's age, although now most women might jokingly avoid the question.

2. Warm up

Read the passage below and answer the questions using Chinese characters.

> 你们好！
> 我叫李元，我家有四口人，爸爸、妈妈、哥哥、我。爸爸是美国人，妈妈是中国人。朋友问我："你是哪国人？"我说 (**shuō**: say)："我是中国人，也 (**yě**: also) 是美国人"。我的哥哥叫李朋，他十二岁，我们不是好朋友。

1. How many people are there in Li Yuan's family?

____

2. Who is Li Peng? How old is he?

____

3. Does Li Yuan like his older brother?

____

3. Vocabulary

	Word	Pinyin	English equivalent
1.	家	**jiā**	family; home
2.	有／没有	**yǒu/méiyǒu**	have/ not have
3.	几口人	**jǐkǒu rén**	how many people (in a family)
4.	多大	**duō dà**	how old (above ten)
5.	几岁	**jǐsuì**	how old (under ten)
6.	哥哥	**gēge**	older brother
7.	姐姐	**jiějie**	older sister
8.	弟弟	**dìdi**	younger brother
9.	妹妹	**mèimei**	younger sister

4. New Characters

Fifteen characters are introduced in this lesson. Use the following explanations to help you understand and remember the characters.

家 有 几 个 口 没 爸 妈 哥 姐 弟 妹 岁 多 大

CHARACTER 46

jiā
home; family

10 STROKES　宀 RADICAL

Useful phrases and sentences

1. 家 **jiā** home

Jīntiān wǎnshang nǐ zài jiā ma?
今天晚上你在家吗？
Will you be home tonight?

2. 家人 **jiārén** family member

Wǒde jiārén dōu huì shuō Zhōngwén.
我的家人都会说中文。
All my family members can speak Chinese.

3. 回家 **huíjiā** go back home

Nǐ shénme shíhou huíjiā?
你什么时候回家？
When will you go back home?

4. 家教 **jiājiào** (home) tutor

Wǒde Zhōngwén jiājiào hěn hǎo.
我的中文家教很好。
My Chinese tutor is very nice.

家

CHARACTER 47

yǒu
have

Useful phrases and sentences

6 STROKES 月 RADICAL

1. 有 **yǒu** have

Nǐ yǒu Zhōngguó péngyou ma?
你有中国朋友吗？
Do you have any Chinese friends?

2. 有趣 **yǒuqù** interesting

Wǒ juéde xué wàiyǔ hěn yǒuqù.
我觉得学外语很有趣。
I think learning a foreign language is very interesting.

3. 有时间 **yǒu shíjiān** have time

Wǒ jīntiān méiyǒu shíjiān.
我今天没有时间。
I do not have time today.

4. 有意思 **yǒu yìsi** interesting

Xué Zhōngwén hěn yǒu yìsi.
学中文很有意思。
Learning Chinese is interesting.

有 1 2 3 4 5 6

CHARACTER 48

jǐ
how many

Useful phrases and sentences

2 STROKES 几 RADICAL

1. 几口人 **jǐkǒu rén** how many people (in a family)

Nǐ jiā yǒu jǐkǒu rén?
你家有几口人？
How many people are there in your family?

2. 几个 **jǐge** how many

Nǐmen bān yǒu jǐge nánshēng?
你们班有几个男生？
How many male students do you have in your class?

3. 几点 **jǐdiǎn** what time

Xiànzài jǐdiǎn zhōng?
现在几点钟？
What time is it now?

4. 几楼 **jǐlóu** which floor

Nǐde bàngōngshì zài jǐlóu?
你的办公室在几楼？
Which floor is your office?

几 1 2

CHARACTER 49

ge
a general measure word

Useful phrases and sentences

3 STROKES 人 RADICAL

1. 一个人 **yíge rén** one person

Jīntiān túshūguǎn lǐ zhǐ yǒu yíge rén.
今天图书馆里只有一个人。
There is only one person in the library today.

2. 两个蛋糕 **liǎngge dàngāo** two cakes

Lǐ Yuán gāng mǎile liǎngge dàngāo.
李元刚买了两个蛋糕。
Li Yuan just bought two cakes.

3. 一个工作 **yíge gōngzuò** one job

Xiànzài hěnduō rén bù zhǐ yǒu yíge gōngzuò.
现在很多人不只有一个工作。
Many people have more than one job nowadays.

4. 四个小时 **sìge xiǎoshí** four hours

Zuótiān wǎnshang wǒ zhǐ shuìle sìge xiǎoshí.
昨天晚上我只睡了四个小时。
I only slept for four hours last night.

个 1 2 3

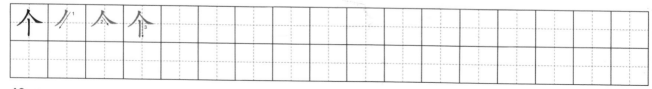

CHARACTER 50

kǒu
mouth; a measure word for people in a family

3 STROKES | 口 RADICAL

Useful phrases and sentences

1. 三口人 **sānkǒu rén** three people

Wǒ jiā yǒu sānkǒu rén.
我家有三口人。
There are three people in my family.

2. 入口 **rùkǒu** entrance

Diànyǐngyuànde rùkǒu zài nǎr?
电影院的入口在哪儿？
Where is the entrance of the cinema?

3. 出口 **chūkǒu** exit

Wǒmen zài chāoshìde chūkǒu jiànmiàn ba.
我们在超市的出口见面吧！
Let's meet at the exit of the supermarket!

4. 口试 **kǒushì** oral exam

Zhècì kǒushì tài nánle, wǒ tīngbudǒng lǎoshīde wèntí.
这次口试太难了，我听不懂老师的问题。
The oral test was very difficult. I couldn't understand teacher's question.

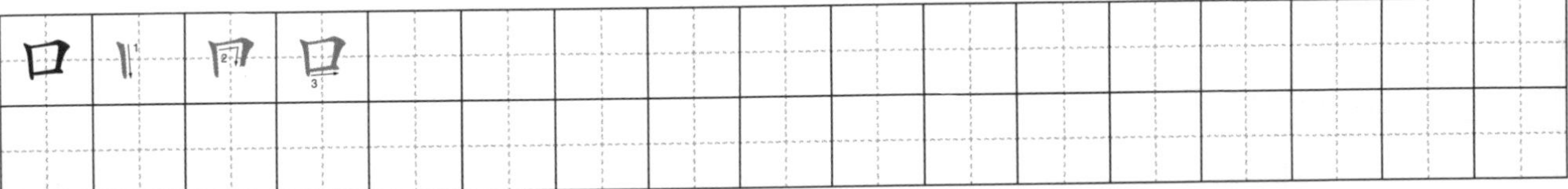

CHARACTER 51

méi
not (negation word for 有)

7 STROKES | 氵 RADICAL

Useful phrases and sentences

1. 没有 **méiyǒu** not have

Wǒ méiyǒu mèimei.
我没有妹妹。
I do not have any younger sisters.

2. 没有钱 **méiyǒu qián** have no money

Wǒ méiyǒu qián mǎi dōngxi le.
我没有钱买东西了。
I have no money for shopping.

3. 没有时间 **méiyǒu shíjiān** have no time

Lǐ Xiānsheng jīntiān méiyǒu shíjiān.
李先生今天没有时间。
Mr. Li has no time today.

4. 没关系 **méi guānxi** that's all right; no connection

A : Duìbùqǐ. **B : Méi guānxi.**
A: 对不起。 B: 没关系。
A: I am sorry. *B: That's all right.*

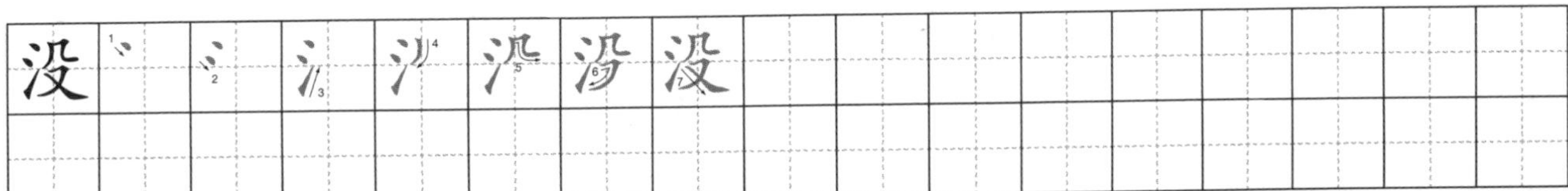

CHARACTER 52

bà
father

8 STROKES | 父 RADICAL

Useful phrases and sentences

1. 爸爸 **bàba** father

Wǒ bàba shì Měiguó rén.
我爸爸是美国人。
My father is American.

2. 爸妈 **bàmā** mom and dad

Wǒ bàmā shì zài Xiānggǎng Dàxué rènshi de.
我爸妈是在香港大学认识的。
My mom and dad met at the University of Hong Kong.

3. 阿爸 **ābà** father (regional use)

Yǒuxiē Zhōngguó rén chēng "bàba" wéi " ābà."
有些中国人称"爸爸"为"阿爸"。
Some Chinese people call their fathers "aba."

4. 干爸 **gānbà** godfather

Wǒ gānbà xìng Zhāng, shì wǒ bàbade péngyou.
我干爸姓张，是我爸爸的朋友。
My godfather is surnamed Zhang. He is a friend of my father.

CHARACTER 53

妈

mā
mother

Useful phrases and sentences

6 STROKES | 女 RADICAL

1. 妈妈 **māma** mother

Wǒ māma bú zài jiā.
我妈妈不在家。
My mother is not home.

2. 干妈 **gānmā** godmother

Lǐ Yuán yǒu yíge gānmā, cóng xiǎo zhàogù tā zhǎngdà.
李元有一个干妈，从小照顾他长大。
Li Yuan has a godmother. She has been looking after him since he was little.

3. 大妈 **dàmā** elderly woman

Gōngyuán shàngwǔ měitiān yǒu hěnduō dàmā zài tiàowǔ.
公园上午每天有很多大妈在跳舞。
Many elderly women are dancing in the park every morning.

4. 姨妈 **yímā** mother's sister

Wǒ yǒu liǎngge yímā, yíge zài Shànghǎi, yíge zài Xī'ān.
我有两个姨妈，一个在上海，一个在西安。
I have two aunts. One is in Shanghai and the other is in Xi'an.

妈 1 2 3 4 5 6

CHARACTER 54

哥

gē
older brother

Useful phrases and sentences

10 STROKES | 一 RADICAL

1. 哥哥 **gēge** older brother

Wǒ gēge jīnnián èrshísuì.
我哥哥今年二十岁。
My older brother is twenty years old.

2. 大哥 **dàgē** oldest brother

Wǒ dàgē zài Bōshìdùn gōngzuò.
我大哥在波士顿工作。
My oldest brother works in Boston.

3. 表哥 **biǎogē** older male cousin

Wǒ biǎogē bú huì shuō Zhōngwén.
我表哥不会说中文。
My older male cousin doesn't speak Chinese.

4. 帅哥 **shuàigē** handsome man

Shuàigē, nǐ jiào shénme míngzi?
帅哥，你叫什么名字？
Handsome man, what is your name?

哥 1 2 3 4 5 6 7 8 9 10

CHARACTER 55

姐

jiě
older sister

Useful phrases and sentences

8 STROKES | 女 RADICAL

1. 姐姐 **jiějie** older sister

Wǒ jiějie méiyǒu nánpéngyou.
我姐姐没有男朋友。
My older sister does not have a boyfriend.

2. 表姐 **biǎojiě** older female cousin

Wǒ biǎojiě hěn yǒu yìsi.
我表姐很有意思。
My older female cousin is very interesting.

3. 小姐 **Xiǎojie** Miss; young lady (sometimes rude)

Xiǎojie, qǐng wèn nǐ duō dà le?
小姐，请问你多大了？
May I ask how old you are, Miss?

4. 姐夫 **jiěfū** older sister's husband

"Jiěfū" jiù shì jiějiede xiānsheng.
"姐夫"就是姐姐的先生。
The term "jiefu" refers to your sister's husband.

姐 1 2 3 4 5 6 7 8

CHARACTER 56

弟

dì

younger brother

7 STROKES | 丷 RADICAL

Useful phrases and sentences

1. 弟弟 **dìdi** younger brother

   Wǒ dìdide Yīngwén hěn hǎo.
   我弟弟的英文很好。
   My younger brother's English is pretty good.

2. 兄弟 **xiōngdì** brothers

   Zhè shì Lǐ jiā sān xiōngdì.
   这是李家三兄弟。
   These are the three brothers of the Li family.

3. 表弟 **biǎodì** younger male cousin

   Wǒ méiyǒu biǎodì.
   我没有表弟。
   I do not have any younger male cousins.

4. 小弟 **xiǎodì** youngest brother

   Zài jiā wǒ shì xiǎodì, wǒ yǒu yíge gēge hé yíge jiějie.
   在家我是小弟，我有一个哥哥和一个姐姐。
   I am the youngest brother in my family. I have one older brother and one older sister.

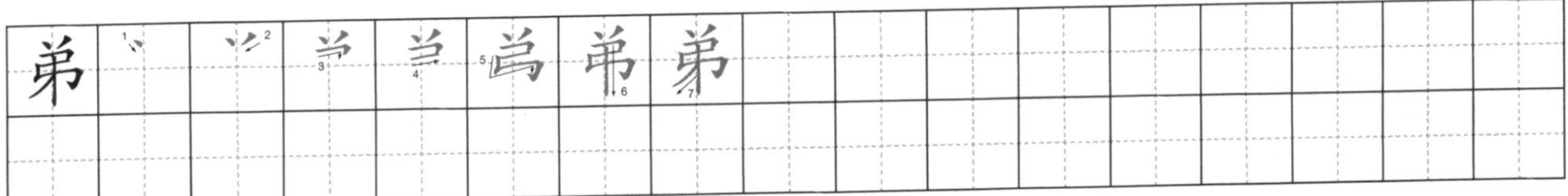

CHARACTER 57

mèi

younger sister

8 STROKES | 女 RADICAL

Useful phrases and sentences

1. 妹妹 **mèimei** younger sister

   Mèimei, zhè shì nǐde péngyou ma?
   妹妹，这是你的朋友吗？
   Is this your friend, younger sister?

2. 姐妹 **jiěmèi** sisters

   Nǐ yǒu jiěmèi ma?
   你有姐妹吗？
   Do you have any sisters?

3. 表妹 **biǎomèi** younger female cousin

   Wǒ biǎomèi bāsuì.
   我表妹八岁。
   My younger female cousin is eight years old.

4. 兄妹 **xiōngmèi** older brother and younger sister

   Nǐmen shì xiōngmèi ma?
   你们是兄妹吗？
   Are you an older brother and a younger sister?

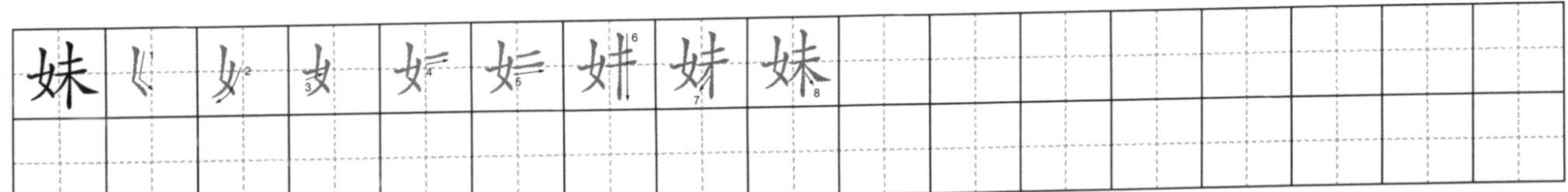

CHARACTER 58

suì

years of age

6 STROKES | 山 RADICAL

Useful phrases and sentences

1. 几岁 **jǐsuì** how old (under ten)

   Nǐ jǐsuì le?
   你几岁了？
   How old are you?

2. 岁数 **suìshu** age

   Nín duō dà suìshu?
   您多大岁数？
   How old are you? (for the elderly)

3. 十八岁 **shíbāsuì** eighteen years old

   Wǒde nǚ'ér jīnnián shíbāsuì.
   我的女儿今年十八岁。
   My daughter is eighteen years old.

4. 岁月 **suìyuè** time

   Zhōngguó rén cháng shuō "suìyuè rú suō."
   中国人常说 "岁月如梭"。
   Chinese people often say "time flies like a shuttle."

CHARACTER 59

duō
many; much

Useful phrases and sentences

6 STROKES | 夕 RADICAL

1. 多大 **duō dà** how old (above ten)
   Nǐ duō dà le?
   你多大了？
   How old are you?

2. 多高 **duō gāo** how tall/high
   Nǐ duō gāo?
   你多高？
   How tall are you?

3. 多重 **duō zhòng** how much weight
   Qǐng nǐ bié wèn wǒ duō zhòng, xíng-bù-xíng?
   请你别问我多重，行不行？
   Can you please not ask me how much I weigh?

4. 多少人 **duōshǎo rén** how many people
   Nǐmen bān yǒu duōshǎo rén?
   你们班有多少人？
   How many people are there in your class?

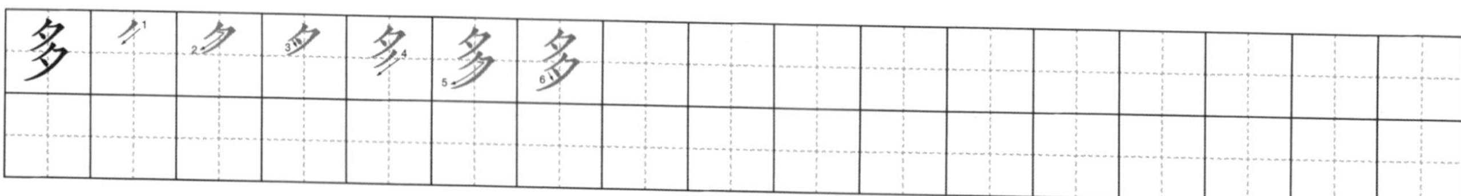

CHARACTER 60

dà
big; large

Useful phrases and sentences

3 STROKES | 大 RADICAL

1. 大学 **dàxué** university; college
   Wǒde dàxué hěn yǒumíng.
   我的大学很有名。
   My university is famous.

2. 大学生 **dàxuésheng** college student
   Nǐ shì dàxuésheng ma?
   你是大学生吗？
   Are you a college student?

3. 大声 **dà shēng** loud voice
   Qǐng nǐ dà sheng yìdiǎnr.
   请你大声一点儿。
   Speak louder, please.

4. 大家 **dàjiā** everyone
   Dàjiā zǎoshang hǎo!
   大家早上好！
   Good morning, everyone!

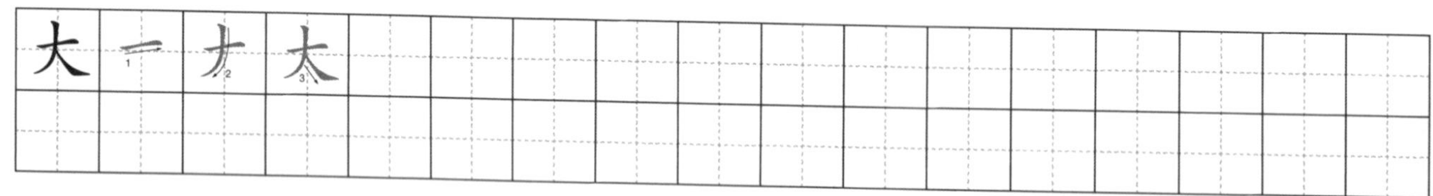

Lesson 4 Exercises

Part 1 Choose from the following words to fill in the blanks.

口、个、问、多大、哪儿、什么

1. 你家有几（　　　　）人？你有几（　　　　）哥哥？
2. 你十八岁，你的中国朋友（　　　　）？

3. 请（　　　），你的爸爸妈妈在（　　　）工作？

4. 你的中文家教叫（　　　）名字？

Part 2 Answer the following questions using Chinese characters.

1. Q: 你家有几口人？

   A: ______________________________。

2. Q: 你的爸爸妈妈是哪国人？

   A: ______________________________。

3. Q: 你今年多大？

   A: ______________________________。

4. Q: 你有没有哥哥、姐姐、弟弟、妹妹？

   A: ______________________________。

Part 3 Use the following prompts to give a one-minute speech.

你们好！

我叫 ______________________________，

我是 ______________________________ 国人。

我的老家在 Pennsylvania。

我家有 __________ 口人，______________________________

______________________________。

我今年 (**jīnnián**: this year) ______________ 岁，

我弟弟 __________ 岁。我有很多中国朋友。

LESSON 5

What do you do for work? 你做什么工作？

1. Introduction

In your opinion, what is a good job? According to a recent survey, three kinds of careers are popular among Chinese young people. The first is a civil service career. Although the pay is not high, such a career is quite secure, which is why it is called an "iron rice-bowl." The second career is working for a foreign company. Although the working hours are long, the salary is generous. The third career is to start one's own business. In recent years, more and more people are starting their own business because of the heated competition in the job market.

2. Warm up

Read the passage below and answer the questions using Chinese characters.

我家有四口人：我爸爸、妈妈、姐姐和我。我爸爸五十岁，他是医生。我妈妈四十八岁，也是医生。我姐姐二十八岁，她是老师。我二十二岁，不是医生，也不是老师，我是学生。

1. What do the author's parents do for work?

____

2. Is the author's older sister a doctor?

____

3. How old is the author? What does he/she do?

____

3. Vocabulary

	Word	Pinyin	English equivalent
1.	父亲	**fùqin**	father (formal)
2.	母亲	**mǔqin**	mother (formal)
3.	父母	**fùmǔ**	parents
4.	工作	**gōngzuò**	job; work
5.	老师	**lǎoshī**	teacher
6.	学生	**xuésheng**	student
7.	医生	**yīsheng**	doctor
8.	女生	**nǚshēng**	female student

4. New Characters

Fifteen characters are introduced in this lesson. Use the following explanations to help you understand and remember the characters.

父 母 亲 和 做 工 作 老 师 学 生 呢 也 医 女

CHARACTER 61

fù
father (formal)

4 STROKES | 父 RADICAL

Useful phrases and sentences

1. 父亲 **fùqin** father (formal)
   Wǒ fùqin zaì Běijīng gōngzuò.
   我父亲在北京工作。
   My father works in Beijing.

2. 父母 **fùmǔ** parents
   Wǒde fùmǔ dōu shì lǎoshī.
   我的父母都是老师。
   My parents are both teachers.

3. 祖父 **zǔfù** paternal grandfather (formal)
   Tāde zǔfù bāshísuì le.
   他的祖父八十岁了。
   His grandfather is eighty years old.

4. 岳父 **yuèfù** father-in-law (wife's father)
   Wǒde yuèfù shì lǎoshī, shēntǐ hěn hǎo.
   我的岳父是老师，身体很好。
   My father-in-law is a teacher. He is in good health.

父 1 2 3 4

CHARACTER 62

mǔ
mother (formal)

Useful phrases and sentences

5 STROKES | 母 RADICAL

1. 母亲 **mǔqin** mother (formal)

Wǒ mǔqin yǒu yíge gēge, yíge jiějie.
我母亲有一个哥哥，一个姐姐。
My mother has one older brother and one older sister.

2. 母语 **mǔyǔ** mother tongue

Wǒde mǔyǔ bú shì Zhōngwén, shì Yīngwén.
我的母语不是中文，是英文。
My mother tongue is not Chinese, but English.

3. 祖母 **zǔmǔ** paternal grandmother (formal)

Wǒde zǔmǔ yǒu hěnduō Yīngguo péngyou.
我的祖母有很多英国朋友。
My grandmother has many English friends.

4. 岳母 **yuèmǔ** mother-in-law (wife's mother)

Tāde yuèmǔ shì Tiānjīn rén, hěn huì zuò jiǎozi.
他的岳母是天津人，很会做饺子。
His mother-in-law is from Tianjin. She is good at making dumplings.

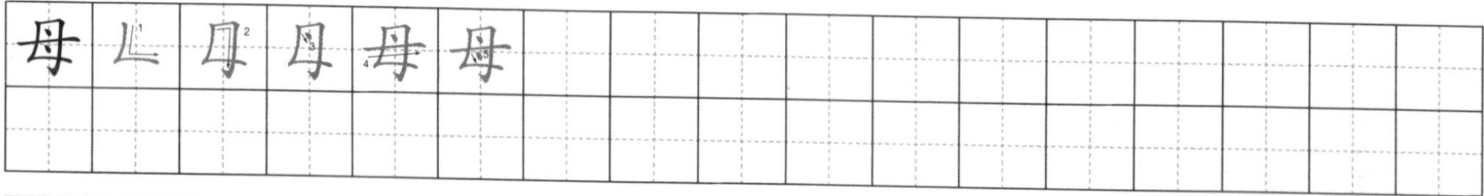

CHARACTER 63

qīn
kin

Useful phrases and sentences

9 STROKES | 立 RADICAL

1. 亲密 **qīnmì** close relationship

Tāliǎde guānxi yuè lái yuè qīnmì.
他俩的关系越来越亲密。
The two of them became more and more intimate.

2. 亲手 **qīnshǒu** personally

Wǒ děi qīnshǒu bǎ zhèběn shū gěi tā.
我得亲手把这本书给他。
I have to hand this book to him in person.

3. 亲戚 **qīnqi** relative

Xiǎo Wáng shì nǐde qīnqi ma?
小王是你的亲戚吗？
Is Xiao Wang one of your relatives?

4. 亲 **qīn** biologically related immediate family

Tā bú shì wǒde qīn dìdi, tāshì wǒ shūshude háizi.
他不是我的亲弟弟，他是我叔叔的孩子。
He is not my biological brother; he is my uncle's son.

CHARACTER 64

hé
and; with

Useful phrases and sentences

8 STROKES | 口 RADICAL

1. 中国和美国 **Zhōngguó hé Měiguó** China and U.S.A.

Zhōngguó hé Měiguó dōu shì dà guó.
中国和美国都是大国。
Both China and U.S.A. are big countries.

2. 老师和学生 **lǎoshī hé xuésheng** teacher and student

Zhèrde lǎoshī hé xuésheng dōu shì wàiguó rén.
这儿的老师和学生都是外国人。
The teachers and students here are all foreigners.

3. 和 **hé** and; with

Wǒ xiǎng hé tā yìqǐ qù Yīngguó.
我想和他一起去英国。
I want to go to Britain with him.

4. 和平 **hépíng** peaceful

Wǒmen dōu xiǎng shēnghuó zài yíge hépíngde shìjiè.
我们都想生活在一个和平的世界。
We all want to live in a peaceful world.

CHARACTER 65

做

zuò
do; make

Useful phrases and sentences

11 STROKES | 亻 RADICAL

1. 做饭 **zuòfàn** cook

Wǒde tóngwū hěn xǐhuan zuòfàn.
我的同屋很喜欢做饭。
My roommate loves cooking.

2. 做作业 **zuò zuòyè** do homework

Wǒ jīntiān méiyǒu shíjiān, wǒ děi zuò zuòyè.
我今天没有时间，我得做作业。
I don't have time today. I need to do homework.

3. 做生意 **zuò shēngyì** do business

Nǐ xiǎng hé wǒ qù Zhōngguó zuò shēngyì ma?
你想和我去中国做生意吗？
Do you want to go to China with me to do business?

4. 做什么 **zuò shénme** do what

Nǐ zhǎngdà xiǎng zuò shénme?
你长大想做什么？
What do you want to do when you grow up?

CHARACTER 66

工

gōng
work

Useful phrases and sentences

3 STROKES | 工 RADICAL

1. 工人 **gōngren** worker

Wǒbàba shì gōngren, tā měitiān hěn máng.
我爸爸是工人，他每天很忙。
My father is a worker and he is busy every day.

2. 工厂 **gōngchǎng** factory

Zài Zhōngguó yǒu hěnduō wàiguo gōngchǎng.
在中国有很多外国工厂。
There are many foreign factories in China.

3. 打工 **dǎgōng** do temporary work

Wǒ xiǎng qù fànguǎnr dǎgōng.
我想去饭馆儿打工。
I want to work part-time in a restaurant.

4. 工资 **gōngzī** wages

Yīshengde gōngzī hěn gāo ma?
医生的工资很高吗？
Are doctors' wages high?

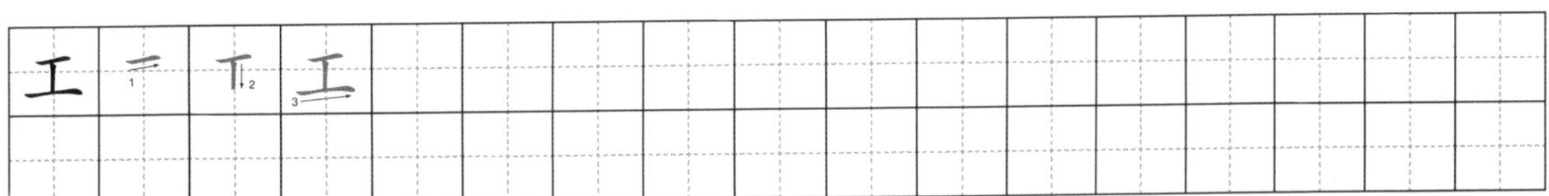

CHARACTER 67

作

zuò
make

Useful phrases and sentences

7 STROKES | 亻 RADICAL

1. 工作 **gōngzuò** work

Nǐ bàba zùo shénme gōngzuò?
你爸爸做什么工作？
What does your father do for work?

2. 作业 **zuòyè** homework

Nǐde Zhōngwén zuòyè duō ma?
你的中文作业多吗？
Do you have a lot of Chinese homework?

3. 作文 **zuòwén** essay

Wǒ bù xǐhuan xiě zuòwén.
我不喜欢写作文。
I don't like writing essays.

4. 作家 **zùojiā** writer

Tāde mǔqin shì yíge hěn yǒumíngde zùojiā.
她的母亲是一个很有名的作家。
Her mother is a famous writer.

CHARACTER 68

lǎo
old

Useful phrases and sentences

6 STROKES | 老 RADICAL

1. 老 **lǎo** old

Wǒde fùmǔ dōu lǎo le, wǒ xiǎng hé tāmen zhù yìqǐ.
我的父母都老了，我想和他们住一起。
My parents are old and I hope to live with them.

2. 老公 **lǎogōng** husband (intimate)

Tāde lǎogōng yězài Běijīng Dàxué gōngzuò.
她的老公也在北京大学工作。
Her husband also works at Beijing University.

3. 老板 **lǎobǎn** boss

Wǒde lǎobǎn rén hěn hǎo.
我的老板人很好。
My boss is a nice person.

4. 老外 **lǎowài** foreigner (some people find it offensive)

Yǒude Zhōngguó rén jiào wàiguo rén "lǎowài."
有的中国人叫外国人“老外”。
Some Chinese people call foreigners "laowai."

CHARACTER 69

师

shī
teacher; master

Useful phrases and sentences

6 STROKES | 丨 RADICAL

1. 老师 **lǎoshī** teacher

Wǒ mèimei shì lǎoshī.
我妹妹是老师。
My younger sister is a teacher.

2. 律师 **lǜshī** laywer

Zuò lǜshī hěn lèi, kěshì gōngzī hěn gāo.
做律师很累，可是工资很高。
Being a lawyer is tiring, but the salary is high.

3. 师傅 **shīfu** master (of a trade); driver

Shīfu, qù Běijīng Dàxué ma?
师傅，去北京大学吗？
Sir, is this going to Peking University?

4. 师弟 **shīdì** junior male student

Tā shì wǒ dàxuéde shīdì.
他是我大学的师弟。
He is a younger fellow student in my college.

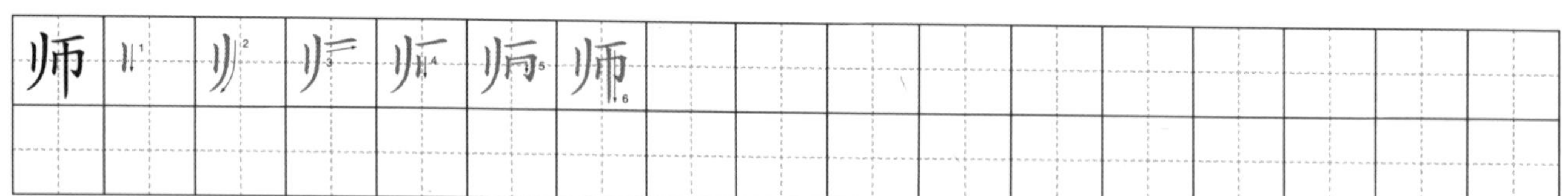

CHARACTER 70

xué
study; learn

Useful phrases and sentences

8 STROKES | 子 RADICAL

1. 学 **xué** study; learn

Xué shùxué hěn nán.
学数学很难。
It's hard to study math.

2. 学生 **xuésheng** student

Zhège lǎoshī hěn xǐhuan hé xuésheng liáotiān.
这个老师很喜欢和学生聊天。
This teacher likes to talk with students.

3. 学费 **xuéfèi** tuition fee

Zài nǐde dàxué, xuéfèi yìnián duōshao qián?
在你的大学，学费一年多少钱？
In your college, how much is your tuition per year?

4. 科学 **kēxué** science

Tā cóng xiǎo jiù xǐhuan kēxué.
他从小就喜欢科学。
He has liked science since he was little.

CHARACTER 71

生

shēng
student; born; live; raw

Note: **shēng** loses its tone in **xuésheng** *(student)*.

5 STROKES | 丿 RADICAL

Useful phrases and sentences

1. 生病 **shēngbìng** to get sick

Tā zuótiān shēngbìngle, méi lái shàngkè.
她昨天生病了，没来上课。
She did not come to the class because she got sick yesterday.

2. 生日 **shēngrì** birthday

Jīntiān shì wǒde shēngrì, wǒ shíbāsuì le.
今天是我的生日，我十八岁了。
Today is my birthday. I am turning 18.

3. 生活 **shēnghuó** life; live

Niǔyuē rén tài duō le, wǒ bù xǐhuan nàrde shēnghuó.
纽约人太多了，我不喜欢那儿的生活。
There are too many people in New York. I don't like the life there.

4. 生词 **shēngcí** new words

Dìsānkède kèwén yǒu hěnduō shēngcí.
第三课的课文有很多生词。
There are too many new words in the text for Lesson Three.

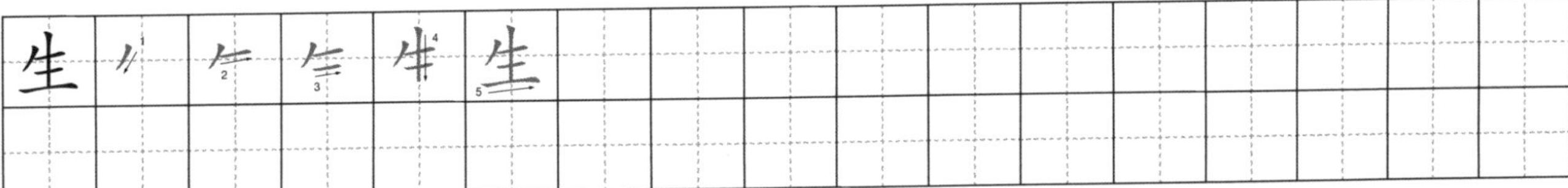

CHARACTER 72

呢

ne
how about; what about

8 STROKES | 口 RADICAL

Useful phrases and sentences

1. 你呢？ **nǐ ne?** How about you?

Wǒ shì Rìběn rén, nǐ ne?
我是日本人，你呢？
I am Japanese. How about you?

2. 你家呢？ **nǐ jiā ne?** How about your family/home?

Wǒ jiā yǒu sānkǒu rén, nǐ jiā ne?
我家有三口人，你家呢？
There are three people in my family. How about your family?

3. 美国呢？ **Měiguó ne?** What about U.S.A.?

Zhōngguóde shǒudū shì Běijīng, Měiguó ne?
中国的首都是北京，美国呢？
The capital city of China is Beijing. What about U.S.A.?

4. 你妹妹呢？ **nǐ mèimei ne?** What about your younger sister?

Nǐ dìdi shì xuésheng, nǐ mèimei ne?
你弟弟是学生，你妹妹呢？
Your younger brother is a student. What about your younger sister?

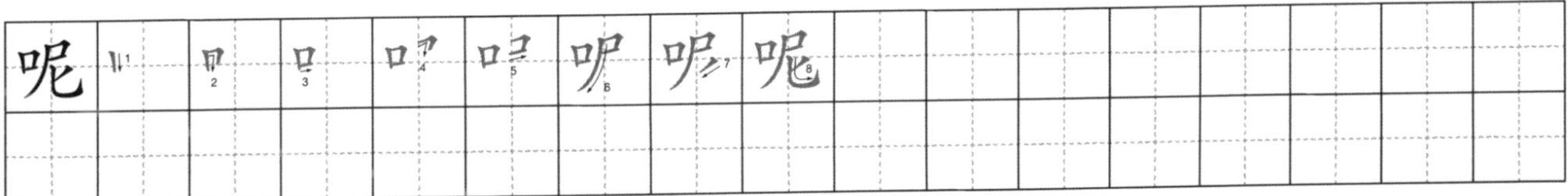

CHARACTER 73

yě
also; too

3 STROKES | 乛 RADICAL

Useful phrases and sentences

1. 也 **yě** also; too

Wǒ dìdi yě shì dàxuésheng.
我弟弟也是大学生。
My younger brother is also a college student.

2. 也好 **yě hǎo** all right

Nǐ lái yě hǎo, bù lái yě hǎo, wǒ dōu wúsuǒwèi.
你来也好，不来也好，我都无所谓。
It's OK if you come or don't come. Either way I don't mind.

3. 也有 **yě yǒu** also have

Wǒ yǒu yíge jiějie, Lǐ Yuán yě yǒu.
我有一个姐姐，李元也有。
I have one older sister and so does Li Yuan.

4. 也许 **yěxǔ** maybe; perhaps

Yěxǔ Lǐ Péng bù xiǎng dāng yīsheng, tā xiǎng dāng lǎoshī.
也许李朋不想当医生，他想当老师。
Maybe Li Peng doesn't want to be a doctor; he wants to be a teacher.

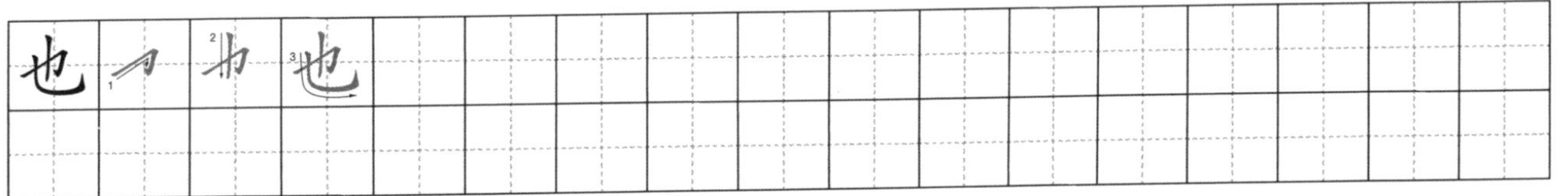

CHARACTER 74

医

yī
doctor; (things relating to medicine)

Useful phrases and sentences

7 STROKES | 匚 RADICAL

1. 医生 **yīsheng** doctor
Yīsheng shuō nǐ yīnggāi dūo hē shuǐ.
医生说你应该多喝水。
The doctor said you should drink more water.

2. 医院 **yīyuàn** hospital
Qǐng wèn, qù yīyuàn zěnme zǒu?
请问，去医院怎么走？
Excuse me, how can I get to the hospital?

3. 医学院 **yīxuéyuàn** medical school
Tīngshuō zài Měiguó kǎo yīxuéyuàn hěn nán.
听说在美国考医学院很难。
I heard that it is very hard to get into medical school in U.S.A.

4. 中医 **Zhōngyī** Traditional Chinese Medicine (TCM)
Wǒ hěn xiǎng qù Zhōngguó xué Zhōngyī.
我很想去中国学中医。
I really want to go to China to learn Traditional Chinese Medicine.

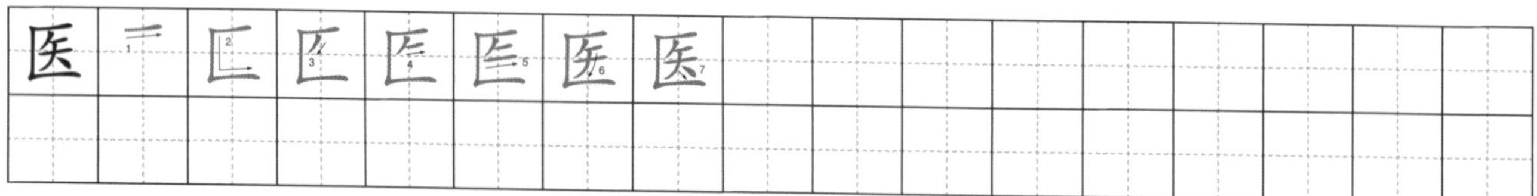

CHARACTER 75

女

nǚ
female

Useful phrases and sentences

3 STROKES | 女 RADICAL

1. 女生 **nǚshēng** female student
Zhège dàxué nǚshēng bù duō.
这个大学女生不多。
There are not many female students in this college.

2. 女人 **nǚrén** woman
Nánrén hé nǚrénde xiǎngfǎ bù yíyàng.
男人和女人的想法不一样。
Men and women have different ways of thinking.

3. 女儿 **nǚ'ér** daughter
Nǐde nǚ'ér yě zài yīxuéyuàn gōngzuò ma?
你的女儿也在医学院工作吗？
Does your daughter also work for the medical school?

4. 子女 **zǐnǚ** children (formal)
Zhège lǎorén méiyǒu zǐnǚ.
这个老人没有子女。
This old man does not have any children.

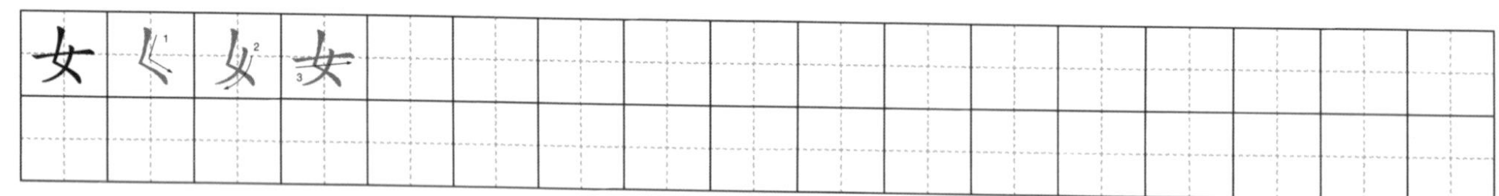

Lesson 5 Exercises

Part 1 Choose from the following words to fill in the blanks.

和、呢、也、做、老板

1. 我家有四口人，你家（　　　　）？

2. 你以后想（　　　　）什么工作？

3. 我的爸爸是公司的（　　　　），他每天都很忙。

4. 我（　　　　　）我的弟弟都是大学生。我喜欢学中文，他（　　　　　）喜欢学中文。

Part 2 Answer the following questions using Chinese characters.

1. Q: 你的父亲和母亲做什么工作？

   A: ______________________________。

2. Q: 你想 (**xiǎng**: want) 做什么工作？

   A: ______________________________。

3. Q: 你有几个老师？

   A: ______________________________。

4. Q: 你有几个好朋友？

   A: ______________________________。

Part 3 Write down the information in the chart below using information about your family members.

Family members	爸爸	妈妈	哥哥	姐姐	弟弟	妹妹
Job						
Like/don't like						

Here is a list of vocabulary for jobs in Chinese:

1. **jǐngchá** police

   警察

2. **yīsheng** doctor

   医生

3. **lǜshī** lawyer

   律师

4. **lǎoshī** teacher

   老师

Lessons 1–5 (Review Exercises)

Part 1 Write the Pinyin and the English meaning of the following words.

	Words	Pinyin	English Equivalent
e.g.,	五元	**wǔyuán**	**five yuan (Chinese dollars, formal)**
1.	九十二	__________	__________
2.	七百八十五	__________	__________
3.	你好	__________	__________
4.	名字	__________	__________
5.	中国	__________	__________
6.	朋友	__________	__________
7.	哥哥	__________	__________
8.	几岁	__________	__________
9.	老师	__________	__________
10.	工作	__________	__________

Part 2 Fill in the blanks according to the English meaning.

1. (　　　) 时间 have time
2. (　　　) 生 student
3. (　　　) 么 what
4. (　　　) 关系 that's all right
5. (　　　) 友 friend
6. 老 (　　　) teacher
7. 打 (　　　) do temporary work
8. 父 (　　　) father
9. 中 (　　　) China
10. 名 (　　　) name

Part 3 Answer the following questions using Chinese characters.

1. Q: 你的<u>室友</u> (**shìyou**: roommate) 叫什么名字？

   A: ____________________ 。

2. Q: 你觉得什么工作很有意思？

A: ____。

3. Q: 你家有几口人？他们是谁？

A: ____。

4. Q: 你今年多大了？你有美国朋友吗？

A: ____。

Part 4 Read the passage below and answer the questions using Chinese characters.

小朋，

我昨天认识了一个新朋友，他是美国人，今年二十三岁。他的中文名字是王国友。

国友家有六口人，爸爸、妈妈、还有两个哥哥，一个妹妹。他的妈妈是英国人，爸爸是中国人。国友的中文不太好，他常常问我很多中文问题，他的问题很有意思。国友人很好，你想认识他吗？

祝好，

李新

1. 国友是哪国人？他今年多大了？

____。

2. 国友家有几口人？他的爸爸、妈妈做什么工作？

____。

3. 国友的中文好不好？

____。

4. 小朋认识国友吗？

____。

LESSON 6

What day is today? 今天是星期几?

1. Introduction

In this lesson you will learn the words for weekdays and months in Chinese. While the vocabulary of months in English comes mostly from Latin, the Chinese describe the twelve months of a year in a relatively linear way. You only need to add the number of the month in front of the word 月 (**yuè:** month). For instance, 一月 (**yīyuè:** January), 三月 (**sānyuè:** March), 四月 (**sìyuè:** April), and 十一月 (**shíyīyuè:** November).

The terms for weekdays in Chinese follow similar rules. The Chinese word for "week" is 星期 (**xīngqī**). If you want to say Monday, it is 星期一 (**xīngqīyī**). Tuesday is 星期二 (**xīngqī'èr**). Friday is 星期五 (**xīngqīwǔ**). So the rule is to put the number of the weekday after 星期 (**xīngqī:** week. There is one exception. For Sunday, we don't say 星期七 (**xīngqīqī**). Instead, we say 星期日 (**xīngqīrì**) or 星期天 (**xīngqītiān**). What months do you like? When is your birthday? What are the busiest days for you?

2. Warm up

Read the passage below and answer the questions using Chinese characters.

> 我叫李元，今天是二零一六年一月二十日，星期三。今天是我十岁的生日 (**shēngrì**: birthday)。我、我爸爸妈妈和我的好朋友们一起吃饭 (**yìqǐ chīfàn**: eat together)、唱歌 (**chànggē**: sing songs)。我很开心 (**hěn kāixīn**: very happy)。你呢？你的生日是几月几号？

1. What day is today?

____

2. How old is he?

____

3. How did he celebrate his birthday?

____

3. Vocabulary

	Word	Pinyin	English equivalent
1.	今天	**jīntiān**	today
2.	昨天	**zuótiān**	yesterday
3.	明天	**míngtiān**	tomorrow
4.	明年	**míngnián**	next year
5.	星期日	**xīngqīrì**	Sunday
6.	谢谢	**xièxie**	thanks
7.	再见	**zàijiàn**	goodbye
8.	一月	**yīyuè**	January
9.	二月	**èryuè**	February

4. New Characters

Fifteen characters are introduced in this lesson. Use the following explanations to help you understand and remember the characters.

今　明　昨　天　年　月　日　星　期　吗　谢　再　见　上　下

CHARACTER 76

jīn
today; now; current

4 STROKES　人 RADICAL

Useful phrases and sentences

1. 今天 **jīntiān** today

Nǐ jīntiān máng ma?
你今天忙吗？
Are you busy today?

2. 今年 **jīnnián** this year

Wǒ jīnnián dàxué bìyè.
我今年大学毕业。
I will graduate from university this year.

3. 今后 **jīnhòu** from now on

Jīnhòu wǒmen shì péngyou le.
今后我们是朋友了。
We are friends from now on.

4. 今晚 **jīnwǎn** tonight

Nǐ jīnwǎn qù nǎr?
你今晚去哪儿？
Where are you going tonight?

CHARACTER 77

míng
tomorrow; bright

8 STROKES | 日 RADICAL

Useful phrases and sentences

1. 明天 **míngtiān** tomorrow
   Míngtiān shì wǒ bàbade shēngrì.
   明天是我爸爸的生日。
   Tomorrow is my father's birthday.

2. 明年 **míngnián** next year
   Wǒ míngnián yào qù Zhōngguó.
   我明年要去中国。
   I will be going to China next year.

3. 明白 **míngbai** understand
   Wǒ bù míngbai nǐ shuō shénme.
   我不明白你说什么。
   I do not understand what you are saying.

4. 聪明 **cōngming** smart
   Wǒ gēge hěn cōngming.
   我哥哥很聪明。
   My older brother is very smart.

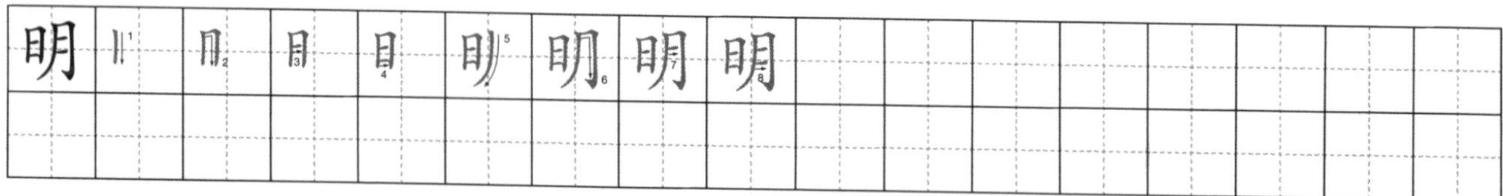

CHARACTER 78

zuó
yesterday

9 STROKES | 日 RADICAL

Useful phrases and sentences

1. 昨天 **zuótiān** yesterday
   Zuótiān shì xīngqī'èr.
   昨天是星期二。
   Yesterday was Tuesday.

2. 昨晚 **zuówǎn** last night
   Wǒ zuówǎn méiyǒu chīfàn.
   我昨晚没有吃饭。
   I did not eat last night.

3. 昨日 **zuórì** yesterday (formal)
   Zuórìde shì wǒ yǐjīng wàngle.
   昨日的事我已经忘了。
   I have forgotten about what happened last night.

4. 昨天晚上 **zuótiān wǎnshang** last night (full version of 昨晚)
   Zuótiān wǎnshang wǒ hé jiārén chīfàn.
   昨天晚上我和家人吃饭。
   I had dinner with my family last night.

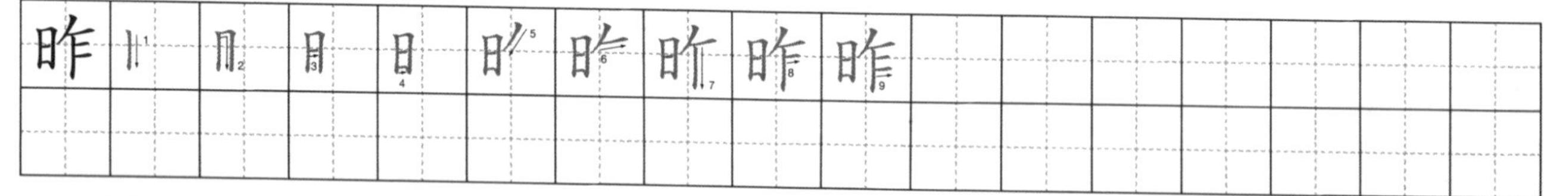

CHARACTER 79

tiān
day; sky; heaven

4 STROKES | 大 RADICAL

Useful phrases and sentences

1. 天亮 **tiānliàng** dawn
   Tiānliàngle, wǒmen chūmén ba.
   天亮了，我们出门吧。
   It's dawn. Let's go outside.

2. 天文 **tiānwén** astronomy
   Tā yǐhòu xiǎng xué tiānwén zhuānyè.
   他以后想学天文专业。
   He wants to study astronomy in the future.

3. 天气 **tiānqì** weather
   Jīntiānde tiānqì hěn hǎo.
   今天的天气很好。
   The weather today is pretty good.

4. 天哪！ **Tiānna** Oh my god!; Good heavens!
   Tiānna! Wǒde qiánbāo diūle!
   天哪！我的钱包丢了！
   Oh my god! I lost my wallet!

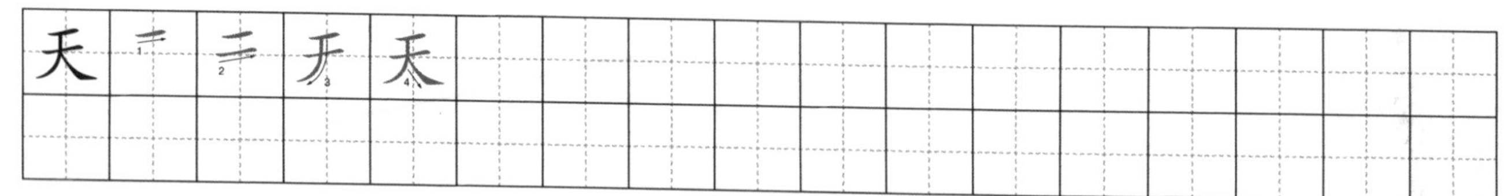

CHARACTER 80

年

nián
year

6 STROKES | 干 RADICAL

Useful phrases and sentences

1. 年轻 **niánqīng** young

Zhème duō nián méi jiàn nǐ, nǐ háishì nàme niánqīng!
这么多年没见你，你还是那么年轻！
I haven't seen you for many years. You still look very young!

2. 年级 **niánjí** grade

Wǒ shì dàxué sìniánjíde xuésheng, tā shì dàxué yīniánjíde xuésheng.
我是大学四年级的学生，她是大学一年级的学生。
I am a senior in college and she is a freshman.

3. 年纪 **niánjì** age

Tā niánjì xiǎo, kěshì dǒng hěnduō shìqing.
他年纪小，可是懂很多事情。
He is young, but he understands quite a lot.

4. 年代 **niándài** age/decade of a century

Wǒ shì bāshí niándài chūshēng de, wǒ jiā zhǐ yǒu wǒ yíge háizi.
我是八十年代出生的，我家只有我一个孩子。
I was born in the 80s. I was the only child in my family.

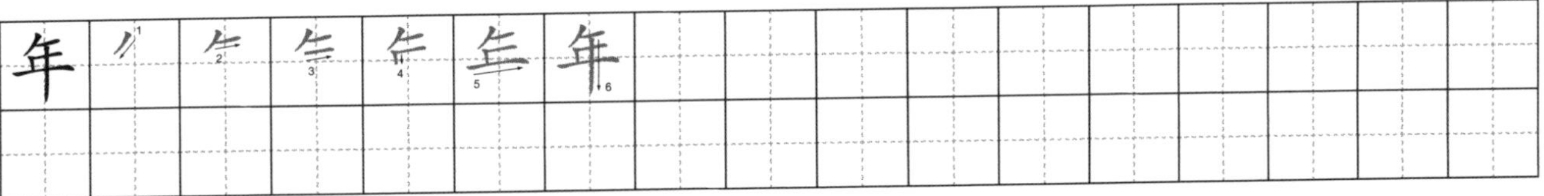

CHARACTER 81

月

yuè
month

4 STROKES | 月 RADICAL

Useful phrases and sentences

1. 九月 **jiǔyuè** September

Nǐ jiǔyuè máng ma?
你九月忙吗？
Are you busy in September?

2. 两个月 **liǎngge yuè** two months

Liǎngge yuède shíjiān hěn cháng.
两个月的时间很长。
Two months is a long time.

3. 月饼 **yuèbǐng** moon cake

Wǒ hěn xǐhuan chī yuèbǐng.
我很喜欢吃月饼。
I like moon cakes.

4. 上个月 **shàngge yuè** last month

Shàngge yuè wǒ hěn máng.
上个月我很忙。
I was very busy last month.

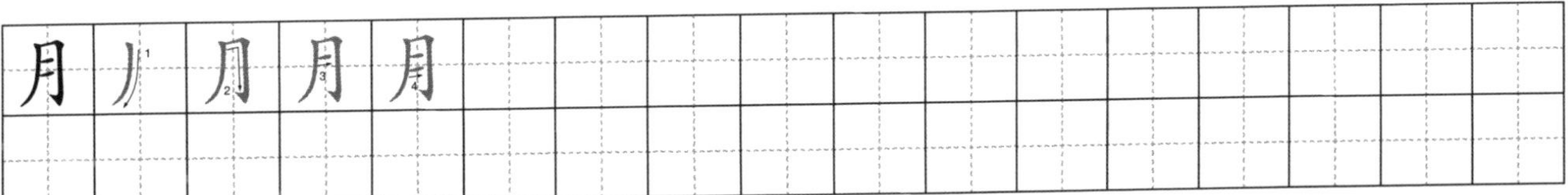

CHARACTER 82

rì
day

4 STROKES | 日 RADICAL

Useful phrases and sentences

1. 几月几日 **jǐyuè jǐrì** which day of which month

Jīntiān shì jǐyuè jǐrì?
今天是几月几日？
What is the date today?

2. 日本 **Rìběn** Japan

Nǐ xiǎng gēn wǒ qù Rìběn lǚyóu ma?
你想跟我去日本旅游吗？
Do you want to travel to Japan with me?

3. 日出 **rìchū** sunrise

Wǒmen míngtiān zǎoshang wǔdiǎn qù hǎibiān kàn rìchū ba.
我们明天早上五点去海边看日出吧。
Let's go and see the sunrise at the seaside at 5 a.m. tomorrow morning.

4. 日记 **rìjì** diary

Wǒ měitiān xiě rìjì.
我每天写日记。
I write in my diary every day.

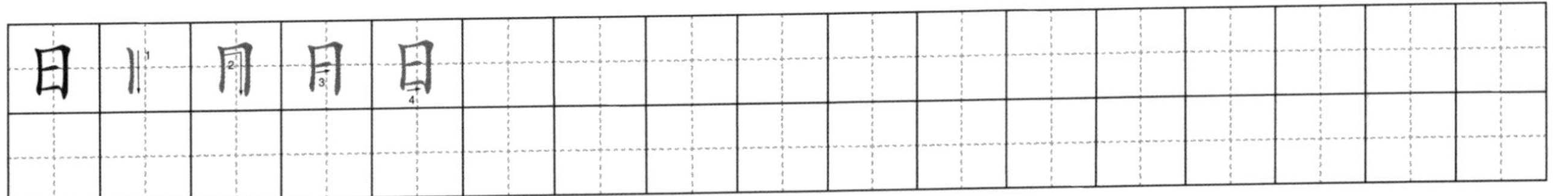

CHARACTER 83

星

xīng
star

Useful phrases and sentences

9 STROKES | 日 RADICAL

1. 星期 **xīngqī** week
   Zhège xīngqī wǒ méiyǒu kè.
   这个星期我没有课。
   I do not have classes this week.

2. 星星 **xīngxing** star
   Tiānkōng zhōng yǒu hěnduō xīngxing.
   天空中有很多星星。
   There are a lot of stars in the sky.

3. 影星 **yǐngxīng** film star
   Wǒ hěn xǐhuan zhèwèi yǐngxīng.
   我很喜欢这位影星。
   I like this film star very much.

4. 三星级 **sānxīngjí** three-star (level of quality)
   Zhèjiā sānxīngjí fàndiàn hěn yǒumíng.
   这家三星级饭店很有名。
   This three-star restaurant is well-known.

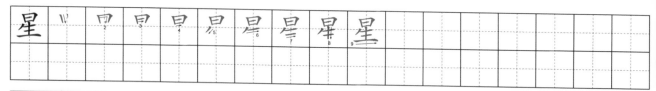

CHARACTER 84

期

qī
period (of time)

Useful phrases and sentences

12 STROKES | 月 RADICAL

1. 星期几 **xīngqījǐ** which day of the week
   Jīntiān shì xīngqījǐ?
   今天是星期几？
   Which day of the week is today?

2. 学期 **xuéqī** school term
   Zhège xuéqī wǒmen xué Zhōngwén.
   这个学期我们学中文。
   We will learn Chinese this term.

3. 期中 **qīzhōng** midterm
   Wǒmen méiyǒu qīzhōng kǎoshì.
   我们没有期中考试。
   We don't have midterm exams.

4. 期末 **qīmò** end of term
   Xiàge xīngqī shì qīmò kǎoshì.
   下个星期是期末考试。
   The final exam is next week.

CHARACTER 85

ma
an interrogative particle

Useful phrases and sentences

6 STROKES | 口 RADICAL

1. ...吗？ **...ma?** (question form)
   Nǐ shì Měiguó rén ma?
   你是美国人吗？
   Are you American?

2. 好吗？ **hǎo ma?** OK?
   Qǐng gēn wǒ yìqǐ qù, hǎo ma?
   请跟我一起去，好吗？
   Please come with me, OK?

3. 在吗？ **zài ma?** be present?
   Lǐ Péng zài ma?
   李朋在吗？
   Is Li Peng present?

4. 对吗？ **duìma?** right?
   Nǐ shì dàxuésheng, duì ma?
   你是大学生，对吗？
   You are a college student, right?

CHARACTER 86

谢

xiè
to thank

12 STROKES | 讠 RADICAL

Useful phrases and sentences

1. 谢谢 **xièxie** "Thank you"

Xièxie!
谢谢！
Thank you!

2. 感谢 **gǎnxiè** thank

Tài gǎnxiè nín le, zhème máng hái lái yīyuàn kàn wǒ.
太感谢您了，这么忙还来医院看我。
Thank you very much for visiting me in hospital although you are very busy.

3. 多谢 **duō xiè** thanks a lot

Duō xiè.
多谢。
Thanks a lot.

4. 谢 **Xiè** (surname)

Xiè Xiānsheng shì Guǎngzhōu rén, yǒu yíge háizi.
谢先生是广州人，有一个孩子。
Mr. Xie is from Guangzhou. He has one child.

CHARACTER 87

zài
again

6 STROKES | 冂 RADICAL

Useful phrases and sentences

1. 再见 **zàijiàn** goodbye; see you again

Bàba, zàijiàn!
爸爸，再见！
Bye, dad!

2. 再来 **zài lái** come again

Qǐng xiàcì zài lái!
请下次再来！
Please come again next time!

3. 再读 **zài dú** read again

Qǐng zài dú yíbiàn.
请再读一遍。
Please read it again.

4. 再说 **zài shuō** say again; additionally

Qǐng zài shuō yíbiàn.
请再说一遍。
Please say it again.

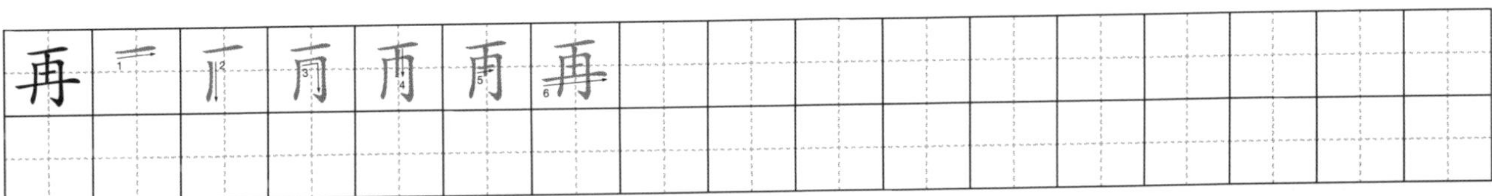

CHARACTER 88

jiàn
to see

4 STROKES | 见 RADICAL

Useful phrases and sentences

1. 明天见 **míngtiān jiàn** see you tomorrow

Wǒmen míngtiān jiàn!
我们明天见！
See you tomorrow!

2. 见多识广 **jiànduōshíguǎng** experienced and knowledgeable

Tā jiànduōshíguǎng, yě yǒu hěnduō péngyou.
他见多识广，也有很多朋友。
He is experienced and knowledgeable, and has many friends.

3. 没看见 **méi kànjiàn** did not see

Wǒ méi kànjiàn nǐ péngyou.
我没看见你朋友。
I did not see your friend.

4. 见面 **jiànmiàn** meet (face to face)

Wǒmen zài nǎr jiànmiàn?
我们在哪儿见面？
Where shall we meet?

见

CHARACTER 89

shàng
above; up; attend; in

Useful phrases and sentences

3 STROKES | 一 RADICAL

1. 上学 **shàngxué** attend school
   Nǐ mèimei shàngxuéle ma?
   你妹妹上学了吗？
   Does your younger sister attend school?

2. 上课 **shàngkè** have class
   Wǒmen shàngwǔ bādiǎn shàngkè.
   我们上午八点上课。
   We have class at eight o'clock in the morning.

3. 上班 **shàngbān** go to work
   Wǒ zài Běijīng shàngbān.
   我在北京上班。
   I work in Beijing.

4. 桌子上 **zhuōzi shàng** on the table
   Zhuōzi shàng yǒu yíge píngguǒ.
   桌子上有一个苹果。
   There is an apple on the table.

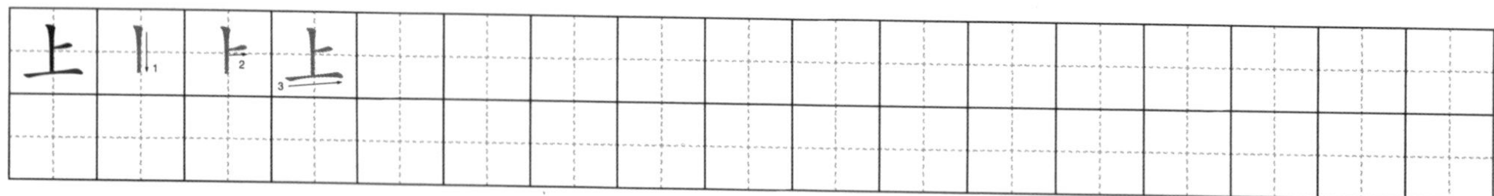

CHARACTER 90

xià
below; down; leave; exit

Useful phrases and sentences

3 STROKES | 一 RADICAL

1. 下班 **xiàbān** get off from work
   Nǐ xiàbān hòu qù nǎr?
   你下班后去哪儿？
   Where are you going after work?

2. 下课 **xiàkè** class is over
   Wǒmen shídiǎn xiàkè.
   我们十点下课。
   Our class is over at ten o'clock.

3. 下回 **xiàhuí** next time
   Nǐ xiàhuí lái Běijīng jìde gàosù wo.
   你下回来北京记得告诉我。
   Please let me know if you come to Beijing next time.

4. 下雪 **xiàxuě** to snow
   Bōshìdùn měinián dōu xiàxuě.
   波士顿每年都下雪。
   In Boston it snows every year.

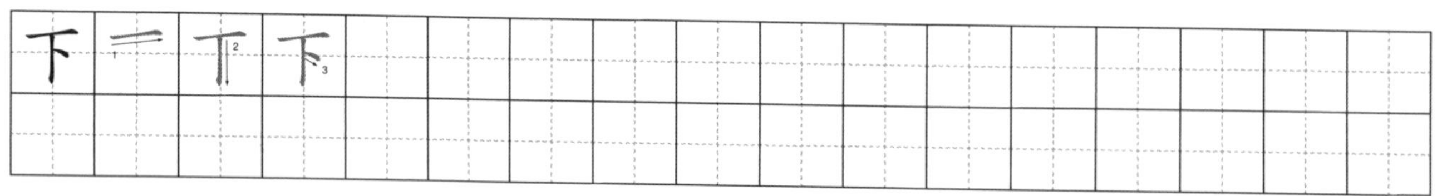

Lesson 6 Exercises

Part 1 Choose from the following words to fill in the blanks.

星期、上、下、昨天、明天、再见

1. 今天是三月五日，（　　　　）是三月四日，（　　　　）是三月六日。

2. 我们每天八点（　　　　）课，九点（　　　　）课。

3. 我这个月没时间，我们下个月（　　　　）。

4. （　　　　）六没有课，我们去吃中国菜吧。

Part 2 Complete the following dialogues using Chinese characters.

1. A: 今天是星期几？

   B: ____。

2. A: 明年你多大？

   B: ____。

3. A: 昨天是星期六吗？

   B: ____。

4. A: 你星期几不忙？

   B: ____。

5. A: 你的生日是几月几日？

   B: ____。

Part 3 Use the following prompts to give a one-minute speech.

我是大一 (**dàyī**: freshman in college) 的学生，每天 __________ 点上课，__________ 点下课。今天是 ______________ 年

__________ 月 __________ 日，星期五。__________ 天是星期六，我想休息 (**xiǎng xiūxi**: want to

rest)、睡觉 (**shuìjiào**: sleep)。

LESSON 7

What is your hobby? 你喜欢做什么？

1. Introduction

Chinese people have various ways to relax and refresh themselves. People like to go to karaoke, hang out with friends at coffee shops, or enjoy fine dining in restaurants. As for exercise, young people go to the gym to work out, while the elderly go to neighborhood parks to exercise. In China, parks attract many elderly people, especially in the morning and evening. They gather to practice various kinds of exercises, such as singing, folk dancing, playing table tennis, as well as doing t'ai chi. What do you like to do in your free time? Do you have any Chinese friends? What are their hobbies?

2. Warm up

Read the passage below and answer the questions using Chinese characters.

> 我今年 21 岁，大三。我平常喜欢看书，有时候看电视。星期六和星期天我常常和朋友们打球、看电影，我们都喜欢看中国功夫 (**gōngfu**: Kung-Fu) 电影。我妈妈和姐姐都喜欢买东西，我不喜欢。

1. What is his hobby?

____

2. What does he usually do on weekends?

____

3. Does he like shopping? What about his mother and older sister?

____

3. Vocabulary

	Word	Pinyin	English equivalent
1.	平常	**píngcháng**	usually
2.	喜欢	**xǐhuan**	like
3.	看书	**kànshū**	reading; studying
4.	看	**kàn**	watch; see
5.	电视	**diànshì**	TV
6.	打球	**dǎqiú**	play ball
7.	电影	**diànyǐng**	movie
8.	都	**dōu**	all; both
9.	买东西	**mǎi dōngxi**	buy things

4. New Characters

Fifteen characters are introduced in this lesson. Use the following explanations to help you understand and remember the characters.

平　常　喜　欢　看　书　电　视　影　打　球　买　东　西　都

CHARACTER 91

píng
common; flat

Useful phrases and sentences

5 STROKES　干 RADICAL

1. 水平 **shuǐpíng** level; standard

Zhōngguó jīngjìde fāzhǎn ràng Zhōngguó rénde shēnghuó shuǐpíng tígāole hěnduō.
中国经济的发展让中国人的生活水平提高了很多。
Economic growth has significantly raised the living standards of the Chinese people.

2. 平静 **píngjìng** calm

Píngjìng yìdiǎn, búyào shēngqì.
平静一点，不要生气。
Calm down. Don't be angry.

3. 公平 **gōngpíng** fair

Zhège bǐsài bù gōngpíng.
这个比赛不公平。
This match is not fair.

4. 平安夜 **píng'ān yè** Christmas Eve

Píng'ān yè shì shénme shíhou?
平安夜是什么时候？
When is Christmas Eve?

平 一 二 三 三 平

CHARACTER 92

cháng
often

Useful phrases and sentences

11 STROKES | 巾 RADICAL

1. 平常 **píngcháng** usually

Nǐ píngcháng xǐhuan zuò shénme?
你平常喜欢做什么？
What do you usually like to do?

2. 常常 **chángcháng** often

Wǒ chángcháng qù nàge fànguǎnr chīfàn.
我常常去那个饭馆儿吃饭。
I often eat at that restaurant.

3. 非常 **fēicháng** very; extraordinarily

Zhège diànyǐng fēicháng hǎokàn.
这个电影非常好看。
This movie is very good.

4. 常见 **chángjiàn** common

Zhèzhǒng bìng hěn chángjiàn, nǐ búyòng tài dānxīn.
这种病很常见，你不用太担心。
This illness is very common. You don't have to worry.

CHARACTER 93

喜

xǐ
happy

Useful phrases and sentences

12 STROKES | 口 RADICAL

1. 喜欢 **xǐhuan** like

Wǒ xǐhuan Xiǎolì.
我喜欢小丽。
I like Xiaoli.

2. 喜爱 **xǐài** like

Zhège diànyǐng shòudàole dàjiāde xǐài.
这个电影受到了大家的喜爱。
The film is widely liked.

3. 喜事 **xǐshì** joyful event (usually a wedding)

Jīntiān yǒu shénme xǐshì?
今天有什么喜事？
Are there any joyful events today?

4. 恭喜 **gōngxǐ** congratulations

Gōngxǐ, gōngxǐ!
恭喜，恭喜！
Congratulations!

CHARACTER 94

欢

huān
happy

Useful phrases and sentences

6 STROKES | 欠 RADICAL

1. 联欢 **liánhuān** have a get-together

Zhège Zhōngguó shèqū měinián dōu jǔbàn chūnjié liánhuān wǎnhuì.
这个中国社区每年都举办春节联欢晚会。
This Chinese community holds a Spring Festival party every year.

2. 欢快 **huānkuài** cheerful

Tā chàngle yìshǒu hěn huānkuàide gē, fēicháng hǎotīng.
他唱了一首很欢快的歌，非常好听。
He sings a very cheerful song. It's very pleasant to hear.

3. 欢笑 **huānxiào** laugh heartily

Wǒmen měitiān zài huānxiào zhōng xué Zhōngwén.
我们每天在欢笑中学中文。
We learn Chinese in a joyful atmosphere every day.

4. 欢送会 **huānsònghuì** farewell party

Wǒmen míngtiān yǒu bìyèshēng huānsònghuì.
我们明天有毕业生欢送会。
We are having a graduation farewell party tomorrow.

CHARACTER 95

kàn
look; see

Useful phrases and sentences

9 STROKES | 目 RADICAL

1. 看见 **kànjiàn** see
Wǒ zuótiān kànjiàn tāde nǚpéngyou.
我昨天看见他的女朋友。
I saw his girlfriend yesterday.

2. 看看 **kànkan** have a look
Nǐ kànkan zhèběn shū ba!
你看看这本书吧！
You should read this book.

3. 看朋友 **kàn péngyou** visit a friend
Wǒ yào qù Niǔyuē kàn yíge péngyou.
我要去纽约看一个朋友。
I am going to New York to visit a friend.

4. 看医生 **kàn yīsheng** see a doctor
Tā míngtiān yàoqù kàn yīsheng, suóyi bù néng lái.
他明天要去看医生，所以不能来。
He will see a doctor tomorrow, so he cannot come.

CHARACTER 96

shū
book

Useful phrases and sentences

4 STROKES | 乛 RADICAL

1. 看书 **kànshū** reading; studying
Wǒ dìdi bù xǐhuan kànshū.
我弟弟不喜欢看书。
My younger brother doesn't like reading.

2. 书法 **shūfǎ** calligraphy
Tā měitiān liànxí shūfǎ liǎngge zhōngtóu.
他每天练习书法两个钟头。
He practices calligraphy for two hours a day.

3. 书房 **shūfáng** study (i.e., a room)
Tāde shūfáng yǒu hǎo jǐbǎiběn shū.
他的书房有好几百本书。
He has hundreds of books in his study.

4. 一本书 **yìběn shū** one book
Yìběn shū èrshíkuài, liǎngběn shū sānshíwǔkuài.
一本书二十块，两本书三十五块。
One book is 20 kuai. 35 kuai for two.

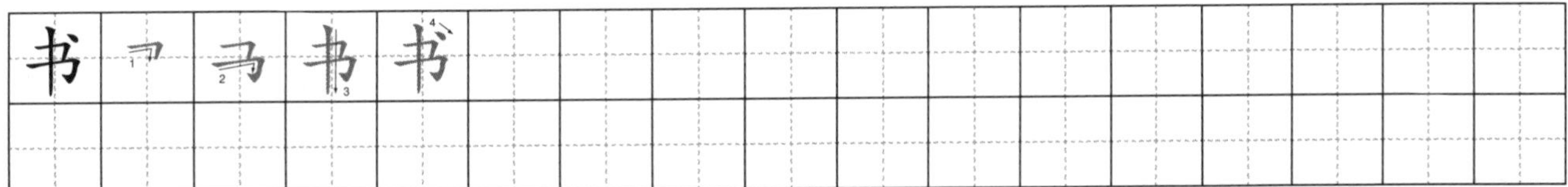

CHARACTER 97

diàn
electric

Useful phrases and sentences

5 STROKES | 田 RADICAL

1. 电子词典 **diànzǐ cídiǎn** electronic dictionary
Nǐde diànzǐ cídiǎn wǒ kěyǐ jièyíxia ma?
你的电子词典我可以借一下吗？
Can I borrow your electronic dictionary?

2. 电费 **diànfèi** electricity bill
Qǐng wèn, yíge yuè diànfèi duōshao qián?
请问，一个月电费多少钱？
Excuse me, how much is your monthly electricity bill?

3. 电器 **diànqì** electronic device
Wǒ jiā yǒu hěnduō diànqì.
我家有很多电器。
There are many electronic devices in my home.

4. 没电了 **méi diàn le** have no electric power
Wǒde shǒujī méi diàn le.
我的手机没电了。
My cell phone has run out of power.

CHARACTER 98

shì
look

Useful phrases and sentences

8 STROKES | 见 RADICAL

1. 电视 **diànshì** television

Měige xiǎoháir dōu xǐhuan kàn diànshì.
每个小孩儿都喜欢看电视。
Every child likes to watch television.

2. 视力 **shìlì** eyesight

Wǒde shìlì hěn hǎo.
我的视力很好。
I have good eyesight.

3. 视频 **shìpín** video

YouTube shì yíge shìpín wǎngzhàn.
YouTube 是一个视频网站。
YouTube is a video website.

4. 重视 **zhòngshì** pay attention to; consider important

Zhège xuéxiào hěn zhòngshì Yīngwén.
这个学校很重视英文。
This school pays much attention to English.

CHARACTER 99

yǐng
shadow; reflection; image

Useful phrases and sentences

15 STROKES | 彡 RADICAL

1. 电影 **diànyǐng** film

Nǐ xǐhuan zhège diànyǐng ma?
你喜欢这个电影吗？
Do you like this film?

2. 影响 **yǐngxiǎng** to influence; to affect; effect; to be influenced

Xīfāng wénhuà duì Zhōngguó wénhuàde yǐngxiǎng yuè lái yuè shēn.
西方文化对中国文化的影响越来越深。
Western culture is affecting Chinese culture more and more.

3. 影片 **yǐngpiàn** movie

Nǐ zhīdao zuìjìn yǒu shénme xīnde yǐngpiàn ma?
你知道最近有什么新的影片吗？
Do you know any latest movies?

4. 影迷 **yǐngmí** movie fan

Diànyǐngyuàn wàimiàn yǒu hěnduō yǐngmí.
电影院外面有很多影迷。
There are many movie fans outside the cinema.

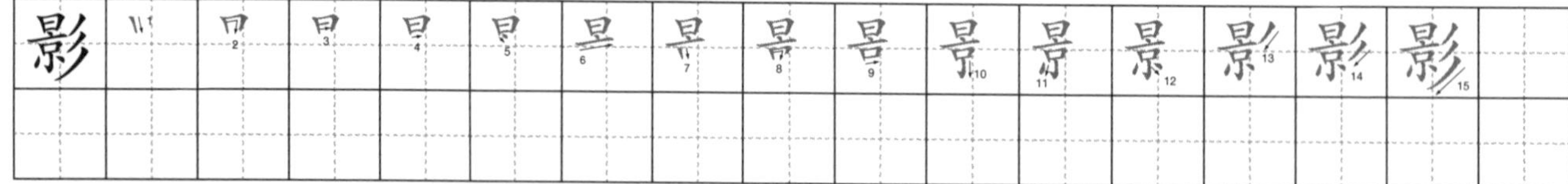

CHARACTER 100

dǎ
play; hit

Useful phrases and sentences

5 STROKES | 扌 RADICAL

1. 打球 **dǎqiú** play ball

Wǒ míngtiān bú qù dǎqiú.
我明天不去打球。
I am not playing ball tomorrow.

2. 打架 **dǎjià** fight

Nàr yǒu liǎngge rén zài dǎjià.
那儿有两个人在打架。
There are two men fighting there.

3. 打扫 **dǎsǎo** clean

Wǒ měitiān dǎsǎo fángjiān.
我每天打扫房间。
I clean my room every day.

4. 打交道 **dǎ jiāodào** to interact with

Nǐ zhīdao zěnme gēn Zhōngguó rén dǎjiāodào ma?
你知道怎么跟中国人打交道吗？
Do you know how to interact with Chinese people?

CHARACTER 101

qiú
ball

Useful phrases and sentences

11 STROKES | 王 RADICAL

1. 打篮球 **dǎ lánqiú** play basketball
   Wǒ xǐhuan dǎ lánqiú.
   我喜欢打篮球。
   I like to play basketball.

2. 踢足球 **tī zúqiú** play football (soccer)
   Wǒ bù xǐhuan hé wǒ gēge tī zúqiú.
   我不喜欢和我哥哥踢足球。
   I do not like to play football with my older brother.

3. 网球 **wǎngqiú** tennis
   Nǐ shénme shíhou qù dǎ wǎngqiú?
   你什么时候去打网球？
   When are you going to play tennis?

4. 足球赛 **zúqiúsài** football (soccer) match
   Míngtiān yǒu yīchǎng zúqiúsài.
   明天有一场足球赛。
   There is a football game tomorrow.

CHARACTER 102

mǎi
buy

Useful phrases and sentences

6 STROKES | 乙 or 大 RADICAL

1. 买书 **mǎi shū** buy books
   Wǒ yào qù shūdiàn mǎi shū.
   我要去书店买书。
   I am going to the bookstore to buy books.

2. 买票 **mǎi piào** buy tickets
   Nǐ mǎi piào le ma?
   你买票了吗？
   Have you bought the tickets?

3. 买衣服 **mǎi yīfu** buy clothes
   Wǒde nǚpéngyou hěn xǐhuan mǎi yīfu.
   我的女朋友很喜欢买衣服。
   My girlfriend likes to buy clothes.

4. 买车 **mǎi chē** buy a car
   Wǒ méi qián mǎi chē.
   我没钱买车。
   I don't have money to buy a car.

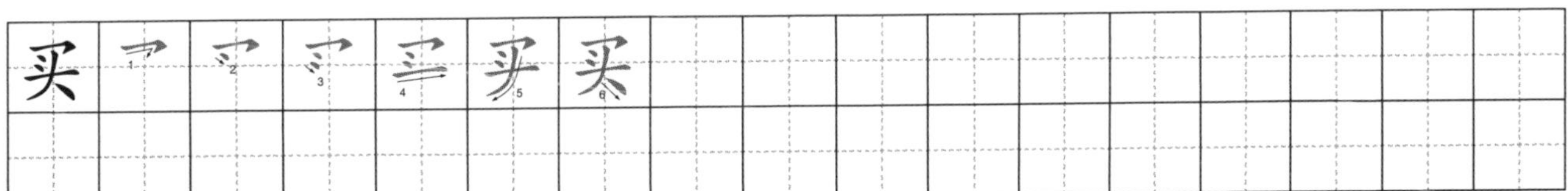

CHARACTER 103

dōng
east

Useful phrases and sentences

5 STROKES | 一 RADICAL

1. 东西 **dōngxi** thing
   Nǐ zhuōshàngde dōngxi tài duō le.
   你桌上的东西太多了。
   You have too many things on your table.

2. 东边 **dōngbiān** east
   Rìběn zài Zhōngguóde dōngbiān.
   日本在中国的东边。
   Japan is to the east of China.

3. 东北 **dōngběi** northeast
   Zhōngguóde dōngběi dōngtiān hěn lěng.
   中国的东北冬天很冷。
   The northeast past of China is very cold in winter.

4. 东南亚 **Dōngnányà** Southeast Asia
   Tàiguó shì yíge Dōngnányà guójiā.
   泰国是一个东南亚国家。
   Thailand is a country in Southeast Asia.

CHARACTER 104

xī
west

Useful phrases and sentences

6 STROKES | 西 RADICAL

1. 西方 **xīfāng** west

Měiguó shì yíge xīfāng guójiā.
美国是一个西方国家。
U.S.A. is a western country.

2. 西餐 **xīcān** western-style food

Zhège fànguǎnrde xīcān fēicháng hǎo.
这个饭馆儿的西餐非常好。
This restaurant has very good western-style food.

3. 西服 **xīfú** western-style clothes (formal clothing)

Zhètào xīfú hěn guì.
这套西服很贵。
This western-style suit is very expensive.

4. 西瓜 **xīguā** watermelon

Wǒ xǐhuan chī xīguā.
我喜欢吃西瓜。
I like to eat watermelon.

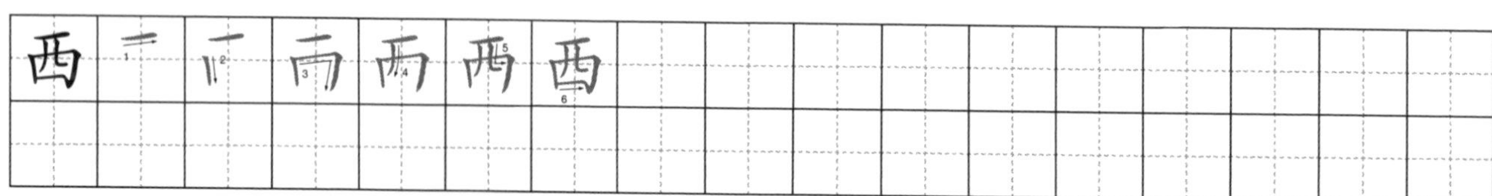

CHARACTER 105

dōu
both; all

Useful phrases and sentences

10 STROKES | 阝 RADICAL

1. 都是 **dōu shì** both/all be

Wǒmen dōu shì xuésheng.
我们都是学生。
We are all students.

2. 都有 **dōu yǒu** both/all have

Tāmen liǎngge rén dōu yǒu jiějie.
他们两个人都有姐姐。
They both have older sisters.

3. 都喜欢 **dōu xǐhuan** both/all like

Dàjiā dōu xǐhuan kàn diànyǐng.
大家都喜欢看电影。
Everyone likes to watch movies.

4. 都在... **dōu zài...** both/all at/in...

Jīntiān wǒde bàba māma dōu zài jiā.
今天我的爸爸妈妈都在家。
Both my parents are at home today.

Lesson 7 Exercises

Part 1 Choose from the following words to fill in the blanks.

喜欢、看、买、看书、电影 、东西

1. 我要去超市（　　　　）（　　　　）。

2. 我哥哥不喜欢（　　　　），我很喜欢。

3. 明天一起（　　　）（　　　）吧，我去买票 (**piào**: ticket)。

4. 他不（　　　）打球。

Part 2 Complete the following dialogues using Chinese characters.

1. A: 你平常喜欢做什么？

   B: ______________________________。

2. A: 你喜欢看书吗？

   B: ______________________________。

3. A: 你平常去哪儿买东西？

   B: ______________________________。

4. A: 你喜欢和谁看电影？

   B: ______________________________。

5. A: 你的家人都是美国人吗？

   B: ______________________________。

Part 3 Use the following prompts to give a one-minute speech.

我是一个大学生，我 ______________ 在学校，我喜欢 ______________，

我不喜欢 ______________________________。

我每天看书，星期六和星期天我 ______________________ 休息 (**xiūxi**: rest)，

我有时候 (**yǒu shíhou**: sometimes) 去超市 (**qù chāoshì**: go to the supermarket) ______________，

有时候和朋友 ______________，有时候和家人 ______________。

LESSON 8

What are your weekend plans? 你周末做什么？

1. Introduction

What do you like to do on the weekends? Do you like to stay at home or go out? Recently, there are two new words in Chinese: 宅男 **zháinán** and 宅女 **zháinǚ**. 宅 **Zhái** is a classical word for house or home. Can you guess the meanings of 宅男 and 宅女? These two words are used to describe young people who spend most of their time staying home surfing the internet or playing online games. They don't like to go outside and engage in social activities. Do you think you are a 宅男 or 宅女?

2. Warm up

Read the passage below and answer the questions using Chinese characters.

> 我是一个学生，平常每天都有课，早上起床 (**qǐchuáng**: get up)、吃饭、上课、下课。我周末没有课，有时候喜欢一个人看书，有时候喜欢和朋友打球，还有时候喜欢买东西。今天是星期日，我想回家 (**huíjiā**: go home) 和爸爸妈妈吃晚饭。

1. What does he usually do during weekdays?

____

2. What does he usually do on weekends?

____

3. What will he do today?

____

3. Vocabulary

	Word	Pinyin	English equivalent
1.	每天	**měitiān**	every day
2.	课	**kè**	class
3.	早上	**zǎoshang**	morning
4.	吃饭	**chīfàn**	eat food
5.	下课	**xiàkè**	class is over
6.	周末	**zhōumò**	weekend
7.	有时候	**yǒu shíhou**	sometimes
8.	还	**hái**	still; or
9.	想	**xiǎng**	want; think
10.	晚饭	**wǎnfàn**	dinner
11.	谁	**shuí/shéi**	who
12.	还是	**háishì**	or (question)
13.	地方	**dìfang**	place
14.	可以	**kěyǐ**	can; may
15.	时候	**shíhou**	moment

4. New Characters

Fifteen characters are introduced in this lesson. Use the following explanations to help you understand and remember the characters.

周 末 想 吃 饭 谁 还 地 方 早 晚 可 以 时 候

CHARACTER 106

周

zhōu
week; cycle

8 STROKES | 口 RADICAL

Useful phrases and sentences

1. 周围 **zhōuwéi** nearby
   Xuéxiào zhōuwéi yǒu bùshǎo hěnhǎode yàzhōu fànguǎnr.
   学校周围有不少很好的亚洲饭馆儿。
   There are many good Asian restaurants near school.

2. 一周 **yìzhōu** a week
   Wǒ yìzhōu yǒu shí'èrjié kè.
   我一周有十二节课。
   I have twelve classes a week.

3. 周二 **zhōu'èr** Tuesday
   Jīntiān shì zhōu'èr.
   今天是周二。
   Today is Tuesday.

4. 上周 **shàngzhōu** last week
   Nǐ shàngzhōu kàn diànyǐng le ma?
   你上周看电影了吗？
   Did you watch a movie last week?

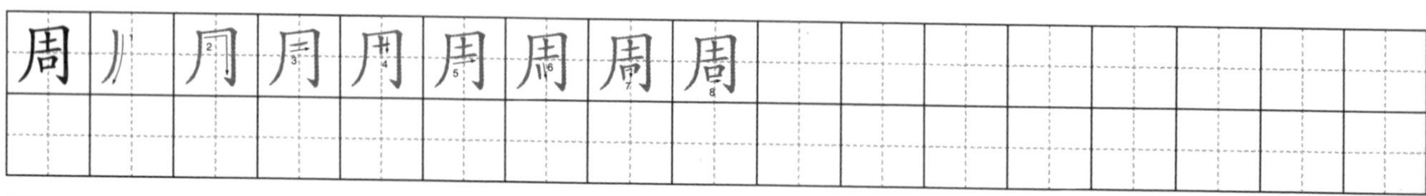

CHARACTER 107

mò
end

5 STROKES | 木 RADICAL

Useful phrases and sentences

1. 周末 **zhōumò** weekend
   Zhège zhōumò nǐ xiǎng zuò shénme?
   这个周末你想做什么？
   What do you want to do this weekend?

2. 月末 **yuèmò** end of month
   Wǒ yuèmò chángcháng méiyǒu qián.
   我月末常常没有钱。
   I often have no money at the end of the month.

3. 年末 **niánmò** end of year
   Wǒmen dōu xǐhuan zài niánmò mǎi dōngxi.
   我们都喜欢在年末买东西。
   We all like to go shopping at the end of the year.

4. 期末考试 **qīmòkǎoshì** final exam
   Zhèige kè méiyǒu qīmòkǎoshì ma?
   这个课没有期末考试吗？
   Isn't there a final exam for this class?

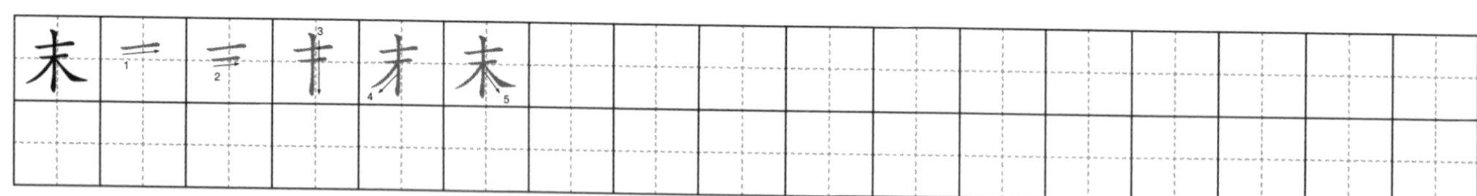

CHARACTER 108

xiǎng
want; think; miss

13 STROKES | 心 RADICAL

Useful phrases and sentences

1. 想… **xiǎng…** want to …
   Nǐ xiǎng-bù-xiǎng qù mǎi dōngxi?
   你想不想去买东西？
   Do you want to go buy things?

2. 不想 **bù xiǎng** do not want to
   Wǒ bù xiǎng hé tā dǎqiú.
   我不想和他打球。
   I do not want to play ball with him.

3. 想法 **xiǎngfǎ** idea
   Nǐ yǒu shénme xiǎngfǎ?
   你有什么想法？
   Do you have any ideas?

4. 想家 **xiǎngjiā** miss home
   Wǒ hěn xiǎngjiā.
   我很想家。
   I miss my home very much.

CHARACTER 109

吃

chī
eat

6 STROKES | 口 RADICAL

Useful phrases and sentences

1. 吃饭 **chīfàn** have meals; eat

Nǐ měitiān zǎoshang jǐdiǎn chīfàn?
你每天早上几点吃饭？
When do you usually eat every morning?

2. 吃东西 **chī dōngxi** eat something

Shàngkède shíhou búyào chī dōngxi.
上课的时候不要吃东西。
Do not eat in class.

3. 吃早饭 **chī zǎofàn** eat breakfast

Wǒ yǒu shíhou méiyǒu shíjiān chī zǎofàn.
我有时候没有时间吃早饭。
Sometimes I don't have time to eat breakfast.

4. 小吃 **xiǎochī** snacks; small bites

Wǒ xǐhuan zhège dìfangde xiǎochī.
我喜欢这个地方的小吃。
I like the snacks in this place.

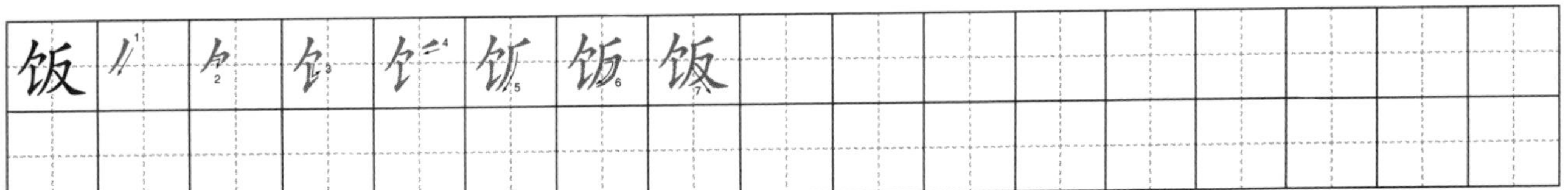

CHARACTER 110

饭

fàn
meal

7 STROKES | 饣 RADICAL

Useful phrases and sentences

1. 饭店 **fàndiàn** hotel; restaurant

Zhège fàndiàn shì wǔxīngjíde.
这个饭店是五星级的。
This is a 5-star hotel.

2. 饭菜 **fàncài** food; meal

Kuài diǎn chī ba, fàncài dōu liángle.
快点吃吧，饭菜都凉了。
Eat your food. It's getting cold.

3. 米饭 **mǐfàn** rice

Nǐ yào mǐfàn háishì miànbāo?
你要米饭还是面包？
Would you like rice or bread?

4. 饭馆儿 **fànguǎnr** restaurant

Wǒ píngcháng lái zhège fànguǎnr chīfàn.
我平常来这个饭馆儿吃饭。
I usually come to this restaurant to eat.

CHARACTER 111

shuí/shéi
who

10 STROKES | 讠 RADICAL

Useful phrases and sentences

1. 谁的 **shéide** whose

Zhè shì shéide shū?
这是谁的书？
Whose book is it?

2. 谁有 **shuí yǒu** who has

Shuí yǒu diànyǐng piào?
谁有电影票？
Who has the movie ticket?

3. 谁是 **shéi shì** who is

Shéi shì Fāng Xiānsheng?
谁是方先生？
Who is Mr. Fang?

4. 谁在 **shuí zài** who is at/in

Xiànzài shuí zài jiā?
现在谁在家？
Who is at home now?

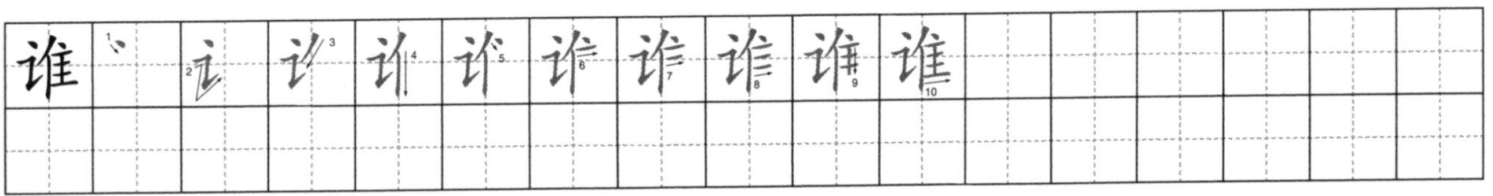

CHARACTER 112

hái/huán
still; or/to return

Useful phrases and sentences

7 STROKES | 辶 RADICAL

1. 还是 **háishì** or (in questions)
Nǐ xǐhuan chá háishì kāfēi?
你喜欢茶还是咖啡？
Do you like tea or coffee?

2. 还有 **hái yǒu** also
Wǒ yǒu yíge jiějie, hái yǒu yíge gēge.
我有一个姐姐，还有一个哥哥。
I have an older sister. I also have an older brother.

3. 还没 **hái méi** not yet
Wǒ shì xuésheng, hái méi gōngzuò.
我是学生，还没工作。
I am a student. I don't work yet.

4. 还行 **hái xíng** not bad
Zhège diànyǐng hái xíng.
这个电影还行。
This movie is not bad.

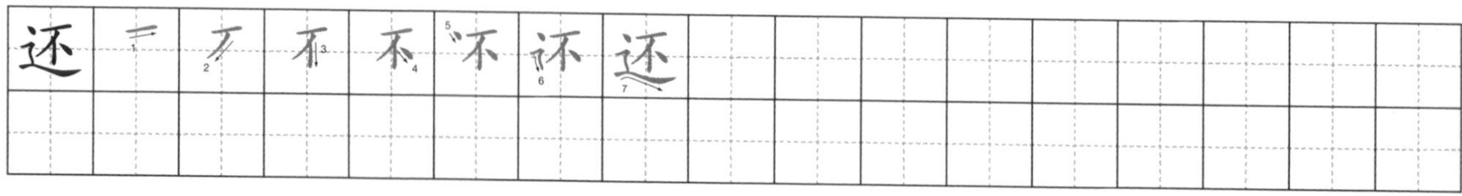

CHARACTER 113

dì
land

Useful phrases and sentences

6 STROKES | 土 RADICAL

1. 地方 **dìfang** place
Zhège dìfang hěn piàoliang.
这个地方很漂亮。
This place is beautiful.

2. 地图 **dìtú** map
Nǐ yǒu Zhōngguó dìtú ma?
你有中国地图吗？
Do you have a map of China?

3. 地址 **dìzhǐ** address
Nǐde dìzhǐ shì shénme?
你的地址是什么？
What is your address?

4. 地道 **dìdao** authentic
Zhège fànguǎnde cài hěn dìdao.
这个饭馆的菜很地道。
The food in this restaurant is authentic.

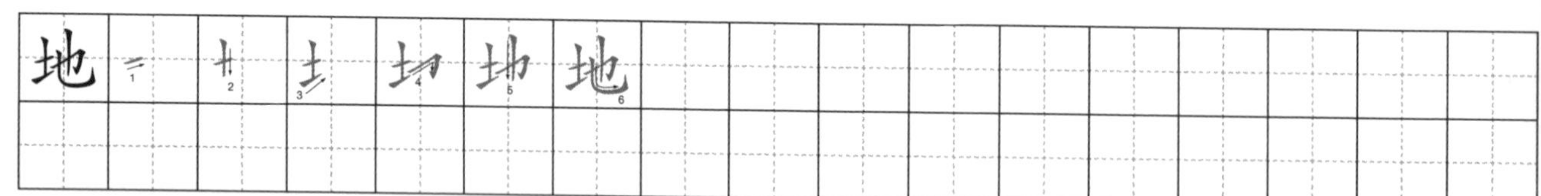

CHARACTER 114

fāng
direction; side; square; place

Useful phrases and sentences

4 STROKES | 方 RADICAL

1. 方向 **fāngxiàng** direction
Wǒ juéde zhège fāngxiàng bú duì.
我觉得这个方向不对。
I think this is the wrong direction.

2. 方面 **fāngmiàn** aspect
Zhōngguó wénhuà, nǐ zuì xǐhuan nǎ fāngmiàn?
中国文化，你最喜欢哪方面？
In Chinese culture, which aspect do you like the most?

3. 方式 **fāngshì** way; method
Kējì gǎibiànle rénmende shēnghuó fāngshì.
科技改变了人们生活的方式。
Technology changes our way of living.

4. 方法 **fāngfǎ** method; solution
Nǐ yǒu shénme hǎo fāngfǎ?
你有什么好方法？
Have you found any good solutions?

方 1 2 3 4

CHARACTER 115

zǎo
early; morning

Useful phrases and sentences

6 STROKES | 日 RADICAL

1. 早上 **zǎoshang** morning
Nǐ píngcháng zǎoshang jǐdiǎn qǐchuáng?
你平常早上几点起床？
When do you usually get up in the morning?

2. 早 **zǎo** "Good morning"
Zǎo!
早！
Good morning!

3. 早点儿 **zǎo diǎnr** earlier
Qǐng nǐ zǎo diǎnr lái shàngkè.
请你早点儿来上课。
Please come to class earlier.

4. 早饭 **zǎofàn** breakfast
Nǐ chī zǎofàn le ma?
你吃早饭了吗？
Did you have breakfast?

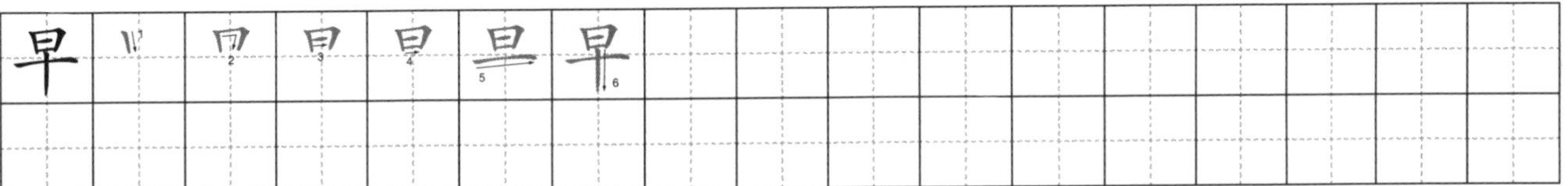

CHARACTER 116

wǎn
late

Useful phrases and sentences

11 STROKES | 日 RADICAL

1. 晚上 **wǎnshang** evening; night
Míngtiān wǎnshang yào-bú-yào lái wǒ jiā chīfàn?
明天晚上要不要来我家吃饭？
Do you want to come to my house to have dinner tomorrow evening?

2. 晚饭 **wǎnfàn** supper; dinner
Wǒ píngcháng hé jiārén yìqǐ chī wǎnfàn.
我平常和家人一起吃晚饭。
I usually have dinner with my family.

3. 晚安 **wǎn'ān** "Good night"
"Wǎn'ān!"
晚安。
"Good night!"

4. 太晚了 **tài wǎn le** too late
Tài wǎn le, wǒmen huíjiā ba.
太晚了，我们回家吧。
It is too late. Let's go home.

CHARACTER 117

kě
can

Useful phrases and sentences

5 STROKES | 口 RADICAL

1. 可是 **kěshì** but
Jīntiān shì xīngqīrì, kěshì wǒ méi shíjiān wánr.
今天是星期日，可是我没时间玩儿。
Today is Sunday, but I do not have time for fun.

2. 可能 **kěnéng** maybe
Tā kěnéng shì Zhōngguó rén.
他可能是中国人。
Maybe he is Chinese.

3. 可爱 **kě'ài** cute
Nǐde mèimei fēicháng kě'ài.
你的妹妹非常可爱。
Your younger sister is very cute.

4. 可乐 **kělè** cola (often slang for the Coca-Cola brand)
Wǒ xiǎng mǎi yīpíng kělè.
我想买一瓶可乐。
I want to buy a bottle of coke.

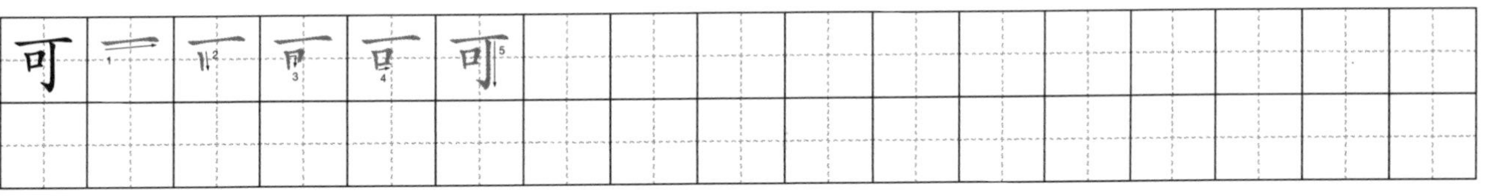

CHARACTER 118

以

yǐ
with

Useful phrases and sentences

4 STROKES | 人 RADICAL

1. 可以 **kěyǐ** can

Wǒ kěyǐ jìnlái ma?
我可以进来吗？
May I come in?

2. 以前 **yǐqián** before; ago

Tā yǐqián shìge yīsheng.
他以前是个医生。
He used to be a doctor.

3. 以后 **yǐhòu** after

Wǒ píngcháng shíyīdiǎn yǐhòu shuìjiào.
我平常十一点以后睡觉。
I usually go to bed after eleven o'clock.

4. 以为 **yǐwéi** mistakenly thought

Tā yǐwéi zuótiān méiyǒu kǎoshì, suóyi tā méiyǒu zhǔnbèi.
他以为昨天没有考试，所以他没有准备。
He mistakenly thought that there was no test yesterday, so he did not do any preparation.

以 1 2 3 4

CHARACTER 119

shí
time

Useful phrases and sentences

7 STROKES | 日 RADICAL

1. 时间 **shíjiān** time

Wǒ jīntiān méi shíjiān dǎ lánqiú.
我今天没时间打篮球。
I do not have time to play basketball today.

2. 时差 **shíchā** time difference; jet lag

Tā gāng cóng Jiānádà huílái, hái yǒu shíchā.
她刚从加拿大回来，还有时差。
She just got back from Canada and she still has jet lag.

3. 准时 **zhǔnshí** on time

Jīntiān dàjiā dōu hěn zhǔnshí.
今天大家都很准时。
Everyone is punctual today.

4. 随时 **suíshí** any time

Nǐ kěyǐ suíshí gěi wǒ dǎ diànhuà.
你可以随时给我打电话。
You can call me any time.

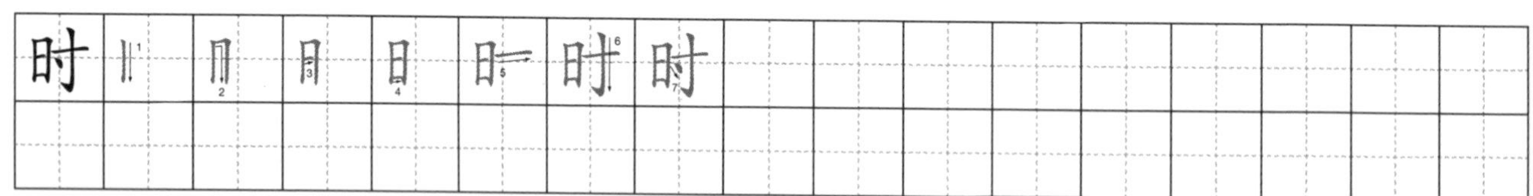

CHARACTER 120

hòu/hou
time; moment

Useful phrases and sentences

10 STROKES | 亻 RADICAL

1. 时候 **shíhou** time; moment

Chīfànde shíhou bié kàn shǒujī.
吃饭的时候别看手机。
Don't look at your cell phone when eating.

2. 有时候 **yǒu shíhou** sometimes

Wǒ yǒu shíhou zhōumò bú huíjiā.
我有时候周末不回家。
Sometimes I don't go home on the weekend.

3. 气候 **qìhòu** climate (sometimes figurative)

Nǐ lǎojiāde qìhòu zěnmeyàng?
你老家的气候怎么样？
How is the climate in your hometown?

4. 候选人 **hòuxuǎnrén** candidate

Wǒ hěn xǐhuan zhège hòuxuǎnrén.
我很喜欢这个候选人。
I like this candidate.

候 1 2 3 4 5 6 7 8 9 10

Lesson 8 Exercises

Part 1 Choose from the following words to fill in the blanks.

时候、周末、吃饭、谁、地方、可以

1. 这儿有没有吃饭的（　　　　　）？

2. （　　　　　）不上课，我们（　　　　　）去打球。

3. 请问，你明天什么（　　　　　）有时间？

4. 你昨天中午和（　　　　　）一起（　　　　　）的？

Part 2 Complete the following dialogues using Chinese characters.

1. A: 你是什么时候学中文的？

   B: ______________________________。

2. A: 你周末做了什么？

   B: ______________________________。

3. A: 你的中文老师是谁？

   B: ______________________________。

4. A: 你明天想做什么？

   B: ______________________________。

5. A: 你平常去什么地方吃饭？

   B: ______________________________。

Part 3 Complete the following chart on your plans for the coming weekend. Write the names of activities using Chinese characters.

我的周末

Time	Activity
9:00 a.m.–noon	
12:00 noon–1:00 p.m.	
1:00 p.m.–4:00 p.m.	
7:00 p.m.–10:00 p.m.	

LESSON 9

Clothes shopping (I) 买衣服 (I)

1. Introduction

Do you like to buy clothes? Nowadays many young people in China are keen to buy luxury brands, and spend a significant portion of their income on them. For them, this represents social status and financial capability. Do you spend money on luxury brands? When purchasing clothes, do you value quality, price, or the brand?

2. Warm up

Read the passage below and answer the questions using Chinese characters.

我平常很忙，只有周末有时间买些东西。我很喜欢买东西，但我不喜欢和我姐姐一起买。她有时候问我，“这个怎么样？”我说，“很不错。”她说，“不好，太贵了，我没钱。那个怎么样？”我说，“也很好。”她说，“我觉得不好看。”我觉得她太小气 (**xiǎoqì**: stingy) 了。

1. When is she not busy?

___

2. Does she like to go shopping with her sister?

___

3. What is the example she gives to support her opinion of her sister?

___

3. Vocabulary

	Word	Pinyin	English equivalent
1.	很	**hěn**	very
2.	忙	**máng**	busy
3.	只	**zhǐ**	only
4.	时间	**shíjiān**	time
5.	些	**xiē**	some
6.	一起	**yìqǐ**	together
7.	问	**wèn**	ask
8.	这个	**zhège**	this one
9.	怎么样	**zěnmeyàng**	how about …
10.	不错	**bú cuò**	not bad
11.	太…了	**tài…le**	too …
12.	贵	**guì**	expensive
13.	那个	**nàge**	that one
14.	觉得	**juéde**	feel
15.	多少钱	**duōshao qián**	how much money
16.	便宜	**piányi**	cheap

4. New Characters

Fifteen characters are introduced in this lesson. Use the following explanations to help you understand and remember the characters.

觉 得 这 那 怎 样 钱 很 太 小 贵 便 宜 错 了

CHARACTER 121

jué/jiào
feel/sleep

Useful phrases and sentences

9 STROKES | 见 RADICAL

1. 觉得 **juéde** feel; think
   Wǒ juéde Xiǎo Lín zhège rén hěn hǎo.
   我觉得小林这个人很好。
   I think Xiao Lin is a good person.

2. 感觉 **gǎnjué** feeling
   Nǐ xiànzài gǎnjué zěnmeyàng?
   你现在感觉怎么样？
   How are you feeling now?

3. 睡觉 **shuìjiào** sleep; go to bed
   Wǒ měitiān shíyīdiǎn shuìjiào.
   我每天十一点睡觉。
   I go to bed at eleven o'clock every day.

4. 午觉 **wǔjiào** afternoon nap
   Nǐ yǒu shíjiān shuì wǔjiào ma?
   你有时间睡午觉吗？
   Do you have time to take a nap?

觉

CHARACTER 122

de
a particle indicating manner

Useful phrases and sentences

11 STROKES | 彳 RADICAL

1. 跑得真快 **pǎode zhēn kuài** run really fast
   Nàge xiǎoháizi pǎode zhēn kuài.
   那个小孩子跑得真快！
   That kid runs really fast!

2. 说得好 **shuōdehǎo** speak well
   Nǐde Zhōngwén shuōde hěn hǎo.
   你的中文说得很好。
   You speak Chinese very well.

3. 看得见 **kàndejiàn** can see
   Nàge rén nǐ kàndejiàn ma?
   那个人你看得见吗？
   Can you see that person?

4. 做得完 **zuòdewán** can finish
   Jīntiānde zuòyè nǐ zuòdewán ma?
   今天的作业你做得完吗？
   Can you finish today's homework?

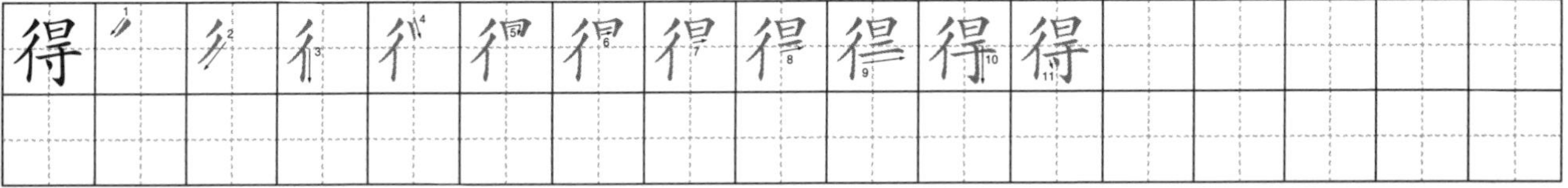

CHARACTER 123

zhè
this; here

Useful phrases and sentences

7 STROKES | 辶 RADICAL

1. 这个 **zhège** this
   Wǒ xǐhuan zhège fànguǎnr.
   我喜欢这个饭馆儿。
   I like this restaurant.

2. 这是 **zhè shì** this is
   Zhè shì wǒde nǚpéngyou.
   这是我的女朋友。
   This is my girlfriend.

3. 这些 **zhèxiē** these
   Zhèxiē dōngxi dōu shì wǒde.
   这些东西都是我的。
   These things are all mine.

4. 这儿 **zhèr** here
   Zhèr yǒu fànguǎn ma?
   这儿有饭馆吗？
   Are there any restaurants here?

这

CHARACTER 124

nà
that; there

Useful phrases and sentences

6 STROKES | 阝 RADICAL

1. 那个 **nàge** that

Nàge nǚháir shì shéi?
那个女孩儿是谁？
Who is that girl?

2. 那是 **nà shì** that is

Nà shì wǒde fángjiān.
那是我的房间。
That is my room.

3. 那些 **nàxiē** those

Nàxiē rén zài zuò shénme?
那些人在做什么？
What are those people doing?

4. 那儿 **nàr** there

Wǒmende Yīngwén lǎoshī zài nàr.
我们的英文老师在那儿。
Our English teacher is over there.

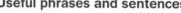

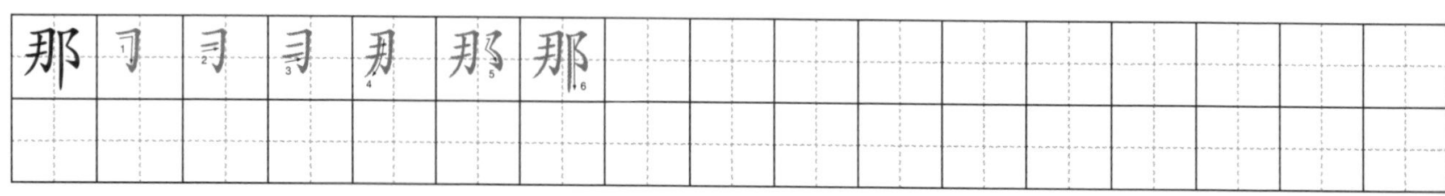

CHARACTER 125

zěn
how

Useful phrases and sentences

9 STROKES | 心 RADICAL

1. 怎么 **zěnme** how to

Zhège dōngxi zěnme chī?
这个东西怎么吃？
How to eat this thing?

2. 怎么写... **zěnme xiě...** how to write ...

Nǐde Zhōngwén míngzi zěnme xiě?
你的中文名字怎么写？
How do you write your Chinese name?

3. 怎么说 **zěnme shuō** how to say it

"Coffee" Zhōngwén zěnme shuō?
"Coffee" 中文怎么说？
How do you say "coffee" in Chinese?

4. 怎么了 **zěnmele** what happened; what's wrong

Nǐ zěnmele?
你怎么了？
What happened to you?

CHARACTER 126

yàng
type; fashion; way

Useful phrases and sentences

10 STROKES | 木 RADICAL

1. 什么样 **shénmeyàng** what kind of

Nǐ xǐhuan shénmeyàngde rén?
你喜欢什么样的人？
What kind of people do you like?

2. 怎么样 **zěnmeyàng** how about

Xiàwǔ yìqǐ dǎqiú zěnmeyàng?
下午一起打球怎么样？
How about playing ball together this afternoon?

3. 一样 **yíyàng** the same

Wǒmende diànnǎo yíyàng.
我们的电脑一样。
Our computers are the same.

4. 样子 **yàngzi** appearance; style

Wǒ xǐhuan zhèjiàn yīfude yàngzi.
我喜欢这件衣服的样子。
I like the style of this shirt/dress.

CHARACTER 127

qián
money

Useful phrases and sentences

10 STROKES | 钅 RADICAL

1. 多少钱 **duōshao qián** how much money
   Zhèpíng shuǐ duōshao qián?
   这瓶水多少钱？
   How much is this bottle of water?

2. 三块钱 **sānkuài qián** three *kuai*
   Wǒ zhǐ yǒu sānkuài qián.
   我只有三块钱。
   I only have three kuai.

3. 有钱 **yǒuqián** rich; to have money
   Tā hěn yǒuqián.
   他很有钱。
   He is very rich.

4. 钱包 **qiánbāo** purse; wallet
   Zhège qiánbāo hěn piàoliang.
   这个钱包很漂亮。
   This purse is pretty.

CHARACTER 128

hěn
very

Useful phrases and sentences

9 STROKES | 彳 RADICAL

1. 很晚 **hěn wǎn** very late
   Xiànzài hěn wǎn le, wǒ děi zǒule.
   现在很晚了，我得走了。
   It's very late now, I have to leave.

2. 很大 **hěn dà** very big; very large
   Zhège fángjiān hěn dà.
   这个房间很大。
   This room is very large.

3. 很远 **hěn yuǎn** very far
   Tāde xuéxiào hěn yuǎn.
   她的学校很远。
   Her school is very far.

4. 很多 **hěnduō** many; much
   Wǒ yǒu hěnduō shū.
   我有很多书。
   I have many books.

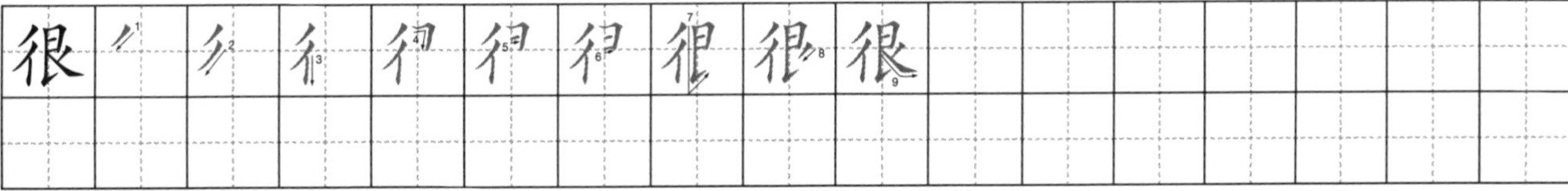

CHARACTER 129

tài
too

Useful phrases and sentences

4 STROKES | 大 RADICAL

1. 太大了 **tài dà le** too big/large
   Zhèjiàn yīfu tài dà le.
   这件衣服太大了。
   This shirt/dress is too big.

2. 太难了 **tài nán le** too difficult
   Jīntiānde kè tài nán le, wǒ méi tīngdǒng.
   今天的课太难了，我没听懂。
   Today's class was really difficult. I couldn't understand.

3. 太高了 **tài gāo le** too tall/high
   Nàge zhuōzi tài gāo le.
   那个桌子太高了。
   That table is too high.

4. 太好了 **tài hǎo le** so wonderful!
   Zhège xiǎngfǎ tài hǎo le!
   这个想法太好了！
   What a wonderful idea!

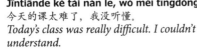

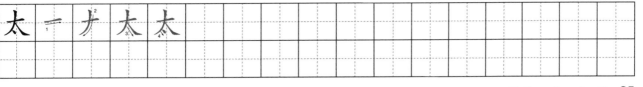

CHARACTER 130

xiǎo
small; little

Useful phrases and sentences

3 STROKES | 小 RADICAL

1. 太小了 **tài xiǎo le** too small/little
Zhège màozi tài xiǎo le.
这个帽子太小了。
This hat is too small.

2. 小时 **xiǎoshí** hour
Cóng zhèr dào Běijīng yào jǐge xiǎoshí?
从这儿到北京要几个小时?
How many hours does it take from here to Beijing?

3. 小学 **xiǎoxué** primary school
Nà shì xiǎoxué háishì zhōngxué?
那是小学还是中学?
Is that a primary school or a middle school?

4. 小说 **xiǎoshuō** novel
Wǒ xǐhuan kàn xiǎoshuō.
我喜欢看小说。
I like reading novels.

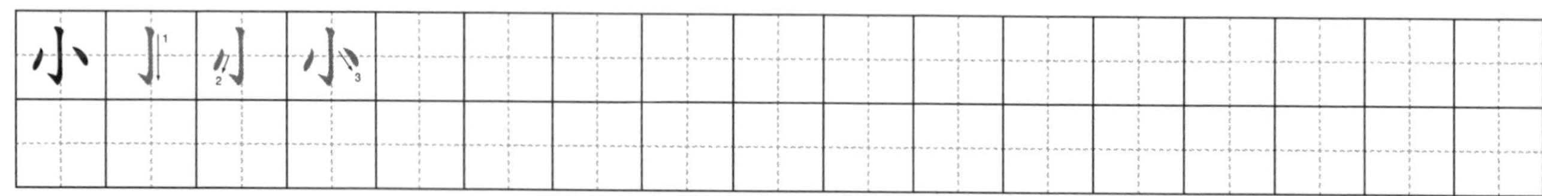

CHARACTER 131

guì
expensive; nobility; your (honorific)

Useful phrases and sentences

9 STROKES | 贝 RADICAL

1. 很贵 **hěn guì** very expensive (speaking of amount)
Wǒmende xuéfèi hěn guì.
我们的学费很贵。
Our tuition fee is expensive.

2. 昂贵 **ángguì** expensive (speaking of objects)
Zhège lǐwù tài ángguì le.
这个礼物太昂贵了。
This gift is too expensive.

3. 贵校 **guìxiào** your school (honorific)
Qǐng wèn, guìxiào zài nǎr?
请问, 贵校在哪儿?
Excuse me, where is your school?

4. 太贵了 **tài guì le** too expensive
Zài Měiguó chī Zhōngguó cài tài guì le!
在美国吃中国菜太贵了!
It is too expensive to eat Chinese food in U.S.A.

CHARACTER 132

pián/biàn
cheap/convenient

Useful phrases and sentences

9 STROKES | 亻 RADICAL

1. 便条 **biàntiáo** note
Yàoshì wǒ bú zài jiā, qǐng nǐ gěi wǒ xiě yíge biàntiáo.
要是我不在家, 请你给我写一个便条。
If I'm not home, please leave me a note.

2. 方便 **fāngbiàn** convenient
Xuésheng zhùzài xuéxiào hěn fāngbiàn.
学生住在学校很方便。
It is convenient for students to live on campus.

3. 方便面 **fāngbiànmiàn** instant noodles
Wǒ bù xǐhuan chī fāngbiànmiàn.
我不喜欢吃方便面。
I don't like to eat instant noodles.

4. 便利店 **biànlìdiàn** convenience store
Wǒ píngcháng qù biànlìdiàn mǎi dōngxi.
我平常去便利店买东西。
I usually go buy things at convenience stores.

CHARACTER 133

宜

yí
appropriate

8 STROKES　宀 RADICAL

Useful phrases and sentences

1. 便宜 **piányi** cheap

Piányide dōngxi bù yīdìng bù hǎo.
便宜的东西不一定不好。
Cheap things are not necessarily bad.

2. 合宜 **héyí** appropriate

Tāde māma zǒngshì chuānzhuó héyí.
他的妈妈总是穿着合宜。
His mother is always well-dressed.

3. 不宜 **bùyí** inadvisable; not suitable

Zhèi jiàn shì jīntiān bùyí shuō.
这件事今天不宜说。
It is inadvisable to mention this today.

4. 宜人 **yírén** pleasant

Jiāzhōude qìhòu yīnián sìjì dōu hěn yírén.
加州的气候一年四季都很宜人。
The climate in California is always pleasant all year round.

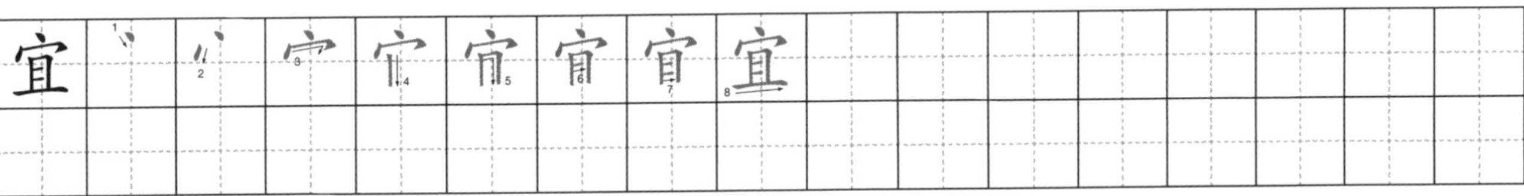

CHARACTER 134

cuò
wrong; mistake

13 STROKES　钅 RADICAL

Useful phrases and sentences

1. 走错 **zǒucuò** walk/go wrong; get lost

Nǐ zǒucuò jiàoshì le.
你走错教室了。
You are in the wrong classroom.

2. 听错 **tīngcuò** hear wrong

Wǒ tīngcuòle kǎoshì shíjiān.
我听错了考试时间。
I heard the test time wrong.

3. 错误 **cuòwù** mistake

Zhècì kǎoshì nǐ yǒu hěnduō cuòwù.
这次考试你有很多错误。
You made many mistakes in this test.

4. 错过 **cuòguo** miss (an opportunity)

Kuàidiǎnr, bié cuòguole hǔochē.
快点儿，别错过了火车！
Hurry up, don't miss the train!

CHARACTER 135

le
a particle indicating completion or change of state

2 STROKES　乛 RADICAL

Useful phrases and sentences

1. 好了 **hǎole** Okay

Hǎole, wǒmen zǒu ba!
好了，我们走吧！
Okay, let's go!

2. 看了 **kànle** looked; watched; read

Wǒ kànle sāngè xiǎoshí shū.
我看了三个小时书。
I read for three hours.

3. 买了 **mǎile** bought

Nǐ mǎile shénme?
你买了什么？
What did you buy?

4. 太…了 **tài…le** too…

Zhèjiàn yīfu tài guì le.
这件衣服太贵了。
This shirt/dress is too expensive.

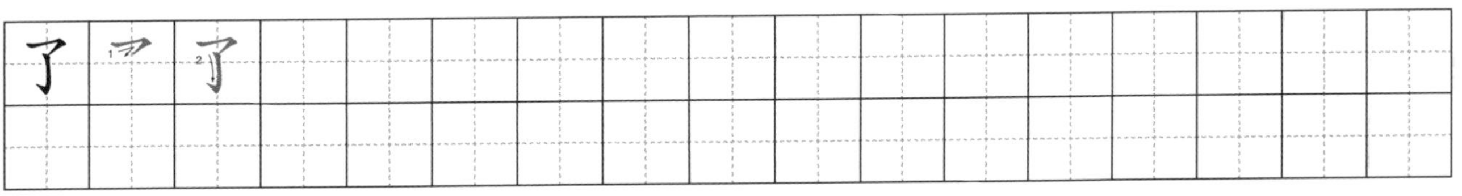

Lesson 9 Exercises

Part 1 Choose from the following words to fill in the blanks.

便宜、觉得、错、怎么样、钱

1. 这本书很不错。你（　　　　）这本书（　　　　）？
2. 请问，这件衣服多少（　　　　）？
3. 这个太贵了，（　　　　）点儿吧！
4. 你听（　　　　）了，他不是中国人。

Part 2 Complete the following dialogues using Chinese characters.

1. A: 你觉得中文课怎么样？

   B: ____。

2. A: 你的学费 (**xuéfèi**: tuition fee) 贵吗？

   B: ____。

3. A: 你平常去哪儿买衣服？

   B: ____。

4. A: 你喜欢和谁去买衣服？

   B: ____。

5. A: 你的学校 (**xuéxiào**: school) 大不大？

   B: ____。

Part 3 Use the following prompts to give a one-minute speech.

我的学校在＿＿＿＿＿＿，我喜欢这儿的＿＿＿＿＿＿，我不喜欢这儿的＿＿＿＿＿＿，

我觉得＿＿＿＿＿＿。我平常去＿＿＿＿＿＿买东西，因为 (**yīnwèi**: because) 那儿＿＿＿＿＿＿。

LESSON 10

Clothes shopping (II) 买衣服 (II)

1. Introduction

As we know, in the US people rush to different stores on Black Friday for good deals. Do you know that there is a similar day in China? On November 11th, many shops have big discounts and numerous items are for sale. This is called "Double Eleven" Day in Chinese. "Double Eleven" was originally for single people as it fell on 11/11. Major online retailers started to have big sales on this day and it has become a nationwide "deal day" in China. Does your country have a similar day like this?

2. Warm up

Read the passage below and answer the questions using Chinese characters.

朋友问我，你喜欢做什么？我说："我喜欢买衣服，特别爱买便宜、好看的衣服！"。我有很多衣服，可是我的衣服都很便宜。这个周末，我和我的室友要一起去买一点儿衣服。我要买两双鞋，一件裤子和三件裙子。你想不想跟我一起去？

1. What is her hobby?

____

2. Is she satisfied with the clothes she has?

____

3. What is she going to buy?

____

3. Vocabulary

	Word	Pinyin	English equivalent
1.	说	**shuō**	say; speak
2.	衣服	**yīfu**	clothes
3.	特别	**tèbié**	especially
4.	爱	**ài**	love
5.	好看	**hǎokàn**	pretty; good looking
6.	可是	**kěshì**	but

	Word	Pinyin	English equivalent
7.	室友	**shìyou**	roommate
8.	要	**yào**	want
9.	去	**qù**	go
10.	一点儿	**yìdiǎnr**	a little bit
11.	双	**shuāng**	pair (measure word)
12.	两双鞋	**liǎngshuāng xié**	two pairs of shoes
13.	件	**jiàn**	measure word for clothes
14.	裤子	**kùzi**	trousers; pants
15.	裙子	**qúnzi**	skirt; dress
16.	少一点	**shǎo yìdiǎn**	a bit less
17.	能	**néng**	can
18.	试穿	**shìchuān**	try on

4. New Characters

Fifteen characters are introduced in this lesson. Use the following explanations to help you understand and remember the characters.

双 鞋 裤 裙 子 件 衣 服 少 点 能 要 吧 试 穿

CHARACTER 136

shuāng
pair

Useful phrases and sentences

4 STROKES | 又 RADICAL

1. 一双 **yìshuāng** a pair
   Wǒ xiǎng mǎi yìshuāng xié.
   我想买一双鞋。
   I want to buy a pair of shoes.

2. 双胞胎 **shuāngbāotāi** twins
   Wǒmen shì shuāngbāotāi.
   我们是双胞胎。
   We are twins.

3. 双号 **shuānghào** even numbers
   Shuānghào fángjiān zài nàbiān.
   双号房间在那边。
   Even-numbered rooms are on that side.

4. 双人床 **shuāngrén chuáng** double bed
   Shuāngrén chuáng bǐ dānrén chuáng dàde duō.
   双人床比单人床大得多。
   A double bed is much bigger than a twin bed.

双 1 2 3 4

CHARACTER 137

鞋

xié
shoe

15 STROKES　革 RADICAL

Useful phrases and sentences

1. 皮鞋 **píxié** leather shoes
   Zhèshuāng píxié tài guì le.
   这双皮鞋太贵了。
   This pair of leather shoes is too expensive.

2. 运动鞋 **yùndòngxié** sports shoes
   Zhèshuāng yùndòngxié hěn shūfu.
   这双运动鞋很舒服。
   This pair of sports shoes is very comfortable.

3. 拖鞋 **tuōxié** slippers
   Wǒ zài jiā chuān tuōxié.
   我在家穿拖鞋。
   I wear slippers at home.

4. 高跟鞋 **gāogēnxié** high-heeled shoes
   Zuótiān wǒ mǎile yìshuāng gāogēnxié.
   昨天我买了一双高跟鞋。
   I bought a pair of high-heeled shoes yesterday.

CHARACTER 138

裤

kù
trousers; pants

12 STROKES　衤 RADICAL

Useful phrases and sentences

1. 裤子 **kùzi** trousers; pants
   Zhèjiàn kùzi zěnmeyàng?
   这件裤子怎么样？
   How about this pair of trousers?

2. 短裤 **duǎnkù** shorts
   Wǒ yǒu hěnduōjiàn duǎnkù.
   我有很多件短裤。
   I have many pairs of shorts.

3. 运动裤 **yùndòngkù** sports pants
   Wǒ píngcháng chuān yùndòngkù.
   我平常穿运动裤。
   I usually wear sports pants.

4. 西裤 **xīkù** suit pants
   Zhèjiàn xīkù yánsè hěn hǎo.
   这件西裤颜色很好。
   The color of this suit pants is good.

CHARACTER 139

qún
skirt; dress

12 STROKES　衤 RADICAL

Useful phrases and sentences

1. 裙子 **qúnzi** skirt
   Zhèjiàn qúnzi tài dà le.
   这件裙子太大了。
   This skirt is too big.

2. 围裙 **wéiqún** apron
   Wǒ māma zuòfàn shí zǒngshì wéi shàng wéiqún.
   我妈妈做饭时总是围上围裙。
   My mother always puts on an apron when cooking.

3. 短裙 **duǎnqún** short skirt
   Nǐ jīntiānde duǎnqún hěn hǎokàn.
   你今天的短裙很好看。
   Your short skirt today is pretty.

4. 长裙 **chángqún** long skirt
   Zhège zhōumò wǒ xiǎng qù mǎi yījiàn chángqún.
   这个周末我想去买一件长裙。
   I want to go buy a long skirt this weekend.

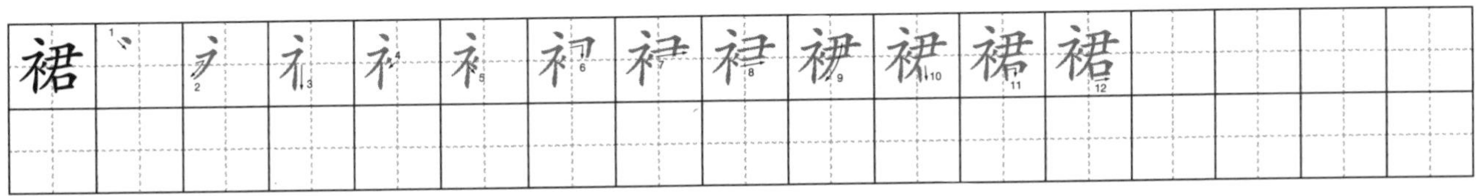

CHARACTER 140

zi
a noun suffix; son

Useful phrases and sentences

3 STROKES | 子 RADICAL

1. 杯子 **bēizi** cup; glass
   Zhège bēizi wǒ zài Měiguó mǎi de.
   这个杯子我在美国买的。
   I bought this cup in U.S.A.

2. 孩子 **háizi** child; kid
   Nǐ yǒu jǐgè háizi?
   你有几个孩子？
   How many children do you have?

3. 椅子 **yǐzi** chair; stool
   Nàge yǐzi yào wǔbǎikuài, tài guì le.
   那个椅子要五百块，太贵了。
   That chair costs 500 kuai.

4. 桌子 **zhuōzi** table; desk
   Zhège zhuōzi hé zhège yǐzi dōu hěn hǎokàn.
   这个桌子和这个椅子都很好看。
   This table and this chair both look good.

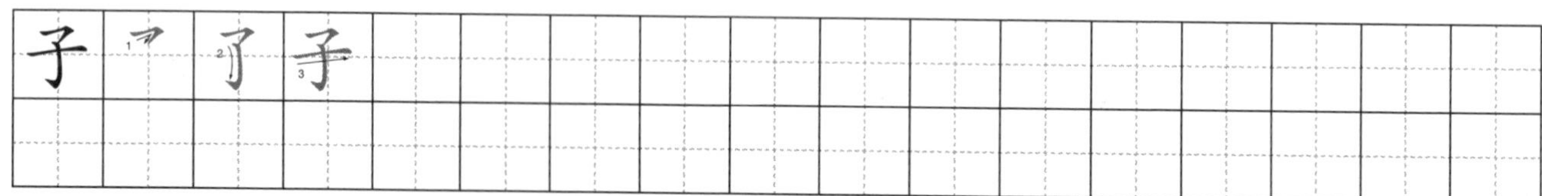

CHARACTER 141

jiàn
piece;
a measure word

Useful phrases and sentences

6 STROKES | 亻 RADICAL

1. 这件衣服 **zhèjiàn yīfu** this piece of clothing
   Nǐ juéde zhèjiàn yīfu zěnmeyàng?
   你觉得这件衣服怎么样？
   What do you think about this piece of clothing?

2. 一件行李 **yíjiàn xíngli** a piece of luggage
   Wǒ zhǐ yǒu yíjiàn xíngli.
   我只有一件行李。
   I only have one piece of luggage.

3. 一件毛衣 **yíjiàn máoyī** a sweater
   Wǒ yǒu yījiàn hóngsède máoyī.
   我有一件红色的毛衣。
   I have a red sweater.

4. 软件 **ruǎnjiàn** software
   Zhège ruǎnjiàn hěn yǒuyòng.
   这个软件很有用。
   This software is very useful.

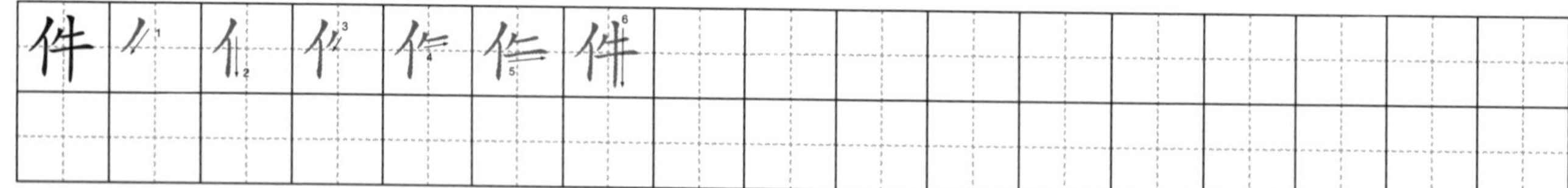

CHARACTER 142

yī
clothes

Useful phrases and sentences

6 STROKES | 衣 RADICAL

1. 毛衣 **máoyī** sweater
   Xiànzài chuān máoyī tài zǎo le.
   现在穿毛衣太早了。
   It is too early to wear a sweater now.

2. 衣架 **yījià** hanger
   Wǒ néng jiè yíge yījià ma?
   我能借一个衣架吗？
   Can I borrow a hanger?

3. 衣柜 **yīguì** wardrobe
   Wǒ yīguìlǐde yīfu tài duō le.
   我衣柜里的衣服太多了。
   There are too many clothes in my wardrobe.

4. 洗衣机 **xǐyījī** washing machine
   Zhège xǐyījī hěn piányi.
   这个洗衣机很便宜。
   This washing machine is cheap.

CHARACTER 143

fú
clothes; service

Useful phrases and sentences

8 STROKES | 月 RADICAL

1. 衣服 **yīfu** clothes
Nǐ zhège yīfu zài nǎr mǎi de?
你这个衣服在哪儿买的？
Where did you buy this shirt/dress?

2. 校服 **xiàofú** school uniform
Wǒmen xuéxiào méiyǒu xiàofú.
我们学校没有校服。
We do not have school uniforms in our school.

3. 制服 **zhìfú** uniform (army, company, etc.)
Zhè shì nǐ gōngsī de zhìfú ma?
这是你公司的制服吗？
Is this your company uniform?

4. 服务员 **fúwùyuán** waiter; service personnel
Fúwùyuán, xiànzài kěyǐ diǎncài ma?
服务员，现在可以点菜吗？
Waiter, can I order now?

CHARACTER 144

shǎo
few; less

Useful phrases and sentences

4 STROKES | 小 RADICAL

1. 太少了 **tài shǎo le** too little
Zhège gōngzuòde qián tài shǎo le.
这个工作的钱太少了。
The money for this job is too little.

2. 少一点 **shǎo yìdiǎn** a little less
Táng shǎo yìdiǎn, xièxie.
糖少一点，谢谢。
Less sugar, thank you.

3. 很少 **hěn shǎo** little; few
Tāde péngyou hěn shǎo.
他的朋友很少。
He has few friends.

4. 少数人 **shǎoshùrén** a few people
Shǎoshùrén yídìng yào tīng duōshùrénde huà ma?
少数人一定要听多数人的话吗？
Is it necessary that the minority needs to listen to the majority?

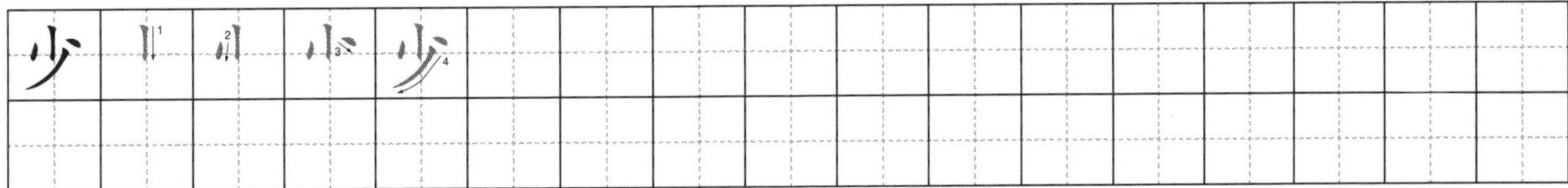

CHARACTER 145

diǎn
a little; dot

Useful phrases and sentences

9 STROKES | 灬 RADICAL

1. 一点儿 **yìdiǎnr** a little
Bēizilǐ yǒu yìdiǎnr shuǐ.
杯子里有一点儿水。
There is a little water in the cup.

2. 有点儿 **yǒudiǎnr** a little bit too ... (negative)
Zhèjiàn yīfu yǒudiǎnr dà.
这件衣服有点儿大。
These clothes are little bit big.

3. 早一点儿 **zǎo yìdiǎnr** a little earlier
Wǒ míngtiān yào zǎo yìdiǎnr qǐchuáng.
我明天要早一点儿起床。
I need to get up a little earlier tomorrow.

4. 快一点儿 **kuài yìdiǎnr** a little faster
Nǐ kěyǐ kuài yìdiǎnr ma?
你可以快一点儿吗？
Could you please be a little faster?

CHARACTER 146

néng
can

Useful phrases and sentences

10 STROKES | 月 RADICAL

1. 不能 **bù néng** cannot

Wǒ gǎn màole, bù néng dǎqiú.
我感冒了，不能打球。
I have a cold. I can't play ball.

2. 能 **néng** can

Nǐ néng guòlái yíxià ma?
你能过来一下吗？
Could you please come over?

3. 能不能 **néng-bù-néng** can or cannot (for yes/no questions)

Wǒ néng-bù-néng shì yíxià?
我能不能试一下？
Could I try?

4. 能力 **nénglì** ability

Tā hěn yǒu nénglì.
他很有能力。
He is very capable.

CHARACTER 147

yào
want; will

Useful phrases and sentences

9 STROKES | 覀 RADICAL

1. 要 **yào** want

Wǒ yào yībēi kāfēi, xièxie.
我要一杯咖啡，谢谢。
I want a cup of coffee, thanks.

2. 要 **yào** will

Wǒ míngtiān yào qù Fǎguó.
我明天要去法国。
I am going to France tomorrow.

3. 不要 **bú yào** don't want

Wǒ bù yào hóngsède, yào lǜsè de.
我不要红色的，要绿色的。
I don't want the red one, I want the green one.

4. 不要 **búyào** do not

Qǐng búyào zài zhèr chōuyān!
请不要在这儿抽烟！
Please do not smoke here!

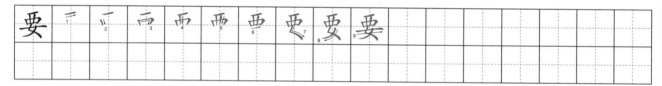

CHARACTER 148

ba
a particle indicating suggestion/ supposition

Useful phrases and sentences

7 STROKES | 口 RADICAL

1. 吧 **ba** indicating suggestion

Wǒmen yìqǐ zǒu ba!
我们一起走吧！
Let's go together!

2. 吧 **ba** indicating supposition

Nǐ shì Zhōngguó rén ba?
你是中国人吧？
I suppose you are Chinese, right?

3. 吧 **ba** indicating suggestion

Wǒmen jīntiān wǎnshang yìqǐ qù dǎqiú ba!
我们今天晚上一起去打球吧！
Let's go play ball tonight!

4. 吧 **ba** indicating supposition

Nǐde shìyou shì Měiguó rén ba?
你的室友是美国人吧？
I suppose your roommate is American, right?

CHARACTER 149

shì
try; test

8 STROKES | **讠 RADICAL**

Useful phrases and sentences

1. 试试 **shìshì** give a try

Wǒ kěyǐ shìshì zhèjiàn hóngsède ma?
我可以试试这件红色的吗？
Can I try this red one?

2. 试吃 **shìchī** try (food sampling)

Zhè shì xīn chǎnpǐn, huānyíng shìchī.
这是新产品，欢迎试吃。
This is a new product. You are welcome to try it.

3. 试穿 **shìchuān** try on

Qǐng wèn, wǒ néng shìchuān yíxià zhèjiàn yīfu ma?
请问，我能试穿一下这件衣服吗？
Excuse me, can I try on these clothes?

4. 笔试 **bǐshì** written examination

Wǒmen míngtiān yǒu yíge bǐshì.
我们明天有一个笔试。
We have a written examination tomorrow.

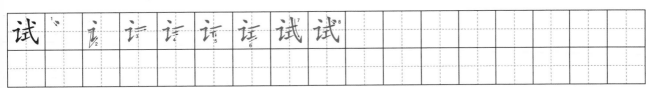

CHARACTER 150

chuān
wear; pass through

9 STROKES | **穴 RADICAL**

Useful phrases and sentences

1. 穿衣服 **chuān yīfu** dress (*verb*); wear clothes

Zhège háizi tài xiǎo le, búhuì zìjǐ chuān yīfu.
这个孩子太小了，不会自己穿衣服。
This child is too young to dress himself.

2. 穿鞋 **chuān xié** wear shoes

Děng yíxià, wǒ zài chuān xié.
等一下，我在穿鞋。
Wait a minute! I am wearing my shoes.

3. 穿上 **chuānshàng** put on

Tiān lěng le, bǎ yīfu chuānshàng ba!
天冷了，把衣服穿上吧！
It's getting cold. Put on your clothes!

4. 穿过 **chuānguò** pass through

Chuānguò huāyuán jiùshì sùshè le.
穿过花园，就是宿舍了。
You will get to the dormitory after passing through the garden.

Lesson 10 Exercises

Part 1 Choose from the following words to fill in the blanks.

件、鞋、衣服、裙子、试

1. 你的这件（　　　　）很好看，我也想买。
2. 你觉得这双（　　　　）怎么样？

3. 这件（　　　　）有点儿大，我（　　　　）一下那件吧。

4. 我不喜欢这（　　　　）裤子，太贵了。

Part 2 Complete the following dialogues using Chinese characters.

1. A: 你常常去买衣服吗？

   B: ____。

2. A: 你有很贵的衣服吗？

   B: ____。

3. A: 你有几双运动鞋？

   B: ____。

4. A: 你这个周末要去哪儿？

   B: ____。

5. A: 买衣服你试穿吗？

   B: ____。

Part 3 Fill out the following chart based on the given information.

Your friend would like to purchase the following goods.	Where do you recommend him/her to shop?	Why do you think he/she should go to those places to shop? (e.g., price, quality)
一双运动鞋		
两条裤子		
一件衣服		

Lessons 6–10 (Review Exercises)

Part 1 Write the Pinyin and the English meaning of the following words.

	Words	Pinyin	English Equivalent
e.g.,	五元	**wŭyuán**	five yuan
1.	星期	____________	____________
2.	谢谢	____________	____________
3.	再见	____________	____________
4.	喜欢	____________	____________
5.	打球	____________	____________
6.	衣服	____________	____________
7.	周末	____________	____________
8.	地方	____________	____________
9.	时间	____________	____________
10.	便宜	____________	____________

Part 2 Fill in the blanks according to the English meaning.

1. (   ) 友 roommate
2. (   ) 是 but
3. (   ) 得 feel
4. (   ) 起 together
5. (   ) 天 every day
6. 可 (   ) can
7. 电 (   ) movie
8. 平 (   ) usually
9. 再 (   ) goodbye
10. 打 (   ) play ball

Part 3 Answer the following questions using Chinese characters.

1. Q: 你平常星期几很忙?

   A: ____。

2. Q: 你的父母周末喜欢做什么？

A: ____。

3. Q: 你买的衣服贵不贵？

A: ____。

4. Q: 你好朋友的生日是几月几号？

A: ____。

Part 4 Read the passage below and answer the questions using Chinese characters.

张欢： 常天，明天是周末，你想做什么？
常天： 我不知道呢。
张欢： 我们去买衣服，怎么样？
常天： 我不喜欢买衣服，衣服太贵了。
张欢： 那我们去打球吧？
常天： 打球……，我这个星期太累了。
张欢： 明天下午去看美国电影吧？
常天： 明天下午我没有时间，不好意思。
张欢： 我们一起去吃晚饭吧？
常天： 不好意思，我要跟别人吃晚饭。
张欢： 你是不是有女朋友了？
常天： ……

1. 周末张欢想跟常天去做什么？

____。

2. 常天为什么不跟张欢去吃晚饭？

____。

3. 你觉得常天有没有女朋友？

____。

LESSON 11

Where is the Great Wall Hotel? 请问，长城宾馆在哪儿？

1. Introduction

In China, a hotel is called **bīnguǎn** or **jiǔdiàn**. The term 宾馆 **bīnguǎn** is composed of 宾 (**bīn:** guest) and 馆 (**guǎn:** building; establishment), while the term 酒店 **jiǔdiàn** is composed of 酒 (**jiǔ:** liquor) and 店 (**diàn:** store). So what is the difference between a **bīnguǎn** and a **jiǔdiàn**? Generally speaking, a **jiǔdiàn** has much more to offer than mere lodging, such as high-end restaurants, business centers, fancy bars, and multifunctional rooms for weddings or conferences. A **bīnguǎn**, in contrast, is mainly for lodging.

No matter whether you stay in a **jiǔdiàn** or a **bīnguǎn** in China, you will find disposable slippers, toothbrushes, and toothpaste in the room. These supplies are considered essential for Chinese people when they choose to stay in a hotel. Have you ever stayed in a hotel in China? Did you find it comfortable?

2. Warm up

Read the passage below and answer the questions using Chinese characters.

林先生：你好！请问，长城宾馆在哪儿？
李先生：长城宾馆？这儿没有长城宾馆，我知道双城宾馆。
林先生：哦，我说错了，是双城宾馆。
李先生：那是火车站，往前走，两分钟就到了。
林先生：谢谢！
李先生：不客气！

1. What hotel is Mr. Lin looking for?

____

2. How long it will take to go to the hotel?

____

3. Vocabulary

	Word	Pinyin	English equivalent
1.	长城	**Chángchéng**	the Great Wall
2.	宾馆	**bīnguǎn**	hotel
3.	知道	**zhīdao**	know
4.	哦	**ò**	"oh"
5.	错	**cuò**	wrong
6.	火车站	**huǒchēzhàn**	train station
7.	往	**wǎng**	to; toward
8.	前	**qián**	ahead; front
9.	走	**zǒu**	walk
10.	城市	**chéngshì**	city
11.	分钟	**fēnzhōng**	minute
12.	就	**jiù**	then; (particle indicating quickness or ease)
13.	到	**dào**	arrive
14.	不客气	**bú kèqi**	you are welcome

4. New Characters

Fifteen characters are introduced in this lesson. Use the following explanations to help you understand and remember the characters.

知 道 城 市 宾 馆 往 前 走 分 钟 就 到 客 气

CHARACTER 151

知

zhī
know

Useful phrases and sentences

8 STROKES | 矢 RADICAL

1. 知足 **zhīzú** be satisfied

Wǒde fángzi búdà, kěshì hěn shūfu. Wǒ yǐjīng zhīzú le.
我的房子不大，可是很舒服。我已经知足了。
My house is not big, but is comfortable. I'm satisfied.

2. 知名 **zhīmíng** well-known

Tāde fùqin shì dāngdì zhīmíngde zuòjiā.
他的父亲是当地知名的作家。
His father is a well-known writer in his hometown.

3. 通知 **tōngzhī** inform; notify; notice

Rúguǒ Wáng Xiǎojie láile, tōngzhī wǒ yíxià.
如果王小姐来了，通知我一下。
Please inform me if Ms Wang arrives.

4. 无知 **wúzhī** ignorant

Wǒ juéde tā yǒudiǎnr wúzhī.
我觉得他有点儿无知。
I feel that he is a bit ignorant.

知 1 2 3 4 5 6 7 8

CHARACTER 152

dào
road

Note: The **dào** in **zhīdao** loses its tone.

Useful phrases and sentences

12 STROKES | 辶 RADICAL

1. 知道 **zhīdao** know

Wǒ bù zhīdao yǐhòu zuò shénme gōngzuò.
我不知道以后做什么工作。
I don't know what job I will do in the future.

2. 道理 **dàolǐ** sense; reason

Tā zhǐ yǒu sìsuì, kěshì tā shuōde huà hěn yǒu dàoli.
她只有四岁，可是她说的话很有道理。
She is only four years old, but what she says makes great sense.

3. 道歉 **dàoqiàn** apologize

Zhèjiàn shì shì nǐde cuò, nǐ yīnggaī dàoqiàn.
这件事是你的错，你应该道歉。
This is your fault. You should apologize.

4. 道别 **dàobié** say goodbye to someone

Tā yǐjīng huíguóle, kěshì wǒ méi shíjiān gēn tā dàobié.
他已经回国了，可是我没时间跟他道别。
He's already returned to his country, but I hadn't had the opportunity to say goodbye to him.

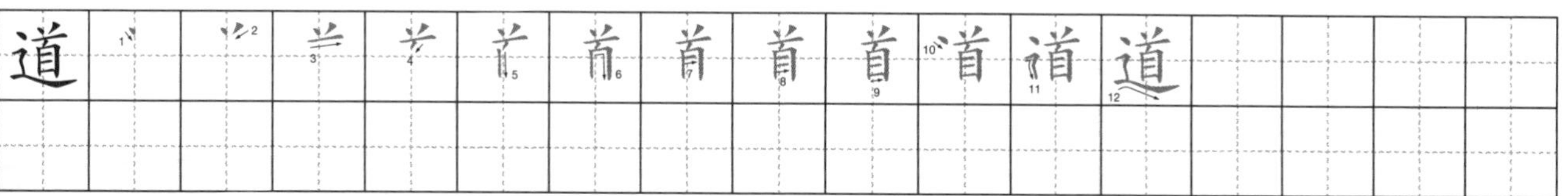

CHARACTER 153

chéng
city

Useful phrases and sentences

9 STROKES | 土 RADICAL

1. 城市 **chéngshì** city

Nǐ zuì xǐhuan nǎge chéngshì?
你最喜欢哪个城市？
What city do you like best?

2. 城里 **chéngli** in the city

Wǒ bù xǐhuan zhù zaì chéngli, tài chǎo le.
我不喜欢住在城里，太吵了。
I don't like to live in the city. It is too noisy.

3. 长城 **Chángchéng** The Great Wall

Nǐ qùguo Chángchéng ma?
你去过长城吗？
Have you been to the Great Wall?

4. 城堡 **chéngbǎo** castle

Sūgélán yǒu hěnduō piàoliangde chéngbǎo.
苏格兰有很多漂亮的城堡。
There are many beautiful castles in Scotland.

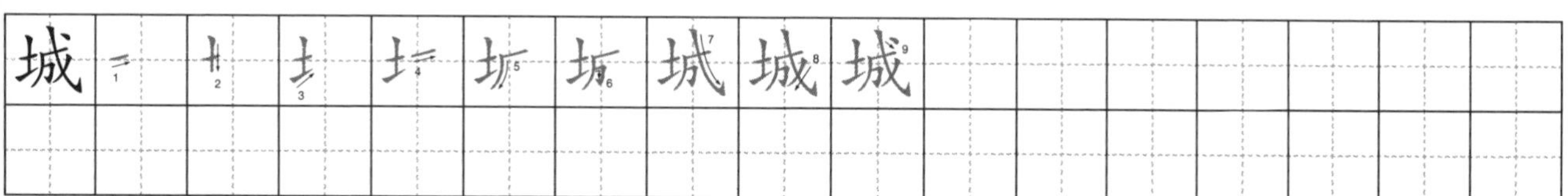

CHARACTER 154

shì
city; market

Useful phrases and sentences

5 STROKES | 巾 RADICAL

1. 市区 **shìqū** urban district

Wǒ bùxiǎng zhùzài shìqū, fángzū tài guìle!
我不想住在市区，房租太贵了！
I don't want to live in the downtown area because the rent is too expensive.

2. 市长 **shìzhǎng** mayor

Xīn shìzhǎng hěn guānxīn chéngshìde jiāotōng wèntí.
新市长很关心城市的交通问题。
The new mayor really cares about the issues of traffic.

3. 市中心 **shìzhōngxīn** downtown

Shìzhōngxīn lí zhèr bù yuǎn.
市中心离这儿不远。
Downtown is not far from here.

4. 夜市 **yèshì** night market

Táiwān měige chéngshì chàbùduō dōu yǒu yèshì.
台湾每个城市差不多都有夜市。
Almost every city in Taiwan has night markets.

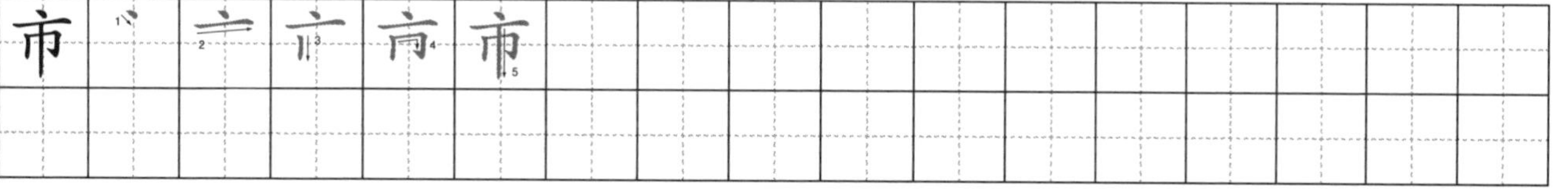

CHARACTER 155

宾

bīn
guest

Useful phrases and sentences

10 STROKES | 宀 RADICAL

1. 宾馆 **bīnguǎn** hotel
   Shìzhōngxīnde bīnguǎn doū hěn guì.
   市中心的宾馆都很贵。
   The hotels downtown are all very expensive.

2. 贵宾 **guìbīn** guest of honor
   Jīntiānde yànhuì yǒu hěnduō guìbīn.
   今天的宴会有很多贵宾。
   There are many guests of honor at the reception today.

3. 来宾 **láibīn** guest
   Jīntiān láibīn chàbùduō yǒu yībǎige.
   今天来宾差不多有一百个。
   There are about one hundred guests today.

4. 外宾 **wàibīn** foreign guest
   Wǒmen jīntiān yě qǐngle yīxiē wàibīn.
   我们今天也请了一些外宾。
   We also invite some foreign guests today.

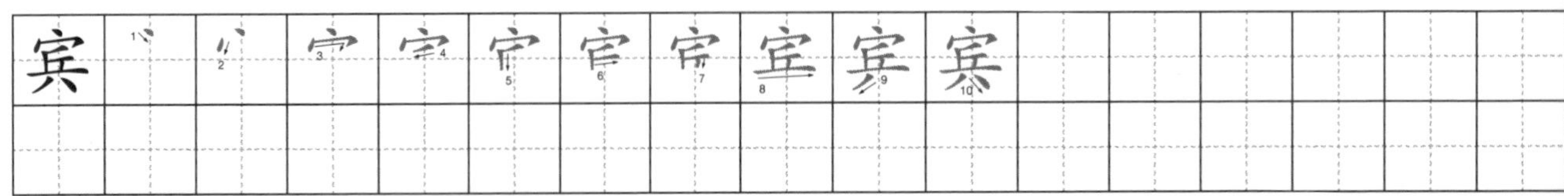

CHARACTER 156

馆

guǎn
building; establishment

Useful phrases and sentences

11 STROKES | 饣 RADICAL

1. 旅馆 **lǚguǎn** inn
   Zhèjiā xiǎo lǚguǎn hěn gānjìng, jiàge yě hěn piányi.
   这家小旅馆很干净，价格也很便宜。
   This inn is very tidy and clean, the price is also very cheap.

2. 体育馆 **tǐyùguǎn** gym
   Nǐ měige xīngqī dōu qù tǐyùguǎn duànliàn shēntǐ ma?
   你每个星期都去体育馆锻炼身体吗？
   Do you go to gym to work out every week?

3. 博物馆 **bówùguǎn** museum
   Wǒ zhōumò chángcháng qù bówùguǎn.
   我周末常常去博物馆。
   I often go to museums on the weekend.

4. 图书馆 **túshūguǎn** library
   Wǒ bù xǐhuan zài túshūguǎn xuéxí.
   我不喜欢在图书馆学习。
   I don't like to study in libraries.

CHARACTER 157

往

wǎng
to; toward

Useful phrases and sentences

8 STROKES | 彳 RADICAL

1. 往前 **wǎng qián** ahead; go straight
   Nǐ wǎng qián zǒu, kāfēiguǎn jiù zài qiánbian.
   你往前走，咖啡馆儿就在前边。
   Go ahead and you'll see the coffee shop in the front.

2. 往哪儿 **wǎng nǎr** to which direction
   Qǐng wèn, Běijīng Bīnguǎn wǎng nǎr zǒu?
   请问，北京宾馆往哪儿走？
   Excuse, how (to which direction) do you walk to the Beijing Hotel?

3. 往后 **wǎng hòu** toward back
   Bié wǎng qián zǒu, wǎng hòu zǒu.
   别往前走，往后走。
   Don't walk ahead, walk back.

4. 交往 **jiāowǎng** to date; associate; contact
   Nǐ hé Lǐ Xiǎojie zài jiāowǎng ma?
   你和李小姐在交往吗？
   Are you and Ms Li dating?

CHARACTER 158

qián
ahead; in front of

Useful phrases and sentences

9 STROKES | 刂 RADICAL

1. 前边 **qiánbian** in front of; proceeding

Qiánbian hái yǒu mài yīfu de, wǒmen qù kànkan.
前边还有卖衣服的，我们去看看。
There are clothes shops in the front. Let's go and see.

2. 前天 **qiántiān** the day before yesterday

Wǒ fùmǔ qiántiān lái kàn wǒ le.
我父母前天来看我了。
My parents came to see me the day before yesterday.

3. 前年 **qiánnián** the year before last

Qiánnián wǒ qùle Rìběn.
前年我去了日本。
I went to Japan the year before last.

4. 前头 **qiántou** ahead

Hépíng Bīnguǎn jiù zài qiántou, zǒu liǎng fēnzhōng jiù dàole.
和平宾馆就在前头，走两分钟就到了。
The Heping Hotel is just ahead, two minutes walk.

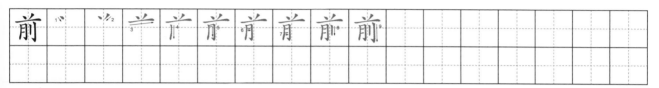

CHARACTER 159

zǒu
walk; go

Useful phrases and sentences

7 STROKES | 走 RADICAL

1. 走路 **zǒulù** to walk

Wǒmen zǒulù qù ba.
我们走路去吧。
Let's walk there.

2. 先走了 **xiān zǒule** go now

Wǒ yǒu yìdiǎn shìr, xiān zǒule.
我有一点事儿，先走了。
I have something to do. I'll be going now.

3. 带走 **dàizǒu** take away

Nǐde dōngxi jìde dàizǒu.
你的东西记得带走。
Remember to take away your belongings.

4. 走走 **zǒuzǒu** go for a walk

Wǒ chūqù zǒuzǒu.
我出去走走。
I am going out for a walk.

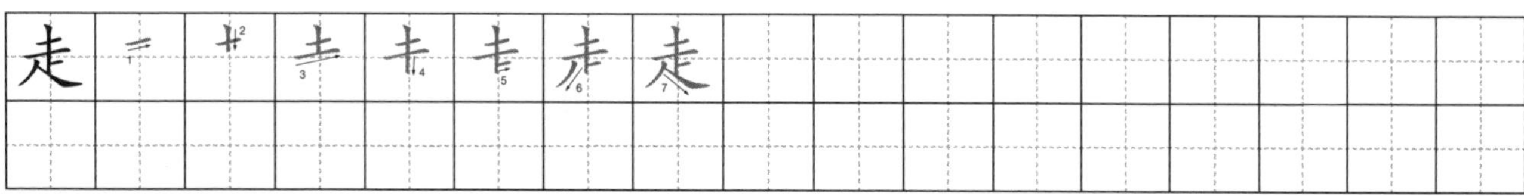

CHARACTER 160

fēn
divide; minutes

Useful phrases and sentences

4 STROKES | 刀 RADICAL

1. 分钟 **fēnzhōng** minutes

Hái yǒu sānfēnzhōng jiù shàngkèle.
还有三分钟就上课了。
Class will start in three minutes.

2. 分数 **fēnshù** grades

Zhècì kǎoshì wǒde fēnshù hěn dī.
这次考试我的分数很低。
My grade for this test is very low.

3. 分开 **fēnkāi** separate

Wǒ yǐjīng shíbā suì le, wǒ xiǎng hé fùmǔ fēnkāi zhù.
我已经十八岁了，我想和父母分开住。
I am already eighteen years old. I want to live separately from my parents.

4. 分享 **fēnxiǎng** share

Tā hěn xǐhuan gēn péngyou fēnxiǎng yǒu yìside shìqing.
她很喜欢跟朋友分享有意思的事情。
She likes to share interesting things with friends.

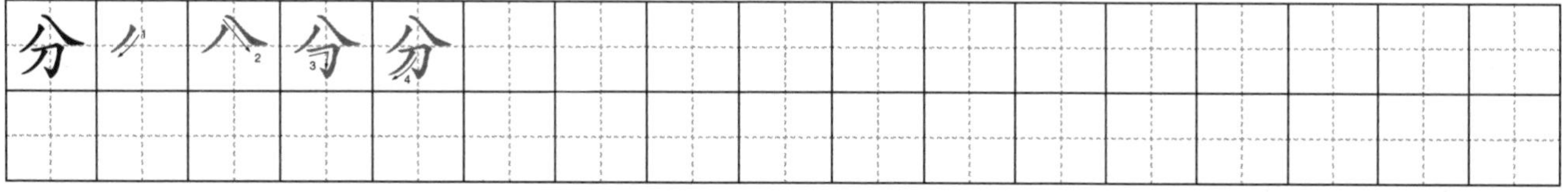

CHARACTER 161

zhōng
clock

Useful phrases and sentences

9 STROKES | 钅 RADICAL

1. 钟 **zhōng** clock

Zài Zhōngguó, bù néng gěi biéren sòng zhōng, nǐ zhīdao wèishénme ma?
在中国，不能给别人送钟，你知道为什么吗？
In China, you cannot give a clock as a gift. Do you know why?

2. 钟头 **zhōngtóu** hour

Tā měitiān liànxí Zhōngwén sānge zhōngtóu.
她每天练习中文三个钟头。
She practices Chinese for 3 hours a day.

3. 闹钟 **nàozhōng** alarm clock

Ài, wǒde nàozhōng huàile.
哎，我的闹钟坏了。
Oh, my alarm clock is not working.

4. 五十分钟 **wǔshífēn zhōng** fifty minutes

Wǒde Zhōngwén kè měitiān wǔshífēn zhōng.
我的中文课每天五十分钟。
My Chinese class is fifty minutes every day.

CHARACTER 162

就

jiù
then

Useful phrases and sentences

12 STROKES | 尢 RADICAL

1. 就到了 **jiù dàole** then you'll have arrived

Nǐ wǎng qián zǒu jiù dàole.
你往前走就到了。
Keep walking straight and you'll be there.

2. 就是 **jiùshì** exactly

Duì, wǒ jiù shì Wáng Xiānsheng.
对，我就是王先生。
Yes, I am Mr. Wang.

3. 就… **jiù…** as early as…

Wǒ jīntiān zǎoshang liùdiǎn jiù qǐchuáng le.
我今天早上六点就起床了。
I got up as early as six o'clock this morning.

4. 就要 **jiù yào** be going to

Wǒ jīnnián wǔyuè jiù yào bìyè le.
我今年五月就要毕业了。
I am graduating this May.

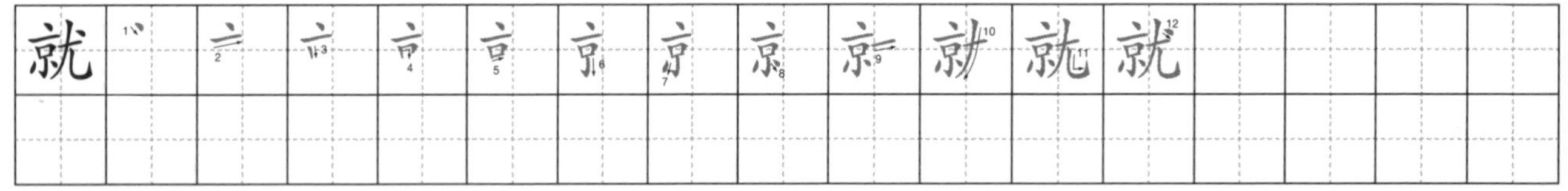

CHARACTER 163

dào
arrive

Useful phrases and sentences

8 STROKES | 刂 RADICAL

1. 到了 **dàole** arrived

Wǒ yǐjīng dàole, nǐ zài nǎr?
我已经到了，你在哪儿？
I have arrived. Where are you?

2. 到处 **dàochù** everywhere

Zài Zhōngguóde dà chéngshì, dàochù dōu néng kàndao kāfēiguǎnr.
在中国的大城市，到处都能看到咖啡馆儿。
Coffee shops can be found everywhere in China's big cities.

3. 到底 **dàodǐ** exactly; on earth

Nǐ dàodǐ xǐhuan shénme?
你到底喜欢什么？
What exactly do you like?

4. 到家 **dàojiā** arrive at home

Wǒ yǐjīng dàojiā le, nǐ bié dānxīn.
我已经到家了，你别担心。
I've arrived at home. Don't worry.

CHARACTER 164

kè
guest

Useful phrases and sentences

9 STROKES　宀 RADICAL

1. 客气 **kèqi** polite

Nǐ bié zhème kèqi.
你别这么客气。
You don't need to be so polite.

2. 不客气 **bú kèqi** you are welcome; no need to be polite

A: Xièxie. **B: Bú kèqi.**
A: 谢谢。 B:不客气。
A: Thank you. B: You are welcome.

3. 做客 **zuòkè** be a guest

Qù Měiguó rén jiāli zuòkè yīnggāi dài shénme?
去美国人家里做客应该带什么？
What should you bring when you are invited as a guest to an American's family?

4. 客人 **kèren** guest

Jīntiān wǒ jiāli huì lái jǐge kèren.
今天我家里会来几个客人。
There will be a few guests coming to my house today.

CHARACTER 165

qì
air; energy

Useful phrases and sentences

4 STROKES　气 RADICAL

1. 生气 **shēngqì** angry

Wǒ zuótiān wàngle nǚpéngyoude shēngrì, tā hěn shēngqì.
我昨天忘了女朋友的生日，她很生气。
I forgot my girlfriend's birthday yesterday. She was very angry.

2. 力气 **lìqì** strength

Tā shēngbìngle, lián shuōhuàde lìqì dōu méiyǒu.
他生病了，连说话的力气都没有。
He's sick. He could barely speak.

3. 气球 **qìqiú** balloon

Qìqiú fēizǒule, háizi kūle.
气球飞走了，孩子哭了。
The balloon flies away, and kid cries.

4. 空气 **kōngqì** air

Zhèrde kōngqì zhēn hǎo.
这儿的空气真好。
The air here is really good.

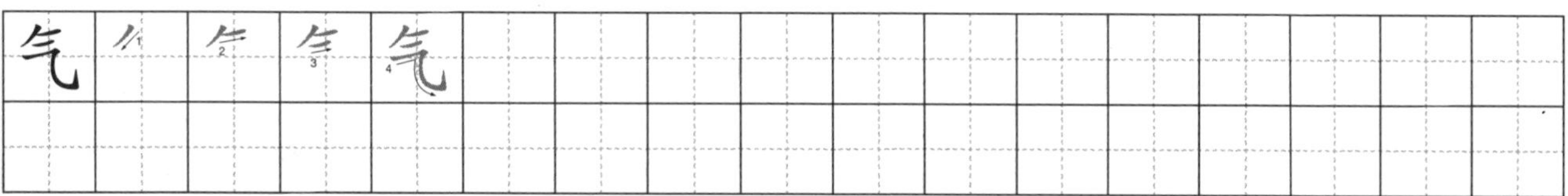

Lesson 11 Exercises

Part 1 Choose from the following words to fill in the blanks.

知道、客气、往、分钟、城市

1. 你（　　　　）她有男朋友吗？
2. 谢谢你请我吃饭，你太（　　　　）了。
3. 我知道你去过很多外国的（　　　　），你最喜欢哪个？
4. 你（　　　　）前走五（　　　　）就到了。

Part 2 Complete the following dialogues using Chinese characters.

1. A: 你知道你爸爸喜欢看什么书吗？

   B: ____。

2. A: 你觉得哪个宾馆很好？

   B: ____。

3. A: 你在哪个城市上学？你喜欢吗？

   B: ____。

4. A: 你觉得哪儿的人很客气？哪儿的人不太客气？

   B: ____。

5. A: 你家在哪个城市？那儿的市中心怎么样？

   B: ____。

Part 3 Word Game

Make as many disyllabic words as you can by using the following characters.

觉	远	方	周	末	都	看	钱
这	得	时	一	那	市	书	可
衣	服	候	宾	城	贵	宜	以
吃	谁	第	方	馆	客	气	便
裙	女	儿	地	件	分	喜	打
子	日	月	谢	钟	今	欢	球
哪	生	口	大	家	几	天	岁

1. ____________ 2. ____________ 3. ____________

4. ____________ 5. ____________ 6. ____________

7. ____________ 8. ____________ 9. ____________

LESSON 12

Where is the bank? 这儿有银行吗？

1. Introduction

There is a Chinese joke that goes that an international student arrived in China after one year of Chinese language study in his home country. One day, he asked his Chinese friend what the characters 很行 (**hěn xíng**: capable) meant, as he frequently saw the sign 中国很行 (**Zhōngguó hěn xíng**: China is capable) on the street. It turned out that what he actually saw was the sign for the Bank of China 中国银行 (**Zhōngguó yínháng**); he misinterpreted 银行 (**yínháng**: bank) as 很行 (**hěn xíng**: capable).

The more Chinese characters you learn, the more similarities you will find between some of them. You will also discover that, a number of Chinese characters have more than one pronunciations, such as 行 (**xíng** or **háng**). Do attend to this along your course of Chinese studies.

2. Warm up

Read the passage below and answer the questions using Chinese characters.

钱小姐：请问，去中国银行怎么走？远不远？
王小姐：很近，过了路口往前走是一个公园，银行在公园的旁边。
钱小姐：谢谢您。
王小姐：今天是星期天，银行不开门。
钱小姐：是啊，今天是星期天，不是星期一。谢谢您！
王小姐：不客气。再见！

1. Where does Ms Qian want to go?

____

2. How to go to the bank?

____

3. Is the bank open today?

____

3. Vocabulary

	Word	Pinyin	English equivalent
1.	银行	**yínháng**	bank
2.	远	**yuǎn**	far
3.	近	**jìn**	close
4.	过	**guò**	pass; go past
5.	路口	**lùkǒu**	intersection
6.	公园	**gōngyuán**	park
7.	在	**zài**	in; at
8.	旁边	**pángbiān**	on the side; beside
9.	开门	**kāimén**	open (for business)
10.	对不起	**duìbùqǐ**	sorry
11.	里边	**lǐbiān**	inside

4. New Characters

Fifteen characters are introduced in this lesson. Use the following explanations to help you understand and remember the characters.

对 起 里 银 行 过 街 路 在 公 园 旁 边 远 近

CHARACTER 166

duì
correct; across; facing

Useful phrases and sentences

5 STROKES 寸 RADICAL

1. 对 **duì** correct
Zhè shì nǐde Zhōngwén míngzi, duì-bú-duì?
这是你的中文名字，对不对？
This is your Chinese name, correct?

2. 对不起 **duìbùqǐ** sorry
Duìbùqǐ, wǒ láiwǎn le.
对不起，我来晚了。
I am sorry. I am late.

3. 对面 **duìmiàn** opposite side
Wǒjiāde duìmiàn shì yíge gōngyuán.
我家的对面是一个公园。
Opposite my house is a park.

4. 对手 **duìshǒu** opponent
Wǒ juéde tā búshì wǒde duìshǒu.
我觉得他不是我的对手。
I feel that he is no competition to me.

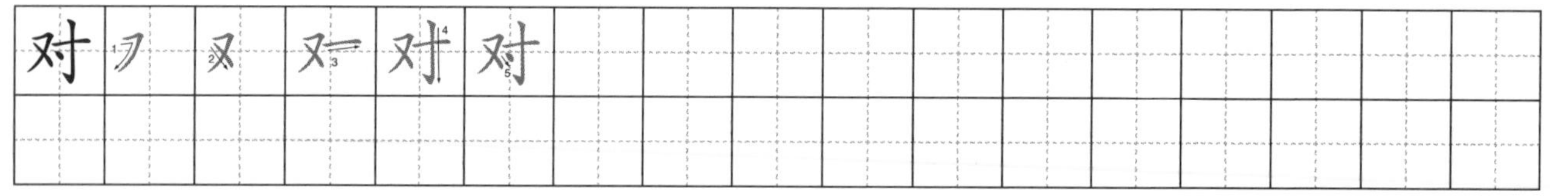

CHARACTER 167

qǐ
rise

Useful phrases and sentences

10 STROKES 走 RADICAL

1. 起床 **qǐchuáng** get up from bed

Nǐ míngtiān jǐdiǎn qǐchuáng?
你明天几点起床？
What time do you get up tomorrow?

2. 看不起 **kànbuqǐ** looked down on

Wǒ bùxǐhuan tā, yīnwèi tā zǒngshì kànbuqi biéren.
我不喜欢他，因为他总是看不起别人。
I don't like him because he always looks down on others.

3. 起来 **qǐlai** used after a verb or an adjective to indicate the beginning of an action

Jīnnián xué Zhōngwénde xuésheng duōqǐlai le.
今年学中文的学生多起来了。
This year the number of students taking Chinese has increased.

4. 看起来 **kànqǐlai** look; seem

Tāde nǚpéngyou zuótiān kànqǐlai bú tài gāoxìng.
他的女朋友昨天看起来不太高兴。
His girlfriend seemed unhappy yesterday.

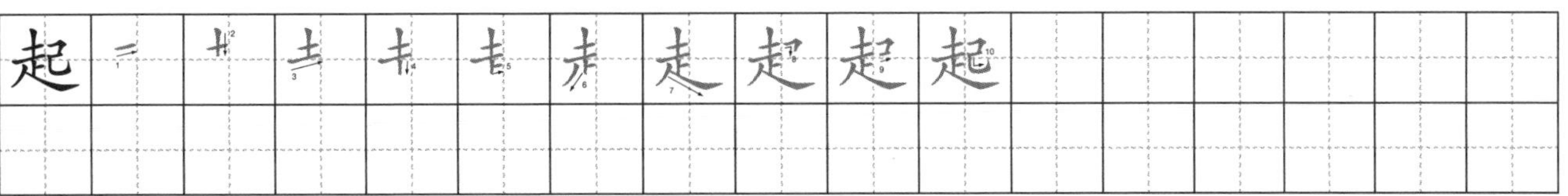

CHARACTER 168

lǐ
inside

Useful phrases and sentences

7 STROKES 里 RADICAL

1. 里 **lǐ** inside

Qǐng wèn, jiāli yǒu rén ma?
请问，家里有人吗？
Excuse me, is anybody home?

2. 里边 **lǐbiān** inside

Nǐ kàn, bīngxiāng lǐbiān yǒu bù shǎo hǎochīde.
你看，冰箱里边有不少好吃的。
Look! There is a lot of yummy food in the fridge.

3. 这里 **zhèli** here

Zhèlide rén dōu hěn hǎo, wǒ xǐhuan zhù zai zhèr.
这里的人都很好，我喜欢住在这儿。
People here are all very nice. I like living here.

4. 那里 **nàli** there

Nǐ jiā zài Zhījiāgē ma? Nàli dōngxi guì ma?
你家在芝加哥吗？那里东西贵吗？
Are you from Chicago? Are things expensive there?

CHARACTER 169

yín
silver

Useful phrases and sentences

11 STROKES 钅 RADICAL

1. 银行 **yínháng** bank

Wǒ jiā pángbiān yǒu yíge yínháng.
我家旁边有一个银行。
There is a bank next to my home.

2. 银色 **yínsè** silver color

Tā qùnián mǎile yíliang yínsède chē.
他去年买了一辆银色的车。
He purchased a silver car last year.

3. 中国银行 **Zhōngguó Yínháng** Bank of China

Zhèr yǒu Zhōngguó Yínháng ma?
这儿有中国银行吗？
Is there a Bank of China here?

4. 银川 **Yínchuān** Yinchuan city

Yínchuān zài Zhōngguóde xīběibiān.
银川在中国的西北边。
Yinchuan is in the northwest of China.

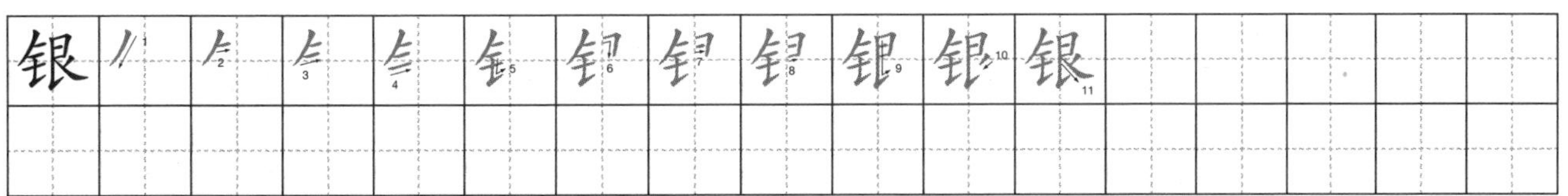

CHARACTER 170

行

háng/xíng
line; row/travel; OK

Useful phrases and sentences

6 STROKES | 行 RADICAL

1. 行 **háng** line; row
Dìyīháng dìsānge zì, nǐ rènshi ma?
第一行第三个字，你认识吗？
Do you know the third character in the first row?

2. 排行 **páiháng** seniority among brothers and sisters
Wǒ zài jiā páiháng lǎoèr, wǒ yǒu yíge jiějie, yíge dìdi.
我在家排行老二，我有一个姐姐，一个弟弟。
I'm the second oldest child in my family. I have an older sister and a younger brother.

3. 行 **xíng** be alright
Nǐ song wǒ qù yíxià jīchǎng, xíng-bù-xíng?
你送我去一下机场，行不行？
Would it be alright for you to take me to the airport?

4. 行李 **xíngli** luggage
Nǐde xíngli tài zhòng le, wǒ nábuqǐlai.
你的行李太重了，我拿不起来。
Your luggage is too heavy. I can't lift it.

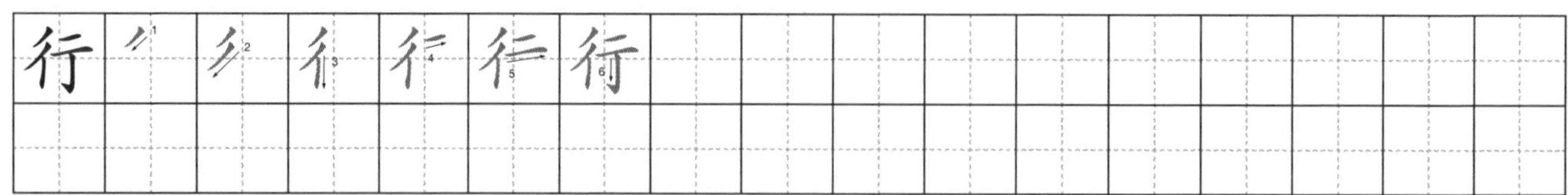

CHARACTER 171

guò
pass

Useful phrases and sentences

6 STROKES | 辶 RADICAL

1. 通过 **tōngguò** pass; by means of
Tā méi tōngguò shùxué kǎoshì, xīnqíng hěn chà.
他没通过数学考试，心情很差。
He didn't pass the math exam. He's in a bad mood.

2. 过去 **guòqu** go over there; in the past
Nǐ xiànzài bié guòqu, tāmen bú zài jiā.
你现在别过去，他们不在家。
Don't go there now. They are not home.

3. 过生日 **guò shēngrì** celebrate one's birthday
Zuótiān wǒ péngyou lái jiāli gěi wǒ guò shēngrì.
昨天我朋友来家里给我过生。
Yesterday my friends came to my house to celebrate my birthday.

4. 过马路 **guò mǎlù** cross a street
Guò mǎlùde shíhou nǐ yào xiǎoxīn yìdiǎnr.
过马路的时候你要小心一点儿。
You should be careful when you cross the street.

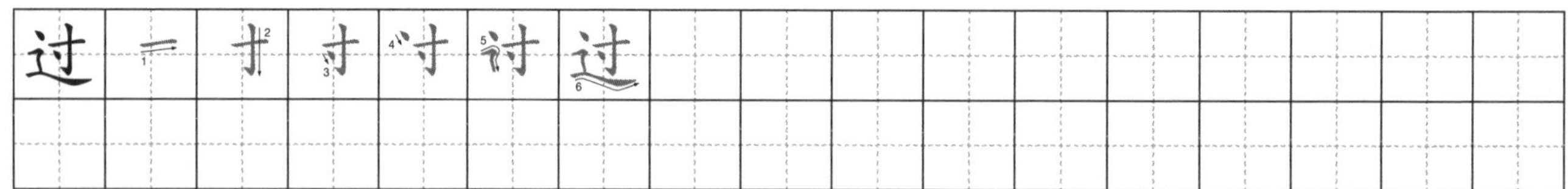

CHARACTER 172

jiē
street

Useful phrases and sentences

12 STROKES | 行 RADICAL

1. 街 **jiē** street
Nǐ jiā zhù zài nǎtiáo jiē?
你家住在哪条街？
What street do you live on?

2. 上街 **shàngjiē** go on the street
Wǒde tóngwū měige zhōumò dōu shàngjiē mǎi dōngxi.
我的同屋每个周末都上街买东西。
My roommate goes on the street to buy things every weekend.

3. 逛街 **guàngjiē** walk on the street (window-shopping)
Wǒ méi qián le, bié ràng wǒ gēn nǐ qù guàngjiē.
我没钱了，别让我跟你去逛街。
Don't ask me to walk on the street with you, as I don't have any money left.

4. 过街 **guòjiē** cross a street
Guòle zhètiáo jiē jiù dào nǐde xuéxiào le.
过了这条街就到你的学校了。
When you cross the street you will arrive at your school.

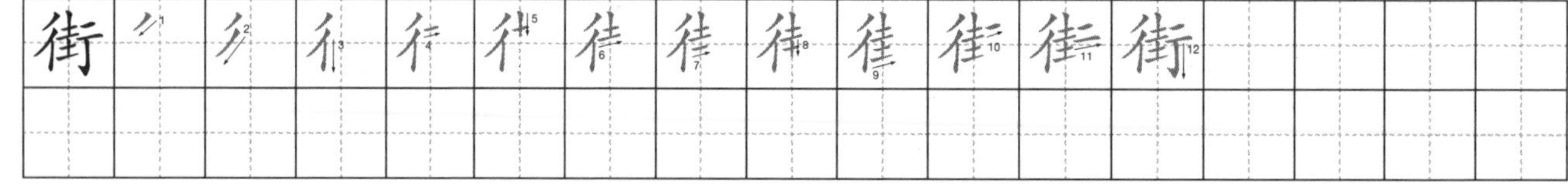

CHARACTER 173

lù
road

Useful phrases and sentences

13 STROKES | 足 RADICAL

1. 马路 **mǎlù** road

Guò mǎlùde shíhou búyào dǎ diànhuà.
过马路的时候不要打电话。
Do not talk on the phone when you're crossing the road.

2. 路过 **lùguò** pass by

Wǒ jīntiān lùguò yìjiā xīnkāide fànguǎnr, kànqǐlai hěn bú cuò.
我今天路过一家新开的饭馆儿，看起来很不错。
Today I passed by a newly opened restaurant. It looked really nice.

3. 路口 **lùkǒu** intersection

Tā shuō shífēnzhōng yǐhòu zài lùkǒu jiàn.
他说十分钟以后在路口见。
He said he will meet us in ten minutes at the intersection.

4. 路 **lù** (for bus route)

Èr-yī-wǔ lù qìchē dào xuéxiào ma?
215路汽车到学校吗？
Does Bus 215 go to school?

CHARACTER 174

zài
at; in; on

Useful phrases and sentences

6 STROKES | 土 RADICAL

1. 在 **zài** at; in; on

Nǐ zhǎo Wáng Lǎoshī ma? Tā bú zài bàngōngshì.
你找王老师吗？他不在办公室。
Are you here to see Teacher Wang? He is not in his office.

2. 在家 **zài jiā** be at home

Nǐ zhège zhōumò zài jiā ma?
你这个周末在家吗？
Are you going to be home this weekend?

3. 坐在 **zuò zài** sit at; on

Bié zuò zài dìshang, bù gānjìng.
别坐在地上，不干净。
Don't sit on the floor. It's not clean.

4. 现在 **xiànzài** now

Nín xiànzài yǒu shíjiān ma? Wǒ yǒu yíge wèntí.
您现在有时间吗？我有一个问题。
Do you have time now? I have a question.

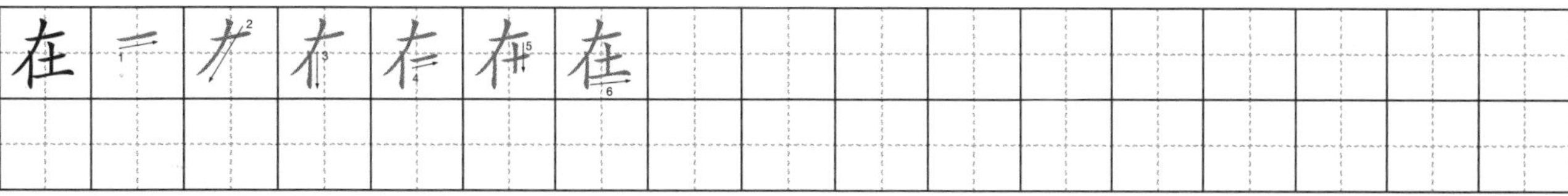

CHARACTER 175

gōng
public; metric

Useful phrases and sentences

4 STROKES | 八 RADICAL

1. 公园 **gōngyuán** park

Zhège gōngyuán wǒ yǐqián láiguo.
这个公园我以前来过。
I've been to this park before.

2. 公里 **gōnglǐ** kilometer

Nǐ jiā lí jīchǎng yǒu jǐ gōnglǐ?
你家离机场有几公里？
How many kilometers are there from your house to the airport?

3. 公共汽车 **gōnggòng qìchē** public bus

Zài Běijīng zuò gōnggòng qìchē hěn piányi.
在北京坐公共汽车很便宜。
It's cheap to take public buses in Beijing.

4. 公车 **gōngchē** bus

Máfan wèn yíxià, yī lù gōngchē jǐdiǎn lái?
麻烦问一下，一路公车几点来？
Excuse me, do you know what time the No. 1 Bus will arrive?

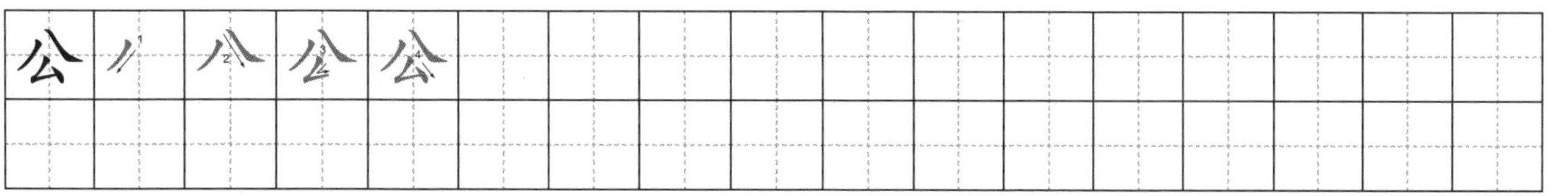

CHARACTER 176

yuán
park; garden

Useful phrases and sentences

7 STROKES | 囗 RADICAL

1. 花园 **huāyuán** (flower) yard
Nǎinai jiā yǒu yíge huāyuán, lǐmiàn yǒu hěnduō huā.
奶奶家有一个花园，里面有很多花。
There is a flower garden at my grandma's house and there are many flowers inside.

2. 动物园 **dòngwùyuán** zoo
Xiǎoshíhou wǒ zuì xǐhuan qù dòngwùyuán kàn xióngmāo.
小时候我最喜欢去动物园看熊猫。
When I was little, I loved going to the zoo to see pandas.

3. 校园 **xiàoyuán** campus
Xiānggǎng Zhōngwén Dàxué xiàoyuán zhēn piàoliang!
香港中文大学校园真漂亮！
The campus of Chinese University of Hong Kong is so pretty!

4. 幼儿园 **yòu'éryuán** kindergarten
Wǒ jiā pángbiān yǒu yíge yòu'éryuán.
我家旁边有一个幼儿园。
There is a kindergarten next to my house.

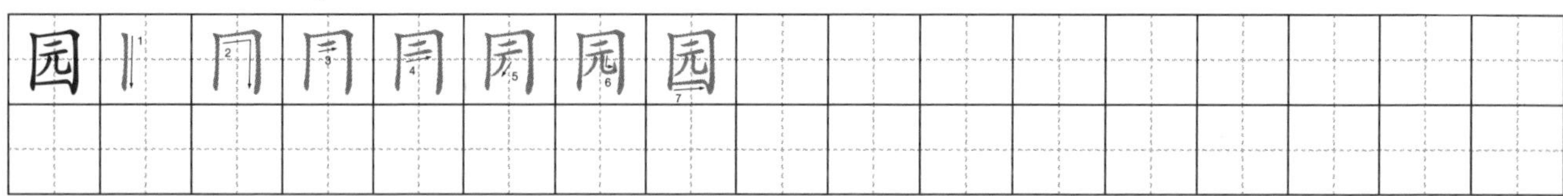

CHARACTER 177

páng
side; beside

Useful phrases and sentences

10 STROKES | 方 RADICAL

1. 旁边 **pángbiān** next to
Zhànzài wǒ nǚpéngyou pángbiānde nàge nánshēng shì shéi?
站在我女朋友旁边的那个男生是谁？
Who is the man standing next to my girlfriend?

2. 两旁 **liǎngpáng** both sides
Mǎlù liǎngpáng xīnkāile yìxiē xiǎo shāngdiàn.
马路两旁新开了一些小商店。
There are some new shops on both sides of the street.

3. 旁听 **pángtīng** audit (a class)
Lǎoshī, nínde kè wǒ kěyǐ pángtīng ma?
老师，您的课我可以旁听吗？
Teacher, may I audit your class?

4. 旁白 **pángbái** background narration
Zhège diànyǐng yǒu hěnduō pángbái.
这个电影有很多旁白。
There are many background narrations in this movie.

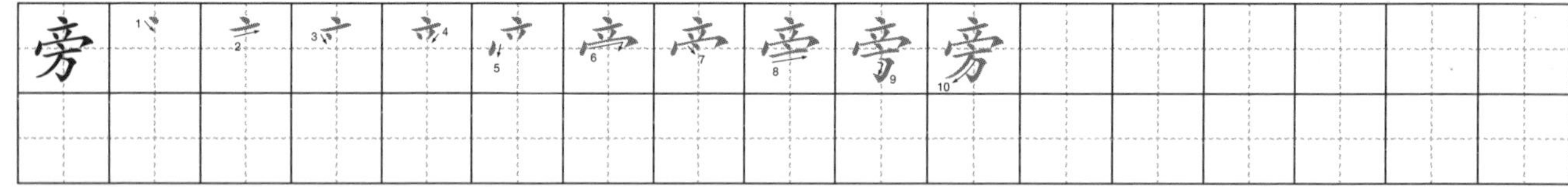

CHARACTER 178

biān
edge; side

Useful phrases and sentences

5 STROKES | 辶 RADICAL

1. 上边 **shàngbian** above; on the top of
Zhuōzi shàngbian nàběn shū shì nǐde ma?
桌子上边那本书是你的吗？
Is that book on the top of the table yours?

2. 下边 **xiàbian** under; down
Wǒ yíge xiǎoshí hòu zài nǐ sùshèlóu xiàbian děng nǐ.
我一个小时后在你宿舍楼下边等你。
I will be waiting for you in one hour downstairs in your dormitory.

3. 海边 **hǎibiān** seaside
Měinián xiàtiān, wǒ dōu gēn jiārén qù hǎibiān wánr.
每年夏天，我都跟家人去海边玩儿。
Every summer, I would go and play at the seaside with my family.

4. 一边…一边… **yìbiān…yìbiān…** (expresses two simultaneous actions)
Nǐ búyào yìbiān kāichē yìbiān dǎ diànhuà.
你不要一边开车一边打电话。
Don't speak on the phone while driving.

CHARACTER 179

yuǎn
far

Useful phrases and sentences

7 STROKES ⻌ RADICAL

1. 远 **yuǎn** far

Wǒ fùqinde gōngsi lí jiā hěn yuǎn, tā měitiān hěn zǎo qù shàngbān.
我父亲的公司离家很远，他每天很早去上班。
My father's company is far from home. He goes to work early in the morning every day.

2. 远近 **yuǎnjìn** distance

Zhè liǎngtiáolù yuǎnjìn chàbuduō.
这两条路远近差不多。
The travel distance of these two roads is nearly the same.

3. 多远 **duō yuǎn** how far

Nǐ jiā lí gòuwù zhōngxīn yǒu duō yuǎn?
你家离购物中心有多远？
How far is your home from the shopping center?

4. 出远门 **chūyuǎnmén** journey away from home

Zhè shì mèimei dìyīcì chūyuǎnmén, fùmǔ yǒudiǎn dānxīn.
这是妹妹第一次出远门，父母有点担心。
This is the first distant trip for my sister. My parents are a bit worried.

CHARACTER 180

jìn
close

Useful phrases and sentences

7 STROKES ⻌ RADICAL

1. 近 **jìn** close

Wǒ hěn xǐhuan wǒde sùshè, yīnwèi lí jiàoshì hé túshūguǎn dōu hěn jìn.
我很喜欢我的宿舍，因为离教室和图书馆都很近。
I like my dorm as it is close to the classrooms and the library.

2. 近年 **jìnnián** in recent years

Jìnnián qù Měiguó liúxué de Zhōngguó xuésheng yuè lái yuè duō.
近年去美国留学的中国学生越来越多。
In recent years, there are more and more Chinese students studying in U.S.A.

3. 近路 **jìnlù** shortcut

Nǐ gēn wǒ zǒu, wǒ zhīdao yìtiáo jìnlù.
你跟我走，我知道一条近路。
Just follow me. I know a shortcut.

4. 附近 **fùjìn** nearby; in the vicinity

Nǐmen xuéxiào fùjìn yǒu shénme shāngdiàn?
你们学校附近有什么商店？
What kinds of shops are there in the vicinity of your school?

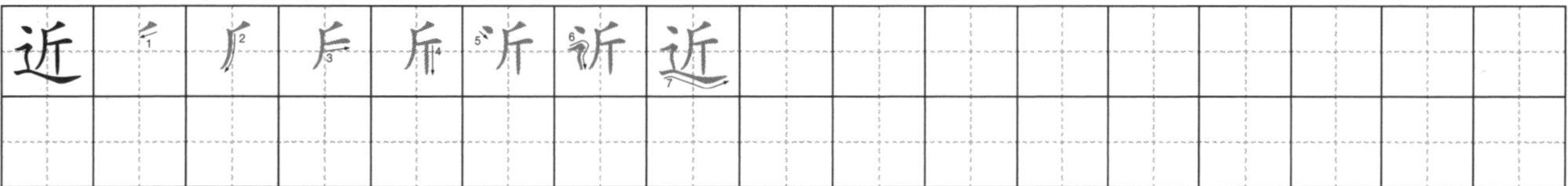

Lesson 12 Exercises

Part 1 Choose from the following words to fill in the blanks.

过、在、旁边、远

1. 请问，中国银行在公园的（　　　　）吗？
2. 你（　　　　）街的时候不要打电话。

3. 我们（　　　　）家吃饭吧，外边的饭太贵了，也不好吃。

4. 那个宾馆有点儿（　　　　），去那儿不太方便。

Part 2 Complete the following dialogues using Chinese characters.

1. A: 你家旁边有没有银行？

   B: ______________________________。

2. A: 你这个周末在家吗？我想去找你。

   B: ______________________________。

3. A: 请问，城市公园在前边吗？

   B: ______________________________。

4. A: 超市 (**chāoshì**: supermarket) 远吗？走路要多长时间？

   B: ______________________________。

5. A: 你明天想上街买东西吗？

   B: ______________________________。

Part 3 Use the following prompts to give a one-minute speech.

这个男生现在在电影院 (**diànyǐngyuàn**: cinema) 的门口，他想去超市。请你告诉 (**gàosù**: tell) 他怎么走？超市离电影院远不远？走路要多长时间？

LESSON 13

Is the school store open today? 学校商店今天开门吗？

1. Introduction

In China's universities, you can often find grocery stores or mid-sized supermarkets on campus. These stores provide various things, from daily groceries to school supplies, and from snack food to fresh fruit. Generally speaking, campus stores are students' top choice to buy things because of their convenience. Students also tend to have a good relationship with the store owners. They often call the female owners 阿姨 (**āyí**: aunt) and male owners 叔叔 (**shūshu**: uncle.) Do you often shop in the stores on campus? What do you buy there?

2. Warm up

Read the passage below and answer the questions using Chinese characters.

小路：喂，小远，你现在去哪儿？
小远：我去学校的商店买东西。你去吗？
小路：我不去商店，我想去旁边的花店。
小远：你要买花吗？
小路：那个花店的花很漂亮，也很便宜。
小远：你给谁买花？你是不是有女朋友了？
小路：我们走吧！

1. What does Xiao Lu want to buy?

____

2. Who does Xiao Yuan think Xiao Lu is buying flowers for?

____

3. Vocabulary

	Word	Pinyin	English equivalent
1.	喂	**wèi**	"Hey"; (greeting used to answer the phone)
2.	现在	**xiànzài**	right now
3.	学校	**xuéxiào**	school
4.	商店	**shāngdiàn**	store
5.	花店	**huādiàn**	flower shop
6.	花	**huā**	flower
7.	漂亮	**piàoliang**	pretty
8.	卖	**mài**	sell
9.	前面	**qiánmiàn**	in the front
10.	后面	**hòumiàn**	in the back
11.	关门	**guānmén**	closed (for business)
12.	左边	**zuǒbiān**	left side
13.	右边	**yòubiān**	right side
14.	左右	**zuǒyòu**	or so

4. New Characters

Fifteen characters are introduced in this lesson. Use the following explanations to help you understand and remember the characters.

商 花 店 卖 校 后 开 关 门 左 右 现 面 漂 亮

CHARACTER 181

shāng
business

Useful phrases and sentences

11 STROKES | 口 RADICAL

1. 商业 **shāngyè** business

Wángfǔjǐng shì Běijīng zuì rènàode shāngyèjiē.
王府井是北京最热闹的商业街。
Wangfujing is the liveliest business district in Beijing.

2. 商人 **shāngrén** business man

Wǒde fùmǔ dōu shì shāngrén, tāmen dōu hěn máng.
我的父母都是商人，他们都很忙。
Both my parents are businesspeople. They are very busy.

3. 商场 **shāngchǎng** mall; market

Shāngchǎngde yīfu tài guì le. Wǒ xǐhuan zài wǎngshang mǎi.
商场的衣服太贵了，我喜欢在网上买。
The clothes in the malls are expensive. I like to shop online.

4. 商量 **shāngliang** discuss; consult

Lǎoshī, wǒ yǒu jiàn shì xiǎng gēn nín shāngliang.
老师，我有件事想跟您商量。
Teacher, I have a matter that I'd like to discuss with you.

商	1	2	3	4	5	6	7	8	9	10	11					

CHARACTER 182

huā
flower; spend (money or time)

Useful phrases and sentences

7 STROKES | 艹 RADICAL

1. 花 **huā** flower
Sānyuè le, huā dōu kāile.
三月了，花都开了。
It's March. The flowers are blossoming.

2. 花钱 **huā qián** spend money
Wǒ měige yuè huā hěnduō qián mǎi shū.
我每个月花很多钱买书。
I spend a lot of money buying books each month.

3. 花时间 **huā shíjiān** spend time
Wǒ yíge xīngqī huā hěnduō shíjiān xué shùxué.
我一个星期花很多时间学数学。
I spend plenty of time learning math every week.

4. 花生 **huāshēng** peanut
Wǒ dìdi bù xǐhuan chī huāsheng.
我弟弟不喜欢吃花生。
My younger brother does not like to eat peanuts.

CHARACTER 183

diàn
store

Useful phrases and sentences

8 STROKES | 广 RADICAL

1. 商店 **shāngdiàn** store
Nǐ píngcháng qù nǎge shāngdiàn mǎi dōngxi?
你平常去哪个商店买东西？
Which store do you usually go shopping at?

2. 书店 **shūdiàn** bookstore
Wǒ zhōumò xǐhuan qù shūdiàn kànshū.
我周末喜欢去书店看书。
I like to read at bookstores on the weekend.

3. 咖啡店 **kāfēidiàn** coffee shop
Zhèr fùjìn nǎr yǒu kāfēidiàn?
这儿附近哪儿有咖啡店？
Where is the coffee shop nearby?

4. 店员 **diànyuán** store clerk
Nàge diànyuán hěn kèqi, zǒngshì xiàoliǎnyíngrén.
那个店员很客气，总是笑脸迎人。
That store clerk is very polite and always smiling.

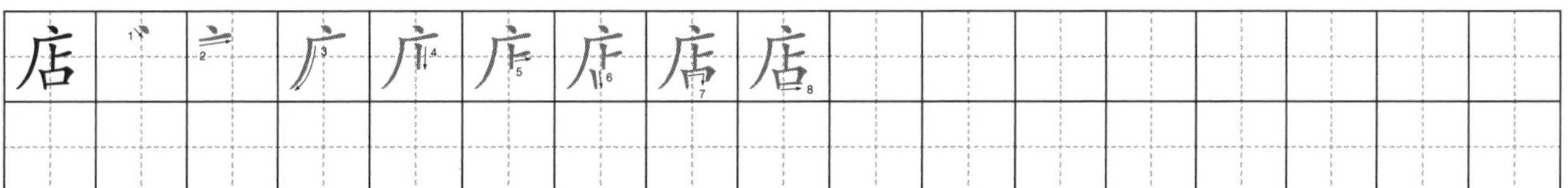

CHARACTER 184

mài
sell

Useful phrases and sentences

8 STROKES | 十 RADICAL

1. 卖 **mài** sell
Zhèshuāng xié mài duōshao qián?
这双鞋卖多少钱？
How much is this pair of shoes?

2. 做买卖 **zuò mǎimài** do business
Wǒ juéde zuò mǎimài hěn yǒu yìsi.
我觉得做买卖很有意思。
I think doing business is interesting.

3. 卖给 **mài gěi** sell to
Wǒ tīngshuō nàge shāngdiàn mài gěi Lǐ Xiānsheng le.
我听说那个商店卖给李先生了。
I heard that that shop was sold to Mr. Li.

4. 专卖店 **zhuānmàidiàn** specialized shop
Nà yǒu yījiā yùndòng yòngpǐn zhuānmàidiàn.
那有一家运动用品专卖店。
There is a shop specialized in sports goods over there.

CHARACTER 185

xiào
school

Useful phrases and sentences

10 STROKES | 木 RADICAL

1. 学校 **xuéxiào** school

Nǐmen xuéxiào yǒu duōshaoge xuésheng?
你们学校有多少个学生？
How many students are there in your school?

2. 校长 **xiàozhǎng** principal of a school

Nǐmen xuéxiàode xiàozhǎng jiào shénme míngzi?
你们学校的校长叫什么名字？
What is the name of your school's principal?

3. 母校 **mǔxiào** alma mater

Nǐde mǔxiào yě shì Běijīng Dàxué ma?
你的母校也是北京大学吗？
Is Peking University your alma mater, too?

4. 校车 **xiàochē** school bus

Měiguóde xiàochē shì huángsède.
美国的校车是黄色的。
American school buses are yellow.

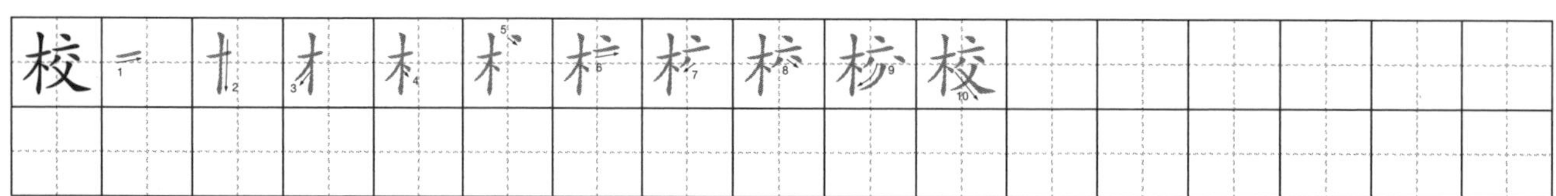

CHARACTER 186

hòu
behind

Useful phrases and sentences

6 STROKES | 口 RADICAL

1. 后面 **hòumiàn** behind

Xuéxiàode hòumiàn yǒu jǐge shāngdiàn.
学校的后面有几个商店。
There are a few stores behind the school.

2. 后悔 **hòuhuǐ** regret

Zuòguode shìqing jiù búyào hòuhuǐ.
做过的事情就不要后悔。
Do not regret what you have done.

3. 后天 **hòutiān** the day after tomorrow

Nǐ hòutiān shì-bú-shì yào qù Xīnjiāpō?
你后天是不是要去新加坡？
Are you going to Singapore the day after tomorrow?

4. 后来 **hòulái** later; afterwards

Tā cóng xiǎo jiù hěn nǔlì, hòulái chéngle dàxué xiàozhǎng.
她从小就很努力，后来成了大学校长。
She had been very hardworking since she was young. She later became a college president.

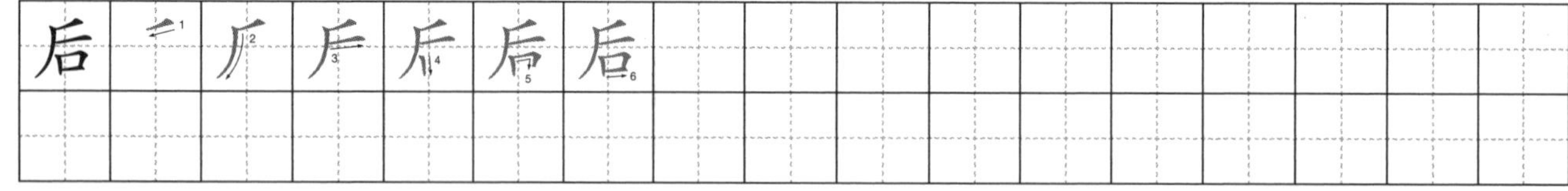

CHARACTER 187

kāi
open; on; drive

Useful phrases and sentences

4 STROKES | 廾 RADICAL

1. 开车 **kāichē** drive

Nǐ bàba kāichē kāide tài kuài le.
你爸爸开车开得太快了！
Your dad drives too fast.

2. 开门 **kāimén** open (for business)

Nàjiā huādiàn jīntiān bù kāimén.
那家花店今天不开门。
That flower shop is not open today.

3. 开发 **kāifā** develop

Píngguǒ gōngsī měinián dōu kāifā xīn chǎnpǐn.
苹果公司每年都开发新产品。
Apple Inc. releases newly developed products every year.

4. 开会 **kāihuì** have a meeting

Bié wàngle, jīntiān xiàwǔ sāndiǎn kāihuì.
别忘了，今天下午三点开会。
Don't forget that we have a meeting at three this afternoon.

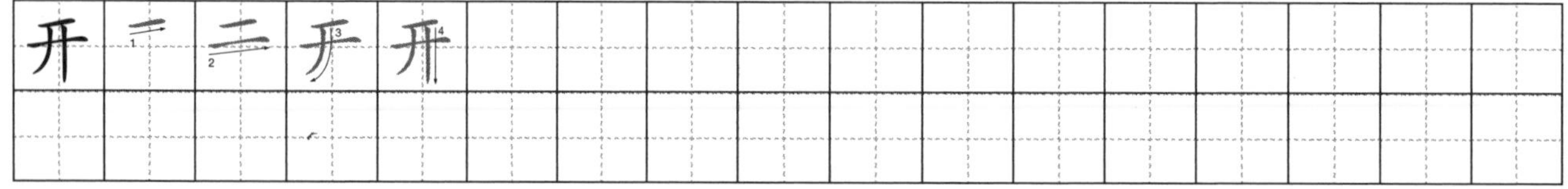

CHARACTER 188

guān
close; off

Useful phrases and sentences

6 STROKES | 丷 RADICAL

1. 关门 **guān mén** close the door

Nǐ chūqùde shíhou bié wàngle guān mén.
你出去的时候别忘了关门。
Don't forget to close the door when you go out.

2. 关门 **guānmén** closed (for business)

Xuéxiàode shāngdiàn jīntiān jǐdiǎn guānmén?
学校的商店今天几点关门？
When is the school's store closed today?

3. 关灯 **guān dēng** turn off the light

Tā chūménde shíhou bù guān dēng.
他出门的时候不关灯。
He does not turn off the light when he leaves.

4. 关电视 **guān diànshì** turn off the TV

Tā zuótiān wàngle guān diànshì.
他昨天忘了关电视。
He forgot to turn off the TV last night.

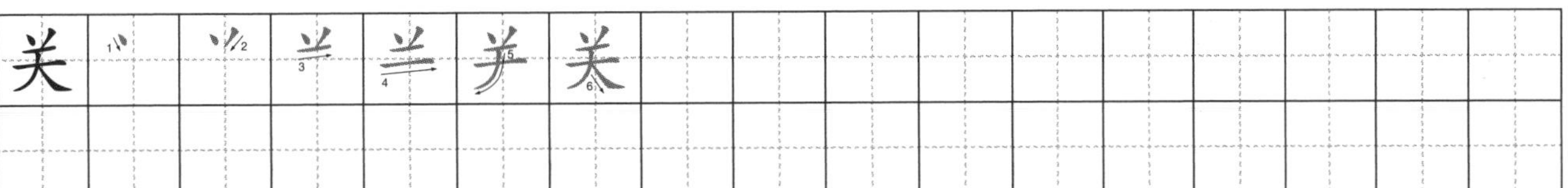

CHARACTER 189

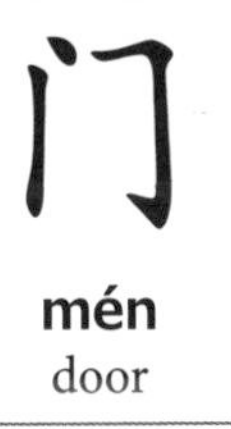

mén
door

Useful phrases and sentences

3 STROKES | 门 RADICAL

1. 开门 **kāimén** open the door

Yǒu rén ma? Qǐng kāimén.
有人吗？请开门。
Anyone there? Please open the door.

2. 门口 **ménkǒu** gate

Nǐ zài xuéxiào ménkǒu děng wǒ, wǒ mǎshang dào.
你在学校门口等我，我马上到。
Please wait for me at the school's gate. I'll be right there.

3. 出门 **chūmén** leave home; go out

Nǐ měitiān tōngcháng jǐdiǎn chūmén?
你每天通常几点出门？
When do you usually leave home every day?

4. 前门 **qiánmén** front door; front gate

Jīntiān qiánmén bù kāi, nǐ cóng hòumén zǒu.
今天前门不开，你从后门走。
The front door is not open today. Please use the back door.

CHARACTER 190

zuǒ
left

Useful phrases and sentences

5 STROKES | 工 RADICAL

1. 左边 **zuǒbiān** left side

Zuò zài nǐ zuǒbiānde rén shì shéi?
坐在你左边的人是谁？
Who is the person sitting to your left?

2. 左手 **zuǒshǒu** left hand

Wǒ yòng zuǒshǒu xiězì, yòng yòushǒu chīfàn.
我用左手写字，用右手吃饭。
I use my left hand to write and my right hand to eat.

3. 往左走 **wǎng zuǒ zǒu** walk to the left

Dàole qiánmiànde kāfēiguǎnr wǎng zuǒ zǒu.
到了前面的咖啡馆儿往左走。
Turn left when you see the coffee shop in the front.

4. 左右 **zuǒyòu** about; approximately; or so

Tā jīnnián sānshísuì zuǒyòu ba!
她今年三十岁左右吧！
I suppose she is around thirty years old.

CHARACTER 191

右

yòu
right

Useful phrases and sentences

5 STROKES | 口 RADICAL

1. 右边 **yòubiān** right side
Túshūguǎnde yòubiān shì yíge bówùguǎn.
图书馆的右边是一个博物馆。
On the right hand side of the library is a museum.

2. 右手 **yòushǒu** right hand
Māma ràng wǒ yòng yòushǒu xiězì, bú ràng yòng zuǒshǒu xiě.
妈妈让我用右手写字，不让用左手写。
Mom makes me use my right hand to write. She doesn't let me use my left hand.

3. 往右走 **wǎng yòu zǒu** walk to the right
Nǐ dào dìyíge lùkǒu wǎng yòu zǒu jiù dàole.
你到第一个路口往右走就到了。
Go to the first intersection and then walk to the right. You'll be there.

4. 左邻右舍 **zuǒlínyòushè** neighbors
Wǒmen gāng bānle xīnjiā, zuǒlínyòushè dōu hěn yǒuhǎo.
我们刚搬了新家，左邻右舍都很友好。
We just moved into a new house. The neighbors are very friendly.

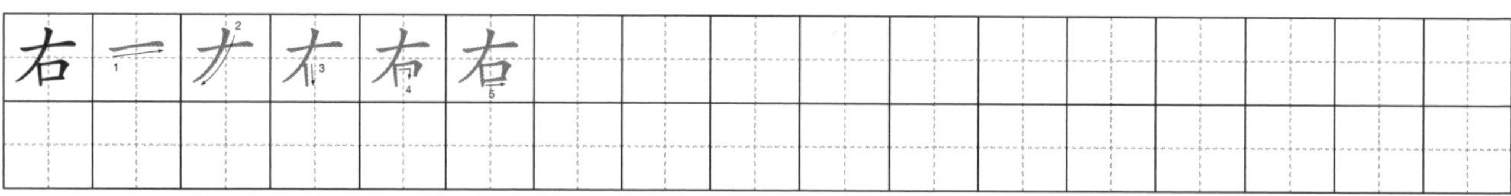

CHARACTER 192

现

xiàn
right now

Useful phrases and sentences

8 STROKES | 见 RADICAL

1. 现代 **xiàndài** modern
Wǒ xǐhuan Běijīng, yīnwèi tā hěn gǔlǎo, yě hěn xiàndài.
我喜欢北京，因为它很古老，也很现代。
I like Beijing because it's ancient, but it's also modern.

2. 现金 **xiànjīn** cash
Wǒ méiyǒu xiànjīn, kěyǐ shuā kǎ ma?
我没有现金，可以刷卡吗？
I do not have any cash. Do you take credit cards?

3. 现场 **xiànchǎng** on-site
Tā qù NBA xiànchǎng kànle bǐsài.
他去NBA现场看了比赛。
He watched an NBA game on-site.

4. 出现 **chūxiàn** appear; emerge
Diànnǎo shì shénme shíhou kāishǐ chūxiànde?
电脑是什么时候开始出现的？
When did computers begin to appear?

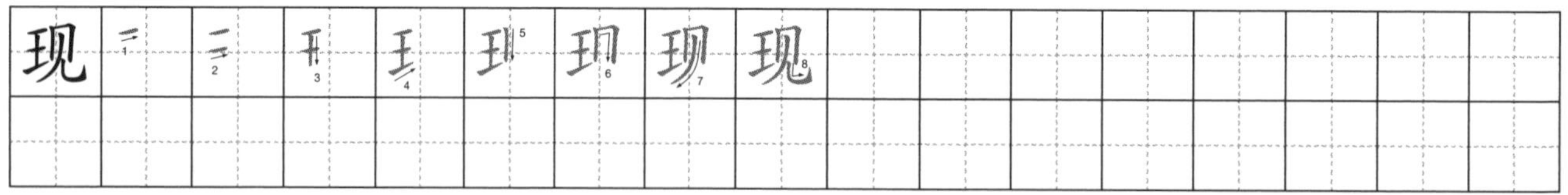

CHARACTER 193

miàn
surface; face; noodle

Useful phrases and sentences

9 STROKES | 面 RADICAL

1. 前面 **qiánmiàn** front
Nǐ kàn, qiánmiàn jiùshì Chángchéng le!
你看，前面就是长城了！
Look! The Great Wall is in front of us.

2. 面条 **miàntiáo** noodle
Zài Zhōngguó, běifāngrén bǐjiào xǐhuan chī miàntiáo.
在中国，北方人比较喜欢吃面条。
In China, northern people love noodles.

3. 上面 **shàngmiàn** on; above
Tā zài shūjià shàngmiàn fàngle hěnduō zhàopiàn.
他在书架上面放了很多照片。
He put many photos on the bookshelf.

4. 下面 **xiàmiàn** underneath
Zhuōzi xiàmiàn yǒu yīzhī kě'àide māo.
桌子下面有一只可爱的猫。
There is a cute cat under the table.

CHARACTER 194

漂

piāo/piào
float/beautiful

Useful phrases and sentences

14 STROKES | 氵 RADICAL

1. 漂 **piāo** float
Héshang piāozhe yīxiē shùyè.
河上漂着一些树叶。
There are some leaves floating on the river.

2. 漂亮 **piàoliang** pretty
Nǐ chuān zhèjiàn yīfu hěn piàoliang.
你穿这件衣服很漂亮。
You look nice in this dress.

3. 漂浮 **piāofú** float
Wǒ xǐhuan piāofú zài shuǐmiàn shàng.
我喜欢漂浮在水面上。
I like floating in the water.

4. 漂流 **piāoliú** drift
Xiànzài, niánqīngrén hěn xǐhuan shuǐshàng piāoliú zhège yùndòng.
现在，年轻人很喜欢水上漂流这个运动。
Now, young people like the water sport "drifting" very much.

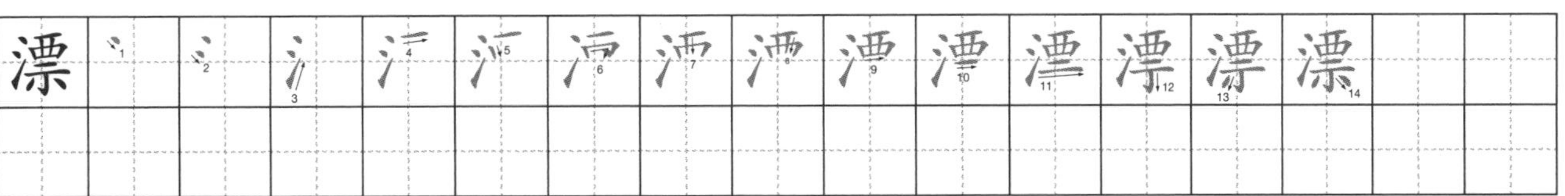

CHARACTER 195

亮

liàng
bright

Useful phrases and sentences

9 STROKES | 亠 RADICAL

1. 亮 **liàng** bright
Zhège wūzi hěn liàng, wǒ hěn xǐhuan.
这个屋子很亮，我很喜欢。
This room is bright. I like it very much.

2. 亮光 **liàngguāng** light
Wàimiàn hěn hēi, yìdiǎnr liàngguāng dōu méiyǒu.
外面很黑，一点儿亮光都没有。
It's very dark outside, not even a bit of light.

3. 月亮 **yuèliang** moon
Jīntiān wǎnshang yuèliang hěn yuán.
今天晚上月亮很圆。
The moon tonight is round.

4. 亮点 **liàngdiǎn** eye-catching highlight
Zhèige shūdiànde liàngdiǎn shì yǒu yījiān hěn hǎode kāfēidiàn.
这个书店的亮点是有一间很好的咖啡店。
The eye-catching highlight of this bookstore is its fine coffee shop.

Lesson 13 Exercises

Part 1 Put the words in the correct order to make sentences.

1. 时间、你、现在、吗、有

____ ?

2. 觉得、衣服、这、漂亮、很、我、件

____ 。

3. 六、开、商店、门、学校、 星期、不

____。

4. 前、就、大学、北京、往、走、是、了

____。

Part 2 Complete the following dialogues using Chinese characters.

1. A: 你学校的商店卖的东西贵吗？

   B: ____。

2. A: 你买过花吗？你给谁买过花？

   B: ____。

3. A: 你的学校的图书馆什么时候开门？

   B: ____。

4. A: 你觉得你的学校漂亮吗？

   B: ____。

5. A: 你以后想做什么工作？

   B: ____。

Part 3 Give a brief introduction about your school's libraries by filling in the information.

	你的学校图书馆的名字	这个图书馆人多不多？	星期几开门？星期几关门？	漂亮吗？大吗？	你一个星期去几次？
1.					
2.					
3.					

LESSON 14

Weather and climate (I) 天气和气候 (I)

1. Introduction

There are four seasons in a year: spring, summer, fall and winter. Which season do you like best? China is so big that the climate varies from one place to another. In China, there is a city that is well known for its quickly-changing weather. There are three other cities that are called "three furnaces" because of their high temperature in the summer. There is also a city called the "ice city." Do you know what cities they are? You will find the answers in this lesson.

2. Warm up

Read the passage below and answer the questions using Chinese characters.

中国人一：你好，你是哪里人？
中国人二：我是上海人。
中国人一：你喜欢北京吗？
中国人二：我不太喜欢这儿的天气。春天风太大了，夏天太热了，冬天太冷了。
中国人一：秋天不冷不热，你喜欢吧？
中国人二：秋天不错，可是上海的秋天比北京舒服。
中国人一：那你为什么来北京工作？

1. Where does the second Chinese person come from? Does he/she like Beijing?

____。

2. Does the second Chinese person like the summer in Beijing? Why?

____。

3. How does the second Chinese person compare the autumn in Beijing and Shanghai?

____。

3. Vocabulary

	Word	Pinyin	English equivalent
1.	上海	**Shànghǎi**	Shanghai
2.	北京	**Běijīng**	Beijing
3.	天气	**tiānqì**	weather
4.	春天	**chūntiān**	spring
5.	风	**fēng**	wind
6.	夏天	**xiàtiān**	summer
7.	热	**rè**	hot
8.	冬天	**dōngtiān**	winter
9.	冷	**lěng**	cold
10.	秋天	**qiūtiān**	autumn
11.	比	**bǐ**	compare
12.	舒服	**shūfu**	comfortable
13.	为什么	**wèishénme**	why
14.	凉快	**liángkuai**	cool
15.	暖和	**nuǎnhuo**	warm
16.	但是	**dànshì**	but
17.	下雨	**xiàyǔ**	rain
18.	下雪	**xiàxuě**	snow

4. New Characters

Fifteen characters are introduced in this lesson. Use the following explanations to help you understand and remember the characters.

冷 热 凉 快 暖 比 但 雨 雪 风 春 夏 秋 冬 舒

CHARACTER 196

lěng
cold

Useful phrases and sentences

7 STROKES | 冫 RADICAL

1. 冷 **lěng** cold

Jīntiān hěn lěng, nǐ duō chuān yìdiǎnr.
今天很冷，你多穿一点儿。
It's cold today. You should put on more clothes.

2. 冷饮 **lěngyǐn** cold drinks

Tài rè le, nǐ xiǎng hē lěngyǐn ma?
太热了，你想喝冷饮吗？
It's too hot. Do you want to have some cold drinks?

3. 冷气 **lěngqì** cool air; air conditioner

Zhège fángjiān méiyǒu lěngqì, yǒu diǎnr rè.
这个房间没有冷气，有点儿热。
There is no air conditioner in this room. It's a bit hot.

4. 冷静 **lěngjìng** calm down; relax

Nǐ lěngjìng yíxià, bié jí.
你冷静一下，别急。
Don't rush; relax.

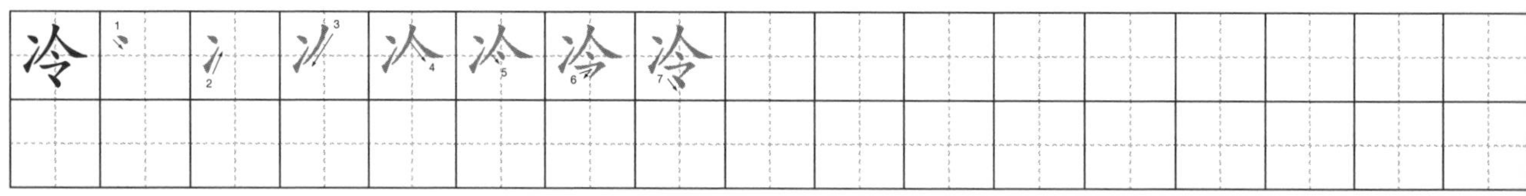

CHARACTER 197

rè
hot

Useful phrases and sentences

10 STROKES | 灬 RADICAL

1. 热 **rè** hot

Nánjīngde xiàtiān zhēn rè.
南京的夏天真热。
Summer in Nanjing is really hot.

2. 热情 **rèqíng** enthusiastic; hospitable

Wǒ juéde Niǔyuē rén bú tài rèqíng, nǐ juéde ne?
我觉得纽约人不太热情，你觉得呢？
I think New Yorkers are not so hospitable. What do you think?

3. 热闹 **rènao** bustling; lively

Wǒ nǎinai xǐhuan zhù zai rènaode dìfang.
我奶奶喜欢住在热闹的地方。
My grandmother likes to live in a lively place.

4. 热水 **rè shuǐ** hot water

Gěi wǒ yìbēi rèshuǐ, xièxie.
给我一杯热水，谢谢！
Please give me a cup of hot water. Thank you!

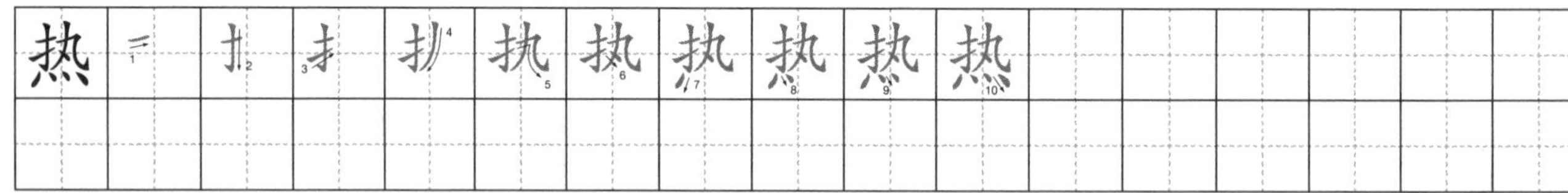

CHARACTER 198

liáng
cool

Useful phrases and sentences

10 STROKES | 冫 RADICAL

1. 凉 **liáng** cool

Tiānqì mànmàn biàn liáng le.
天气慢慢变凉了。
The weather is slowly getting cooler.

2. 凉菜 **liáng cài** cold dish

Wǒmen diǎn jǐge liáng cài ba.
我们点几个凉菜吧。
Let's order some cold dishes.

3. 凉快 **liángkuai** pleasantly cool

Zhèrde xiàtiān hěn liángkuai.
这儿的夏天很凉快。
The summer here is pleasantly cool.

4. 凉茶 **liáng chá** cold herbal tea

Zhèjiā diànde liáng chá hěn yǒumíng.
这家店的凉茶很有名。
The cold herbal tea in this shop is well-known.

CHARACTER 199

kuài
fast

Useful phrases and sentences

7 STROKES | 忄 RADICAL

1. 快 **kuài** fast; quick

Nǐ kuài lái, wǒmen yào chīfàn le.
你快来，我们要吃饭了。
Come quickly. We are eating now.

2. 快乐 **kuàilè** happy

Zhù nǐ měiyītiān dōu jiànkāng kuàilè.
祝你每一天都健康快乐！
Wishing you health and happiness every day!

3. 快餐 **kuàicān** fast food

Zài Zhōngguó yǒu hěnduō Měiguóde kuàicān diàn.
在中国有很多美国的快餐店。
There are many American fast food restaurants in China.

4. 尽快 **jǐnkuài** as quickly as possible

Wǒ jǐnkuài guòqù.
我尽快过去。
I am heading over as quickly as I can.

CHARACTER 200

nuǎn
warm

Useful phrases and sentences

13 STROKES | 日 RADICAL

1. 暖 **nuǎn** warm

Zhèr sānyuè jiù nuǎn le.
这儿三月就暖了。
The weather is getting warmer here in March.

2. 温暖 **wēnnuǎn** warm (temperature); warm-hearted

Xiǎo Wáng shì yíge hěn wēnnuǎnde rén, zǒngshì yuànyì bāngzhùbiérén.
小王是一个很温暖的人，总是愿意帮助别人。
Xiao Wang is warm-hearted. He is always willing to help other people.

3. 暖气 **nuǎnqì** heating

Zhōngguóde nánfāng dōngtiān xūyào nuǎnqì ma?
中国的南方冬天需要暖气吗？
Do you need heating in the winter in southern China?

4. 保暖 **bǎonuǎn** stay warm

Tiānqì liángle, zhùyì bǎonuǎn.
天气凉了，注意保暖。
It's getting chilly; stay warm.

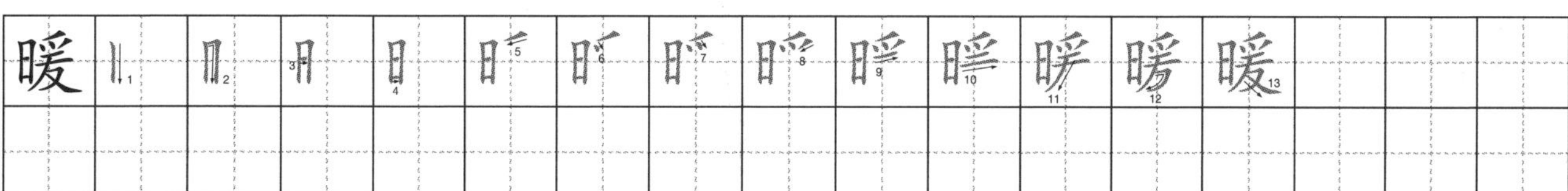

CHARACTER 201

bǐ
compare

Useful phrases and sentences

4 STROKES | 比 RADICAL

1. 比 **bǐ** compare

Xī'ānde xiàtiān bǐ Chéngdū rè.
西安的夏天比成都热。
Summer in Xi'an is hotter than in Chengdu.

2. 比较 **bǐjiào** comparatively; to compare

Niánqīng rén juéde shàngwǎng mǎi dōngxi bǐjiào fāngbiàn.
年轻人觉得上网买东西比较方便。
Young people think that shopping online is comparatively convenient.

3. 比方说 **bǐfāngshuō** for example

Tā juéde zài Xiānggǎng shēnghuó bú tài shūfu, bǐfāngshuō rén tài duō le, fángjiān tài xiǎo le.
他觉得在香港生活不太舒服，比方说人太多了，房间太小了。
He thinks that living in Hong Kong is uncomfortable. For example, it's crowded and the rooms are too small.

4. 比赛 **bǐsài** competition; game

Nǐ xiǎng gēn wǒ yìqǐ qù kàn bīngqiú bǐsài ma?
你想跟我一起去看冰球比赛吗？
Do you want to go to a hockey game with me?

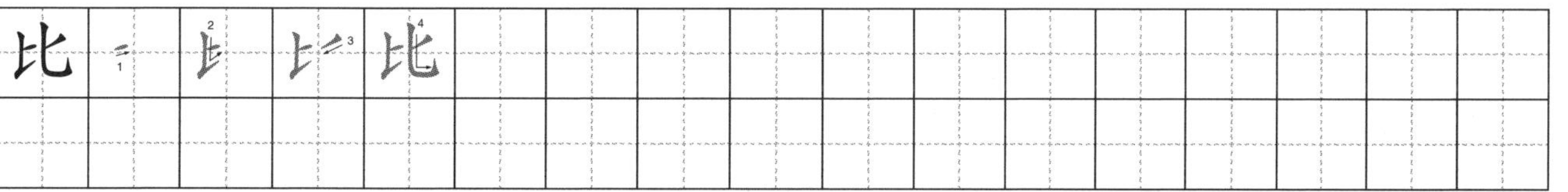

CHARACTER 202

dàn
but

Useful phrases and sentences

7 STROKES | 亻 RADICAL

1. 但是 **dànshì** but

Tā juéde tāde gōngzuò hěn yǒu yìsi, dànshì qián yǒudiǎnr shǎo.
她觉得她的工作很有意思，但是钱有点儿少。
She thinks that her job is interesting, but not well paid.

2. 但愿 **dànyuàn** I wish

Dànyuàn dàjiā bìyè hòu dōu néng zhǎodào hǎo gōngzuò.
但愿大家毕业后都能找到好工作。
I hope everyone would find an excellent job after graduation.

3. 不但… 而且… **búdàn…érqiě…** not only… but also…

Zhèr búdàn tiānqì hǎo, érqiě kōngqì yě hǎo.
这儿不但天气好，而且空气也好。
Not only the weather is good, but the air is also good here.

4. 但凡 **dànfán** as long as; in any case

Dànfán rènshi tāde rén, dōu shuō tā rén hěn hǎo.
但凡认识他的人，都说他人很好。
Everyone who knows him says he's a nice guy.

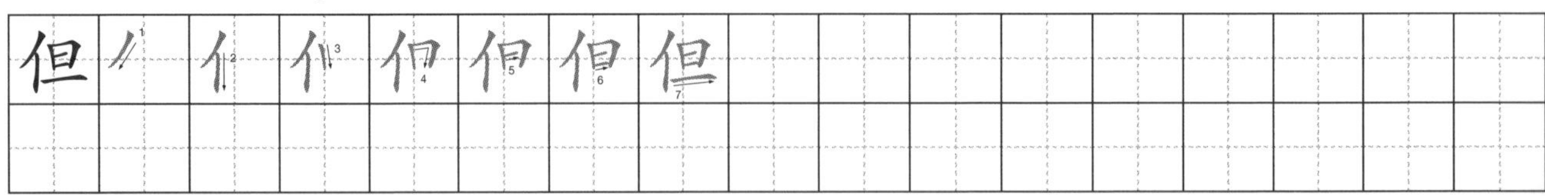

CHARACTER 203

yǔ
rain

Useful phrases and sentences

8 STROKES | 雨 RADICAL

1. 有雨 **yǒu yǔ** have rain

Míngtiān hǎoxiàng yǒu yǔ.
明天好像有雨。
It seems that it's going to rain tomorrow.

2. 下雨 **xiàyǔ** rain *(verb)*

Wàimiàn zài xiàyǔ, nǐ xiān bié zǒu.
外面在下雨，你先别走。
It's raining outside. You'd better not leave right now.

3. 雨伞 **yǔsǎn** umbrella

Wǒ jīntiān yòu wàngle dài yǔsǎn.
我今天又忘了带雨伞。
I forgot to bring my umbrella again today.

4. 雨天 **yǔtiān** rainy day

Zěnme míngtiān yòu shì yǔtiān?
怎么明天又是雨天？
How come it's another rainy day tomorrow?

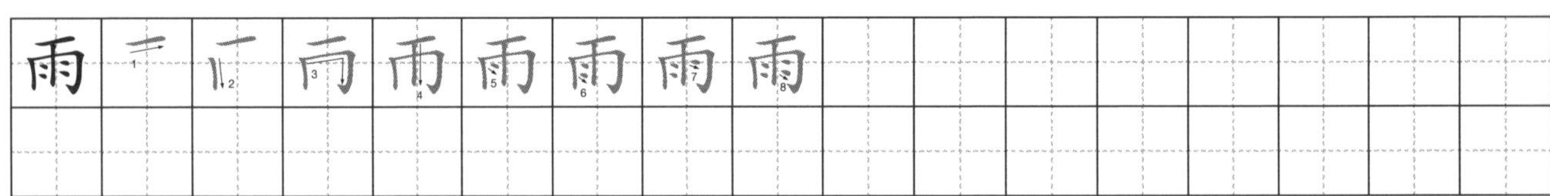

CHARACTER 204

xuě
snow

Useful phrases and sentences

11 STROKES | 雨 RADICAL

1. 雪 **xuě** snow *(noun)*

Zhè shì wǒ dìyīcì kànjiàn xuě.
这是我第一次看见雪。
This is my first time to see snow.

2. 雪景 **xuějǐng** snowscape

Wǒ shì nánfāngrén, zhè shì wǒ dìyīcì kàn xuějǐng, tài měi le.
我是南方人，这是我第一次看雪景，太美了！
I'm a southerner, so this is my first time seeing snow. It's gorgeous!

3. 雪人 **xuěrén** snowman

Wǒmen zuòge xuěrén ba?
我们做个雪人吧？
Let's make a snowman, shall we?

4. 滑雪 **huáxuě** ski

Nǐ huì huáxuě ma?
你会滑雪吗？
Do you ski?

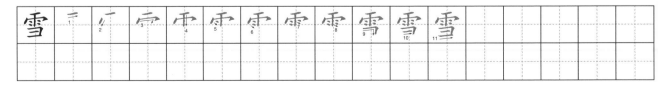

CHARACTER 205

fēng
wind

Useful phrases and sentences

4 STROKES | 风 RADICAL

1. 风 **fēng** wind

Jīntiānde fēng bǐ zuótiān dà.
今天的风比昨天大。
The wind today is stronger than yesterday.

2. 刮风 **guā fēng** windy; blowing (wind)

Běijīng chūntiān chángcháng guā fēng.
北京春天常常刮风。
It is often windy in spring in Beijing.

3. 风景 **fēngjǐng** scenery

Wǒ xǐhuan zuò hǔochē, yīnwèi kěyǐ kàn wàimiànde fēngjǐng.
我喜欢坐火车，因为可以看外面的风景。
I love to take trains, as I can enjoy the view outside.

4. 飓风 **jùfēng** hurricane

Měiguó nánfāng xiàtiān cháng yǒu jùfēng.
美国南方夏天常有飓风。
There are frequent hurricanes in the south of America during the summer.

CHARACTER 206

chūn
spring

Useful phrases and sentences

9 STROKES | 日 RADICAL

1. 春天 **chūntiān** spring

Zài Zhōngguó, rénmen shuō Kūnmíng shì "chūnchéng", yīnwèi yìnián sìjì dōu shì chūntiān.
在中国，人们说昆明是“春城”，因为一年四季都是春天。
In China, people call Kunming a city of spring, as it feels like spring all the year long.

2. 春节 **chūnjié** Spring Festival/Chinese New Year

Jīnnián chūnjié nǐ huíjiā ma?
今年春节你回家吗？
Are you going home this Chinese New Year?

3. 春假 **chūnjià** spring break

Wǒ chūnjià bù xiǎng chūqu, zhǐ xiǎng zài sùshè xiūxi.
我春假不想出去，只想在宿舍休息。
I don't want to go anywhere in spring break. I just want to rest in my dormitory.

4. 长春 **Chángchūn** Changchun (name of a city)

Chángchūn shì Jílínshěngde shěnghuì.
长春是吉林省的省会。
Changchun is the capital city of Jilin Province, China.

CHARACTER 207

xià
summer

Useful phrases and sentences

10 STROKES | 夂 RADICAL

1. 夏 **Xià** (surname)

Xià Tàitai kāile yījiā huādiàn, shēngyì bú cuò.
夏太太开了一家花店，生意不错。
Mrs. Xia opened a flower shop. She has good business.

2. 初夏 **chūxià** early summer

Xiànzài chūxià, hái búshì tài rè.
现在初夏，还不是太热。
It's early summer and not too hot yet.

3. 夏天 **xiàtiān** summer

Chóngqìng, Wǔhàn, Nánjīngde xiàtiān dōu tài rè le.
重庆、武汉、南京的夏天都太热了。
Summers in Chongqing, Wuhan, and Nanjing are all too hot.

4. 夏令营 **xiàlìngyíng** summer camp

Nǐ cānjiāguo shénme xiàlìngyíng?
你参加过什么夏令营？
What kind of summer camp did you go to before?

CHARACTER 208

qiū
autumn

Useful phrases and sentences

9 STROKES | 禾 RADICAL

1. 秋天 **qiūtiān** autumn; fall

Jīnnián qiūtiān bǐ qùnián lěng yìdiǎnr.
今年秋天比去年冷一点儿。
Fall this year is colder than last year.

2. 中秋节 **Zhōngqiūjié** The Mid-Autumn Festival

Zhōngqiūjié shì nónglì bāyuè shíwǔhào.
中秋节是农历八月十五号。
The Mid-Autumn Festival is on the 15th day of the 8th month.

3. 秋收 **qiūshōu** autumn harvest

Jīnniánde qiūshōu bú cuò, dàjiā dōu hěn gāoxìng.
今年的秋收不错，大家都很高兴。
The autumn harvest this year is good. Everyone is happy.

4. 秋季学期 **qiūjì xuéqī** Fall semester

Wǒmen xuéxiàode qiūjì xuéqī jiǔyuè kāishǐ.
我们学校的秋季学期九月开始。
Our Fall Semester begins in September.

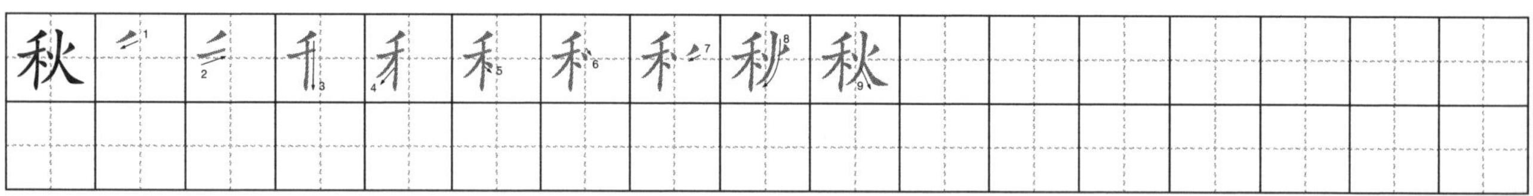

CHARACTER 209

dōng
winter

Useful phrases and sentences

5 STROKES | 夂 RADICAL

1. 冬天 **dōngtiān** winter

Hā'ěrbīn yějiào "bīngchéng", yīnwèi nàrde dōngtiān tèbié lěng, yě xià hěnduō xuě.
哈尔滨也叫"冰城"，因为那儿的冬天特别冷，也下很多雪。
Harbin is also called "ice city," as the winter there is very cold and sees heavy snow.

2. 冬瓜 **dōngguā** winter melon

Dōngguā tāng hěn hǎohē.
冬瓜汤很好喝。
Winter melon soups are tasty.

3. 冬令营 **dōnglìngyíng** winter camp

Wǒde nǚ'ér yīyuè cānjiā yíge dōnglìngyíng.
我的女儿一月参加一个冬令营。
My daughter joined a winter camp in January.

4. 暖冬 **nuǎndōng** warm winter

Jīnniánde dōngtiān bú tài lěng, shì nuǎndōng.
今年的冬天不太冷，是暖冬。
This winter is not too cold; it's a warm winter.

CHARACTER 210

shū
comfortable

Useful phrases and sentences

12 STROKES | 舌 RADICAL

1. 舒服 **shūfu** comfortable

Zhè shuāng xié hěn shūfu, nǐ yě mǎi ba.
这双鞋很舒服，你也买吧。
This pair of shoes is very comfortable. Why don't you buy one too?

2. 舒服 **shūfu** physically well

Lǐ Lǎoshī jīntiān yǒudiǎnr bù shūfu, zài jiā xiūxi.
李老师今天有点儿不舒服，在家休息。
Teacher Li is not feeling well today. She is resting at home.

3. 舒适 **shūshì** (space) comfy

Zhège fángjiān hěn dà, hěn shūshì.
这个房间很大，很舒适。
This room is big and comfy.

4. 舒 **Shū** (surname)

Shū Lǎoshī shì Táiwān rén, hòulái zhù zài Xīnjiāpō.
舒老师是台湾人，后来住在新加坡。
Teacher Shu is from Taiwan. He later lived in Singapore.

Lesson 14 Exercises

Part 1 Choose from the following words to fill in the blanks.

比、舒服、但是、天气

1. 我没去过南京，南京的（　　　　）怎么样？
2. 这里的春天很漂亮，（　　　　）春天很短。
3. 哥哥的房间（　　　　）弟弟的大一点儿。
4. 你怎么了？你看起来不太（　　　　）。

Part 2 Complete the following dialogues using Chinese characters.

1. A: 你喜欢哪个<u>季节</u> (**jìjié**: season) ？

   B: ______________________________。

2. A: 你的<u>老家</u> (**lǎojiā**: hometown) 冬天下雪吗？

   B: ______________________________。

3. A: 要是我去你的老家，几月去比较好？

   B: ______________________________。

4. A: 明年夏天你想去哪儿？做什么？

   B: ______________________________。

5. A: 你觉得你的房间舒服不舒服？为什么？

   B: ______________________________。

Part 3 Use the following prompts to give a one-minute speech.

你们好，

今天我想说说我老家的天气。我家住在 __________，我最喜欢的季节是 __________，我最不喜欢的季节是 __________。春天 __________，我喜欢去 __________；夏天 __________，我喜欢跟朋友 __________；秋天 __________，我常常 __________；冬天这儿 __________，我有时候 __________。你想来我的老家玩儿吗？要是你想来，你 ________ (which month) 来比较好，因为 __________。

LESSON 15

Weather and climate (II) 天气和气候 (II)

1. Introduction

Westerners frequently start their casual conversations by talking about the weather. In the past, Chinese people didn't usually talk about the weather when they met; instead, they greeted each other with questions like "Are you busy?" "Have you eaten?" or "What are you up to?" Recently, air pollution has become a serious issue in China, so people talk more and more the weather and the air quality when they meet. What do people like to talk about when they meet in your culture? What kind of greetings do you usually use?

2. Warm up

Read the passage below and answer the questions using Chinese characters.

小雨: 你去过昆明吗？
小雪: 只去过一次。
小雨: 昆明在哪儿？
小雪: 在中国的西南边，在四川旁边。
小雨: 昆明天气怎么样？
小雪: 昆明春夏秋冬都很舒服，不冷不热，而且很少下雨。你会喜欢的！

1. Where is Kunming?

____

2. Did Xiao Xue go to Kunming before?

____

3. How does Xiao Xue describe the weather in Kunming?

____

3. Vocabulary

	Word	Pinyin	English equivalent
1.	去	**qù**	go
2.	-过	**-guo**	(verb particle indicating experience)
3.	昆明	**Kūnmíng**	Kunming (city name)
4.	只	**zhǐ**	only
5.	次	**cì**	time
6.	西南	**xīnán**	southwest
7.	四川	**Sìchuān**	Sichuan (province name)
8.	而且	**érqiě**	moreover
9.	很少	**hěn shǎo**	seldom; rarely
10.	来	**lái**	come
11.	上午	**shàngwǔ**	morning
12.	下午	**xiàwǔ**	afternoon
13.	所以	**suóyi**	so
14.	晚上	**wǎnshang**	evening
15.	南	**nán**	south
16.	西	**xī**	west
17.	北	**běi**	north
18.	每次	**měicì**	every time
19.	同意	**tóngyì**	agree

4. New Characters

Fifteen characters are introduced in this lesson. Use the following explanations to help you understand and remember the characters.

来 去 次 南 只 北 外 同 意 每 而 且 所 午 夜

CHARACTER 211

lái
come

Useful phrases and sentences

7 STROKES | 木 RADICAL

1. 来 **lái** come
   Nǐ jīntiān wǎnshang huì lái ma ?
   你今天晚上会来吗？
   Are you coming tonight?

2. 过来 **guòlai** come over
   Wǒ māma shuō míngtiān guòlai kàn wǒ.
   我妈妈说明天过来看我。
   My mother said that she will come over tomorrow.

3. 来回 **láihuí** round trip journey
   Cóng bīnguǎn dào shìzhōngxīn láihuí yào liǎngge xiǎoshí.
   从宾馆到市中心来回要两个小时。
   From the hotel to downtown, round trip takes two hours.

4. 来不及 **láibují** not have enough time
   Wǒmen děi zǒule, yǐjīng kuài láibují le.
   我们得走了，已经快来不及了。
   We have to go. We are running late.

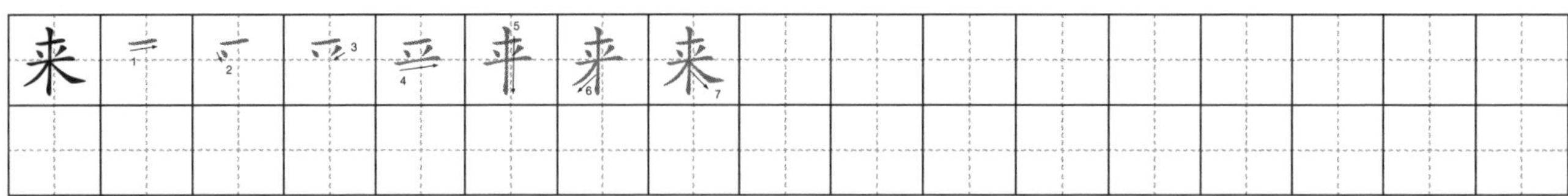

CHARACTER 212

去

qù
go

Useful phrases and sentences

5 STROKES | 厶 RADICAL

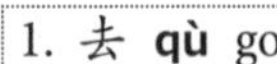

1. 去 **qù** go
   Nǐ zhège zhōumò xiǎng qù nǎr?
   你这个周末想去哪儿？
   Where do you want to go this weekend?

2. 去年 **qùnián** last year
   Wǒmen shì qùnián rènshide.
   我们是去年认识的。
   We met last year.

3. 拿去 **náqu** take away
   Zhèxiē qiǎokèlì nǐ náqu chī ba, bié kèqi.
   这些巧克力你拿去吃吧，别客气。
   Help yourself to those chocolates.

4. 去世 **qùshì** pass away
   Wǒde nǎinai qùnián qùshìle, wǒ hěn xiǎng tā.
   我的奶奶去年去世了，我很想她。
   My grandmother passed away last year. I miss her very much.

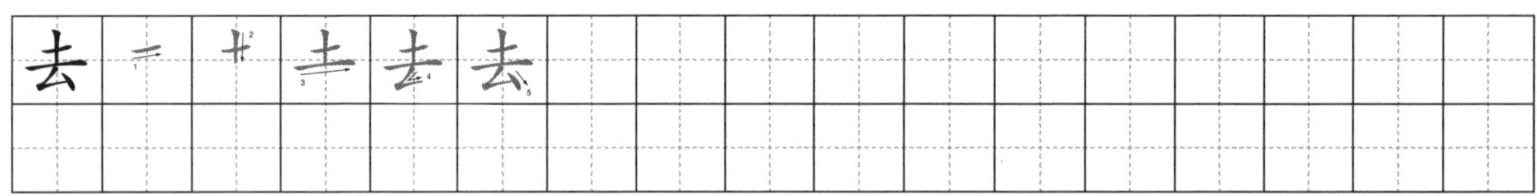

CHARACTER 213

次

cì
an instance; a time

Useful phrases and sentences

6 STROKES | 欠 RADICAL

1. 每次 **měicì** every time
   Nǐ tài kèqi le, měicì lái dōu dài lǐwù.
   你太客气了，每次来都带礼物。
   You always bring gifts every time. You are too polite.

2. 第一次 **dìyīcì** the first time
   Zhè shì wǒ dìyīcì lái Táiběi lǚyóu.
   这是我第一次来台北旅游。
   This is my first tour of Taipei.

3. 这次 **zhècì** this time
   Wǒ zhècì lái jiù shì xiǎng kànkan nǐ.
   我这次来就是想看看你。
   The reason I am here is to see you.

4. 上次 **shàngcì** last time
   Nǐ shàngcì lái Táiwān shì shénme shíhou?
   你上次来台湾是什么时候？
   When was the last time you visited Taiwan?

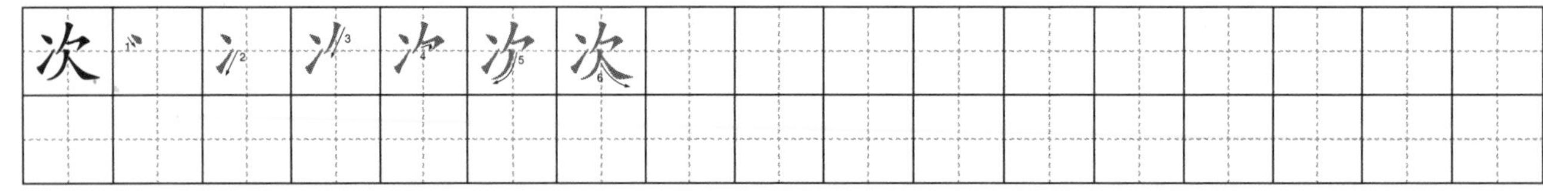

CHARACTER 214

nán
south

Useful phrases and sentences

9 STROKES | 十 RADICAL

1. 南 **nán** south

Nǐ wǎng nán zǒu yíhuìr jiù dàole.
你往南走一会儿就到了。
Walk south and you will arrive soon.

2. 南方 **nánfāng** south; the south; southern

Wǒ shì nánfāngrén, bú tài xíguàn běifāngde shēnghuó.
我是南方人，不太习惯北方的生活。
I am from the south. I am not used to the life style in the north.

3. 东南 **dōngnán** southeast

Shēnzhèn zài Zhōngguóde dōngnánbiān, nàrde tiānqì hěn hǎo.
深圳在中国的东南边，那儿的天气很好。
Shenzhen is in southeast China. The weather there is nice.

4. 西南 **xīnán** southwest

Sìchuān zài Zhōngguóde xīnánbiān, Sìchuānrén hěn xǐhuan dǎ májiàng.
四川在中国的西南边，四川人很喜欢打麻将。
Sichuan is in southwest China. People there like to play mahjong.

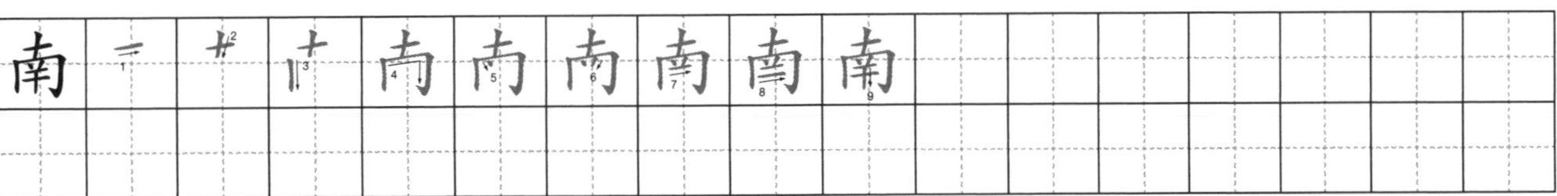

CHARACTER 215

zhǐ/zhī
only/a measure word for certain animals

Useful phrases and sentences

5 STROKES | 口 RADICAL

1. 只有 **zhǐ yǒu** only have

Wǒde sùshè zhǐ yǒu yìzhāng zhuōzi, yìbǎ yǐzi.
我的宿舍只有一张桌子，一把椅子。
I only have one desk and one chair in my dorm room.

2. 只想 **zhǐ xiǎng** only want

Wǒ xiànzài zhǐ xiǎng shuìjiào.
我现在只想睡觉。
I only want to sleep now.

3. 只 **zhī** measure word for a cat

Nàzhī māo hěn kě'ài.
那只猫很可爱。
That cat is very cute.

4. 只 **zhī** measure word for a young dog

Tā hěn xiǎng yǎng yīzhī gǒu, kěshì tāde shìyou bù xǐhuan gǒu.
他很想养一只狗，可是他的室友不喜欢狗。
He wants to keep a dog, but his roommate doesn't like dogs.

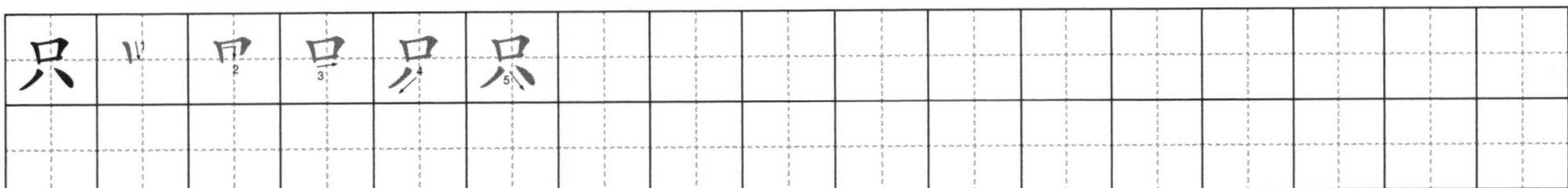

CHARACTER 216

běi
north

Useful phrases and sentences

5 STROKES | 匕 RADICAL

1. 北方 **běifāng** north; the north

Wǒde lǎojiā zài Zhōngguó běifāngde yíge xiǎochéng.
我的老家在中国北方的一个小城。
My hometown is a small town in northern China.

2. 北美 **Běiměi** North America

Wǒ qùguo Běiměi sāncì, jīnnián xiǎngqù nánměi kànkan.
我去过北美三次，今年想去南美看看。
I've been to North America three times. I want to go to South America this year.

3. 西北 **xīběi** northwest

Xī'ān zài Zhōngguóde xīběi, shì yíge hěn gǔlǎode chéngshì.
西安在中国的西北，是一个很古老的城市。
Xi'an is in northwest China. It's an ancient city.

4. 北方话 **běifānghuà** northern dialect

Běifānghuà hé pǔtōnghuà bǐjiào xiàng.
北方话和普通话比较像。
Northern dialects are similar to Mandarin Chinese.

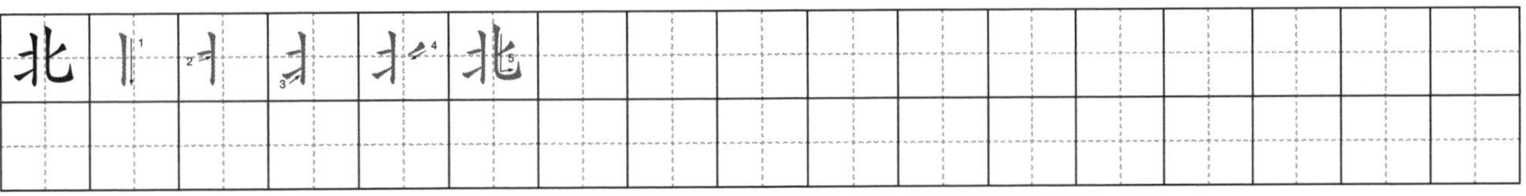

CHARACTER 217

wài
outside

Useful phrases and sentences

5 STROKES | 夕 RADICAL

1. 外面 **wàimiàn** outside

Shéi zài wàimiàn shuōhuà? Xiǎoshēng yìdiǎnr!
谁在外面说话？小声一点儿！
Who is talking outside? Please lower your voice.

2. 外出 **wàichū** go out

Wǒ děi wàichū yíge xīngqī, děng wǒ huílai zài jiànmiànba.
我得外出一个星期，等我回来再见面吧。
I need to be away for a week. Let's meet when I come back.

3. 国外 **guówài** overseas

Xiànzài, hěnduō Zhōngguó xuésheng xiǎng qù guówài xuéxí hé gōngzuò.
现在，很多中国学生想去国外学习和工作。
Today many Chinese students want to go overseas to study and work.

4. 外地人 **wàidìrén** people from other places

Běijīngde wàidìrén yuè lái yuè duō le.
北京的外地人越来越多了。
There are more and more people from other places in Beijing.

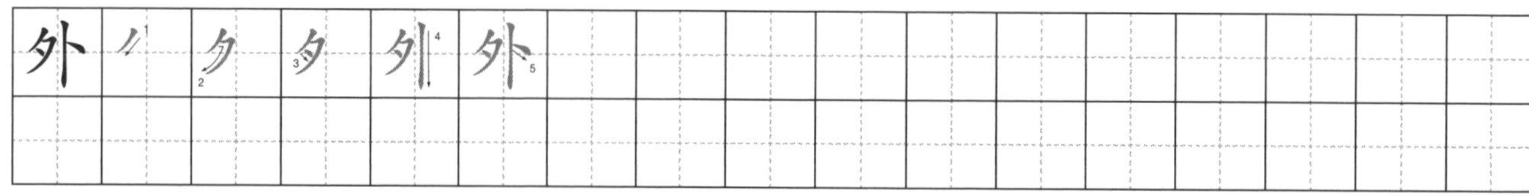

CHARACTER 218

tóng
be similar

Useful phrases and sentences

6 STROKES | 口 RADICAL

1. 同意 **tóngyì** agree

Nǐ fùmǔ tóngyì nǐ qù guówài xuéxí ma?
你父母同意你去国外学习吗？
Do your parents agree that you will study overseas?

2. 同学 **tóngxué** classmate

Zhōumò wǒ huì cānjiā yíge gāozhōng tóngxué jùhuì.
周末我会参加一个高中同学聚会。
I will attend a high school reunion this weekend.

3. 同事 **tóngshì** colleague

Tóngshì jiào wǒ xiàbān hòu yìqǐ qù hē kāfēi.
同事叫我下班后一起去喝咖啡。
My colleague asked me to grab a cup of coffee with him after work.

4. 相同 **xiāngtóng** same

Zài hěnduō wèntí shàng, wǒmen dōu yǒu xiāngtóngde kànfǎ.
在很多问题上，我们都有相同的看法。
We share the same opinions on many things.

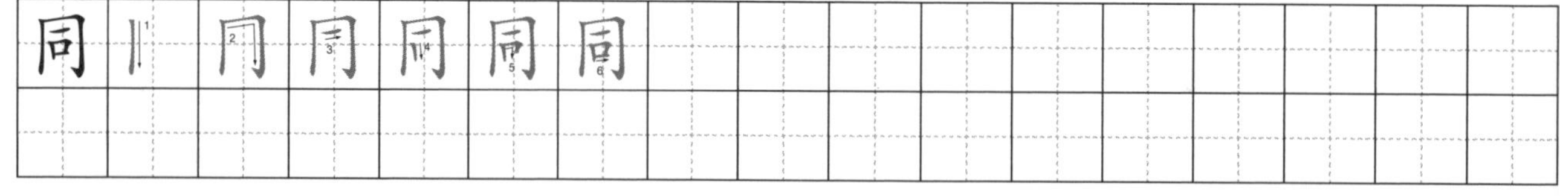

CHARACTER 219

yì
meaning

Useful phrases and sentences

13 STROKES | 心 RADICAL

1. 意思 **yìsi** meaning

Lǎoshī, zhèjù huà shì shénme yìsi?
老师，这句话是什么意思？
Teacher, what does this sentence mean?

2. 意见 **yìjiàn** comment; opinion; recommendation

Nǐ yǒu shénme yìjiàn, qǐng gàosù wǒ.
你有什么意见，请告诉我。
If you have any comments, please let me know.

3. 小意思 **xiǎo yìsi** small token of appreciation

Zhè shì yìdiǎnr xiǎo yìsi, xièxie nínde bāngmáng.
这是一点儿小意思，谢谢您的帮忙。
This is a small token of appreciation. Thank you for your help.

4. 注意 **zhùyì** pay attention to

Zhùyì yíxià: "jǐ" hé "yǐ" zhè liǎngge zì bù yíyàng.
注意一下： "己" 和 "已" 这两个字不一样。
Please pay attention: "ji" and "yi" are two different characters.

CHARACTER 220

měi
every

Useful phrases and sentences

7 STROKES | 母 RADICAL

1. 每天 **měitiān** every day

Yào xuéhǎo wàiyǔ jiù yào měitiān liànxí.
要学好外语就要每天练习。
If you want to master a foreign language, you need to practice everyday.

2. 每年 **měinián** every year

Tā fùqin zài guówài gōngzuò, měinián zhǐ huí yícì jiā.
他父亲在国外工作，每年只回一次家。
His father works overseas. He returns home only once a year.

3. 每个星期 **měige xīngqī** every week

Wǒmen měige xīngqī qù yícì tǐyùguǎn, zěnmeyàng?
我们每个星期去一次体育馆，怎么样？
Let's go to the gym once a week. How about that?

4. 每个月 **měige yuè** every month

Nǐ zhīdao Zhōngguó rén měige yuè cún duōshao qián ma? Měiguó rén nē?
你知道中国人每个月存多少钱吗？美国人呢？
Do you know how much money Chinese people save per month? What about the Americans?

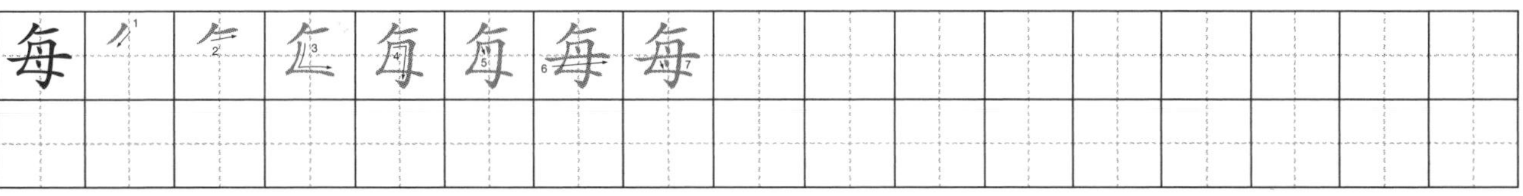

CHARACTER 221

ér
but; and

Useful phrases and sentences

6 STROKES | 而 RADICAL

1. 然而 **rán'ér** however

Zhèjiàn shì zuòqǐlái hěn nán, rán'ér hěn zhídé qù zuò.
这件事做起来很难，然而很值得去做。
This task is quite difficult, however it's worth it.

2. 而已 **éryǐ** only

Wǒde xiǎohái jīnnián wǔsuì éryǐ, hái xiǎo.
我的小孩今年五岁而已，还小。
My child is only five years old this year. She is still little.

3. 反而 **fǎn'ér** instead; on the contrary

Wǒ bāngle tā, tā méi xièxie wǒ, fǎn'ér guài wǒ.
我帮了他，他没谢谢我，反而怪我。
I helped him. He didn't say "thank you." Instead, he blamed me.

4. 不是...而是... **bú shì ···érshì···** not…rather…

Měiguóde shǒudū bú shì Niǔyuē, érshì Huáshèngdùn.
美国的首都不是纽约，而是华盛顿。
The capital city of U.S.A is not New York; it's Washington D.C.

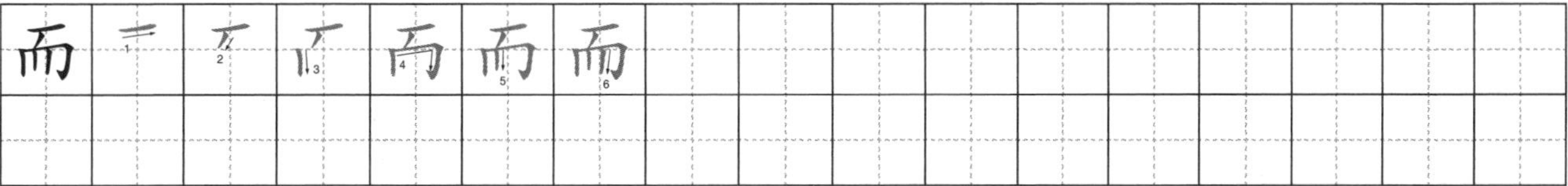

CHARACTER 222

qiě
moreover

Useful phrases and sentences

5 STROKES | 一 RADICAL

1. 而且 **érqiě** moreover

Zhège gōngyuán rén shǎo, érqiě fēngjǐng hěn piàoliang.
这个公园人少，而且风景很漂亮。
This park is less crowded. Moreover, its scenery is beautiful.

2. 且慢 **qiěmàn** hold on a second; wait a moment

Qiěmàn, nǐ gāng shuōde wǒ méi tīngdǒng. Néng-bù-néng qǐng nǐ zài shuō yībiàn?
且慢，你刚说的我没听懂。能不能请你再说一遍？
Hold on a second. I don't understand what you just said. Could you please repeat it?

3. 并且 **bìngqiě** and also

Lǎoshī bāngwǒ zhǎodàole wèntí, bìngqiě bāngwǒ jiějuéle wèntí.
老师帮我找到了问题，并且帮我解决了问题。
My teacher helped me find the problem and she also helped me solve it.

4. 姑且 **gūqiě** for the time being; tentatively

Zuótiānde shì gūqiě bù shuō, jīntian nǐ yòu rěshì.
昨天的事姑且不说，今天你又惹事。
Put aside what happened yesterday for now. You are making trouble again today.

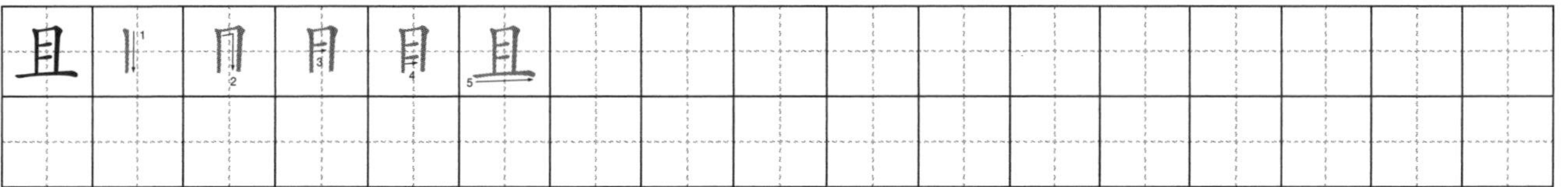

CHARACTER 223

所

suǒ
place

Useful phrases and sentences

8 STROKES 户 RADICAL

1. 所以 **suóyi** so

Wǒ nǎinai zhǐ huì shuō Zhōngwén, suóyi wǒ xiǎng xué Zhōngwén, yǐhòu kěyǐ gēn tā liáotiān.
我奶奶只会说中文，所以我想学中文，以后可以跟她聊天。
My grandmother can only speak Chinese, so I want to learn Chinese in order to chat with her.

2. 所谓 **suǒwèi** so-called

Zhōngguó yǐqián suǒwèide "Cháng'ān" jiùshì xiànzàide "Xī'ān."
中国以前所谓的"长安"就是现在的"西安"。
The so-called "Chang'an" in ancient China refers to "Xi'an" nowadays.

3. 厕所 **cèsuǒ** restroom

Zài Zhōngguó, hěnduō gōnggòng cèsuǒ dōu méiyǒu wèishēngzhǐ.
在中国，很多公共厕所都没有卫生纸。
In China, many public restrooms don't offer any toilet paper.

4. 研究所 **yánjiūsuǒ** graduate school

Yǒude xuésheng bìyè yǐhòu zhǎobúdào hǎode gōngzuò, jiù qù niàn yánjiūsuǒ le.
有的学生毕业以后找不到好的工作，就去念研究所了。
Some students cannot find a good job after graduation, so they go to graduate school.

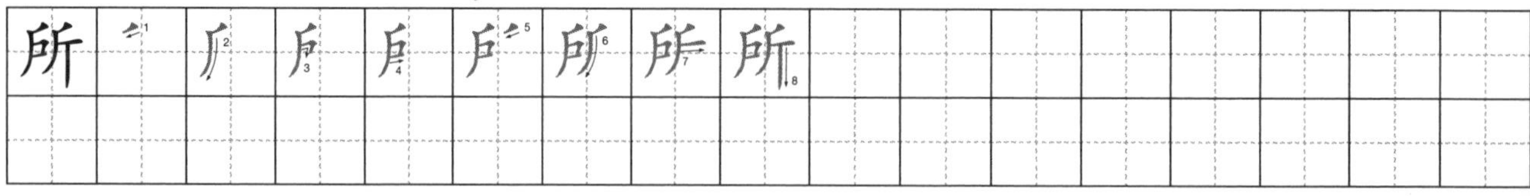

CHARACTER 224

午

wǔ
midday

Useful phrases and sentences

4 STROKES 十 RADICAL

1. 上午 **shàngwǔ** morning

Zhège xuéqī wǒ měitiān shàngwǔ bādiǎn yǒu kè.
这个学期我每天上午八点有课。
This semester I have class at 8 a.m. every morning.

2. 下午 **xiàwǔ** afternoon

Xiàwǔ liǎngdiǎn chángcháng shì wǒ zuì lèide shíhou.
下午两点常常是我最累的时候。
I often feel the most tired at two o'clock in the afternoon.

3. 中午 **zhōngwǔ** noon

Zài Zhōngguó, xuésheng zhōngwǔ dōu yào huí sùshè shuì yíhuir, suóyi méi kè.
在中国，学生中午都要回宿舍睡一会儿，所以没课。
In China, students often go back to the dorm to take a nap at noon, so they have no class.

4. 午饭 **wǔfàn** lunch

Jīntiān wǔfàn nǐ chīle shénme?
今天午饭你吃了什么？
What did you have for lunch today?

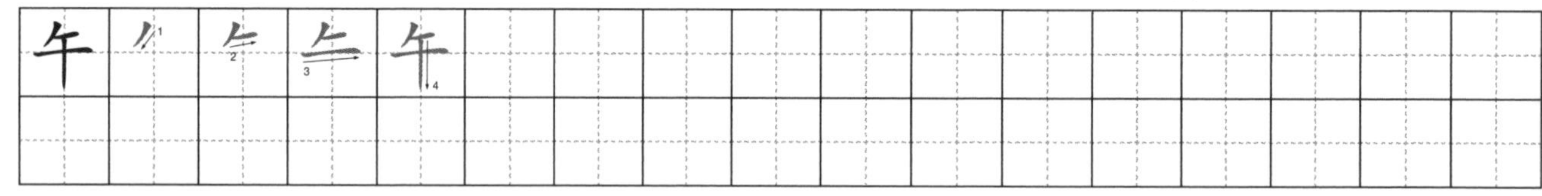

CHARACTER 225

夜

yè
night

Useful phrases and sentences

8 STROKES 夕 RADICAL

1. 夜里 **yèlǐ** in the night

Tā qiántiān yèlǐ liǎngdiǎn cái xiūxi.
他前天夜里两点才休息。
He didn't go to bed until 2 a.m. the day before yesterday.

2. 半夜 **bànyè** midnight

Zuótiān shéi bànyè gěi nǐ dǎ diànhuà?
昨天谁半夜给你打电话？
Who called you midnight yesterday?

3. 夜景 **yèjǐng** night scene

Táiběide yèjǐng zhēn hǎokàn!
台北的夜景真好看！
The night scene of Taipei is so beautiful.

4. 夜生活 **yèshēnghuó** night-life

Zhège chéngshì méi shénme yèshēnghuó, wǎnshang zhǐ néng dāizài jiālǐ.
这个城市没什么夜生活，晚上只能呆在家里。
This city lacks night-life; one can only stay at home at night.

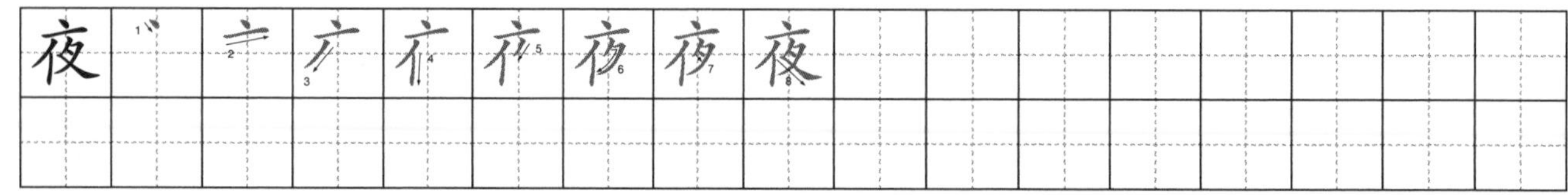

Lesson 15 Exercises

Part 1 Choose from the following words to fill in the blanks.

所以、同意、而且、每次

1. 今天我请你吃饭吧，不能（　　　　）都让你请我。
2. 上中学的时候，父母不（　　　　）我找男朋友。
3. 这个宾馆的房间有点儿小，（　　　　）也不便宜，我们去别的宾馆看看吧。
4. 他没找到工作，（　　　　）这几天不太高兴。

Part 2 Complete the following dialogues using Chinese characters.

1. A: 你为什么想学中文？

   B: ____。

2. A: 要是你做什么事情，你父母会不同意？

   B: ____。

3. A: 你知道<u>青海</u> (**Qīnghǎi**) 在中国的什么地方吗？

   B: ____。

4. A: 你上午几点起床？晚上几点睡觉？

   B: ____。

5. A: 你去过国外吗？你去过什么<u>国家</u> (**guójiā**: country)？

   B: ____。

Part 3 **Sūzhōu** (苏州) is a famous city for sight-seeing in China. Have you ever been to Suzhou? Do some search online about Suzhou and answer the following questions.

1. 苏州在中国什么地方？

____

2. 苏州的天气怎么样？

____

3. 在苏州有很多漂亮的公园吗？

____

Lessons 11–15 (Review Exercises)

Part 1 Write the Pinyin and the English meaning of the following words.

	Words	Pinyin	English Equivalent
e.g.,	五元	**wǔyuán**	five yuan
1.	知道	____________	____________
2.	城市	____________	____________
3.	公园	____________	____________
4.	旁边	____________	____________
5.	里边	____________	____________
6.	漂亮	____________	____________
7.	商店	____________	____________
8.	舒服	____________	____________
9.	天气	____________	____________
10.	同意	____________	____________

Part 2 Fill in the blanks according to the English meaning.

1. (   ) 钟 minute
2. (   ) 以 so
3. (   ) 意 agree
4. (   ) 快 cool
5. (   ) 天 spring
6. 现 (   ) right now
7. 学 (   ) school
8. 城 (   ) city
9. 对不 (   ) sorry
10. 下 (   ) snow

Part 3 Answer the following questions using Chinese characters.

1. Q: 你在哪个城市工作？ 你喜欢那儿吗？

   A: ____。

2. Q: 你家旁边有没有公园？

   A: ____。

3. Q: 对不起，请问银行几点关门？

   A: ____。

4. Q: 你喜欢冬天吗？为什么？

   A: ____。

Part 4 Read the passage below and answer the questions using Chinese characters.

我家旁边有一个公园。公园不大，可是很漂亮。公园每天早上七点开门，晚上九点半关门。我每个周末都跟父母去公园走走，从我的家到公园，走路只要五分钟。

春天和夏天的时候，公园里常常有很多人。春天不冷不热，公园里很舒服；夏天公园里很凉快；秋天去公园的人比较少，因为风很大。冬天很冷，常常下雪，所以很少有人去公园。可是，我家的狗（**gǒu:** dog）球球冬天喜欢去公园，他很喜欢雪。

1. “我”家旁边的公园怎么样？

   ____。

2. 公园几点开门、几点关门？

   ____。

3. 什么时候公园里的人很多？什么时候不多？

   ____。

4. “我”常常什么时候去公园？球球喜欢什么时候去公园？

   ____。

LESSON 16

Chinese language learning 中文听说读写

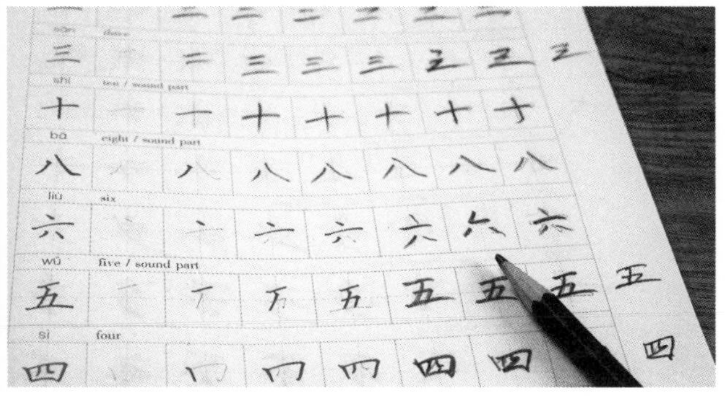

1. Introduction

How do you enjoy Chinese language learning so far? Compared to the other foreign languages you have learned before, is Chinese more difficult or easier? Among the skills of listening, speaking, reading, and writing, which do you find the most challenging? Also, how many Chinese characters can you recognize by now? Are you able to write all of them?

2. Warm up

Read the passage below and answer the questions using Chinese characters.

中国人：你的中文说得很好。
美国人：哪里，哪里。
中国人：中文很难吧！
美国人：开始很难，但是后来就容易了。
中国人：中文听说读写，哪个难？
美国人：我觉得说和写比听和读难。
中国人：你汉语学了多久了？
美国人：学了三年了。我认识两千个汉字左右，有的会写，有的不会。

1. Does the American think that learning Chinese is hard?

____。

2. How does the American compare the learning of the four skills in Chinese?

____。

3. How long has the American been learning Chinese? How many Chinese characters can he/she write?

____。

3. Vocabulary

	Word	Pinyin	English equivalent
1.	中文	**Zhōngwén**	Chinese language
2.	-得	**-de**	(indicates manner)
3.	哪里	**nǎlǐ**	"not at all"
4.	难	**nán**	difficult; hard
5.	开始	**kāishǐ**	in the beginning
6.	后来	**hòulái**	later
7.	容易	**róngyì**	easy
8.	听	**tīng**	listening; listen
9.	读	**dú**	reading; read
10.	写	**xiě**	writing; write
11.	汉语	**Hànyǔ**	Chinese language (language of Han people)
12.	多久	**duō jiǔ**	how long
13.	认识	**rènshi**	know
14.	有的	**yǒude**	some
15.	会	**huì**	can; know how

4. New Characters

Fifteen characters are introduced in this lesson. Use the following explanations to help you understand and remember the characters.

文 京 始 汉 语 久 认 识 会 听 说 写 难 容 易

CHARACTER 226

wén
written language; culture

Useful phrases and sentences

4 STROKES | 文 RADICAL

1. 文明 **wénmíng** civilized

Zài diànyǐngyuàn dàshēng shuōhuà hěn bù wénmíng.
在电影院大声说话很不文明。
It's very impolite to speak loudly in a cinema.

2. 文件 **wénjiàn** file; document

Qǐng wèn, nín shōudào wǒ fāgěi nǐde wénjiànle ma?
请问，您收到我发给你的文件了吗？
Excuse me, have you received the file that I sent you?

3. 文化 **wénhuà** culture

Hěnduō rén xué Zhōngwén shì yīnwèi xǐhuan Zhōngguó wénhuà.
很多人学中文是因为喜欢中国文化。
Many people learn Chinese because they like the Chinese culture.

4. 文学 **wénxué** literature

Nǐ duì wénxué yǒu xìngqù ma?
你对文学有兴趣吗？
Are you interested in literature?

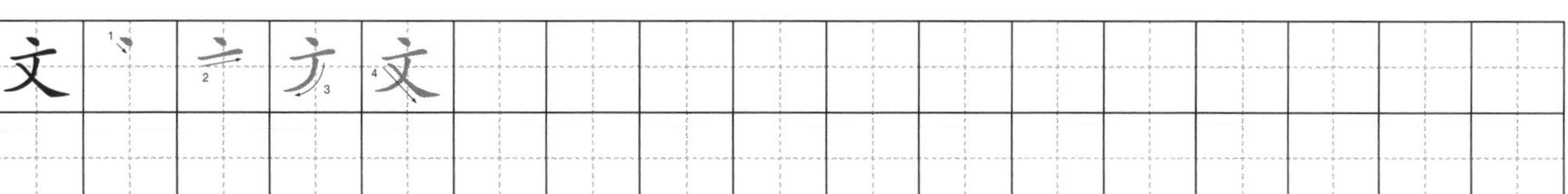

CHARACTER 227

jīng
capital of a country

Useful phrases and sentences

8 STROKES | 亠 RADICAL

1. 北京 **Běijīng** Beijing

Běijīng shì Zhōngguóde shǒudū.
北京是中国的首都。
Beijing is the capital of China.

2. 京剧 **jīngjù** Beijing opera

Bìyè yǐhòu wǒ xiǎng qù Běijīng xué jīngjù.
毕业以后我想去北京学京剧。
I plan to go to Beijing to study the Beijing Opera after graduation.

3. 东京 **Dōngjīng** Tokyo

2020 nián Àoyùnhuì zài Dōngjīng jǔxíng.
2020年奥运会在东京举行。
Tokyo is the host city for the 2020 Olympic games.

4. 南京 **Nánjīng** Nanjing

Nánjīng lí Shànghǎi bù yuǎn, zuò huǒchē yíge xiǎoshí zuǒyòu.
南京离上海不远，坐火车一个小时左右。
Nanjing is not far from Shanghai. It's about an hour away by train.

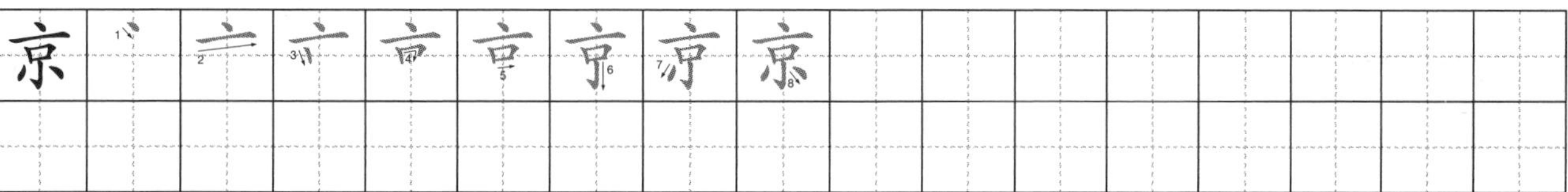

CHARACTER 228

shǐ
beginning; start

Useful phrases and sentences

8 STROKES | 女 RADICAL

1. 开始 **kāishǐ** in the beginning; to start

Zhège Zhōngguó zì cóng nǎr kāishǐ xiě?
这个中国字从哪儿开始写？
Where do you start to write this Chinese character?

2. 创始人 **chuàngshǐ rén** founder

Zhèjiā gōngsīde chuàngshǐ rén xìng Chén, Húnán rén.
这家公司的创始人姓陈，湖南人。
The founder of this company is surnamed Chen. He/She is from Hunan province.

3. 始祖 **shǐzǔ** ancestor

Nǐ zhīdao rénlèide shǐzǔ shì shénme ma?
你知道人类的始祖是什么吗？
Do you know who our human ancestors were?

4. 始末 **shǐmò** whole story; from the beginning to the end

Nǐ néng-bù-néng bǎ zhèjiàn shìde shǐmò gàosù wǒ?
你能不能把这件事的始末告诉我？
Can you tell me the whole story of this matter?

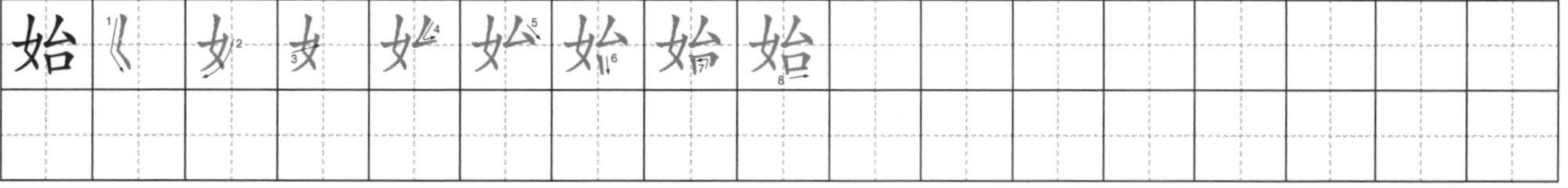

CHARACTER 229

hàn
Han ethnic group

Useful phrases and sentences

5 STROKES | 氵 RADICAL

1. 汉人 **Hànrén** people of Han ethnicity

Dà duōshùde Zhōngguó rén shì Hànrén.
大多数的中国人是汉人。
The majority of Chinese people are of the Han ethnicity.

2. 汉字 **Hànzì** Chinese character

Yīnwèi dà duōshùde Zhōngguó rén shì Hànrén, suóyi Zhōngguó zì yě jiào Hànzì.
因为大多数的中国人是汉人，所以中国字也叫汉字。
Because the majority of Chinese people are of the Han ethnicity, Chinese characters are also called Hanzi.

3. 汉朝 **Hàncháo** the Han dynasty

Hàncháo cóng Xīyuán qián èr-líng-èr nián dào Xīyuán hòu èr-èr-líng nián.
汉朝从西元前二零二年到西元后二二零年。
The Han dynasty was from 202 BC to 220 AD.

4. 汉学 **Hànxué** Sinology

Tā shì yánjiū Hànxuéde, duì Zhōngguó lìshǐ hěn liǎojiě.
他是研究汉学的，对中国历史很了解。
His research is Sinology. He knows Chinese history very well.

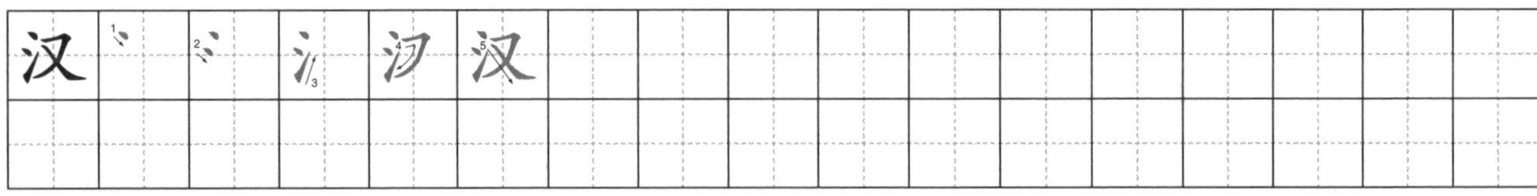

CHARACTER 230

yǔ
language (especially spoken)

Useful phrases and sentences

9 STROKES | 讠 RADICAL

1. 汉语 **Hànyǔ** Chinese (language of Han people)

Hànyǔ jiù shì Zhōngwén. Xiànzài hěnduō wàiguó rén Hànyǔ dōu shuōde hěn hǎo.
汉语就是中文。现在很多外国人汉语都说得很好。
Chinese is also called "Hanyu." Nowadays many foreigners speak good Chinese.

2. 语法 **yǔfǎ** grammar

Zhōngwénde yǔfǎ hé Yīngwén xiàng ma?
中文的语法和英文像吗？
Is Chinese grammar similar to English?

3. 外语 **wàiyǔ** foreign language

Duō xué wàiyǔ kěyǐ duō liǎojiě bùtóngde wénhuà.
多学外语可以多了解不同的文化。
The more foreign languages you learn, the more you can understand different cultures.

4. 语言 **yǔyán** language

Zhāng Xiǎojie duì xué yǔyán hěn yǒu xìngqu, tā huì shuō Zhōngwén, Rìwén, Yīngwén hé Déwén.
张小姐对学语言很有兴趣，她会说中文、日文、英文和德文。
Ms Zhang is interested in learning languages. She speaks Chinese, Japanese, English, and German.

CHARACTER 231

久

jiǔ
long (time ago)

Useful phrases and sentences

3 STROKES | 丿 RADICAL

1. 多久 **duō jiǔ** how long (time)

Nǐ Zhōngwén xuéle duō jiǔ le?
你中文学了多久了？
How long have you been studying Chinese?

2. 很久 **hěn jiǔ** long

Tā qùle hěn jiǔ le, zěnme hái méi huílai?
他去了很久了，怎么还没回来？
He has gone for a long time. Why isn't he back yet?

3. 不久 **bù jiǔ** not long

Wǒ Déwén gāng xué bù jiǔ, shuōde bú tài hǎo.
我德文刚学不久，说得不太好。
I just studied German not long ago. My German is not very good.

4. 好久不见 **hǎo jiǔ bú jiàn** "long time no see"

Hǎo jiǔ bú jiàn, nǐ hǎo ma?
好久不见，你好吗？
I haven't seen you for a long time. How have you been?

久 丿 ク 久

CHARACTER 232

rèn
recognize; know

Useful phrases and sentences

4 STROKES | 讠 RADICAL

1. 认出 **rènchū** recognize; differentiate

Zhēn bùhǎoyìsi, wǒ gāngcái méi rènchū nǐ.
真不好意思，我刚才没认出你。
I feel very sorry that I did not recognize you.

2. 认为 **rènwéi** think

Nǐ rènwéi Lín Xiānshengde yìjiàn zěnmeyàng?
你认为林先生的意见怎么样？
What do you think about Mr. Lin's comments?

3. 承认 **chéngrèn** admit; acknowledge

Wǒ chéngrèn zhècì shì wǒ bù hǎo.
我承认这次是我不好。
I admit that it's my fault this time.

4. 认真 **rènzhēn** hardworking; upright and proper

Wǒde tóngwū fēicháng rènzhēn, měitiān xuéxí dào hěn wǎn.
我的同屋非常认真，每天学习到很晚。
My roommate is really hardworking. She studies until late every day.

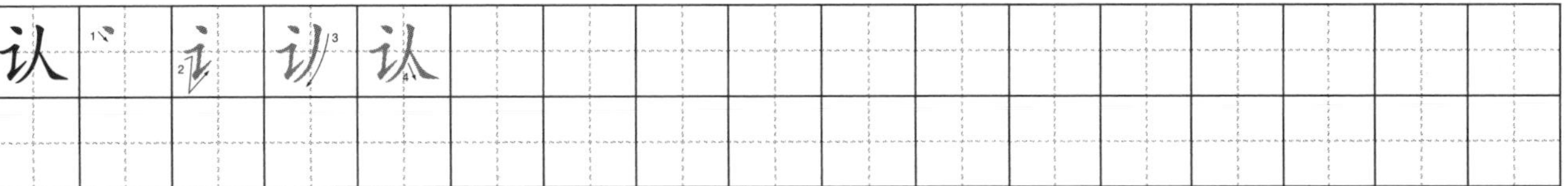

CHARACTER 233

shí
know;
knowledge

Note: **shí** loses its tone in **rènshi, zhīshi** and **chángshi**.

Useful phrases and sentences

7 STROKES | 讠 RADICAL

1. 认识 **rènshi** know; become acquainted with

Zhège Hànzì nǐ rènshi-bú-rènshi?
这个汉字你认识不认识？
Do you know this Chinese character?

2. 识字 **shízì** literate

Zhège cūnzi shízìde rén yǒu duōshǎo?
这个村子识字的人有多少？
How many literate people are there in this village?

3. 知识 **zhīshi** knowledge

Zhīshi jiù shì lìliang.
知识就是力量。
Knowledge is power.

4. 常识 **chángshi** common sense

Zhè shì chángshi, měige rén dōu zhīdao.
这是常识，每个人都知道。
This is common sense; everyone knows it.

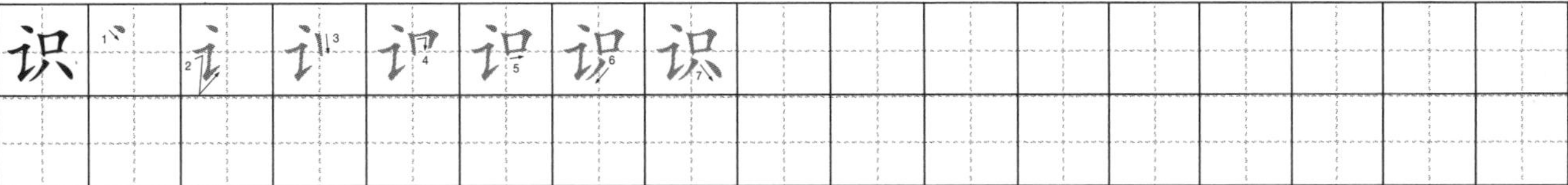

CHARACTER 234

huì
know how to;
will

Useful phrases and sentences

6 STROKES | 人 RADICAL

1. 会 **huì** will

Míngtiān wǒmen huì xué yíge Zhōngguóde gùshì.
明天我们会学一个中国的故事。
We will learn a Chinese story tomorrow.

2. 会 **huì** know how to

Yǒude Shànghǎi rén bú huì shuō Zhōngwén, zhǐ huì shuō Shànghǎi huà.
有的上海人不会说中文，只会说上海话。
Some Shanghainese people don't speak Chinese; they only speak Shanghainese.

3. 机会 **jīhuì** opportunity

Zhè shì hǎo jīhuì. Bié cuòguò.
这是好机会，别错过 。
This is a good opportunity. Don't miss it.

4. 会议 **huìyì** conference

Zhège huìyì shì guānyú yǔyán xuéxí hé yánjiūde.
这个会议是关于语言学习和研究的。
The meeting is about language study and research.

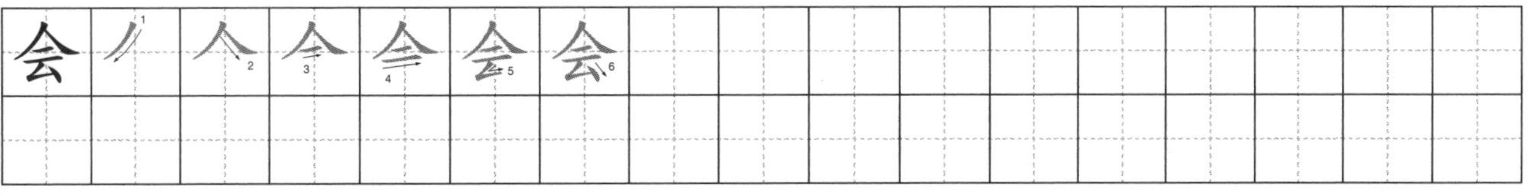

CHARACTER 235

tīng
listen; listening; hear

Useful phrases and sentences

7 STROKES | 口 RADICAL

1. 听 **tīng** listen
Xué Zhōngwénde xuésheng děi duō tīng Zhōngwén.
学中文的学生得多听中文。
Students of Chinese need to listen to Chinese more.

2. 听力 **tīnglì** listening proficiency
Tāde Fǎwén tīnglì hěn hǎo, shuōde yě bú cuò.
他的法文听力很好，说得也不错。
His French listening proficiency is good, and so is his speaking.

3. 听不到 **tīngbúdào** cannot hear
Wǒ tīngbúdào nǐ shuō shénme, qǐng dà sheng yīdiǎn.
我听不到你说什么，请大声一点。
I can't hear what you say. Please speak louder.

4. 听说 **tīngshuō** hear it said that; hearsay
Wǒ tīngshuō tā jīnnián jiǔyuè yào huí Zhōngguó le.
我听说她今年九月要回中国了。
I heard she is returning to China in September.

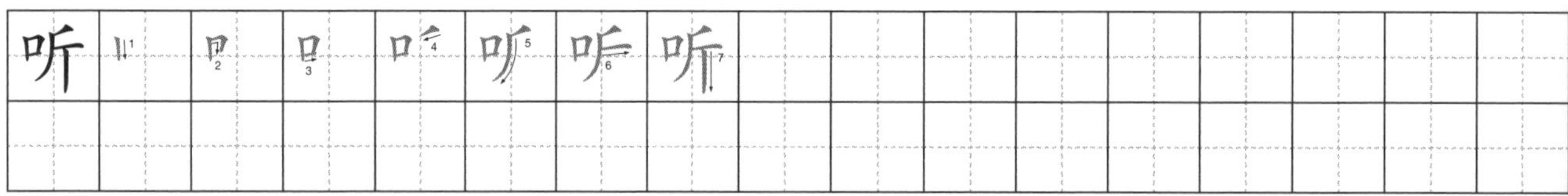

CHARACTER 236

说

shuō
speak; say

Useful phrases and sentences

9 STROKES | 讠 RADICAL

1. 说 **shuō** speak; say
Mànman shuō, bié jí.
慢慢说，别急。
Speak slowly, don't rush.

2. 说到 **shuō dào** speak of
Shuō dào zhèjiàn shì, Wáng Xiānsheng jiù bú tài gāoxìng.
说到这件事，王先生就不太高兴。
Mr. Wang is a bit upset when speaking of this matter.

3. 说话 **shuōhuà** talking; talk
Xiǎo háizi jǐsuì kāishǐ huì shuōhuà?
小孩子几岁开始会说话？
When do children start to talk?

4. 说谎 **shuōhuǎng** tell a lie
Nǐ yīnggāi xiāngxìn tā, tā cónglái bù shuōhuǎng.
你应该相信他，他从来不说谎。
You should trust him; he never lies.

说 1 2 3 4 5 6 7 8 9

CHARACTER 237

写

xiě
write; writing

Useful phrases and sentences

5 STROKES | 冖 RADICAL

1. 写 **xiě** write
Nǐ huì xiě duōshǎoge Hànzì?
你会写多少个汉字？
How many Chinese characters can you write?

2. 听写 **tīngxiě** dictation
Zhōngwén kè chángcháng yǒu tīngxiě, dànshi bù nán.
中文课常常有听写，但是不难。
We frequently take dictation in Chinese class, but it is not difficult.

3. 写作 **xiězuò** writing
Wén Xiānshengde zhuāncháng shì xiězuò.
文先生的专长是写作。
Writing is Mr. Wen's expertise.

4. 写信 **xiěxìn** write a letter
Nǐ xiànzài hái yòng shǒu xiěxìn ma?
你现在还用手写信吗？
Do you still do handwritten letters now?

写 1 2 3 4 5

CHARACTER 238

nán
difficult; hard

Useful phrases and sentences

10 STROKES | 又 RADICAL

1. 难 **nán** difficult; hard
Shuō Zhōngwén bǐjiào nán, háishì xiě Hànzì nán?
说中文比较难，还是写汉字难？
Is speaking Chinese more difficult or is writing Chinese characters?

2. 难过 **nánguò** sad
Wàn Xiānshengde fùqin zǒule, tā hěn nánguò.
万先生的父亲走了，他很难过。
Mr. Wan's father passed away. He is very sad.

3. 难怪 **nánguài** no wonder
Tā cóng xiǎo jiù xué yīnyuè, nánguài gāngqín tánde zhème hǎo!
他从小就学音乐，难怪钢琴弹得这么好！
He has learned music since little. No wonder he plays the piano so well.

4. 难吃 **nánchī** bad-tasting
Zhège fànguǎnde cài yǒudiǎnr nánchī.
这个饭馆的菜有点儿难吃。
The food in this restaurant is a bit bad-tasting.

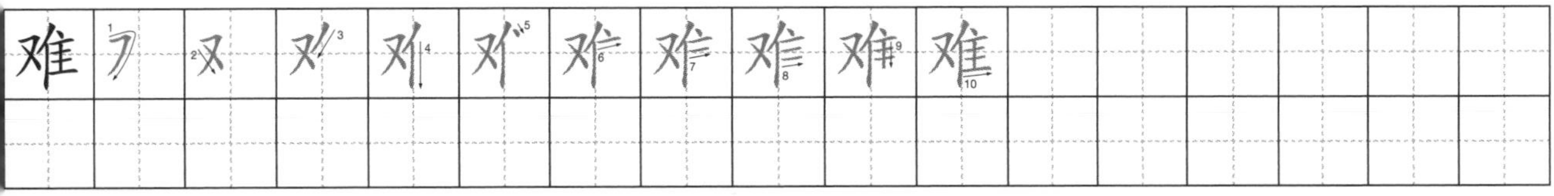

CHARACTER 239

róng
appearance; tolerate

Useful phrases and sentences

10 STROKES | 宀 RADICAL

1. 容貌 **róngmào** appearance; look
Shínián le, nǐde róngmào háishì méi biàn.
十年了，你的容貌还是没变。
It's been ten years. You haven't changed at all.

2. 内容 **nèiróng** content
Jīntiānde kè nèiróng búdàn duō, érqiě hěn nándǒng.
今天的课内容不但多，而且很难懂。
The contents of today's class is not only extensive, but also hard to understand.

3. 容忍 **róngrěn** tolerate; bear
Nǐ zuì bù néng róngrěnde shì shì shénme?
你最不能容忍的事是什么？
What is the thing you can least tolerate?

4. 宽容 **kuānróng** tolerant
Fùmǔ cháng gàosù wǒ, duì biérén yīnggāi kuānróng yìdiǎnr.
父母常告诉我，对别人应该宽容一点儿。
My parents always tell me to be tolerant towards others.

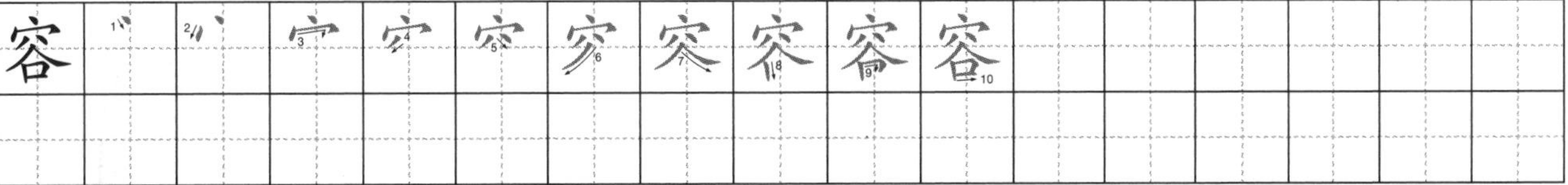

CHARACTER 240

yì
easy; trade

Useful phrases and sentences

8 STROKES | 日 RADICAL

1. 容易 **róngyì** easy
Zhōngguó hé Měiguó yíyàng, yào shàng yíge hǎo dàxué bù róngyì.
中国和美国一样，要上一个好大学不容易。
China and U.S.A. is the same in that it is not easy to attend a good college.

2. 轻易 **qīngyì** lightly; easily
Tā cóngbù qīngyì fàngqì.
他从不轻易放弃。
He never gives up easily.

3. 贸易 **màoyì** trade; business
Tā xuéde shì guójì màoyì, zhǎo gōngzuò yīnggāi bù nán.
他学的是国际贸易，找工作应该不难。
He studies international business. It shouldn't be difficult to find a job.

4. 易经 **Yìjīng** *The Book of Changes*
"Yìjīng" shì Zhōngguóde yīběn gǔshū.
"易经"是中国的一本古书。
The Book of Changes *is an Chinese ancient classic.*

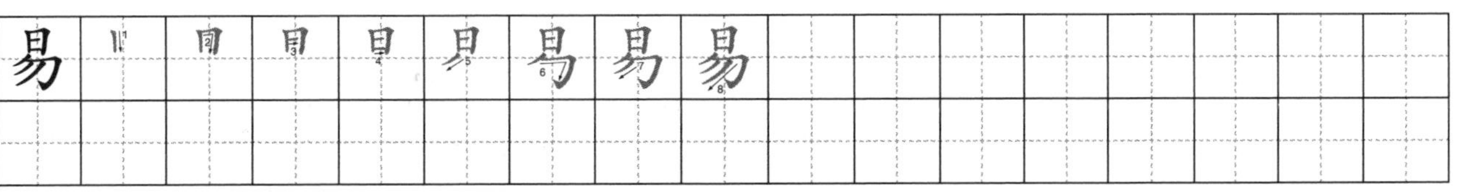

Lesson 16 Exercises

Part 1 Choose from the following words to fill in the blanks.

开始、会、左右、容易

1. 从我家走到学校要半个钟头（　　　　）。

2. 你是什么时候（　　　　）学中文的？

3. 我听别人说学中文很难，你为什么觉得很（　　　　）。

4. 明天你（　　　　）跟我们一起去吗？

Part 2 Complete the following dialogues using Chinese characters.

1. A: 你哪年开始学中文？你觉得中文难学吗？为什么？

   B: ______________________________。

2. A: 你觉得中文听、说、读、写，什么最难？

   B: ______________________________。

3. A: 今年你上什么课？什么课难？什么课容易？

   B: ______________________________。

4. A: 你最好的朋友叫什么名字？你们认识多久了？

   B: ______________________________。

5. A: 大学以后你会去哪儿工作？为什么？

   B: ______________________________。

Part 3 Make as many disyllabic words as you can by using the following characters.

很	远	方	周	好	也	容	易
吃	左	间	一	这	读	书	可
衣	右	侯	写	子	贵	认	以
喝	谁	舒	服	馆	客	识	便
后	来	儿	地	开	分	高	打
读	日	月	谢	始	昨	欢	人
哪	里	口	大	家	几	天	岁

1. ____________ 2. ____________ 3. ____________

4. ____________ 5. ____________ 6. ____________

7. ____________ 8. ____________ 9. ____________

LESSON 17

My Chinese class 我的中文课

1. Introduction

Have you wondered how Chinese people learn English at school? Traditionally, due to class size and limited resources, the majority of class time in an English class in China was allotted to vocabulary memorization, grammar, and translation. As a result, it was not uncommon for Chinese learners of English to have difficulty engaging in daily conversations in English when they go abroad. Recently, this situation has been somewhat ameliorated by the schools' recruitment of native English teachers to help with English instruction.

Does your school offer any Chinese language classes? If so, what kind of activities do you usually do in class? Are there any Chinese culture events on your campus as well? What is your favorite event?

2. Warm up

Read the passage below and answer the questions using Chinese characters.

> 我很喜欢我的中文课。我的中文老师姓王，她是西安人，已经在美国十年了。王老师常常说，中文听说读写都很重要。上课的时候，我们先练习听和说，然后学读汉字和写汉字，还有复习。王老师也常常说很多中国文化、历史跟节日的事，都很有意思。学中文我很高兴，只有一件事我不太喜欢，那就是考试，请你不要跟王老师说。

1. Who is the speaker's Chinese teacher? Where is she from?

   ____。

2. What do they do in a Chinese class?

   ____。

3. Besides the Chinese language, what else does Teacher Wang also introduce in class?

   ____。

3. Vocabulary

	Word	Pinyin	English equivalent
1.	西安	**Xī'ān**	Xi'an (city name)
2.	常常	**chángcháng**	frequent; often
3.	重要	**zhòngyào**	important
4.	上课	**shàngkè**	in class
5.	先	**xiān**	first
6.	练习	**liànxí**	practice
7.	然后	**ránhòu**	then
8.	复习	**fùxí**	review
9.	文化	**wénhuà**	culture
10.	历史	**lìshǐ**	history
11.	跟	**gēn**	and
12.	节日	**jiérì**	holiday
13.	事	**shì**	thing; affair
14.	有意思	**yǒu yìsi**	interesting
15.	高兴	**gāoxìng**	happy
16.	考试	**kǎoshì**	test; exam
17.	不要	**búyào**	don't

4. New Characters

Fifteen characters are introduced in this lesson. Use the following explanations to help you understand and remember the characters.

考 最 练 复 习 话 先 然 用 历 史 化 节 跟 课

CHARACTER 241

kǎo
test; check

Useful phrases and sentences

6 STROKES | 老 RADICAL

1. 考试 **kǎoshì** test; exam

Zhècì kǎoshì hěn nán, dàjiā dōu kǎode bù hǎo.
这次考试很难，大家都考得不好。
This test was hard. No one did well.

2. 高考 **Gāokǎo** College Entrance Examination (China)

"Gāokǎo" shì Zhōngguó shàng dàxué zuì zhòngyàode kǎoshì.
"高考"是中国上大学最重要的考试。
"Gaokao" is the most important examination to enter college in China.

3. 考虑 **kǎolǜ** consider; think over

Qù Zhōngguó háishì zài Měiguó gōngzuò, wǒ děi kǎolǜ yíxià.
去中国还是在美国工作，我得考虑一下。
I need to think about working in China or the U.S.A.

4. 考验 **kǎoyàn** task; test

Yíge rén zài guówài shēnghuó shì hěn dàde kǎoyàn.
一个人在国外生活是很大的考验。
It is a big task for a person to live on his/her own in a foreign country.

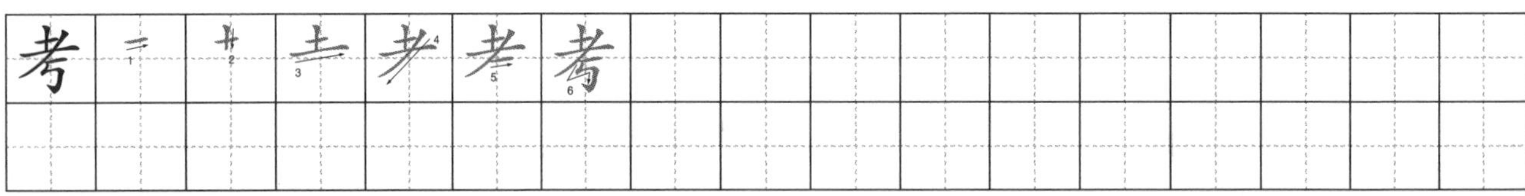

CHARACTER 242

zuì
most

Useful phrases and sentences

12 STROKES | 日 RADICAL

1. 最后 **zuìhòu** the last

Tā xǐhuan zuòzài zuìhòu yìpái.
他喜欢坐在最后一排。
He likes to sit in the back row.

2. 最好 **zuìhǎo** had better; the best

Nǐ zuìhǎo qù kàn yíxià yīsheng.
你最好去看一下医生。
You'd better go see a doctor.

3. 最近 **zuìjìn** recent time

Zuìjìn tiānqì tèbié rè, wǒ nǎr dōu bù xiǎng qù.
最近天气特别热，我哪儿都不想去。
It's been very hot recently. I do not want to go anywhere.

4. 最初 **zuìchū** at first

Wǒ zuìchū rènshi tā shì zài wǒ shàng zhōngxué de shíhou.
我最初认识他是在我上中学的时候。
I first got to know him in my middle school days.

CHARACTER 243

liàn
practice; train

Useful phrases and sentences

8 STROKES | 纟 RADICAL

1. 锻炼 **duànliàn** work out

Wǒ měige xīngqī dōu yào chūqu duànliàn liǎngsāncì.
我每个星期都要出去锻炼两三次。
I work out 2-3 times every week.

2. 训练 **xùnliàn** training; train

Yīnwèi píngshíde xùnliàn, suóyi tā shàngtái shí yìdiǎnr dōu bù jǐnzhāng.
因为平时的训练，所以她上台时一点儿都不紧张。
Because of her regular training, she is not nervous at all when she is on stage.

3. 熟练 **shúliàn** skilled; proficient

Zhège dòngzuò wǒ cháng liànxí, suóyi hěn shúliàn.
这个动作我常练习，所以很熟练。
I practice this movement quite often, so I am skilled.

4. 教练 **jiàoliàn** sports coach; trainer

Nèiwèi shì wǒde wǎngqiú jiàoliàn, tā shì Bōshìdùn rén.
那位是我的网球教练，他是波士顿人。
That is my tennis coach. He is from Boston.

CHARACTER 244

fù
repeat; return

Useful phrases and sentences

9 STROKES | 夂 RADICAL

1. 复印 **fùyìn** photocopy

Nǐ kěyǐ fùyìn yíxià zhèpiān kèwén ma?
你可以复印一下这篇课文吗？
Could you please make one copy of this lesson text?

2. 回复 **huífù** respond; reply

Wǒ gěi tā xiěle yīfēng diànzǐ yóujiàn, kěshì tā méi huífù.
我给他写了一封电子邮件，可是他没回复。
I wrote him an email, but he didn't respond.

3. 重复 **chóngfù** repeat; repeatedly

Zhège dōngxi kěyǐ chóngfù shǐyòng.
这个东西可以重复使用。
This thing can be used repeatedly.

4. 复活节 **Fùhuójié** Easter

Fùhuójié zài Ōuměi shì zhòngyàode jiérì.
复活节在欧美是重要的节日。
Easter is an important holiday in Europe and the US.

复

CHARACTER 245

xí
study; habit

Useful phrases and sentences

3 STROKES | 乙 RADICAL

1. 练习 **liànxí** practice

Jìzhù Hànzì zuì hǎode fāngfǎ jiùshì duō dú hé měitiān liànxí xiě.
记住汉字最好的方法就是多读和每天练习写。
The best way to remember Chinese characters is to read more and practice writing them every day.

2. 复习 **fùxí** review

Lǎoshī shuō: kèqián yùxí, shàngkè zhuānxīn, kèhòu fùxí.
老师说：课前预习，上课专心，课后复习。
The teacher says: preview before class, concentrate in class, and review after class.

3. 学习 **xuéxí** learning; learn

Xiǎo Fāng hěn xǐhuan xuéxí, tā duì shùxué hé kēxué tèbié yǒu xìngqù.
小方很喜欢学习，他对数学和科学特别有兴趣。
Xiao Fang loves learning. He is particularly interested in math and science.

4. 习惯 **xíguàn** habit; become accustomed to

Měige rén dōu yǒu zìjǐde xíguàn.
每个人都有自己的习惯。
Everyone has their own habits.

习

CHARACTER 246

huà
language; speech

Useful phrases and sentences

8 STROKES | 讠 RADICAL

1. 话题 **huàtí** topic

Nǐmende Zhōngwénkè tǎolùnguo shénme huàtí?
你们的中文课讨论过什么话题？
What topics did you discuss in your Chinese class?

2. 会话 **huìhuà** conversation; dialogue

Zhōngwén yī hé Zhōngwén èr xuéde dōu shì shēnghuó huìhuà.
中文一和中文二学的都是生活会话。
Chinese I and Chinese II are all about daily conversations.

3. 打电话 **dǎ diànhuà** make a phone call

Míngtiān shì māmade shēngrì, jìde gěi tā dǎ diànhuà.
明天是妈妈的生日，记得给她打电话。
Tomorrow is mother's birthday. Remember to call her.

4. 多话 **duōhuà** talkative; verbose

Wáng Lǎoshī rén hěn hǎo, jiùshi yǒu yìdiǎnr duōhuà.
王老师人很好，就是有一点儿多话。
Teacher Wang is a nice person. It's just that he/she is a little talkative.

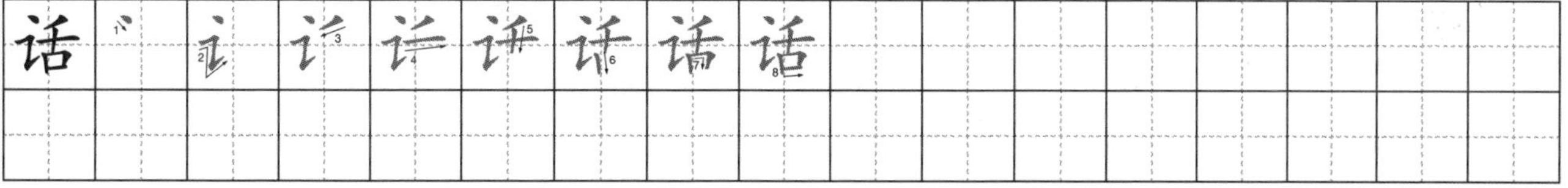

CHARACTER 247

xiān
first; prior

Useful phrases and sentences

6 STROKES | 儿 RADICAL

1. 先 **xiān** first

Jīntiān wǒmen xiān fùxí, ránhòu kǎoshì.
今天我们先复习，然后考试。
Today we review first and then we take a test.

2. 先生 **Xiānsheng** Mr.

Wén Xiānsheng niánjì bú dà, chàbùduō sìshísuì zuǒyòu.
文先生年纪不大，差不多四十岁左右。
Mr. Wen is not that old. He is about forty.

3. 事先 **shìxiān** in advance

Jīntiān shì xīngqīwǔ. Yàoshì nǐ xiǎng dào nàjiā fànguǎn chīfàn, zuìhǎo shìxiān dìngwèi.
今天是星期五。要是你想到那家饭馆吃饭，最好事先订位。
Today is Friday. If you want to go to that restaurant, you'd better book in advance.

4. 祖先 **zǔxiān** ancestor

Nǐde zǔxiān shì cóng shénme dìfang láide?
你的祖先是从什么地方来的？
Where were your ancestors from?

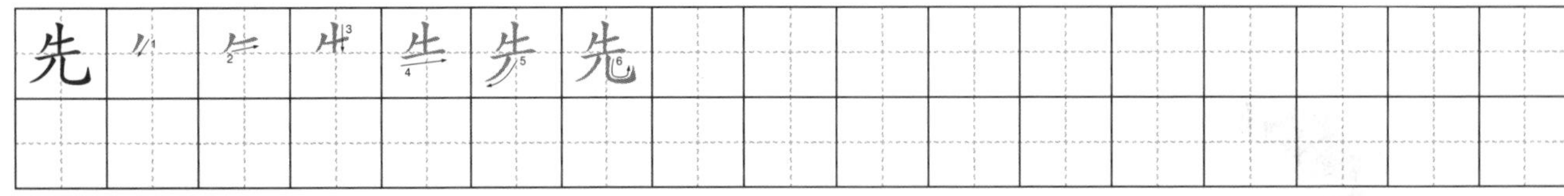

CHARACTER 248

rán
so; thus

Useful phrases and sentences

12 STROKES | 灬 RADICAL

1. 然后 **ránhòu** then

Nǐ xiān wǎng qián zǒu, ránhòu wǎng yòu zhuǎn, jiù dàole.
你先往前走，然后往右转，就到了。
You go straight first and then turn right. You'll be there.

2. 当然 **dāngrán** of course; without doubt; certainly

Zhège dōngxi shǎo, dāngrán bù piányi.
这个东西少，当然不便宜。
There are few of these things, so it is of course not cheap.

3. 突然 **tūrán** suddenly

Jīntiān wǒ zǒulù huíjiāde shíhou, tūrán xià qǐle dà yǔ.
今天我走路回家的时候，突然下起了大雨。
When I was walking home today, it suddenly began to rain heavily.

4. 虽然 **suīrán** although

Suīrán Hànzì hěn nán xiě, dànshì yuè xué yuè yǒu yìsi.
虽然汉字很难写，但是越学越有意思。
Although Chinese characters are difficult to write, the more I learn, the more interesting I find them.

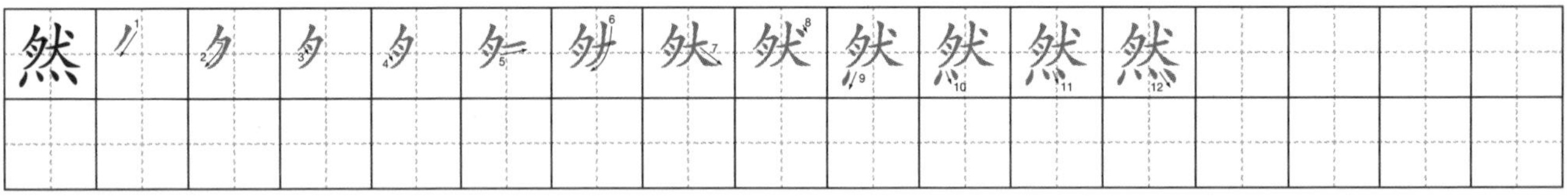

CHARACTER 249

yòng
use; employ

Useful phrases and sentences

5 STROKES | 用 RADICAL

1. 有用 **yǒuyòng** useful

Zhège dōngxi duì nǐ hěn yǒuyòng, duì wǒ méi yǒuyòng.
这个东西对你很有用，对我没有用。
This thing is useful for you, but not for me.

2. 用功 **yònggōng** diligent; hardworking

Wáng Tàitàide nǚ'ér hěn yònggōng, tiāntiān xuéxí.
王太太的女儿很用功，天天学习。
Mrs. Wang's daughter is diligent. She studies every day.

3. 使用 **shǐyòng** use

Kě-bù-kěyǐ qǐng nǐ jiāo wǒ zěnme shǐyòng zhège APP?
可不可以请你教我怎么使用这个APP？
Can you teach me how to use this app?

4. 用品 **yòngpǐn** goods; utensils

Rúguǒ nǐ hái xūyào shénme shēnghuó yòngpǐn, ràng wǒ zhīdao.
如果你还需要什么生活用品，让我知道。
If you still need any other daily utensils, let me know.

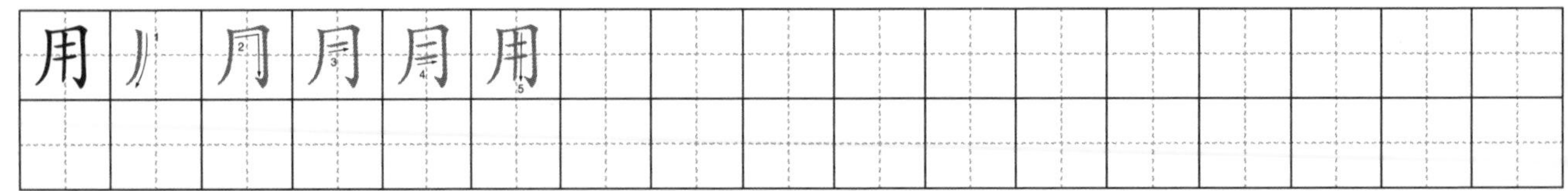

CHARACTER 250

lì
history; experience

Useful phrases and sentences

4 STROKES | 厂 RADICAL

1. 日历 **rìlì** calendar

Nǐ xīnmǎide rìlì hěn piàoliang.
你新买的日历很漂亮。
The new calendar you bought looks very pretty.

2. 经历 **jīnglì** experience

Yǒule zhège jīnglì, wǒ yǐhòu yídìng tíqián sānge xiǎoshí dào jīchǎng.
有了这个经历，我以后一定提前三个小时到机场。
With this experience, I will be sure to arrive at the airport three hours in advance in the future.

3. 学历 **xuélì** academic degree

Nǐ juéde xuélì zhòngyào háishì jīnglì zhòngyào?
你觉得学历重要还是经历重要？
Which one do you think is more important? Experience or academic degree?

4. 简历 **jiǎnlì** curriculum vitae

Yàoshì nǐ duì wǒmende gōngzuò yǒu xìngqu, máfan jì yīfèn jiǎnlì.
要是你对我们的工作有兴趣，麻烦寄一份简历。
If you are interested in our job, please send us your CV.

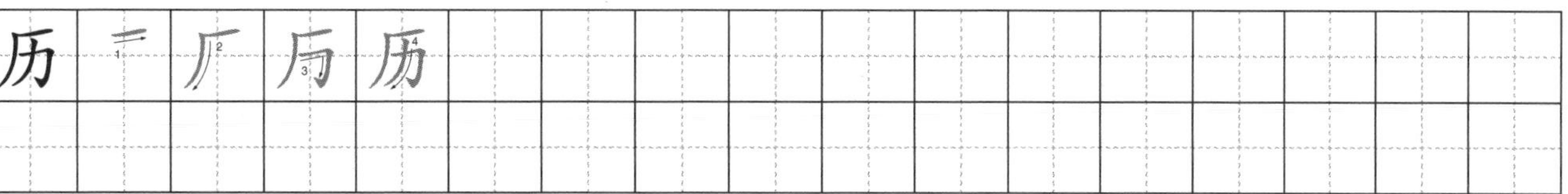

CHARACTER 251

shǐ
history; annal

Useful phrases and sentences

5 STROKES | 口 RADICAL

1. 历史 **lìshǐ** history

Tā fùqin shì yíwèi lìshǐ jiàoshòu, zhuānmén yánjiū Zhōngdōng lìshǐ.
他父亲是一位历史教授，专门研究中东历史。
His father is a history professor. His expertise is the history of the Middle East.

2. 史料 **shǐliào** historical material

Zhèxiē shǐliào duì wǒde yánjiū huì hěn yǒuyòng.
这些史料对我的研究会很有用。
These historical materials will be very useful for my research.

3. 史诗 **shǐshī** epic tale/poem

Nǐ zuì xǐhuan nǎgè xīyáng shǐshī?
你最喜欢哪个西洋史诗？
Which western epic is your favorite?

4. 史 **Shǐ** (surname)

Shǐ Lǎoshī shì Tiānjīn rén, xiànzài zhù zài Měiguó dōngàn.
史老师是天津人，现在住在美国东岸。
Teacher Shi is from Tianjin. He/She now lives on the East Coast of the U.S.A.

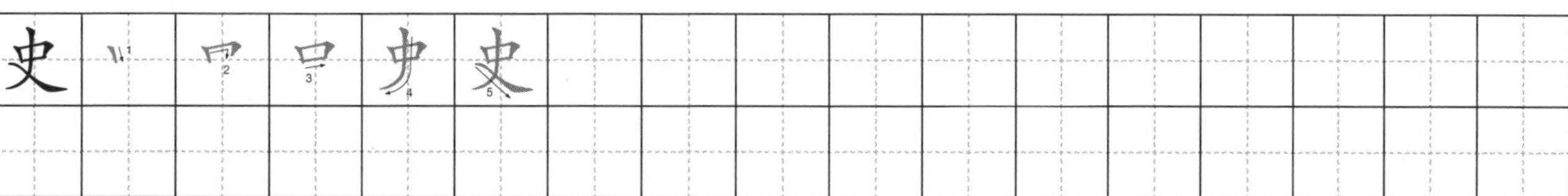

CHARACTER 252

huà
transform; make into

Useful phrases and sentences

4 STROKES | 亻 RADICAL

1. 化 **huà** melt

Xuě yǐjīng huàle.
雪已经化了。
The snow has melted.

2. 全球化 **quánqiúhuà** globalization

Quánqiúhuà ràng bùtóng wénhuàde rén yǒu yuè lái yuè duōde hùdòng.
全球化让不同文化的人有越来越多的互动。
Globalization provides more and more opportunities for people of different cultures to interact.

3. 变化 **biànhuà** change

Shínián le, zhège dìfang háishì méiyǒu shénme biànhuà.
十年了，这个地方还是没有什么变化。
It has been ten years, and this place still has not changed.

4. 西化 **xīhuà** westernized

Yǒurénshuō Zhōngguó rénde shēnghuó xíguàn yǐjīng xīhuàle.
有人说中国人的生活习惯已经西化了。
Some people say that the Chinese people's lifestyle is getting westernized.

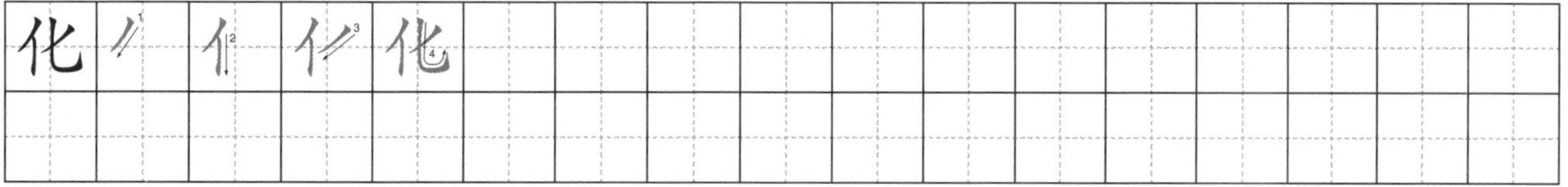

CHARACTER 253

节

jié
festival; holiday

Useful phrases and sentences

5 STROKES | 艹 RADICAL

1. 节日 **jiérì** holiday

Zhōngguó zuì zhòngyàode jiérì shì shénmē?
中国最重要的节日是什么？
What is the most important holiday in China?

2. 节庆 **jiéqìng** festival

Měi nián bāyuè zhège xiǎozhèn huì yǒu yíge dàde jiéqìng.
每年八月这个小镇会有一个大的节庆。
There is a big festival in this town in August every year.

3. 节省 **jiéshěng** save

Jiéshěng yìdiǎnr, bié huā tài duō qián.
节省一点儿，别花太多钱。
Save some money. Don't spend too much.

4. 圣诞节 **Shèngdànjié** Christmas

Shèngdànjié shì shí'èryuè èrshíwǔhào.
圣诞节是十二月二十五号。
Christmas is on December 25th.

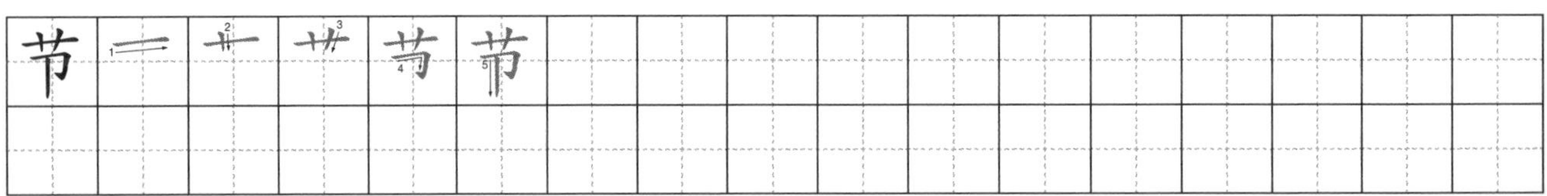

CHARACTER 254

跟

gēn
and; with

Useful phrases and sentences

13 STROKES | 足 RADICAL

1. 跟 **gēn** and

Lǐ Xiānsheng gēn Lǐ Tàitài dōu shì lìshǐ lǎoshī.
李先生跟李太太都是历史老师。
Mr. Li and Mrs. Li are both history teachers.

2. 跟 **gēn** with

Jīntiān wǎnshang yǒu-méi-yǒukòng? Yào-bú-yào gēn wǒ yìqǐ qù kàn diànyǐng?
今天晚上有没有空？要不要跟我一起去看电影？
Do you have time this evening? Do you want to go to a movie with me?

3. 跟着 **gēnzhe** follow

Wǒ zhīdao nàge fànguǎnr, nǐ gēnzhe wǒ zǒuba.
我知道那个饭馆儿，你跟着我走吧。
I know that restaurant. You can just follow me.

4. 跟前 **gēnqián** vicinity

Nǐde shūbāo jiù zài zhuōzi gēnqián, nǐ méi kàndào ma?
你的书包就在桌子跟前，你没看到吗？
Your bag is just next to your desk. Can't you see it?

CHARACTER 255

课

kè
class; course

Useful phrases and sentences

10 STROKES | 讠 RADICAL

1. 中文课 **Zhōngwénkè** Chinese class

Wǒ yàoqù shàng Zhōngwénkè le, xiàwǔ jiàn.
我要去上中文课了，下午见！
Now I will go to Chinese class. See you this afternoon.

2. 课本 **kèběn** textbook

Kèběn yìnián bǐ yìnián guì, wǒ dōu shàngbuqixué le.
课本一年比一年贵，我都上不起学了！
Textbooks are getting more expensive every year. I can't afford to go to school any more.

3. 课外 **kèwài** after-class time; extracurricular

Zài Zhōngguó, xuésheng kèwài chángcháng zuò shénme?
在中国，学生课外常常做什么？
In China, what do students do after class?

4. 选修课 **xuǎnxiūkè** elective course

Zhè xuéqī wǒ huìshàng liǎngmén xuǎnxiūkè.
这学期我会上两门选修课。
I will take two elective courses this semester.

Lesson 17 Exercises

Part 1 Choose from the following words to fill in the blanks.

然后、有意思、常常 、跟

1. 你想（　　　　）我一起去吃晚饭吗？

2. 我想先去买东西，（　　　　）回宿舍写作业。

3. 这个电影很（　　　　），大家一边看一边笑。

4. 你（　　　　）跟老师练习说中文，是吗？

Part 2 Complete the following dialogues using Chinese characters.

1. A: 你喜欢学习中国文化吗？

   B: ____。

2. A: 你周末的时候常常做什么？

   B: ____。

3. A: 你喜欢一个人学习还是跟朋友一起学习？

   B: ____。

4. A: 你每天几点上中文课？一个星期有几节中文课？

   B: ____。

5. A: 你觉得什么节日最有意思？为什么？

   B: ____。

Part 3 Practice writing emails using Chinese characters. You may use the following closing part to conclude your email.

Your friend, 小王, wants to take the beginning-level Chinese class next year. He wrote you an email with several questions. Respond to 小王 by writing an email in Chinese characters. Please use the provided format and follow the instructions:

- Answer the question: 中文听说读写难不难？
- Answer the question: 中文考试多不多？
- Answer the question: 中文课有多少学生？
- Answer the question: 你的中文老师怎么样？
- Conclude your email with "这是我的想法，要是你还有别的问题，请告诉我。" followed by "祝好，" in the beginning of a separate line.
- Sign your name.

小王:

你说你明年也想学中文，我觉得这是一个很好的决定。

____

____

____

____

____

____

LESSON 18

A typical day 我的一天

1. Introduction

What is your typical day like? If you are a student, your typical day may include getting-up, going to class, hanging out with friends, and studying. If you are raising a family, your daily activities will be understandably different from your time as a student. Research shows that people engage in no more than ten conversational scenarios on a daily basis, such as parent-child, teacher-student, friend-friend, supervisor-subordinate, clerk-customer, etc. The research also applies cross-culturally.

2. Warm up

Read the passage below and answer the questions using Chinese characters.

我姓史，今年四十二岁。我有太太，一个儿子跟一个女儿。儿子今年十七岁，女儿今年十五岁。我平常工作很忙，很晚回家。回家以后，看看新闻就睡觉了。周末的时候，我喜欢在家休息，也喜欢和女儿跟儿子聊天、运动。我的儿子明年要读大学了，可是他现在每天上网，看电脑，还跟我说他有"半个"女朋友。我问他"半个女朋友"是什么意思，他说"半个"就是"不是一个"，他也还没决定。我的天啊！

1. Who is the narrator? Can you briefly describe his family?

____。

2. What does the narrator like to do on the weekend?

____。

3. Why is the narrator a bit concerned about his son?

____。

3. Vocabulary

	Word	Pinyin	English equivalent
1.	史	**Shǐ**	Shi (surname)
2.	今年	**jīnnián**	this year
3.	...以后	**...yǐhòu**	after …
4.	新闻	**xīnwén**	news
5.	睡觉	**shuìjiào**	sleep
6.	休息	**xiūxi**	rest; take a break
7.	聊天	**liáotiān**	chat
8.	运动	**yùndòng**	exercise; work out
9.	大学	**dàxué**	university; college
10.	上网	**shàngwǎng**	surf the internet
11.	电脑	**diànnǎo**	computer
12.	半	**bàn**	half
13.	意思	**yìsi**	meaning
14.	决定	**juédìng**	decide
15.	我的天啊	**Wǒde tiān a**	Oh, my goodness!

4. New Characters

Fifteen characters are introduced in this lesson. Use the following explanations to help you understand and remember the characters.

事 睡 半 间 脑 邮 网 读 新 闻 运 动 休 息 聊

CHARACTER 256

shì
thing; affair

Useful phrases and sentences

8 STROKES | 一 RADICAL

1. 事情 **shìqing** thing; affair
   Jīntiān xiàwǔ wǒ yǒu hěnduō shìqing.
   今天下午我有很多事情。
   I have many things to do this afternoon.

2. 事故 **shìgù** accident
   Tā zài jiāotōng shìgù zhōng shòule shāng.
   他在交通事故中受了伤。
   He was injured in a car accident.

3. 故事 **gùshì** story
   Tā hěn xǐhuan kàn tónghuà gùshì.
   她很喜欢看童话故事。
   She likes to read fairy tales.

4. 有事 **yǒu shì** have something to do
   Duìbùqǐ, wǒ yǒu shì, xiān zǒule.
   对不起，我有事，先走了。
   Sorry, I have something to do. I'll be going.

CHARACTER 257

shuì
sleep

Useful phrases and sentences

13 STROKES | 目 RADICAL

1. 睡着 **shuìzháo** fall asleep
   Míngtiān yào kǎoshì, wǒ yīwǎnshang méi shuìzháo.
   明天要考试，我一晚上没睡着。
   My exam is tomorrow. I could not sleep the whole night.

2. 睡眠 **shuìmián** sleep *(noun)*
   Tā zuìjìn yālì bǐjiào dà, shuìmián yǒu diǎnr wèntí.
   他最近压力比较大，睡眠有点儿问题。
   He has been pretty stressed recently. He has some problems with sleep.

3. 睡 **shuì** sleep *(verb)*
   Wǒmen xuéxiàode xuésheng měitiān shuì chàbùduō liùge xiǎoshí.
   我们学校的学生每天睡差不多六个小时。
   Our students sleep about six hours per day.

4. 午睡 **wǔshuì** afternoon nap
   Zhège guójiāde rén yǒu wǔshuìde xíguàn.
   这个国家的人有午睡的习惯。
   People in this country have the habit of taking afternoon naps.

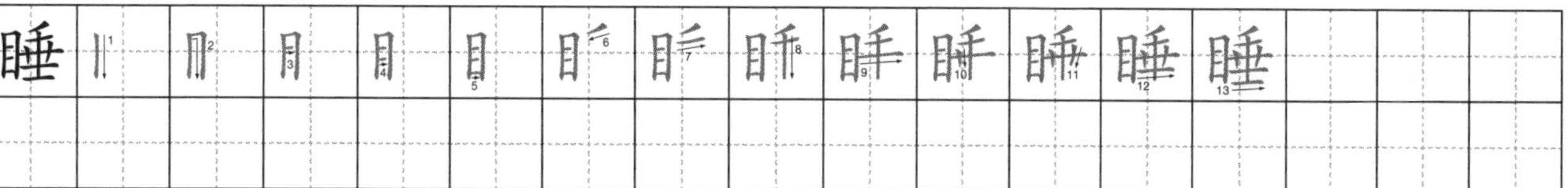

CHARACTER 258

bàn
half

Useful phrases and sentences

5 STROKES | 十 RADICAL

1. 一半 **yíbàn** half
   Wǒ érzi bānshàng yǒu yíbànde xuésheng lái zì Shēnzhèn.
   我儿子班上有一半的学生来自深圳。
   Half of the students in my son's class are from Shenzhen.

2. 半年 **bànnián** half a year
   Wǒ lái Xiānggǎng yǐjīng bànniánle.
   我来香港已经半年了。
   I have been in Hong Kong for half a year.

3. 多半 **duōbàn** most; mostly
   Zhōumòde shíhou xuéshengmen duōbàn zài xiūxi huò shuìjiào.
   周末的时候学生们多半在休息或睡觉。
   Students are mostly resting or sleeping on the weekend.

4. 半个月 **bàn'ge yuè** half a month (2 weeks)
   Tā xiàge yuè yào qù Mòxīgē bàn'ge yuè.
   他下个月要去墨西哥半个月。
   He is going to Mexico for two weeks next month.

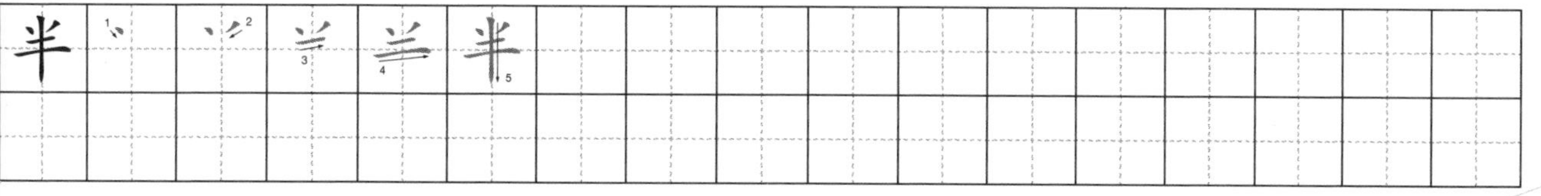

CHARACTER 259

jiān
room; a definite time or space

Useful phrases and sentences

7 STROKES | 门 RADICAL

1. 间 **jiān** measure word for smallest units of a house or classroom
   Zhèjiān jiàoshì hěn xiǎo, kěshì hěn gānjìng.
   这间教室很小，可是很干净。
   This classroom is small but clean.

2. 房间 **fángjiān** room
   Niǔyuē lǚguǎnde fángjiān dōu bú dà, dàn dōu hěn guì.
   纽约旅馆的房间都不大，但都很贵。
   The hotel rooms in New York city are not big, but they are all expensive.

3. 中间 **zhōngjiān** middle
   Xiǎo Qián jiā yǒu sānge háizi, tā yǒu yíge jiějie, yíge dìdi, tā zài zhōngjiān.
   小钱家有三个孩子，他有一个姐姐，一个弟弟，他在中间。
   There are three children in Xiao Qian's family. He has an older sister and a younger brother. He is in the middle.

4. 空间 **kōngjiān** space
   Zhège fángzi yǒu sìge fángjiān, kōngjiān hěn dà.
   这个房子有四个房间，空间很大。
   This house has four rooms. It has a lot of space.

CHARACTER 260

nǎo
brain; mind

Useful phrases and sentences

10 STROKES | 月 RADICAL

1. 电脑 **diànnǎo** computer
   Yǒuxiē shì diànnǎo néng zuòde gèng jīngquè.
   有些事电脑能做得更精确。
   Computers can do certain things more accurately.

2. 大脑 **dànǎo** brain
   Xīyī juéde dànǎo shì rénlèi zuì zhòngyàode qìguān.
   西医觉得大脑是人类最重要的器官。
   Western medicine thinks that the brain is the most important human organ.

3. 头脑 **tóunǎo** brain
   Tāde tóunǎo hěn hǎo, fǎnyìng hěn kuài.
   他的头脑很好，反应很快。
   His brain is good. He is quick at responding.

4. 电脑科学 **diànnǎo kēxué** computer science
   Máshěng Lǐgōng Xuéyuànde diànnǎo kēxué hěn yǒu míng.
   麻省理工学院的电脑科学很有名。
   MIT's computer science department is quite well-known.

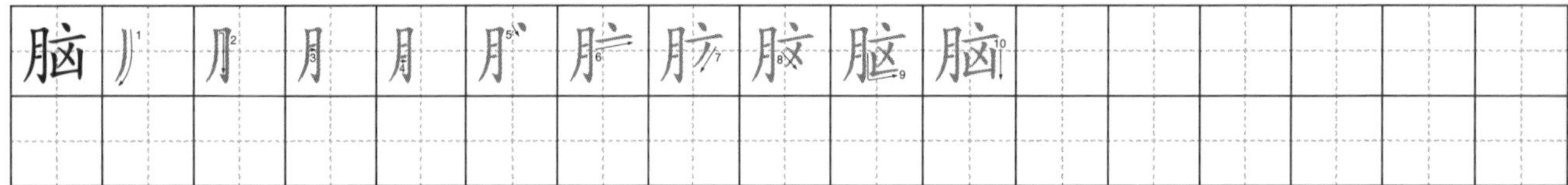

CHARACTER 261

yóu
post

Useful phrases and sentences

7 STROKES | 阝 RADICAL

1. 邮局 **yóujú** post office
   Qǐng wèn, zhèr nǎr yǒu yóujú?
   请问，这儿哪儿有邮局？
   Excuse, is there a post office around here?

2. 电子邮件 **diànzǐ yóujiàn** emails
   Nǐ yǒu jǐge diànzǐ yóujiàn?
   你有几个电子邮件？
   How many emails do you have?

3. 邮箱 **yóuxiāng** mailbox
   Qǐng wèn, zhèr nǎr yǒu yóuxiāng?
   请问，这儿哪儿有邮箱？
   Excuse me, are there any mail boxes around here?

4. 邮票 **yóupiào** stamp
   Cóng Zhōngguó dào Hánguó děi tiē jǐkuài qiánde yóupiào?
   从中国到韩国得贴几块钱的邮票？
   How much is a stamp for a letter from China to Korea?

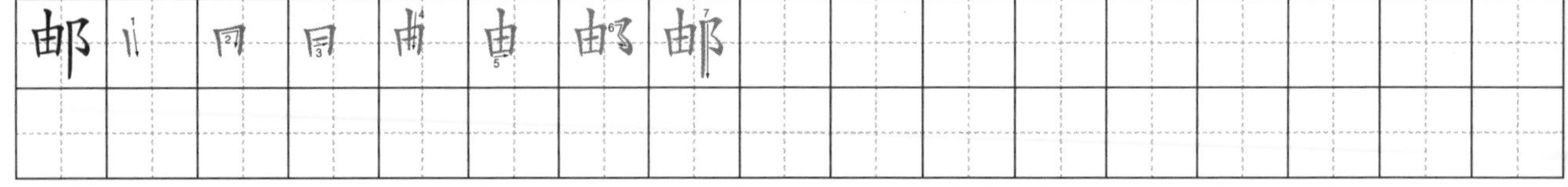

CHARACTER 262

wǎng
net; internet

Useful phrases and sentences

6 STROKES | 冂 RADICAL

1. 上网 **shàngwǎng** surf the internet

Xiànzài hěnduō rén dàole yíge xīn dìfang, dìyíge wèntí shì "zhèlǐ kěyǐ shàngwǎng ma"?
现在很多人到了一个新地方，第一个问题是"这里可以上网吗"？
Nowadays when people arrive at a new place, their first question is "How can I get on the internet here?"

2. 网站 **wǎngzhàn** website

Nǐ zuì xǐhuande wǎngzhàn shì nǎge?
你最喜欢的网站是哪个？
What is your favorite website?

3. 网路 **wǎnglù** internet

Shìjiè shàng hái yǒu hěnduō dìfang méiyǒu wǎnglù.
世界上还有很多地方没有网路。
There are still many places in the world that don't have the internet.

4. 网上 **wǎng shàng** on the internet

Wǎng shàng yǒu hěnduō xìnxī, yǒude duì, yǒude bú duì.
网上有很多信息，有的对，有的不对。
There is a lot of information on the internet. Some is correct while some is not.

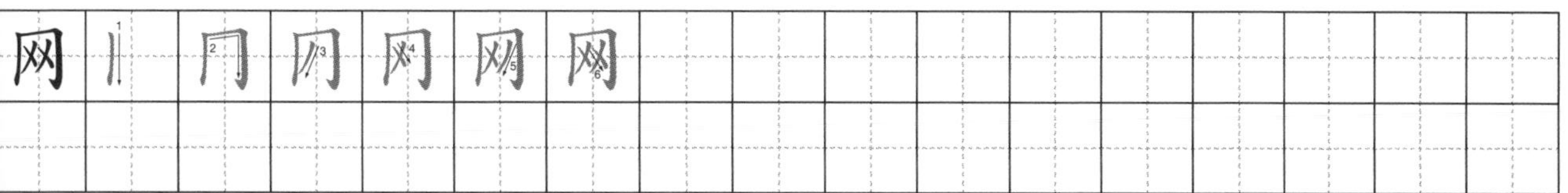

CHARACTER 263

dú
read; study

Useful phrases and sentences

10 STROKES | 讠 RADICAL

1. 读书 **dúshū** studying; study

Xiǎo shíhou wǒ dìdi bú tài xǐhuan dúshū, juéde hěn méiyǒu yìsi.
小时候我弟弟不太喜欢读书，觉得很没有意思。
My younger brother didn't like studying when he was little. He felt bored with it.

2. 听说读写 **tīng shuō dú xiě** listening, speaking, reading and writing

Xué Zhōngwén tīng shuō dú xiě dōu hěn zhòngyào.
学中文听说读写都很重要。
Listening, speaking, reading, and writing are all important for learning Chinese.

3. 工读 **gōngdú** work part-time (while you study)

Wèile bāngzhù fùmǔ, Xiǎo Chén xiàle kè yǐhòu zài sùshídiàn gōngdú.
为了帮助父母，小陈下了课以后在速食店工读。
To help his parents, Xiao Chen works as a part-timer at a fast food restaurant after class.

4. 阅读 **yuèdú** reading

Wǒde àihào shì yuèdú, nǐ ne?
我的爱好是阅读，你呢？
My hobby is reading. How about you?

CHARACTER 264

xīn
new

Useful phrases and sentences

13 STROKES | 斤 RADICAL

1. 新潮 **xīncháo** fashionable

Tā chuānde yīfu tài xīncháo le.
他穿的衣服太新潮了。
Her clothes were overly fashionable.

2. 新年 **xīnnián** new year

Xīnnián shì Zhōngguó zuì zhòngyàode jiérì.
新年是中国最重要的节日。
Chinese New Year is the most important holiday in China.

3. 新鲜 **xīnxiān** fresh

Nèijiā diàn màide qīngcài dōu hěn xīnxiān.
那家店卖的青菜都很新鲜。
The vegetables sold at that store are all fresh.

4. 新生 **xīnshēng** new student

Tā jīnnián shíqīsuì, míngnián jiù shì dàyī xīnshēng le.
她今年十七岁，明年就是大一新生了。
She is seventeen years old. She will be a college freshman next year.

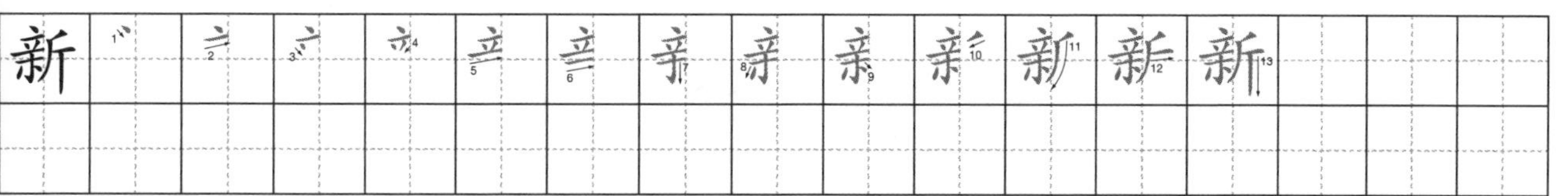

CHARACTER 265

wén
news; famous

Useful phrases and sentences

9 STROKES | 门 RADICAL

1. 新闻 **xīnwén** news

Hǎoxiàng niánqīng rén bú tài kàn xīnwén.
好像年轻人不太看新闻。
It seems that young people don't read the news.

2. 传闻 **chuánwén** rumor

Zuìjìn yǒu chuánwén wǒmen gōngsī yào hé lìngwài yìjiā gōngsī hébìng.
最近有传闻我们公司要和另外一家公司合并。
Recently a rumor says that our company and the other one will merge.

3. 以…闻名 **yǐ...wénmíng** famous for …

Gēlúnbǐyà yǐ kāfēi wénmíng.
哥伦比亚以咖啡闻名。
Colombia is famous for its coffee.

4. 要闻 **yàowén** important news

Zuìjìn yǒu shénme yàowén ma?
最近有什么要闻吗？
Is there any important news recently?

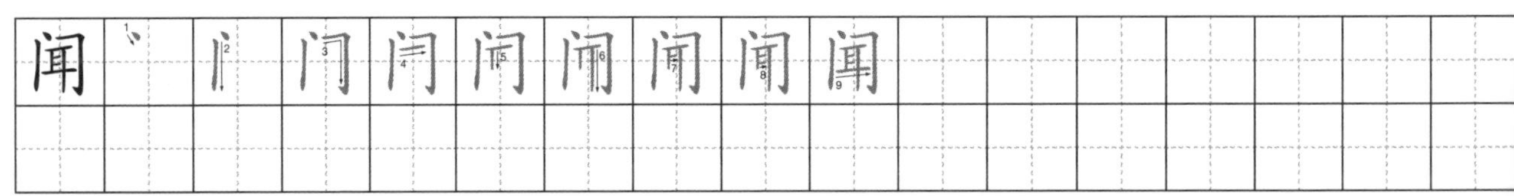

CHARACTER 266

yùn
move; luck

Useful phrases and sentences

7 STROKES | 辶 RADICAL

1. 运气 **yùnqi** luck

Jīntiān yùnqi bú cuò, huídào jiā yǐhòu cái xiàqi dàxuě.
今天运气不错，回到家以后才下起大雪。
I was lucky today. The heavy snow started after I came back home.

2. 运动 **yùndòng** exercise

Wǒ píngcháng gōngzuò tài máng, méiyǒu shíjiān yùndòng.
我平常工作太忙，没有时间运动。
I am usually busy and don't have time to exercise.

3. 运用 **yùnyòng** apply

Xuéle yíge jùxíng yǐhòu, děi zhīdao zěnme yùnyòng.
学了一个句型以后，得知道怎么运用。
You need to know how to apply it after learning a new sentence pattern.

4. 命运 **mìngyùn** fate; destiny

Nǐ xiāngxìn mìngyùn ma?
你相信命运吗？
Do you believe in fate?

CHARACTER 267

dòng
move; stir (the emotions)

Useful phrases and sentences

6 STROKES | 力 RADICAL

1. 动作片 **dòngzuòpiàn** action movie

Nǐ xǐhuan kàn dòngzuòpiàn ma?
你喜欢看动作片吗？
Do you like watching action movies?

2. 感动 **gǎndòng** moved; touched (emotionally)

Zhèbù diànyǐng tài bàng le, wǒ fēicháng gǎndòng.
这部电影太棒了，我非常感动。
This movie is excellent. It really moved me.

3. 动物 **dòngwù** animal

Xīnqíng bù hǎode shíhou, wǒ xǐhuan qù dòngwùyuán kàn dòngwù.
心情不好的时候，我喜欢去动物园看动物。
I like to go to the zoo to see animals when I am in a bad mood.

4. 活动 **huódòng** activity; event

Wǒmen xì shàng chángcháng jǔbàn huódòng.
我们系上常常举办活动。
Our department often holds activities.

CHARACTER 268

xiū
rest

Useful phrases and sentences

6 STROKES | 亻 RADICAL

1. 休学 **xiūxué** suspend schooling

Yīnwèi shēntǐde yuányīn, tā xiūxuéle liǎngnián.
因为身体的原因，他休学了两年。
He suspended his studies for two years due to health issues.

2. 退休 **tuìxiū** retire

Wén Jiàoshòu zài zhège xuéxiào jiāoshū jiāole sānshínián, míngnián yào tuìxiū le.
文教授在这个学校教书教了三十年，明年要退休了。
Prof. Wen has been teaching at this school for thirty years. She is retiring next year.

3. 休息 **xiūxi** take a break; close

Xīngqīliù hěnduō shāngdiàn wǔdiǎn jiù xiūxile.
星期六很多商店五点就休息了。
Many shops are closed as early as five o'clock on Saturday.

2. 休假 **xiūjià** on vacation

Zhège xīngqī Lǐ Xiǎojie xiūjià, rén bú zài bàngōngshì.
这个星期李小姐休假，人不在办公室。
Ms Li is on vacation this week. She is not in the office.

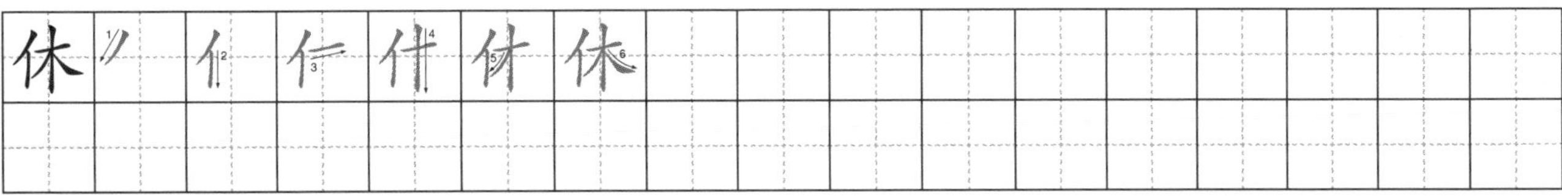

CHARACTER 269

xi/xī
information/rest

Useful phrases and sentences

10 STROKES | 心 RADICAL

1. 消息 **xiāoxi** news

Wǒ hǎocháng shíjiān dōu méi tīngdào Xiǎo Wáng de xiāoxile.
我好长时间都没听到小王的消息了。
I haven't heard from Wang for a very long time.

2. 作息 **zuòxī** (daily) rhythm

Wáng Xiānsheng měitiān shídiǎn shuìjiào, qīdiǎn qǐchuáng, zuòxī zhèngcháng.
王先生每天十点睡觉，七点起床，作息正常。
Mr. Wang goes to bed at ten o'clock and get up at seven o'clock every day. He keeps a regular daily routine.

3. 信息 **xìnxī** information

Tài duō xìnxī le, wǒde tóunǎo yǒu diǎnr shòubùliao.
太多信息了，我的头脑有点儿受不了。
There is too much information. My brain can barely take it in.

4. 有出息 **yǒu chūxi** successful; have good prospects

Zhège háizi cōngming yòu nǔlì, yǐhòu yídìng yǒu chūxi.
这个孩子聪明又努力，以后一定有出息。
This child is both clever and hardworking. He/She will have good prospects.

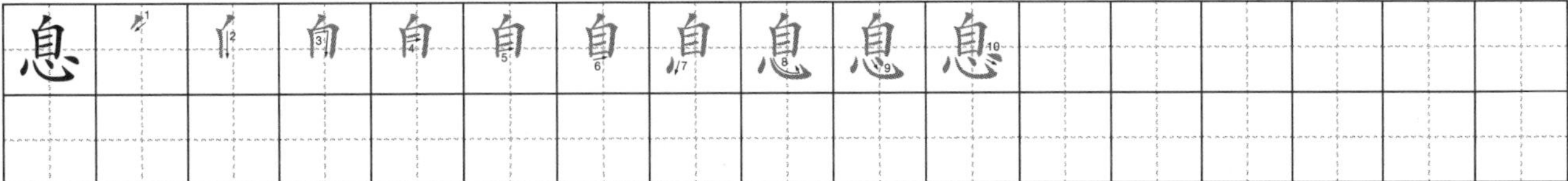

CHARACTER 270

liáo
chat

Useful phrases and sentences

11 STROKES | 耳 RADICAL

1. 聊天 **liáotiān** chat

Zǎoshang hěnduō lǎonián rén zài gōngyuán liáotiān.
早上很多老年人在公园聊天。
Many elderly people chat in the park in the morning.

2. 无聊 **wúliáo** bored

Tā jīntiān yǒu diǎnr wúliáo, xiǎng zhǎo jǐge péngyou liáotiān.
他今天有点儿无聊，想找几个朋友聊天。
He is a bit bored today. He wants to look for his friends to chat.

3. 无聊 **wúliáo** boring

Wǒ juéde kàn diànyǐng hěn wúliáo, wǒmen qù yùndòng ba.
我觉得看电影很无聊，我们去运动吧！
I feel that watching movies is boring. Let's go work out.

4. 聊天室 **liáotiānshì** chat room

Wǎngluò shàng yǒu hěnduō liáotiānshì, nǐ kěyǐ liànxí Zhōngwén.
网络上有很多聊天室，你可以练习中文。
There are many chat rooms online where you can practice your Chinese.

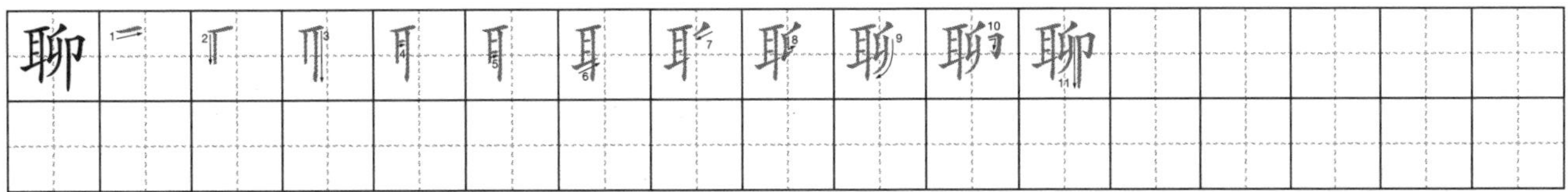

Lesson 18 Exercises

Part 1 Put the words in the correct order to make sentences.

1. 睡觉、昨天、点、几、晚上、你

   ____？

2. 他、大学、明年、读、开始

   ____。

3. 我、朋友、喜欢、男、很、运动

   ____。

4. 常常、家人、跟、周末、她、聊天

   ____。

Part 2 Complete the following dialogues using Chinese characters.

1. A: 你每天晚上几点休息？

   B: ____。

2. A: 你一个星期运动几次？你喜欢什么运动？

   B: ____。

3. A: 你常常上网吗？你上网做什么？

   B: ____。

4. A: 你喜欢你的大学生活吗？为什么？

   B: ____。

5. A: 你常常跟谁聊天？你们聊什么？

   B: ____。

Part 3 Practice writing letters using Chinese characters.

你是一个大一新生，你的父母很想知道你的大学生活。请你写信 (**xìn**: letter) 告诉他们:

1. 你每天忙不忙？你一个星期上几节课？
2. 你常常几点睡觉？几点起床？
3. 你每个星期有没有时间去运动？
4. 你有时间跟朋友聊天吗？你们喜欢去哪儿聊天？

爸爸、妈妈:
你们最近都好吗？我很好，可是我很想你们。

LESSON 19

Visiting a friend's home (I) 到朋友家(I)

1. Introduction

Visiting other people's homes as a guest involves various customs and formulaic expressions in every culture, and Chinese is no exception. When you enter a Chinese home it is customary to remove your shoes and put on the 拖鞋 (**tuōxié:** slippers) the host has prepared for you. Also, always bring a 小意思 (**xiǎo yìsi:** little gift) or 小东西 (**xiǎo dōngxi:** little things), such as fruit, tea leaves, or pastries. The gift does not need to be extravagant, but it should be nicely packed or wrapped. This shows your appreciation for the host's invitation.

2. Warm up

Read the passage below and answer the questions using Chinese characters.

我上个星期和我的中国朋友张文去了他的老家。我们到的时候，他的爸爸妈妈在门前欢迎我们。他们先请我到客厅坐，然后喝点儿茶。他们家很大，有四个房间，一个院子，还有两只狗和一只猫。我给他们带了礼物，他们很高兴。吃晚饭的时候，他们要我喝喝中国的酒，我说我还没二十一岁，所以喝水就好了。他们笑了笑，说我是一个好孩子。

1. Where did the narrator go last week? Did he go alone?

____。

2. Describe Zhang Wen's house.

____。

3. What was the narrator's response when he was invited to have alcohol?

____。

3. Vocabulary

	Word	Pinyin	English equivalent
1.	张	**Zhāng**	(surname)
2.	老家	**lǎojiā**	hometown
3.	门前	**ménqián**	in front of the door
4.	欢迎	**huānyíng**	welcome
5.	客厅	**kètīng**	living room
6.	坐	**zuò**	sit; by (car/bus)
7.	喝	**hē**	drink
8.	茶	**chá**	tea
9.	房间	**fángjiān**	room
10.	院子	**yuànzi**	yard
11.	只	**zhī**	measure word for animals
12.	狗	**gǒu**	dog
13.	猫	**māo**	cat
14.	礼物	**lǐwù**	gift; present
15.	酒	**jiǔ**	wine; alcoholic beverage
16.	水	**shuǐ**	water
17.	笑	**xiào**	smile; laugh
18.	孩子	**háizi**	child

4. New Characters

Fifteen characters are introduced in this lesson. Use the following explanations to help you understand and remember the characters.

张 迎 礼 物 猫 狗 坐 喝 茶 水 酒 房 室 厅 院

CHARACTER 271

张

Zhāng
(surname); open; spread out

Useful phrases and sentences

7 STROKES 弓 RADICAL

1. 张 **Zhāng** (surname)

Zhāng Wénde lǎojiā zài yíge xiǎo cūnzi, lí Nánjīng bù yuǎn.
张文的老家在一个小村子，离南京不远。
Zhang Wen's hometown is in a small village not far from Nanjing.

2. 张 **zhāng** measure word for flat objects

Nǐde shuǐ zài nèizhāng zhuōzi shàng.
你的水在那张桌子上。
Your water is on that table.

3. 紧张 **jǐnzhāng** nervous

Míngtiān wǒ yǒu yíge gōngzuò miànshì, yǒu diǎnr jǐnzhāng.
明天我有一个工作面试，有点儿紧张。
I have a job interview tomorrow. I am a bit nervous.

4. 张家 **Zhāngjiā** The Zhang family

Zhāngjiāde háizi dōu hěn yǒu lǐmào.
张家的孩子都很有礼貌。
The children in the Zhang family are all well-mannered.

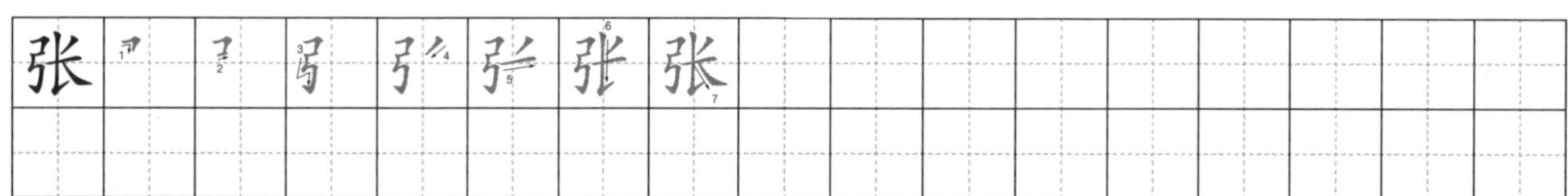

CHARACTER 272

yíng
to welcome; go towards

Useful phrases and sentences

7 STROKES 辶 RADICAL

1. 迎面 **yíngmiàn** in one's face (of wind)

Fēng yíngmiàn chuīlái, wǒ juéde yǒudiǎn lěng.
风迎面吹来，我觉得有点冷。
The wind is blowing on my face. I feel a little bit cold.

2. 迎接 **yíngjiē** enthusiastically welcome or greet

Zhōngguó rén xǐhuan chuān hóngsède yīfu yíngjiē xīnnián.
中国人喜欢穿红色的衣服迎接新年。
Chinese people like to wear red clothes to welcome the New Year.

3. 欢迎 **huānyíng** welcome

Huānyíng, huānyíng! Qǐng zuò, qǐng zuò!
欢迎，欢迎！请坐，请坐！
Welcome, welcome. Please have a seat!

4. 欢迎光临 **Huānyíng guānglín** Welcome! (store clerks welcoming customers)

Huānyíng guānglín! Xiānsheng, xūyào shénme?
欢迎光临！先生，需要什么？
Welcome! What can I get you, sir?

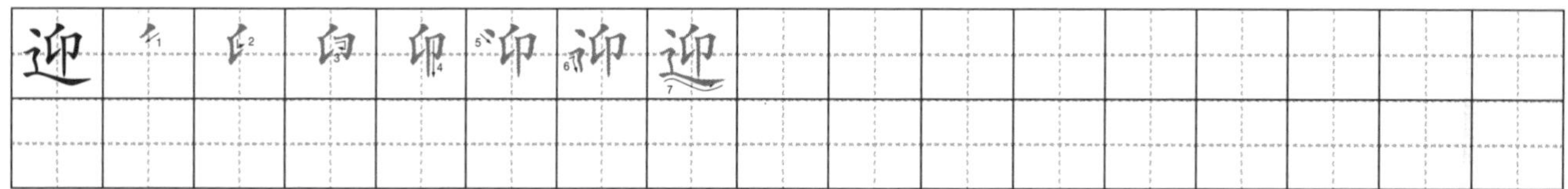

CHARACTER 273

lǐ
gift; etiquette

Useful phrases and sentences

5 STROKES 礻 RADICAL

1. 送礼 **sònglǐ** give somebody a present

Zhōngguó rén sònglǐde xíguàn gēn Měiguó rén hěn bù yíyàng.
中国人送礼的习惯跟美国人很不一样。
The way Chinese people give gifts is quite different from Americans.

2. 有礼貌 **yǒu lǐmào** well-mannered

Nàge xiǎohái hěn yǒu lǐmào, jiàndào rén zǒngshì dǎ zhāohū.
那个小孩很有礼貌，见到人总是打招呼。
That child is well-mannered. He/She also greets people when seeing them.

3. 礼拜 **lǐbài** week

Zhège lǐbài hěn lěng, yìdiǎnr dōu bú xiàng chūntiān.
这个礼拜很冷，一点儿都不像春天。
It's cold this week; it's not like spring at all.

4. 婚礼 **hūnlǐ** wedding

Zhège lǐbàitiān wǒ yào qù Táiběi cānjiā yíge péngyoude hūnlǐ.
这个礼拜天我要去台北参加一个朋友的婚礼。
I am going to Taipei to attend my friend's wedding this Sunday.

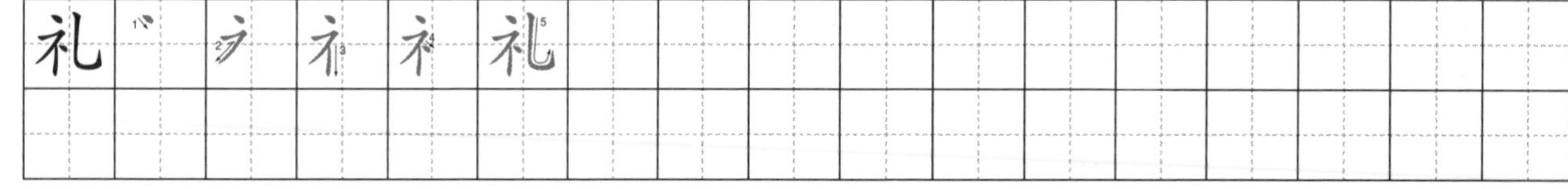

CHARACTER 274

物

wù
object; matter

Useful phrases and sentences

8 STROKES | 牜 RADICAL

1. 物理 **wùlǐ** physics

Cóng gāozhōng kāishǐ, wǒ jiù duì wùlǐ hěn gǎn xìngqu.
从高中开始，我就对物理很感兴趣。
Starting from high school, I was very interested in physics.

2. 物品 **wùpǐn** goods; object

Zuìjìn wùpǐnde jiàqián yuè lái yuè guì.
最近物品的价钱越来越贵。
Recently, goods are getting more and more expensive.

3. 生物 **shēngwù** biology

Zhāng Jiàoshòude zhuānyè shì shēngwù, tā zài Qīnghuá Dàxué jiāoshū.
张教授的专业是生物，他在清华大学教书。
Professor Zhang's expertise is biology. He teaches at Tsinghua University.

4. 礼物 **lǐwù** gift; present

Nǐ gěi tā zhǔnbèile shénme lǐwù?
你给他准备了什么礼物？
What gift did you prepare for him?

CHARACTER 275

猫

māo
cat

Useful phrases and sentences

11 STROKES | 犭 RADICAL

1. 猫 **māo** cat

Wǒ yǎngle yīzhī māo, wǒ jiào tā "māo zhǔxí."
我养了一只猫，我叫她"猫主席"。
I keep a cat. I call her "Chairman Mao."

2. 熊猫 **xióngmāo** panda

Xióngmāo zhēn shì tài kě'ài le, nánguài dàrén xiǎohái dōu xǐhuan.
熊猫真是太可爱了，难怪大人小孩都喜欢。
Pandas are so adorable. No wonder both adults and children love them.

3. 白猫 **bái māo** white cat

Nàr yǒu yīzhī bái māo.
那儿有一只白猫。
There is a white cat over there.

4. 黑猫 **hēi māo** black cat

Yǒuxiē rén juéde hēi māo bù jílì.
有些人觉得黑猫不吉利。
Some people feel that black cats are inauspicious.

CHARACTER 276

狗

gǒu
dog

Useful phrases and sentences

8 STROKES | 犭 RADICAL

1. 狗 **gǒu** dog

Tā zhēnshì ài gǒu, yígòng yǎngle wǔzhī.
她真是爱狗，一共养了五只。
She really loves dogs. She keeps five in total.

2. 热狗 **règǒu** hot dog

Chī règǒu yídìng yào jiāshàng kělè.
吃热狗一定要加上可乐。
Coke is a must when eating hot dogs.

3. 狗粮 **gǒuliáng** dog food

Zhèr mài gǒuliáng ma?
这儿卖狗粮吗？
Do you have dog food for sale?

4. 狗仔 **gǒuzǎi** paparazzi

"Gǒuzǎi" shì yíge xīnde cí, yìsi shì tōu pāi míngrénde rén.
"狗仔"是一个新的词，意思是偷拍名人的人。
"Paparazzi" is a new word, which refers to people who take pictures of celebrities.

CHARACTER 277

zuò
sit; by (car/bus)

Useful phrases and sentences

7 STROKES | 土 RADICAL

1. 坐 **zuò** sit

Nǐ xiān zuò yíxià, wǒ qù pào diǎn chá.
你先坐一下，我去泡点茶。
You have a seat first. I'll go make some tea.

2. 坐班 **zuòbān** on duty

Jīntiān Xiǎo Wáng zuòbān, tā shàngwǔ bādiǎn dào xiàwǔ sìdiǎn dōu zài.
今天小王坐班，他上午八点到下午四点都在。
Xiao Wang is on duty today. He will be in from 8 a.m. to 4 p.m.

3. 坐出租车 **zuò chūzūchē** by taxi

Kuài láibùjí le, wǒmen zuò chūzūchē qù ba!
快来不及了，我们坐出租车去吧！
We are late. Let's go by taxi.

4. 坐飞机 **zuò fēijī** by airplane

Wǒ māma cháng zuò fēijī chūchāi.
我妈妈常坐飞机出差。
My mother often travels by airplane for business.

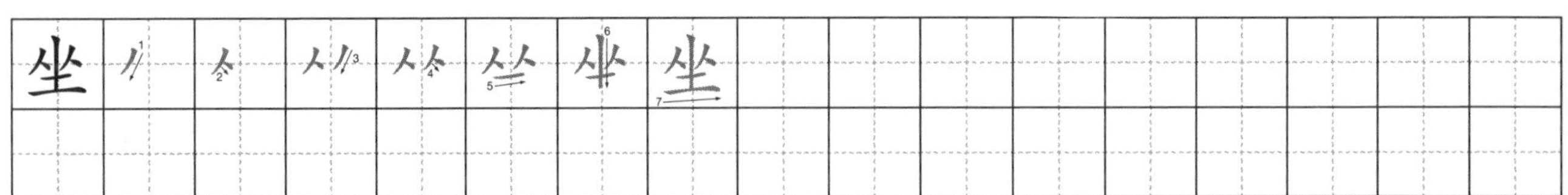

CHARACTER 278

喝

hē
drink

Useful phrases and sentences

12 STROKES | 口 RADICAL

1. 好喝 **hǎohē** good to drink

Zhè shì shénme yǐnliào? Zhēn hǎohē.
这是什么饮料？真好喝。
What drink is this? It tastes good.

2. 喝酒 **hē jiǔ** drink alcoholic beverage

Bié lǎo hē jiǔ, duì nǐde shēntǐ bù hǎo.
别老喝酒，对你的身体不好。
Don't always drink alcoholic beverages. It's not good for your health.

3. 喝茶 **hē chá** drink tea

Nǐ hē shuǐ háishì hē chá?
你喝水还是喝茶？
Would you like water or tea?

4. 喝水 **hē shuǐ** drink water

Zhōngguó rén juéde gǎnmàode shíhou yīnggāi duō hē shuǐ.
中国人觉得感冒的时候应该多喝水。
Chinese people feel that you should drink more water when having a cold.

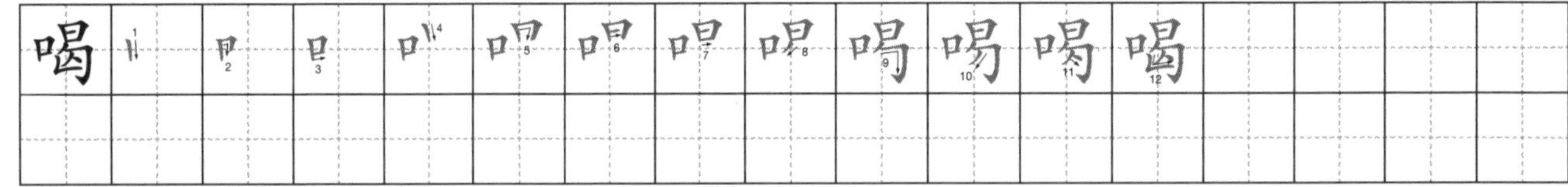

CHARACTER 279

茶

chá
tea

Useful phrases and sentences

9 STROKES | 艹 RADICAL

1. 茶 **chá** tea

Nǐ xiǎng hē shuǐ háishi hē chá?
你想喝水还是喝茶？
Would you like to drink water or tea?

2. 茶馆 **cháguǎn** tea house

Xiànzài chuántǒngde lǎo cháguǎn yuè lái yuè shǎo le.
现在传统的老茶馆越来越少了。
There are fewer and fewer traditional tea houses now.

3. 绿茶 **lǜchá** green tea

Qǐng wèn nín yǒu lǜchá ma? Hóngchá yě kěyǐ.
请问您有绿茶吗？红茶也可以。
Excuse me, do you have green tea? Black tea would be fine as well.

4. 泡茶 **pàochá** make tea

Zhōumòde shíhou, Zhāng Lǎoshī xǐhuan hé péngyou pàochá liáotiān.
周末的时候，张老师喜欢和朋友泡茶聊天。
Teacher Zhang likes to make tea and chat with friends on the weekend.

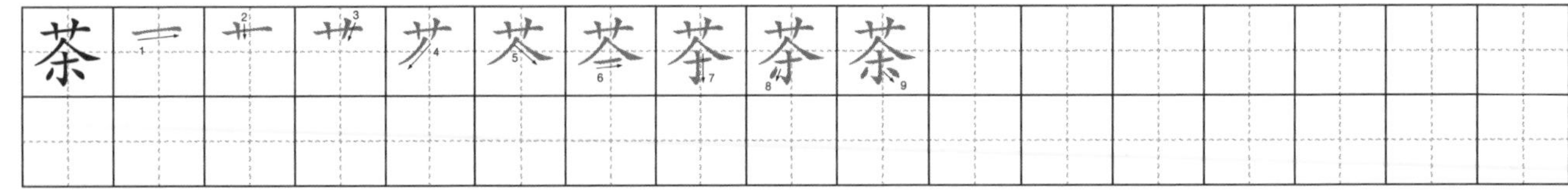

CHARACTER 280

shuǐ
water

Useful phrases and sentences

4 STROKES | 水 RADICAL

1. 水 **shuǐ** water

Zhège dìfang yǒu shān yǒu shuǐ, fēicháng piàoliang.
这个地方有山有水，非常漂亮。
This place is pretty with the mountains and water around.

2. 汽水 **qìshuǐ** soda

Wǒ bù hē qìshuǐ, hē chá jiù kěyǐ le, xièxie.
我不喝汽水，喝茶就可以了，谢谢。
I don't drink soda. Tea is fine. Thank you.

3. 水果 **shuǐguǒ** fruit

Yīnwèi Táiwān zài yàrèdài, suóyi shuǐguǒ hěnduō.
因为台湾在亚热带，所以水果很多。
Because Taiwan is in the subtropical zone, it has many different kinds of fruit.

4. 水饺 **shuǐjiǎo** water-boiled dumpling

Zhège fànguǎnde shuǐjiǎo tèbié hǎochī, yě hěn piányi.
这个饭馆的水饺特别好吃，也很便宜。
The water boiled dumplings in this restaurant are especially good. They are also cheap.

CHARACTER 281

jiǔ
alcohol; alcoholic drink

Useful phrases and sentences

10 STROKES | 西 RADICAL

1. 酒 **jiǔ** alcoholic beverage

Wǒ děi kāichē, suóyi bù néng hē jiǔ.
我得开车，所以不能喝酒。
I need to drive, so I can't drink.

2. 啤酒 **píjiǔ** beer

"Qīngdǎo Píjiǔ" shì Zhōngguó hěn yǒumíngde píjiǔ.
"青岛啤酒"是中国很有名的啤酒。
Qingdao Beer is a famous brand in China.

3. 敬酒 **jìngjiǔ** to toast

Zài Zhōngguó shāowēi zhèngshì yìdiǎnrde wǎnyàn, nǐ děi xué huì jìngjiǔ.
在中国稍微正式一点儿的晚宴，你得学会敬酒。
You need to learn how to toast at a rather formal banquet in China.

4. 酒吧 **jiǔbā** bar

Měiguó měige dìfang dōu yǒu dāngdìde jiǔbā.
美国每个地方都有当地的酒吧。
Every place in the U.S.A. has its local bars.

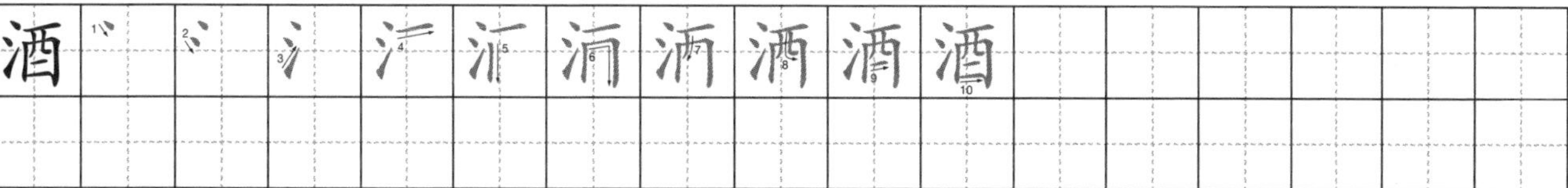

CHARACTER 282

fáng
house; room

Useful phrases and sentences

8 STROKES | 户 RADICAL

1. 房子 **fángzi** house; apartment

Zhège lǎo fángzi shì yī-jiǔ-yī-líng nián jiàn de.
这个老房子是一九一零年建的。
This old house was built in 1910.

2. 房租 **fángzū** rent (money)

Zhèrde fángzū tèbié guì, yíge yuè yào hǎo jǐqiān kuài.
这儿的房租特别贵，一个月要好几千块。
The house rent here is particularly expensive. It costs several thousand kuai a month.

3. 卧房 **wòfáng** bedroom

Zhège fángzi yǒu wǔjiān wòfáng.
这个房子有五间卧房。
This is a five-bedroom house.

4. 房东 **fángdōng** landlord

Nèiwèi fángdōng shì Jiānádà rén, hěn hǎo xiāngchǔ.
那位房东是加拿大人，很好相处。
That landlord is Canadian. He/She is very easygoing.

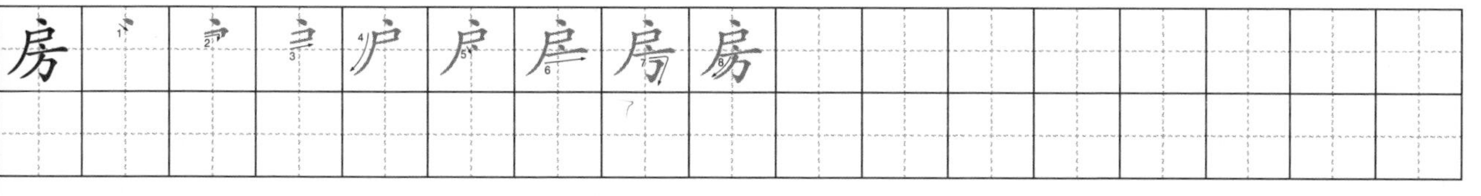

CHARACTER 283

shì
room

Useful phrases and sentences

9 STROKES | 宀 RADICAL

1. 教室 **jiàoshì** classroom

Wǒmende jiàoshì lí túshūguǎn hěn jìn.
我们的教室离图书馆很近。
Our classroom is close to the library.

2. 浴室 **yùshì** bathroom (with a shower or bath)

Zhège gōngyù yǒu jǐge yùshì?
这个公寓有几个浴室？
How many bathrooms does this apartment have?

3. 室内 **shìnèi** indoor

Míngtiān xiàyǔ, wǒmen jiù zài shìnèi jùhuì ba.
明天下雨，我们就在室内聚会吧。
It's going to rain tomorrow. Let's have an indoor party.

4. 办公室 **bàngōngshì** office

Nǐ zhīdao Zhāng Lǎoshīde bàngōngshì zài nǎr ma?
你知道张老师的办公室在哪儿吗？
Do you know where Teacher Zhang's office is?

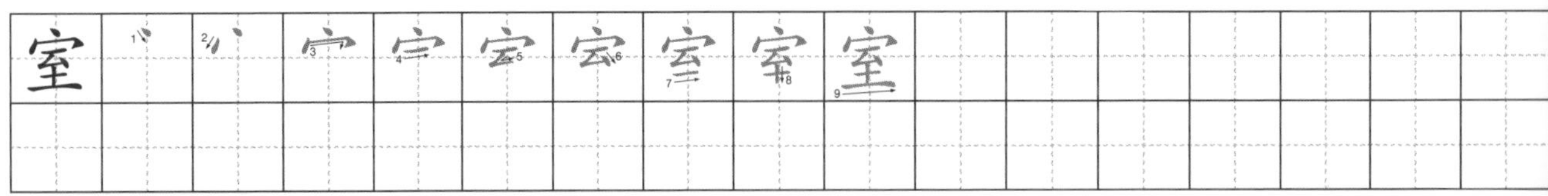

CHARACTER 284

厅

tīng
hall

Useful phrases and sentences

4 STROKES | 厂 RADICAL

1. 大厅 **dàtīng** reception hall; lounge

Wǒmen bànxiǎoshí hòu dàtīng jiàn.
我们半小时后大厅见。
Let's meet at the reception hall in half an hour.

4. 客厅 **kètīng** living room

Chīwán fàn hòu, qǐng dàjiā dào kètīng liáotiān, hē diǎn chá.
吃完饭后，请大家到客厅聊天，喝点茶。
After the meal, please go to the living room to chat and have some tea.

3. 交际舞厅 **jiāojì wǔtīng** ballroom

Zhège jiāojì wǔtīng zhēnshì piàoliang!
这个交际舞厅真是漂亮！
This ballroom is really gorgeous!

4. 餐厅 **cāntīng** restaurant

Zhège cāntīng suīrán bú dà, kěshì zǒngshì kèmǎn.
这个餐厅虽然不大，可是总是客满。
Although this restaurant is not big, it's always full.

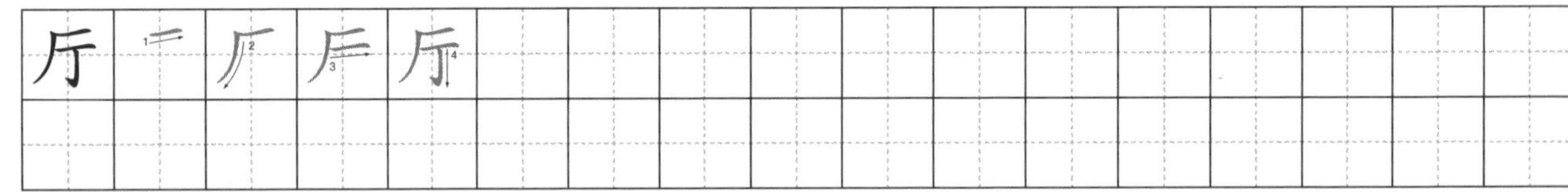

CHARACTER 285

yuàn
courtyard; establishment

Useful phrases and sentences

9 STROKES | 阝 RADICAL

1. 院子 **yuànzi** yard

Zhège shèqū měige rénjiāde yuànzi dōu hěn piàoliang.
这个社区每个人家的院子都很漂亮。
Every family's yard in this community is pretty.

2. 学院 **xuéyuàn** school; college

Hěnduō xuésheng bìyèhou xiǎngqù fǎxuéyuàn xuéxí.
很多学生毕业后想去法学院学习。
After graduation, many students plan to go to law school.

3. 电影院 **diànyǐngyuàn** movie theater

Nǐ xǐhuan qù diànyǐngyuàn kàn diànyǐng háishì zài jiālǐ kàn?
你喜欢去电影院看电影还是在家里看？
Do you like to watch movies in the movie theater or at home?

4. 住院 **zhùyuàn** hospitalize

Tā zuìjìn shēntǐ bú tài hǎo, děi zhùyuàn jiǎnchá yíxià.
他最近身体不太好，得住院检查一下。
He is not feeling well recently. He needs to be hospitalized for a check-up.

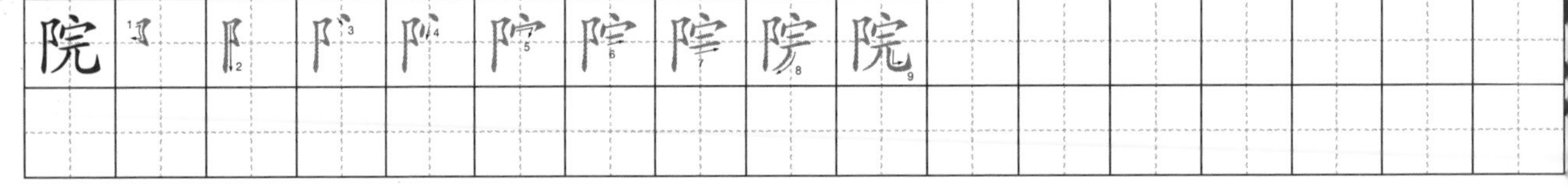

Lesson 19 Exercises

Part 1 Choose from the following words to fill in the blanks.

欢迎、礼物、只、喝

1. 去中国人家里带什么（　　　　）比较好？
2. 她很喜欢小动物，她家有两（　　　　）小狗。
3. 如果你下个周末不忙，（　　　　）你来我家坐坐。
4. 你想（　　　　）点儿什么？我家有茶、可乐。

Part 2 Complete the following dialogues using Chinese characters.

1. A: 要是你去中国人家里做客，你带什么礼物？

   B: ______________________________。

2. A: 在你的国家，去做客带什么礼物好？

   B: ______________________________。

3. A: 在你的国家，多少岁可以喝酒？

   B: ______________________________。

4. A: 你喜欢小动物吗？你家有没有猫和狗？

   B: ______________________________。

5. A: 你有没有室友？你的室友人怎么样？

   B: ______________________________。

Part 3 You are 天明. Reply this email from your friend 大卫.

To: tianming123@gmail.com

Cc:

Subject: 买什么礼物

天明，你好！

这个周末我要去我的中国朋友家做客，可是我不知道带什么礼物比较好。
有的朋友说带中国茶，有的朋友说带点吃的。你觉得我应该怎么做？

谢谢你！

祝好，

大卫

LESSON 20

Visiting a friend's home (II) 到朋友家(II)

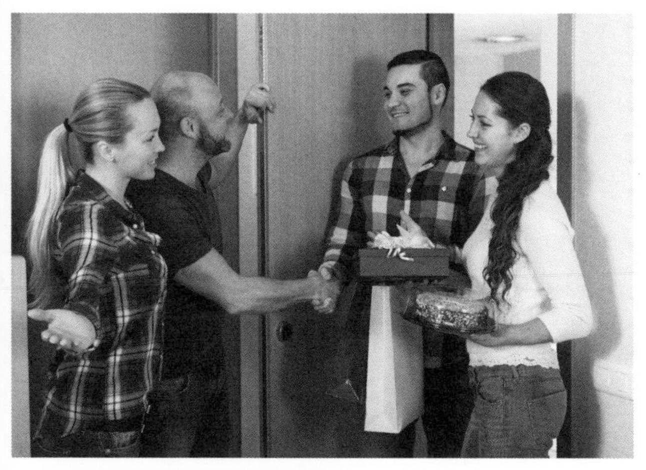

1. Introduction

客气 (**kèqi**: politeness) is an important and well-appreciated social value in Chinese society. Its purpose is to maintain social and interpersonal harmony through interactions, behaviors and the language. 客气 is expected from both parties in a host-guest scenario and many formulaic expressions are involved.

For instance, a host accepts a guest's gift by saying 你太客气了 (**nǐ tài kèqi le**: you are too polite) instead of 谢谢 (**xièxie**: thanks). A common response by the guest in this case would be 应该的 (**yīnggāide**: this is something I ought do).

2. Warm up

Read the passage below and answer the questions using Chinese characters.

> 第二天，张文带我到他家附近走走。我们先到了一个公园，公园里有很多不同颜色的花，红的、黄的、白的、粉红的，都很漂亮。那天因为公园刚好有一个音乐会，所以我们找了一个地方坐下来听音乐。我在张文家住了三天，每天都吃了不同的菜和不同的水果。我自己坐飞机回北京的那一天，张文的爸爸妈妈跟我说，以后常来。我会的。

1. Where did the narrator and Zhang Wen go the next day?

   ____。

2. What did they see and do in the park?

   ____。

3. Do you think that the narrator enjoyed his/her stay at Zhang Wen's home? Why?

   ____。

3. Vocabulary

	Word	Pinyin	English equivalent
1.	带	**dài**	bring; take
2.	附近	**fùjìn**	vicinity; nearby
3.	不同	**bùtóng**	different
4.	颜色	**yánsè**	color
5.	红	**hóng**	red
6.	黄	**huáng**	yellow
7.	白	**bái**	white
8.	粉红	**fěnhóng**	pink
9.	因为	**yīnwèi**	because
10.	刚好	**gānghǎo**	happen to; coincidentally; exactly
11.	音乐	**yīnyuè**	music
12.	音乐会	**yīnyuèhuì**	concert
13.	住	**zhù**	live
14.	菜	**cài**	dish
15.	水果	**shuǐguǒ**	fruit
16.	自己	**zìjǐ**	self
17.	飞机	**fēijī**	airplane
18.	回	**huí**	return
19.	以后	**yǐhòu**	in the future

4. New Characters

Fifteen characters are introduced in this lesson. Use the following explanations to help you understand and remember the characters.

因 为 颜 色 白 黄 粉 音 乐 自 己 果 住 找 慢

CHARACTER 286

yīn
because; reason

Useful phrases and sentences

6 STROKES | 口 RADICAL

1. 因为 **yīnwèi** because

Wǒ yīnwèi jīntiān yǒu shì, suóyi bù néng qù yīnyuèhuì.
我因为今天有事，所以不能去音乐会。
Because I have things to do, I can't go to the concert today.

2. 原因 **yuányīn** reason; cause

Qǐng nǐ gàosù wǒ nǐ zuò zhèjiàn shìqingde yuányīn.
请你告诉我你做这件事情的原因。
Please tell me your reason for doing this.

3. 基因 **jīyīn** genes

Zuìjìn kēxuéjiāmen zhǎodàole lǎonián chīdāizhèngde jīyīn.
最近科学家们找到了老年痴呆症的基因。
Recently scientists have found the genes for Alzheimer's.

4. 主因 **zhǔyīn** main reason

Nǐ shēngbìngde zhǔyīn shì shuǐ hēde bú gòu.
你生病的主因是水喝得不够。
The main reason of your illness is that you don't drink enough water.

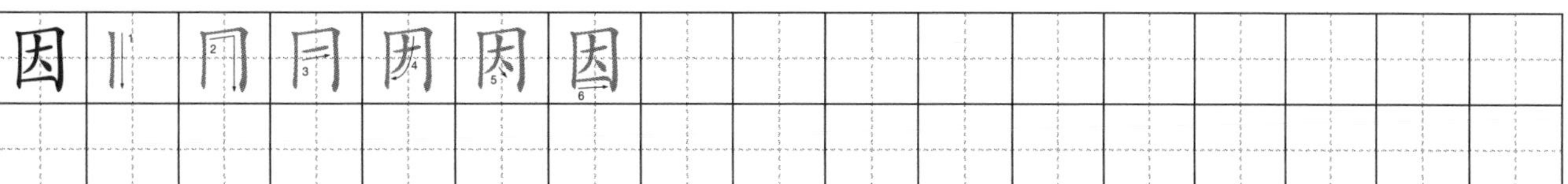

CHARACTER 287

wèi
for

Useful phrases and sentences

4 STROKES | 丶 RADICAL

1. 为何 **wèihé** why (formal)

Nǐ jīntiān wèihé zhème gāoxìng?
你今天为何这么高兴？
Why do you look so happy today?

2. 为什么 **wèishénme** why

Xiǎo Bái hěn cōngming, cóngxiǎo jiù xǐhuan wèn "wèishénme."
小白很聪明，从小就喜欢问"为什么"。
Little Bai is smart. He has always liked to ask "why" since he was little.

3. 为了家人 **wèile jiārén** for the family

Māmā wèile jiārén chángcháng zǎoqǐ zuòfàn.
妈妈为了家人常常早起做饭。
My mother often gets up early to cook for the family.

4. 为了 **wèile** for the sake of

Wèile shēntǐ jiànkāng, nǐ děi duō xiūxi, shǎo áoyè.
为了身体健康，你得多休息，少熬夜。
For the sake of your health, you need to rest more and stay up late less.

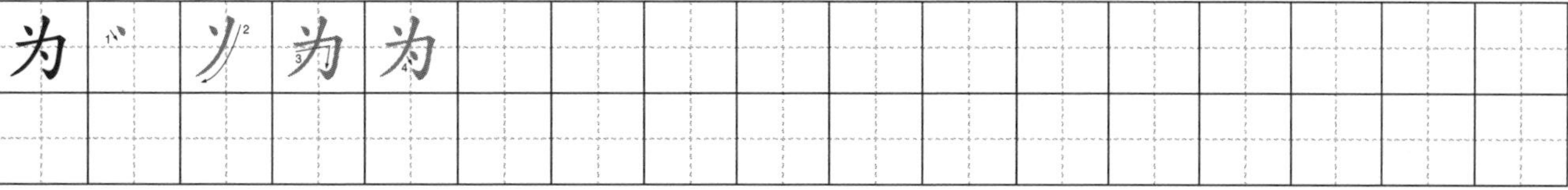

CHARACTER 288

yán
color; appearance

Useful phrases and sentences

15 STROKES | 页 RADICAL

1. 颜色 **yánsè** color

Zhōngguó rén Chūnjiéde shíhou xǐhuan chuān hóng yánsède yīfu.
中国人春节的时候喜欢穿红颜色的衣服。
Chinese people like to wear red-colored clothes on the New Year.

2. 颜值 **yánzhí** attractiveness index (1 to 10 rating)

Zhèwèi nǚ míngxīng yánzhí gāo, yǒu xǔduō yǐngmí.
这位女明星颜值高，有许多影迷。
This female celebrity is very pretty. She has many fans.

3. 容颜 **róngyán** appearance; complexion

Wǒde Zhōngwén lǎoshī jīnnián wǔshísuì, yǒu cíxiángde róngyán.
我的中文老师今年五十岁，有慈祥的容颜。
My Chinese teacher is fifty years old this year. He/She has a kind complexion.

4. 颜 **Yán** (surname)

Yán Xiānsheng shì yíge yīnyuèjiā.
颜先生是一个音乐家。
Mr. Yan is a musician.

CHARACTER 289

sè
color

Useful phrases and sentences

6 STROKES | 色 RADICAL

1. 咖啡色 **kāfēisè** coffee color

Nǐ zuì xǐhuande yánsè shì kāfēisè ma?
你最喜欢的颜色是咖啡色吗？
Do you like coffee color the most?

2. 彩色 **cǎisè** multi-colored

Xiànzàide zhàopiān dōu shì cǎisède, dànshì yǒude rén tèbié xǐhuan hēibái zhàopiān.
现在的照片都是彩色的，但是有的人特别喜欢黑白照片。
Photos nowadays are all in color, but some people like black and white photos better.

3. 绿色 **lǜsè** green

Hónglǜdēng yǒu hóngsè, huángsè hé lǜsè sānzhǒng yánsè.
红绿灯有红色、黄色和绿色三种颜色。
Traffic lights have three colors: red, yellow, and green.

4. 脸色 **liǎnsè** facial look

Jīnglǐ jīntiānde liǎnsè bú tài hǎokàn, bù zhīdao shì-bú-shì bìngle?
经理今天的脸色不太好看，不知道是不是病了？
The manager doesn't look good today. I wonder if he/she is sick?

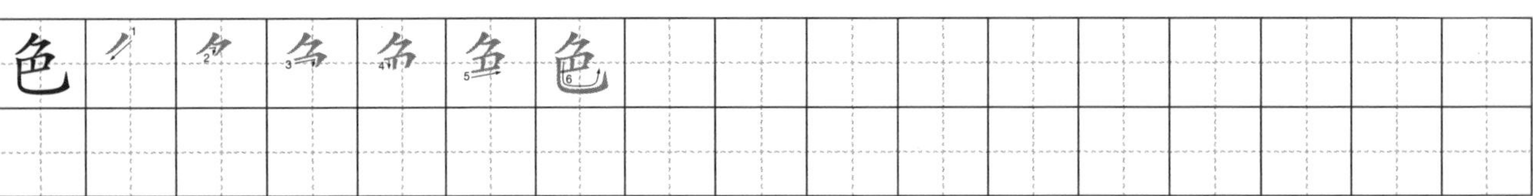

CHARACTER 290

bái
white; blank

Useful phrases and sentences

5 STROKES | 白 RADICAL

1. 白色 **báisè** white

Xiǎo Měi jīntiān chuānle yíjiàn báisède yángzhuāng.
小美今天穿了一件白色的洋装。
Little Mei wore a white dress today.

2. 白天 **báitiān** daytime

Wǒ míngtiān báitiān bú zài jiā, qǐng nǐ wǎnshang zài dǎ.
我明天白天不在家，请你晚上再打。
I am not home during the daytime tomorrow. Please call me in the evening.

3. 空白 **kòngbái** blank

Tāde kǎojuàn shàng yípiàn kòngbái, shénme yě méi xiě.
他的考卷上一片空白，什么也没写。
His test was left blank; he didn't write anything.

4. 白酒 **báijiǔ** *baijiu* (a strong Chinese spirit)

Zhōngguóde báijiǔ hé xīfāngde "spirits" wánquán bù yíyàng.
中国的白酒和西方的"spirits"完全不一样。
Chinese spirits are completely different from the western spirits.

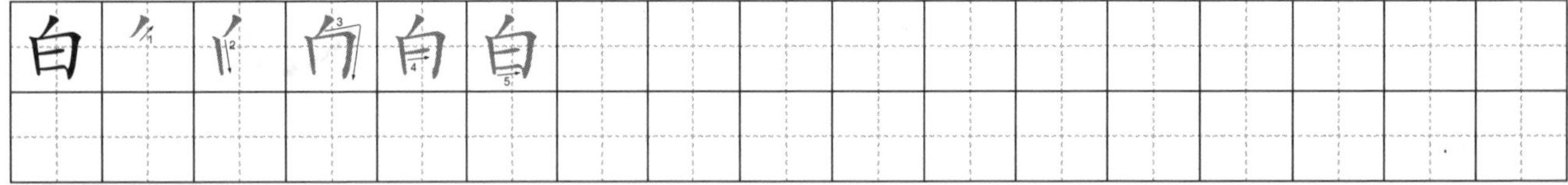

CHARACTER 291

huáng
yellow

Useful phrases and sentences

11 STROKES | 黄 RADICAL

1. 黄色 **huángsè** yellow

Xiǎo Lǐ chuān huángsède yīfu tèbié hǎokàn.
小李穿黄色的衣服特别好看。
Little Li looks especially good on yellow clothes.

2. 黄金 **huángjīn** gold

Nàge xiǎozhèn yīnwèi huángjīn zhuànle hěnduō qián.
那个小镇因为黄金赚了很多钱。
That small town made a fortune because of gold.

3. 黄豆 **huángdòu** soybean

Zhōngguóde dòujiāng shì yòng huángdòu zuò de.
中国的豆浆是用黄豆做的。
Chinese soy milk is made of soybeans.

4. 黄昏 **huánghūn** dusk

Zhège hǎibiān huánghūnde shíhou zuì měi.
这个海边黄昏的时候最美。
Dusk is the prettiest time at this beach.

黄 1 2 3 4 5 6 7 8 9 10 11

CHARACTER 292

fěn
powder

Useful phrases and sentences

10 STROKES　米 RADICAL

1. 粉红色 **fěnhóngsè** pink

Yùjīnxiāng yǒu hěnduō bùtóngde yánsè, wǒ zuì xǐhuan fěnhóngsède.
郁金香有很多不同的颜色，我最喜欢粉红色的。
Tulips have many colors. My favorite is pink.

2. 奶粉 **nǎifěn** milk powder

Zài Zhōngguó hěnduō rén yòng nǎifěn chōngpào niúnǎi.
在中国很多人用奶粉冲泡牛奶。
People people use milk powder to make milk in China.

3. 面粉 **miànfěn** flour

Miànfěn shì zuò gāodiǎn zuì zhòngyàode yuánliào.
面粉是做糕点最重要的原料。
Flour is the most important ingredient in pastries.

4. 洗衣粉 **xǐyīfěn** laundry detergent

Nǐ yòng nǎge páizide xǐyīfěn?
你用哪个牌子的洗衣粉？
Which brand of laundry detergent do you use?

CHARACTER 293

yīn
sound;
musical note

Useful phrases and sentences

9 STROKES　音 RADICAL

1. 音乐 **yīnyuè** music

Nǐ xǐhuan shénme lèixíngde yīnyuè?
你喜欢什么类型的音乐？
What type of music do you like?

2. 音乐会 **yīnyuèhuì** music concert

Zhège zhōumò xuéxiào yǒuge yīnyuèhuì, yào-bú-yào yìqǐ qù?
这个周末学校有个音乐会，要不要一起去？
There is a music concert on campus this weekend. Do you want to go together?

3. 声音 **shēngyīn** voice; sound

Wáng Lǎoshīde shēngyīn hěn hǎotīng, hěn shìhé lùyīn.
王老师的声音很好听，很适合录音。
Teacher Wang has a very good voice. It's ideal for recordings.

4. 发音 **fāyīn** pronunciation

Xué yíge wàiyǔ, fāyīn hé yǔfǎ dōu hěn zhòngyào.
学一个外语，发音和语法都很重要。
Pronunciations and grammar are both important when you learn a foreign language.

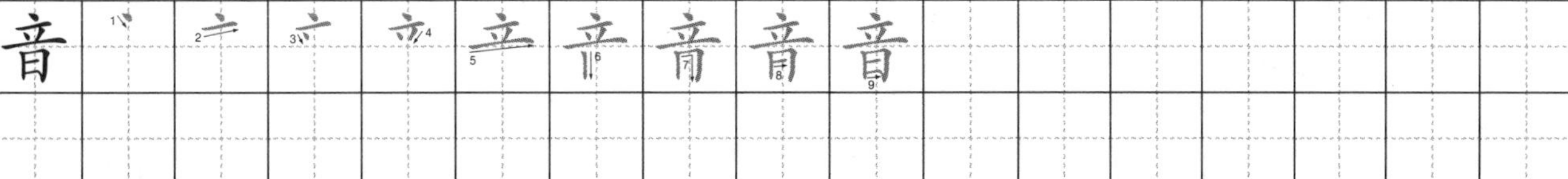

CHARACTER 294

yuè
music

Useful phrases and sentences

5 STROKES　丿 RADICAL

1. 声乐 **shēngyuè** vocal music

Wǒ tèbié xǐhuan zhèwèi shēngyuè lǎoshī.
我特别喜欢这位声乐老师。
I especially like this vocal teacher.

2. 乐器 **yuèqì** music instrument

Qǐng wèn, zhè shì shénme yuèqì?
请问，这是什么乐器？
Excuse me, what music instrument is this?

3. 乐谱 **yuèpǔ** music score; written music

Nǐ kàndedǒng yuèpǔ ma? Wǒ kànbùdǒng.
你看得懂乐谱吗？我看不懂。
Can you read music? I can't.

4. 乐团 **yuètuán** band; orchestra

Wéiyěnà Jiāoxiǎng Yuètuán shìjiè wénmíng.
维也纳交响乐团世界闻名。
The Vienna Philharmonic Orchestra is world famous.

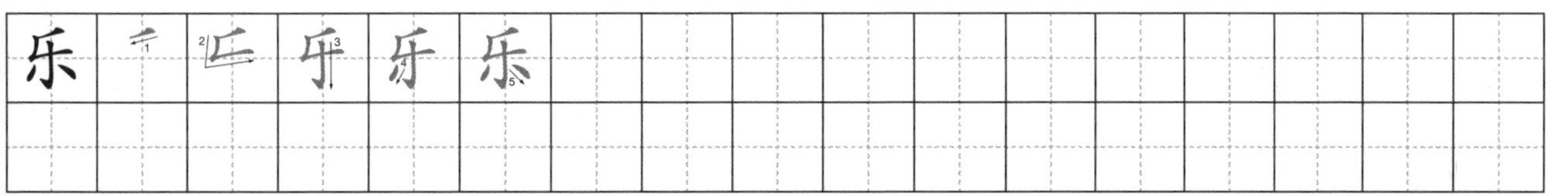

CHARACTER 295

zì
self; from

Useful phrases and sentences

6 STROKES | 自 RADICAL

1. 自学 **zìxué** to teach oneself

Tā zìxué Yīngwén hé Fǎwén.
他自学英文和法文。
He taught himself English and French.

2. 自由 **zìyóu** freedom; free

Zài nǐde guójiā, rénmen yǒu shénme zìyóu?
在你的国家，人们有什么自由？
What kind of freedom do people have in your country?

3. 来自 **láizì** come from

Zhège gēshǒu láizì Ài'ěrlán, yīnyuè hěn dútè.
这个歌手来自爱尔兰，音乐很独特。
This singer is from Ireland. His/Her music is unique.

4. 亲自 **qīnzì** in person

Xièxie nǐ qīnzì gěi wǒ dǎ diànhuà gàosù wǒ zhège hǎo xiāoxi.
谢谢你亲自给我打电话告诉我这个好消息。
Thank you for calling me in person to inform me of this good news.

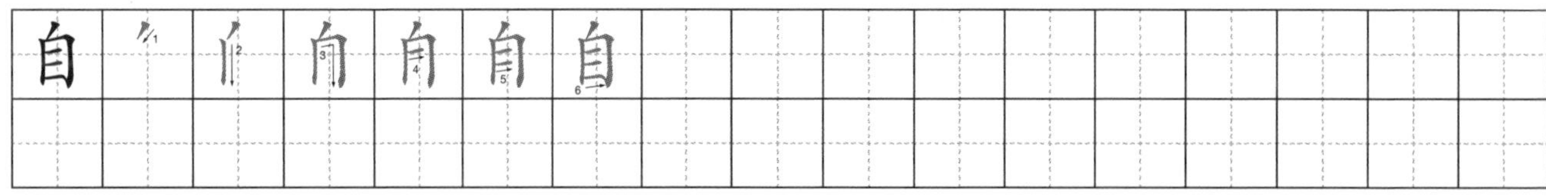

CHARACTER 296

jǐ
self

Useful phrases and sentences

3 STROKES | 己 RADICAL

1. 己 **jǐ** self

Jǐ" hé "yǐ" zhè liǎngge zì bù yíyàng.
"己"和"已"这两个字不一样。
"Ji" and "yi" are two different characters.

2. 知己 **zhījǐ** know oneself; intimate friends

Tā búdàn shì wǒde tóngwū, háishì wǒde zhījǐ.
他不但是我的同屋，还是我的知己。
He's not only my roommate, but also my intimate friend.

3. 自己 **zìjǐ** self; on one's own

Míngtiān wǒ kěyǐ zìjǐ qù jīchǎng, búyòng máfan nǐ.
明天我可以自己去机场，不用麻烦你。
I can go to the airport myself. No need to bother you.

4. 利己 **lìjǐ** to benefit oneself

Zhèjiàn shì sǔnrén yòu bù lìjǐ, nǐ wèishénme yào jiānchí?
这件事损人又不利己，你为什么要坚持？
This matter is harmful to other people and not beneficial to yourself. Why do you insist on this?

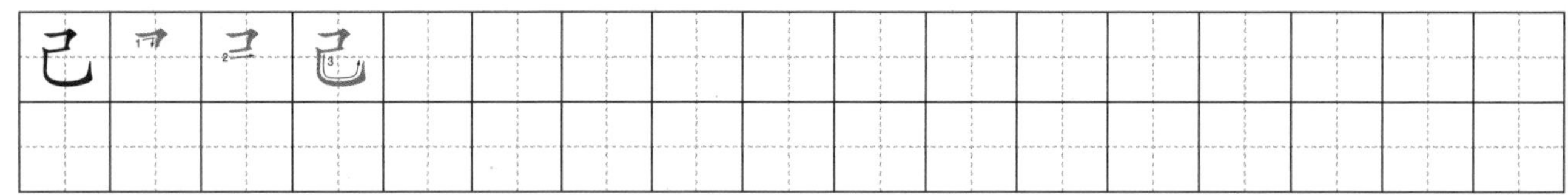

CHARACTER 297

guǒ
fruit; result

Useful phrases and sentences

8 STROKES | 木 RADICAL

1. 结果 **jiéguǒ** result

Zhècì hángbān yánwù shì diànnǎo xìtǒng gùzhàngde jiéguǒ.
这次航班延误是电脑系统故障的结果。
The flight delay this time is the result of a computer system failure.

2. 果酱 **guǒjiàng** jam

Tā zǎocān chángcháng chī guǒjiàng hé miànbāo.
她早餐常常吃果酱和面包。
She eats bread and jam for breakfast.

3. 果汁 **guǒzhī** juice

Zhèzhǒng guǒzhī hǎohē shì hǎohē, dànshì tài tián le.
这种果汁好喝是好喝，但是太甜了。
This kind of juice is tasty, but it's too sweet.

4. 苹果 **píngguǒ** apple

Píngguǒ diànnǎo zài Zhōngguó fēicháng shòu huānyíng.
苹果电脑在中国非常受欢迎。
Apple computers are very popular in China.

果 | 日 | 旦 | 甲 | 果 (stroke-order practice grid)

CHARACTER 298

zhù
live; reside; stop

Useful phrases and sentences

7 STROKES | 亻 RADICAL

1. 住 **zhù** live; reside

Wǒde tóngshìmen dōu zhù zài jiāoqū, zhǐ yǒu wǒ zhù zài chéngshì lǐ.
我的同事们都住在郊区，只有我住在城市里。
My colleagues all live in the suburbs; I am the only one who lives in the city.

2. 住址 **zhùzhǐ** (home) address

Měiguóde zhùzhǐ hé Zhōngguó zhùzhǐde jiégòu bù yíyàng.
美国的住址和中国住址的结构不一样。
The structure of American addresses and Chinese addresses are different.

3. 住房 **zhùfáng** housing

Zhège chéngshìde zhùfáng wèntí hěn yánzhòng, niánqīng rén mǎibuqǐ fángzi.
这个城市的住房问题很严重，年轻人买不起房子。
Housing is a serious issue in this city. Young people can't afford to buy houses.

4. 忍不住 **rěnbuzhù** cannot help

Kàndào tā zhème rènzhēn, wǒ rěnbuzhù xiàole chūlái.
看到他这么认真，我忍不住笑了出来。
I cannot help laughing when I saw him being so serious.

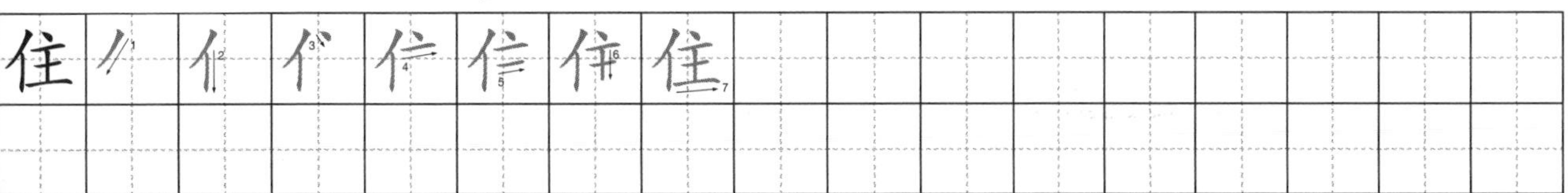

CHARACTER 299

zhǎo
look for; find

Useful phrases and sentences

7 STROKES | 扌 RADICAL

1. 找 **zhǎo** look for; find

Nǐ zài zhǎo shénme? Yào-bú-yào bāngmáng?
你在找什么？要不要帮忙？
What are you looking for? Do you need help?

2. 找工作 **zhǎo gōngzuò** look for work

Xiànzài dàxué bìyèshēng zhǎo gōngzuò róngyì ma?
现在大学毕业生找工作容易吗？
Is it easy for college graduates to find a job now?

3. 找谁 **zhǎo shéi** look for whom

Qǐng wèn, nín zhǎo shéi?
请问，您找谁？
May I ask who you are looking for?

4. 找到 **zhǎodào** find; found

Zhǎodào zìjǐ xǐhuande xìngqù bú shì róngyìde shì.
找到自己喜欢的兴趣不是容易的事。
It's not easy to find a hobby that you really like.

CHARACTER 300

màn
slow

Useful phrases and sentences

14 STROKES | 忄 RADICAL

1. 慢 **màn** slow

Nǐmen mànman chī, wǒ yǒu shì xiān zǒule.
你们慢慢吃，我有事先走了。
Enjoy your meal. I have something to attend to.

2. 慢跑 **mànpǎo** jogging

Bái Xiānsheng xǐhuan mànpǎo, měitiān pǎo yíge xiǎoshí.
白先生喜欢慢跑，每天跑一个小时。
Mr. Bai likes jogging. He jogs an hour every day.

3. 缓慢 **huǎnmàn** slow-moving

Zhège dìfang chéngzhǎng huǎnmàn shì yīnwèi zhèngfǔ xiàolǜ bù hǎo.
这个地方成长缓慢是因为政府效率不好。
Progress in this place is slow-moving because of government inefficiency.

4. 说慢一点儿 **shuō màn yìdiǎnr** speak a bit more slowly

Bù hǎo yìsi, néng-bù-néng qǐng nǐ shuō màn yìdiǎnr?
不好意思，能不能请你说慢一点儿？
I am sorry. Can you speak a bit more slowly?

Lesson 20 Exercises

Part 1 Choose from the following words to fill in the blanks.

因为、颜色、慢、找

1. 他只有黑色的衣服，没有别的（　　　　）的衣服。
2. 上中学的时候，父母不让我(　　　　)男朋友。
3. 他说中文说得很清楚，不过有点儿（　　　　）。
4. 不好意思，我（　　　　）明天还有考试，所以不跟你们去玩儿了。

Part 2 Complete the following dialogues using Chinese characters.

1. A: 你为什么不喜欢你的同屋？

   B: ____。

2. A: 你现在自己住还是跟你的父母一起住？

   B: ____。

3. A: 你毕业以后想去哪儿找工作？

   B: ____。

4. A: 你喜欢什么颜色，不喜欢什么颜色？

   B: ____。

5. A: 去中国人家里做客，可以带水果吗？

   B: ____。

Part 3

你喜欢去朋友家做客吗？还记得上次去朋友家里做客是什么时候吗？请你说说:

1. 上次去朋友家做客是什么时候？

   ____。

2. 你是一个人去的还是跟朋友一起去的？

   ____。

3. 你带了什么礼物？你的朋友喜欢吗？

   ____。

4. 你去朋友家做了什么有意思的事情吗？

   ____。

Lessons 16–20 (Review Exercises)

Part 1 Write the Pinyin and the English meaning of the following words.

	Words	Pinyin	English Equivalent
e.g.,	五元	**wǔyuán**	five yuan
1.	哪里	______	______
2.	容易	______	______
3.	重要	______	______
4.	文化	______	______
5.	休息	______	______
6.	聊天	______	______
7.	房间	______	______
8.	孩子	______	______
9.	音乐	______	______
10.	水果	______	______

Part 2 Fill in the blanks according to the English meaning.

1. (　　　) 始 in the beginning
2. (　　　) 识 know
3. (　　　) 日 holiday
4. (　　　) 试 test
5. (　　　) 脑 computer
6. 决 (　　　) decide
7. 意 (　　　) meaning
8. 礼 (　　　) gift
9. 欢 (　　　) welcome
10. 因 (　　　) because

Part 3 Answer the following questions using Chinese characters.

1. Q: 你觉得学中文有意思吗?

   A: ______________________________。

2. Q: 你每天上网多长时间？

A: ____。

3. Q: 你喜欢跟你的老师聊天吗？

A: ____。

4. Q: 你上次去朋友家做客是什么时候？

A: ____。

Part 4 Read the passage below and answer the questions using Chinese characters.

张老师好，

我是大中。下个星期我们有中文考试，我有点儿紧张（**jǐnzhāng:** nervous）。这个星期我每天很早起床去图书馆复习中文课，练习写汉字。我还常常跟我的室友用中文聊天，可是我还是觉得中文很难学，你觉得我应该怎么办？

我很想跟你聊聊，想请你帮帮我。我今天下午和明天早上都有时间，不知道您几点有时间？

谢谢老师，

大中

1. 张老师是谁？

____。

2. 大中常常学中文吗？他觉得中文难吗？

____。

3. 大中为什么想跟张老师聊聊？

____。

4. 大中想什么时候见张老师？

____。

Appendix

You have been introduced the 300 most common Chinese characters in this book. With only a few additions in this appendix, you will be equipped with all the characters covered in the HSK Level 1 and Level 2.

报纸

bàozhǐ
newspaper

Useful phrases and sentences

1. **Nǐ jīntiān kànle bàozhǐ ma?**
   你今天看了报纸吗？
   Did you read the newspaper today?
2. **Qǐng wèn, nǎr mài bàozhǐ?**
   请问，哪儿卖报纸？
   Excuse me, where can I buy newspapers?
3. **Bàozhǐ yīfèn duōshao qián?**
   报纸一份多少钱？
   How much is the newspaper?
4. **Xiànzài niánqīngrén kàn bàozhǐ ma?**
   现在年轻人看报纸吗？
   Do young people read newspapers nowadays?

船

chuán
boat; ship; ferry

Useful phrases and sentences

1. **Zhè shì shénme chuán?**
   这是什么船？
   What kind of ship is this?
2. **Nǐ zuòguo chuán ma?**
   你坐过船吗？
   Have you taken a boat before?
3. **Nàge dìfang nǐ zhǐ néng zuò chuán qù.**
   那个地方你只能坐船去。
   You can only go to that place by boat.
4. **Nǐ xǐhuan zuò chuán háishì zuò fēijī?**
   你喜欢坐船还是坐飞机？
   Do you prefer boats or airplanes?

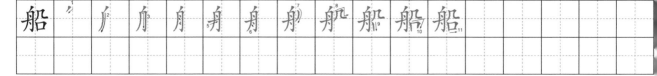

从

cóng
from

Useful phrases and sentences

1. **Cóng Zhōngguó dào Měiguó.**
   从中国到美国。
   From China to the U.S.A.
2. **Cóng jīn yǐhòu.**
   从今以后。
   From now on.
3. **Cóng zhè dào nà.**
   从这到那。
   From here to there.
4. 从小学到大学。
   Cóng xiǎoxué dào dàxué.
   From elementary school to college.

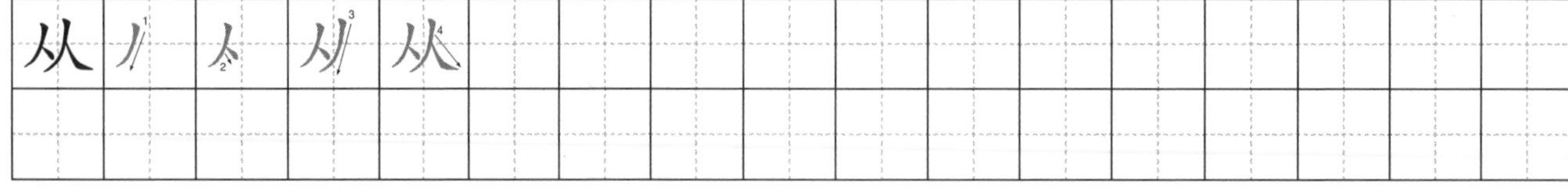

děng
wait; level

Useful phrases and sentences

1. **Qǐng děng yíxià.**
   请等一下。
   Please wait.
2. **Píngděng.**
   平等。
   Equal.
3. **Děngjí.**
   等级。
   Level.
4. **Gāoděng.**
   高等。
   Higher level.

公斤

gōngjīn
kilogram

Useful phrases and sentences

1. **Yīgōngjīn.**
   一公斤。
   One kilogram.
2. **Shígōngjīn.**
   十公斤。
   Ten kilograms.
3. **Yīgōngjīn shì jǐbàng?**
   一公斤是几磅?
   How many pounds are equivalent to one kilogram?
4. **Zhèzhī jī yǒu jǐgōngjīn?**
   这只鸡有几公斤?
   How many kilograms does this chicken weigh?

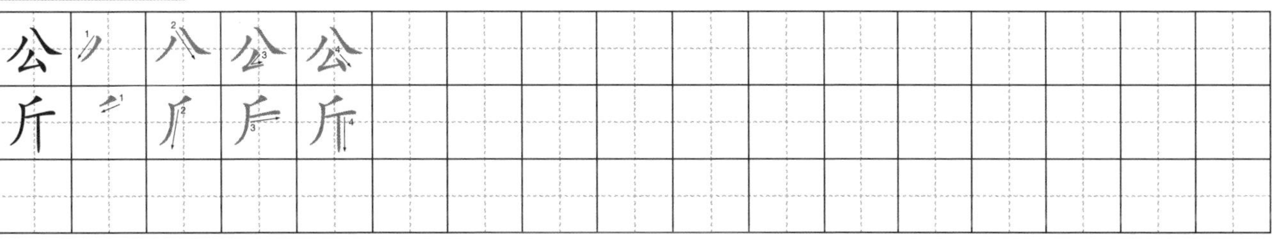

鸡蛋

jīdàn
chicken egg

Useful phrases and sentences

1. **Yīgōngjīn jīdàn.**
   一公斤鸡蛋。
   One kilogram of chicken eggs.
2. **Yīdǎ jīdàn.**
   一打鸡蛋。
   One dozen chicken eggs.
3. **Shíkē jīdàn.**
   十颗鸡蛋。
   Ten chicken eggs.
4. **Jīntiān jīdàn duōshao qián?**
   今天鸡蛋多少钱?
   How much are the chicken eggs today?

晴

qíng
clear sky; sunny

Useful phrases and sentences

1. **Qíngtiān.**
   晴天。
   Clear sky./A sunny day.
2. **Míngtiān shì qíngtiān.**
   明天是晴天。
   It's clear tomorrow.
3. **Xiànzài xiàyǔ, yī huìr jiù huì biàn qíng.**
   现在下雨，一会儿就会变晴。
   It's raining now. It will become clear later.
4. **Nèiwèi nǚháirde míngzi shì Chén Qíng.**
   那位女孩儿的名字是陈晴。
   That girl's name is Qing Chen.

介绍

jièshào
introduce; introduction

Useful phrases and sentences

1. **Zìwǒ jièshào.**
   自我介绍。
   Self-introduction.
2. **Wǒ gěi nǐmen jièshào yíxià.**
   我给你们介绍一下。
   Let me introduce you.
3. **Jièshào chǎnpǐn.**
   介绍产品。
   Introduce products.
4. **Wǒ gēn dàjiā jièshào yíxià wǒmen gōngsī zuì xīnde chǎnpǐn.**
   我跟大家介绍一下我们公司最新的产品。
   Let me introduce to you our company's latest products.

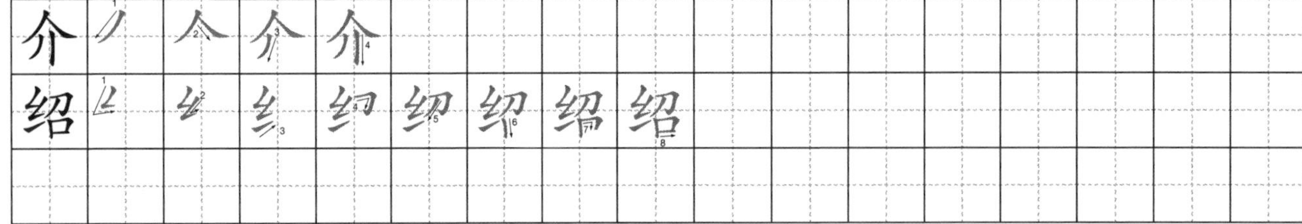

跑步

pǎobù
jog; run

Useful phrases and sentences

1. **Wǒ měitiān pǎobù.**
   我每天跑步。
   I go jogging every day.
2. **Nǐ xǐhuan pǎobù ma?**
   你喜欢跑步吗？
   Do you like jogging?
3. **Nǐ píngcháng zài nǎr pǎobù?**
   你平常在哪儿跑步？
   Where do you usually go jogging?
4. **Wǒmen qù pǎobù ba!**
   我们去跑步吧！
   Let's go jogging!

题

tí
topic; theme

Useful phrases and sentences

1. **Wèntí.**
   问题。
   Question.
2. **Tímù.**
   题目。
   Title.
3. **Zhǔtí.**
   主题。
   Main topic./Main theme.
4. **Nántí.**
   难题。
   Difficulty.

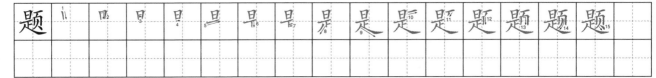

向

xiàng
toward; direction

Useful phrases and sentences

1. **fāngxiàng.**
   方向。
   Direction.
2. **yīxiàng.**
   一向。
   Tend to.
3. **Qīngxiàng.**
   倾向。
   Tendency./Orientation.
4. **Xiàng qián zǒu.**
   向前走。
   Walk straight.

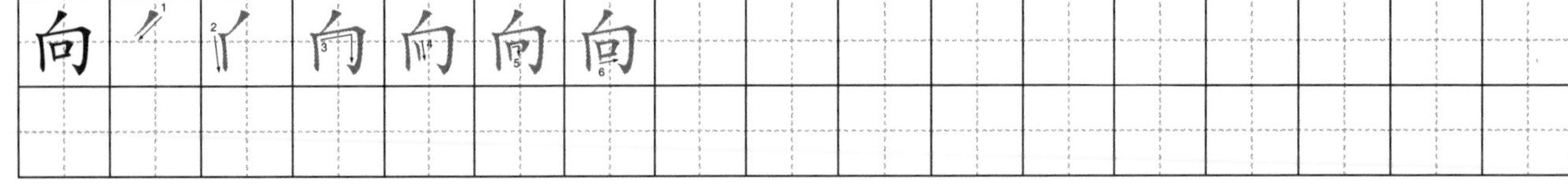

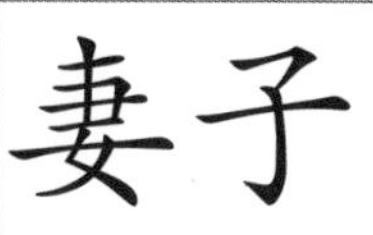

qīzi
wife

Useful phrases and sentences

1. **Yíge qīzi.**
   一个妻子。
   A wife.
2. **Wáng Xiānshengde qīzi.**
   王先生的妻子。
   Mr. Wang's wife.
3. **Wǒde qīzi shì Hánguó rén.**
   我的妻子是韩国人。
   My wife is Korean.
4. **Lǐ Xiānshengde qīzi hé háizi dōu zài Xīnjiāpō.**
   李先生的妻子和孩子都在新加坡。
   Mr. Li's wife and children are all in Singapore.

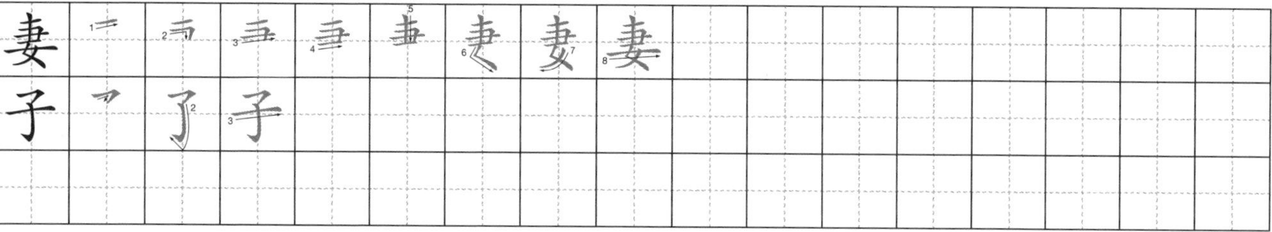

手表

shǒubiǎo
wristwatch

Useful phrases and sentences

1. **Yìzhī shǒubiǎo.**
   一只手表。
   One wristwatch.
2. **Zhège shǒubiǎo zhēn guì.**
   这个手表真贵。
   This wristwatch is really expensive.
3. **Nǐde shǒubiǎo hěn hǎokàn.**
   你的手表很好看。
   Your wristwatch is pretty.
4. **Zhège shǒubiǎo shì nǎge páizide?**
   这个手表是哪个牌子的？
   What brand is this wristwatch?

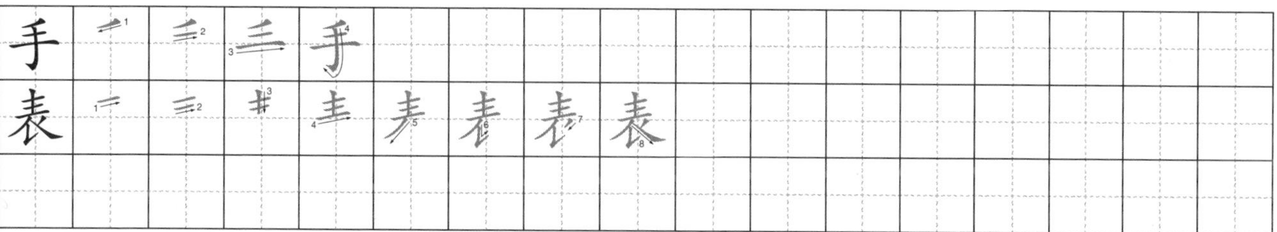

它

tā
it

Useful phrases and sentences

1. **Qítā.**
   其它。
   Other.
2. **Chúle Zhōngwén, nǐ hái huì shuō qítāde yǔyán ma?**
   除了中文，你还会说其他的语言吗？
   Do you speak any other languages besides Chinese?
3. **Tāde yèzi.**
   它的叶子。
   Its leaves.
4. **Zhèkē shù bìngle, tāde yèzi dōu méi le.**
   这棵树病了，它的叶子都没了。
   This tree is sick. Its leaves are all gone.

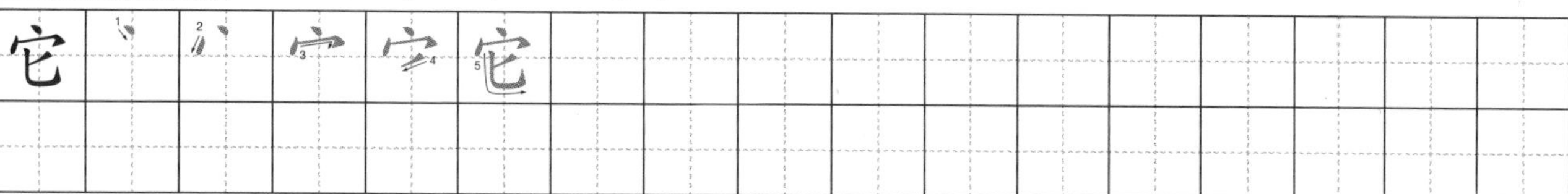

药

yào
medicine;
medication

Useful phrases and sentences

1. **Zhōngyào.**
   中药。
   Chinese medicine.
2. **Xīyào.**
   西药。
   Western medicine.
3. **Yàojú.**
   药局。
   Pharmacy.
4. **Nǐ zuótiān bú tài shūfu, chīle yào ma?**
   你昨天不太舒服，吃了药吗？
   You were not feeling well yesterday. Did you take any medicine?

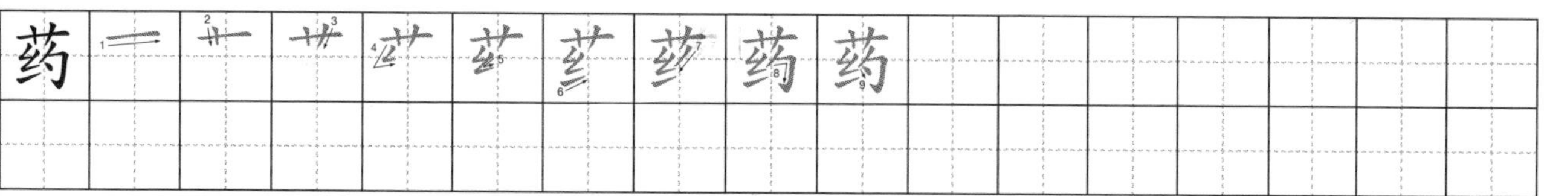

希望

xīwàng
hope

Useful phrases and sentences

1. **Xīwàng shìjiè hépíng.**
   希望世界和平。
   I hope for world peace.
2. **Xīwàng nǐ zǎorì kāngfù.**
   希望你早日康复。
   I hope you recover swiftly.
3. **Háizi shì fùmǔde xīwàng.**
   孩子是父母的希望。
   Children carry the hopes of their parents.
4. **Wǒ juéde zhèjiàn shì méiyǒu xīwàng.**
   我觉得这件事没有希望。
   I feel that this matter is hopeless.

眼睛

yǎnjīng
eye

Useful phrases and sentences

1. **Tāde yǎnjīng.**
   她的眼睛。
   Her eyes.
2. **Yúde yǎnjīng.**
   鱼的眼睛。
   Fish's eyes.
3. **Zhè xiǎoháirde yǎnjīng xiàng bàba.**
   这小孩儿的眼睛像爸爸。
   This child's eyes look like his/her father's.
4. **Wǒde yǎnjīng jīntiān yǒu diǎnr suān.**
   我的眼睛今天有点儿酸。
   My eyes are a bit sore today.

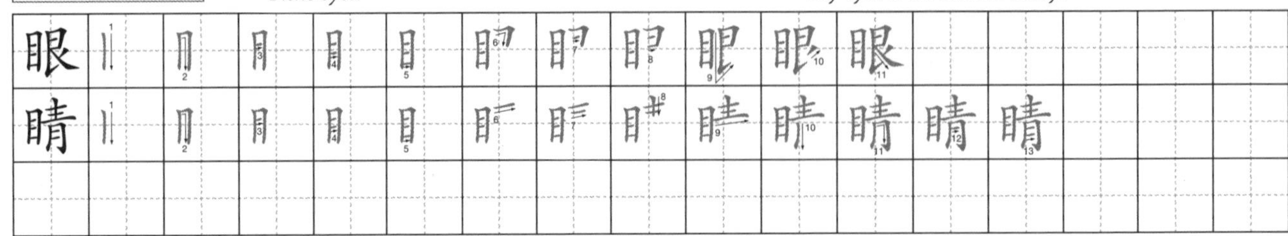

阴

yīn
cloudy; overcast; yin (i.e., yin and yang)

Useful phrases and sentences

1. **Yīntiān.**
   阴天。
   A cloudy day.
2. **Yīn Yáng.**
   阴阳。
   Yin and yang.
3. **Yīnmóu.**
   阴谋。
   Plot, conspiracy.
4. **Yīn'àn.**
   阴暗。
   Dark and gloomy.

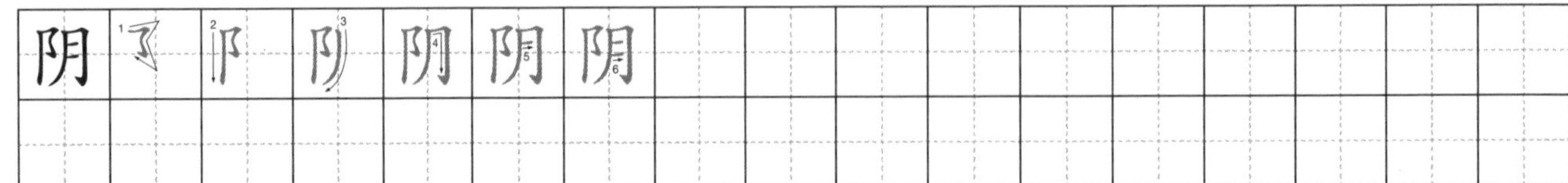

出

chū
exit; out

Useful phrases and sentences

1. **Chūkǒu.**
   出口。
   Exit.
2. **Chūqù.**
   出去。
   Go out.
3. **Chūxiàn.**
   出现。
   Appear.
4. **Zhège dìfang bù zhǔn jìnchū.**
   这个地方不准进出。
   No entry or exit at this place.

yángròu
lamb

Useful phrases and sentences

1. **Liǎngjīn yángròu.**
   两斤羊肉。
   Two jin (jin=500 grams) of lamb.
2. **Zhèkuài yángròu.**
   这块羊肉。
   This piece of lamb.
3. **Nǐ chī yángròu ma?**
   你吃羊肉吗？
   Do you eat lamb?
4. **Zhège cāntīng zuòde yángròu hěn hǎochī.**
   这个餐厅做的羊肉很好吃。
   This restaurant makes tasty lamb.

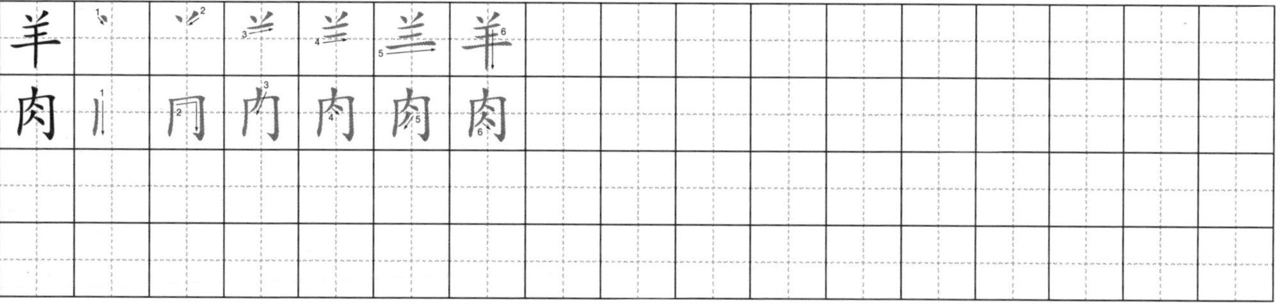

旅游

lǚyóu
travel

Useful phrases and sentences

1. **Guónèi lǚyóu.**
   国内旅游。
   Domestic travel
2. **Guówài lǚyóu.**
   国外旅游。
   International travel
3. **Lǚyóu jǐngdiǎn.**
   旅游景点。
   Tourist attraction
4. **Wǒ dǎsuàn jīnnián xiàtiān qù Éluósī lǚyóu.**
   我打算今年夏天去俄罗斯旅游。
   I plan to travel to Russia this summer.

zhàngfu
husband

Useful phrases and sentences

1. **Yíge zhàngfu.**
   一个丈夫。
   One husband.
2. **Ān Tàitaide zhàngfu.**
   安太太的丈夫。
   Mrs. An's husband.
3. **Zhào Tàitàide zhàngfu zài Shēnzhèn gōngzuò.**
   赵太太的丈夫在深圳工作。
   Mrs. Zhao's husband works in Shenzhen.
4. **Gāo Tàitaide zhàngfu shì Déguó rén.**
   高太太的丈夫是德国人。
   Mrs. Gao's husband is German.

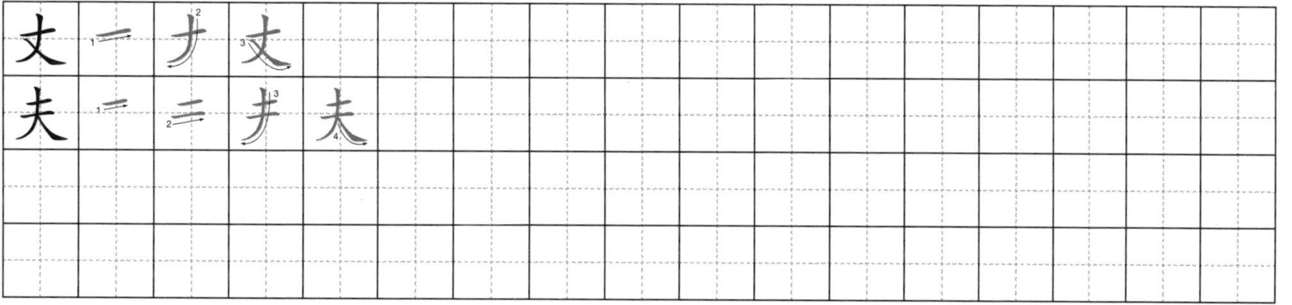

yú
fish

Useful phrases and sentences

1. **Yītiáo yú.**
   一条鱼。
   One fish.
2. **Yúròu.**
   鱼肉。
   Fish meat.
3. **Yú shìchǎng.**
   鱼市场。
   Fish market.
4. **Nǐ huì diàoyú ma?**
   你会钓鱼吗？
   Do you know how to fish?

正在

zhèng zài
(progressive marker)

Useful phrases and sentences

1. **Tā láide shíhou, wǒ zhèng zài xuéxí.**
   他来的时候，我正在学习。
   I was studying when he came.
2. **Wǒ qù zhǎo Xiǎo Lǐde shíhou, tā zhèng zài shuìjiào.**
   我去找小李的时候，他正在睡觉。
   Xiao Li was sleeping when I went to his place.
3. **Wǒ māmā gěi wǒ dǎ diànhuàde shíhou, wǒ zhèng zài shàngkè.**
   我妈妈给我打电话的时候，我正在上课。
   I was in class when my mother called me.
4. **Xiànzài zhèng zài xiàyǔ.**
   现在正在下雨。
   It's raining now.

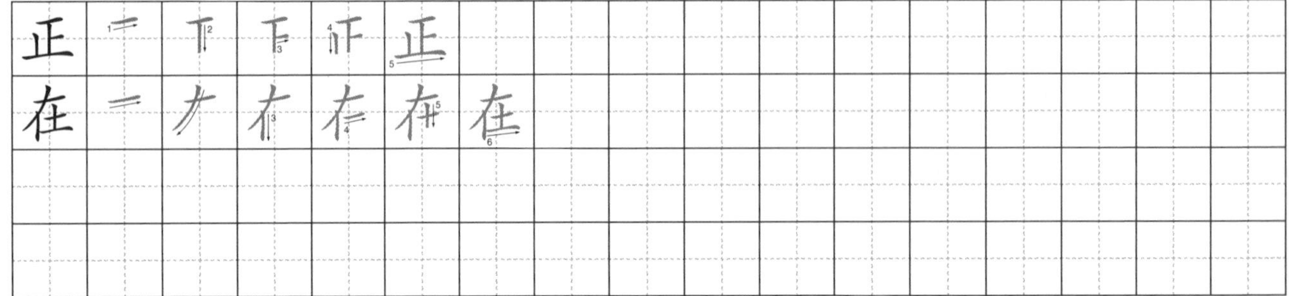

自行车

zìxíngchē
bike

Useful phrases and sentences

1. **Yīliàng zìxíngchē.**
   一辆自行车。
   A bike.
2. **Wǒde zìxíngchē.**
   我的自行车。
   My bike.
3. **Lánsède zìxíngchē.**
   蓝色的自行车。
   A blue bike.
4. **Tiānqì hǎode shíhou, wǒ qí zìxíngchē qù shàngbān.**
   天气好的时候，我骑自行车去上班。
   I go to work by bike when the weather is good.

自 行 车

Answers to Exercises

LESSON 1

Warm up

1. 819 元　　2. 378 元　　3. 69 元

Exercise

Part 1

1. 9　2. 48　3. 76　4. 63　5. 71　6. 99
7. 202　8. 859

Part 2

1. 六十七　2. 二十三　3. 九十二　4. 一百零八
5. 九百八十七　6. 四百七十六　7. 五百二十　8. 九百一十四

Part 3

1. 九七四六八九五五三七　2. 七三四九零八五七九
3. 六零三　4. 三二八

Part 4

Item	Price in China	Price in your country
A cup of Starbucks coffee	四十二块	三美元
A pair of Nike shoes	七百八十块	六十七美元
A bottle of orange juice	十五块	三美元
A movie ticket	六十块	二十美元

LESSON 2

Warm up

1. 李元　2. 王美　3. 李友

Exercise

Part 1

1. 你好！我是学生、你呢？　2. 我叫李友、你叫什么名字？
3. 他姓王、他叫王男。　4. 她是你的朋友吗？

Part 2

1. 我叫王元。　2. 我姓李。　3. 我朋友姓张。
4. 我朋友叫张一朋。

Part 3

你好！我姓王、我叫王友美、我有三个朋友、他们的名字是王元、张朋、李一。我们是好朋友。

LESSON 3

Warm up

1. Kevin 不是中国人。　2. Kevin 是英国人。
3. Kevin 的爸妈是中国人。

Exercise

Part 1

朋友、英文、请问、哪儿、人们、中国

Part 2

	姓	名	他/她是哪国人？
1.	王	梦	她是中国人。
2.	赵	洁	她是美国人。
3.	高	文	他是英国人。

Part 3

1. 我不是中国人。　2. 请问. 你是哪国人？
3. 我的好朋友是英国人。　4. 我的男朋友是美国人。
5. 我一个老师是中国人。一个老师是英国人。

LESSON 4

Warm up

1. 四口人　2. 李元的哥哥。他十二岁。　3. 李元不喜欢哥哥

Exercise

Part 1

1. 你家有几口人？你有几个哥哥？
2. 你十八岁、你的中国朋友多大？
3. 请问、你的爸爸妈妈在哪儿工作？
4. 你的中文家教叫什么名字？

Part 2

1. 我家有三口人。　2. 我的爸爸妈妈是中国人。
3. 我今年二十五岁。　4. 我有一个姐姐。两个弟弟。

Part 3

你们好！
我叫泰勒斯威夫特、我是美国人。我的老家在 Pennsylvania。我家有四口人、爸爸、妈妈、弟弟和我。我今年(**jīnnián**: this year) 二十七岁、我弟弟二十三岁。我有很多中国朋友。

LESSON 5

Warm up

1. 爸爸和妈妈都是医生。　2. 姐姐是老师。
3. 二十二岁；她是学生。

Exercise

Part 1

1. 我家有四口人、你家呢？　　2. 你以后想做什么工作？
3. 我的爸爸是公司的老板，他每天都很忙。
4. 我和我的弟弟都是大学生。我喜欢学中文，他也喜欢学中文。

Part 2

1. 我的父亲是老师、母亲不工作。　3. 我有三个老师。
2. 我以后想去公司工作。　4. 我有六个好朋友。

Part 3

Family members	爸爸	妈妈	哥哥	姐姐	弟弟	妹妹
Job	医生	老师	律师	N/A	学生	学生
Like/don't like	喜欢	喜欢	不喜欢	N/A	不喜欢	喜欢

Review Exercises (Lesson 1–5)

Part 1

1. **jiǔshíèr** ninety two
2. **qībǎibāshíwǔ** seven hundred and eighty five
3. **nǐ hǎo** hello　4. **míngzi** name　5. **Zhōngguó** China
6. **péngyou** friend　7. **gēge** older brother
8. **jǐsuì** how old　9. **lǎoshī** teacher　10. **gōngzuò** job

Part 2

1. 有时间　2. 学生　3. 什么　4. 没关系　5. 朋友
6. 老师　7. 打工　8. 父亲　9. 中国　10. 名字

Part 3

1. 我的室友叫李大中。
2. 我是老师、我觉得我的工作很有意思。
3. 我家有四口人。爸爸、妈妈、姐姐和我。
4. 我今年二十七岁了、我有两个美国朋友。

Part 4

1. 国友是美国人。他今年二十三岁。
2. 六口人。不知道国友的父母做什么工作。
3. 国友的中文不太好。　4. 小朋不认识国友。

LESSON 6

Warm up

1. 2016年1月20日. 星期三　2. 十岁　3. 吃饭、唱歌。

Exercise

Part 1

1. 今天是三月五日。 昨天是三月四日。 明天是三月六日。
2. 我们每天八点上课。 九点下课。
3. 我这个月没时间。 我们下个月再见。
4. 星期六没有课。我们去吃中国菜吧。

Part 2

1. 今天星期二。　4. 我星期四不忙。
2. 明年我三十七岁。　5. 我的生日是八月十五日。
3. 昨天是星期六。

Part 3

我是大一的学生、每天九点上课、下午三点下课。今天是2016年9月8日、星期五。明天是星期六、我想休息 (**xiǎngxiūxi**: want to rest)、睡觉 (**shuìjiào**: sleep)。

LESSON 7

Warm up

1. 喜欢看书、看电视。　2. 和朋友们打球、看功夫电影。
3. 我不喜欢买东西。我姐姐和妈妈喜欢买东西。

Exercise

Part 1

1. 我要去超市买东西。　3. 明天一起看电影吧。 我去买票。
2. 我哥哥不喜欢看书、我很喜欢。　4. 他不喜欢打球。

Part 2

1. 我平常喜欢看电视。　2. 我喜欢看中文书. 不喜欢看英文书。
3. 我平常去 Market Basket 买东西。
4. 我喜欢和女朋友看电影。
5. 我的家人都不是美国人。我们都是新加坡人。

Part 3

我是一个大学生、我住在学校、我喜欢我的宿舍。 我不喜欢学校的餐厅。我每天看书、星期六和星期天我常常休息、我有时候去超市买东西、有时候和朋友打球。有时候和家人看电影。

LESSON 8

Warm up

1. 吃饭、上课、下课。
2. 看书、打球、买东西。
3. 回家和父母吃晚饭。

Exercise

Part 1

1. 这儿有没有吃饭的地方？
2. 周末不上课、我们可以去打球。
3. 请问、你明天什么时候有时间？
4. 你昨天中午和谁一起吃饭的？

Part 2

1. 我是去年开始学中文的。　2. 我周末去买东西了。
3. 我的中文老师是高老师、她是美国人。
4. 我明天想看书。　5. 我平常自己做饭。

Part 3

我的周末

Time	Activity
9:00 a.m.–noon	看书、洗衣服
12:00 noon–1:00 p.m.	吃饭
1:00 p.m.–4:00 p.m.	休息、打球
7:00 p.m.–10:00 p.m.	看电视

LESSON 9

Warm up

1. 周末的时候。
2. 她不喜欢和姐姐去买东西。
3. 我觉得很好的东西、姐姐觉得太贵了／不好看。

Exercise

Part 1

1. 这本书很不错。你觉得这本书怎么样？
2. 请问、这件衣服多少钱？
3. 这个太贵了、便宜点儿吧。
4. 你听错了、他不是中国人。

Part 2

1. 我觉得中文课很有意思。
2. 我的学费不贵。
3. 我喜欢去 Macey's 买衣服。
4. 我喜欢和哥哥去买衣服。
5. 我的学校很大。

Part 3

我的学校在中国的南边、我喜欢这儿的老师、不喜欢这儿的学生、我觉得这儿的学生不喜欢看书。我平常去学校的商店买东西、因为那儿的东西很便宜。

LESSON 10

Warm up

1. 她喜欢买衣服。
2. 不。她觉得她的衣服很便宜。
3. 鞋、裤子和裙子。

Exercise

Part 1

1. 你的这件衣服很好看、我也想买。
2. 你觉得这双鞋怎么样？
3. 这件裙子有点儿大、我试一下那件吧。
4. 我不喜欢这件裤子、太贵了。

Part 2

1. 我常常去买衣服。
2. 我没有很贵的衣服。
3. 我有三双。
4. 我这个周末要去买衣服。
5. 我有时候试穿、有时候不试穿。

Part 3

Your friend would like to purchase the following goods.	Where do you recommend him/her to buy?	Why do you think he/she should go to those places to buy? (e.g., price. quality)
一双运动鞋	耐克商店	有点儿贵，可是很好看
两件裤子	T.J. MAXX	很便宜，也很好看
一件衣服	Gap商店	很好看

REVIEW EXERCISES (LESSON 6–10)

Part 1

1. **xīngqī** week
2. **xièxie** thanks
3. **zàijiàn** goodbye
4. **xǐhuan** like
5. **dǎqiú** play ball
6. **yīfu** cloth
7. **zhōumò** weekend
8. **dìfang** place
9. **shíjiān** time
10. **piányi** cheap

Part 2

1. 室友
2. 可是
3. 觉得
4. 一起
5. 每天
6. 可以
7. 电影
8. 平常
9. 再见
10. 打球

Part 3

1. 我平常星期一和星期五很忙。
2. 我的父母周末常常在家休息、看书。
3. 我有的衣服很贵、有的衣服很便宜。
4. 我好朋友的生日是七月二十一日。

Part 4

1. 张欢想跟常天去买衣服、打球、看电影、吃饭。
2. 常天要跟别人去吃晚饭。
3. 我觉得常天有女朋友。

LESSON 11

Warm up

1. 双城宾馆
2. 两分钟

Exercise

Part 1

1. 你知道她有男朋友吗？
2. 谢谢你请我吃饭、你太客气了。
3. 我知道你去过很多外国的城市、你最喜欢哪个？
4. 你往前走五分钟就到了。

Part 2

1. 我爸爸喜欢看历史书。
2. 我觉得四季宾馆很好。
3. 我在北京上学、我不喜欢、人太多了。
4. 我觉得西安人很客气、上海人不太客气。
5. 我家住在成都、市中心很漂亮。

Part 3

1. 觉得
2. 周末
3. 看书
4. 裙子
5. 客气
6. 地方
7. 衣服
8. 可以
9. 时候

LESSON 12

Warm up

1. 中国银行
2. 过了路口往前走
3. 不开门

Exercise

Part 1

1. 请问、中国银行在公园的旁边吗？
2. 你过街的时候不要打电话。
3. 我们在家吃饭吧、外边的饭太贵了、也不好吃。
4. 那个宾馆有点儿远、去那儿不太方便。

Part 2

1. 我家旁边没有银行。
2. 这个周末我不在家。不好意思。
3. 对、城市公园就在前边。
4. 超市不远、走路五分钟就到了。
5. 我没有钱、我不想上街买东西。

Part 3

超市不远，请你往前走，到了第二个路口往左走，走三分钟就到了。

LESSON 13

Warm up

1. 买花
2. 女朋友

Exercise

Part 1

1. 你现在有时间吗？
2. 我觉得这件衣服很漂亮。
3. 学校商店星期六不开门。
4. 往前走就是北京大学了。

Part 2

1. 学校商店的东西不太贵。
2. 我买过花。我给妈妈买过花。
3. 图书馆早上八点开门。
4. 我的学校很漂亮。
5. 我想去纽约的公司工作。

Part 3

你的学校图书馆的名字	这个图书馆人多不多？	星期几开门？星期几关门？	漂亮吗？大吗？	你一个星期去几次？
1. 燕京图书馆	多	星期六关门	不大. 很漂亮	一次
2.中文图书馆	不太多	星期六、星期天关门	有点小. 很漂亮	一次
3. 科技图书馆	很多	不关门	很大. 不漂亮	三次

LESSON 14

Warm up

1. 上海人；不喜欢
2. 不喜欢；太热了
3. 上海的秋天比北京的秋天舒服

Exercise

Part 1

1. 我没去过南京、南京的天气怎么样？
2. 这里的春天很漂亮、但是春天也很短。
3. 哥哥的房间比弟弟的大一点儿。
4. 你怎么了？你看起来不太舒服。

Part 2

1. 我喜欢春天、不冷也不热。
2. 我的老家冬天不常下雪。
3. 九月去比较好、很舒服。
4. 明年夏天我想去咖啡馆儿打工。
5. 我的房间不太舒服。太小了。

Part 3

你们好、今天我想说说我老家的天气。我家住在北京、我最喜欢的季节是秋天、我最不喜欢的季节是夏天。春天不冷也不热、我喜欢去爬山；夏天太热了、我喜欢跟朋友去游泳；秋天很舒服、也很漂亮、我常常跟家人出去走走；冬天这儿会下雪、我有时候出去玩儿雪。你想来我的老家玩儿吗？要是你想来、你九月来比较好、因为我那时候不忙、可以跟你一起玩儿。

LESSON 15

Warm up

1. 昆明在中国的西南边。
2. 小雪去过昆明一次。
3. 昆明春夏秋冬四个季节都很舒服。

Exercise

Part 1

1. 今天我请你吃饭吧、不能每次都让你请我。
2. 上中学的时候、父母不同意我找男朋友。
3. 这个宾馆的房间有点儿小、而且也不便宜、我们去别的宾馆看看吧。
4. 他没找到工作、s所以这几天不太高兴。

Part 2

1. 我以后想去中国工作。
2. 要是我现在找女朋友、我父母会不同意。
3. 青海在中国的西北边。
4. 我上午六点半起床、晚上十一点睡觉。
5. 我去过国外、我去过日本和泰国。

Part 3

1. 苏州在中国的南方。
2. 苏州的天气很好、很舒服。
3. 对. 苏州有很多漂亮的公园、有的公园很有名。

REVIEW EXERCISES (LESSON 11–15)

Part 1

1. **zhīdao** know
2. **chéngshì** city
3. **gōngyuán** park
4. **pángbiān** side
5. **lǐbiān** inside
6. **piàoliang** pretty
7. **shāngdiàn** store
8. **shūfu** comfortable
9. **tiānqì** weather
10. **tóngyì** agree

Part 2

1. 分钟
2. 所以
3. 同意
4. 凉快
5. 春天
6. 现在
7. 学校
8. 城市
9. 对不起
10. 下雪

Part 3

1. 我在青岛工作。我很喜欢青岛，很干净也很漂亮。
2. 我家旁边有一个很大的公园。公园里常常有很多人。
3. 银行下午五点关门。 4. 我喜欢冬天，我不喜欢热的天气。

Part 4

1. 公园不大. 可是很漂亮。
2. 公园七点开门. 晚上九点半关门。
3. 春天和夏天的时候公园常常有很多人，秋天的时候人不多。
4. 我常常周末去公园。球球喜欢冬天去公园。

LESSON 16

Warm up

1. 开始很难，后来容易了。
2. 说和写难
3. 学了三年了；差不多两千个汉字

Exercise

Part 1

1. 从我家走到学校要半个钟头左右。
2. 你是什么时候开始学中文的？
3. 我听别人说学中文很难，你为什么觉得很容易？
4. 明天你会跟我们一起去吗？

Part 2

1. 我前年开始学中文。我觉得中文不难，因为我喜欢学过日文。
2. 我觉得说中文最难。
3. 今年我上中文、数学、化学课。化学课很容易。
4. 我最好的朋友叫王天，我们认识两年了。
5. 大学以后我会去台湾工作，我喜欢吃台湾饭。

Part 3

1. 认识
2. 哪里
3. 开始
4. 读书
5. 容易
6. 舒服
7. 大家
8. 可以
9. 左右

LESSON 17

Warm up

1. 王老师；西安
2. 练习听和说；读汉字和写汉字
3. 中国文化，历史跟节日。

Exercise

Part 1

1. 你想跟我一起去吃晚饭吗？
2. 我想先去买东西，然后回宿舍写作业。
3. 这个电影很有意思，大家一边看一边笑。
4. 你常常跟老师练习说中文，是吗？

Part 2

1. 我喜欢学习中国文化。
2. 我周末常常在宿舍睡觉，跟朋友聊天。
3. 我喜欢一个人学习。
4. 我每天九点上中文课。一个星期有四节中文课。
5. 我觉得圣诞节很有意思。因为我妈妈会做很多菜(**cài**:dish), 我也有很多礼物(**lǐwù**: present)

Part 3

小王:

你说你明年也想学中文，我觉得这是一个很好的决定。中文读和写有点难，可是说和听不太难。我们的中文课有十六个学生，他们的中文都很好。我们每个星期有一个考试，考试不太难。我有两个中文老师，一个是中国人，一个是美国人，我很喜欢他们。我觉得上中文课很有意思，你也应该上中文课。这是我的想法，要是你还有别的问题，请告诉我。

祝好,

李为

LESSON 18

Warm up

1. 史先生；他有太太、儿子和女儿。
2. 他喜欢在家休息，和孩子聊天、运动。
3. 儿子每天上网、看电脑，不学习。

Exercise

Part 1

1. 你昨天晚上几点睡觉？
2. 他明年开始读大学。
3. 我男朋友很喜欢运动。
4. 周末她常常跟家人聊天。

Part 2

1. 我每天晚上十一点休息。
2. 我一个星期运动一次、我喜欢游泳。
3. 我喜欢上网、我上网看电影。
4. 我喜欢我的大学生活、我的朋友都很有意思。
5. 我常常跟我的历史老师聊天。我们聊很多国家的历史。

Part 3

爸爸、妈妈:

你们最近都好吗？

我每天都很忙。我一个星期上十节课、早上六点半起床、晚上两点睡觉。你们知道我很喜欢运动、可是我没有很多时间、一个星期只能去一次。

我的室友人很好。我常常跟他们一起吃晚饭、聊天。

我很想你们。

祝好,

儿子

LESSON 19

Warm up

1. 去了中国朋友的老家；我跟张文一起去。
2. 他们家很大、四个房间、一个院子。
3. “我”不喝酒、因为还没二十一岁。

Exercise

Part 1

1. 去中国人家里带什么礼物比较好？
2. 她很喜欢小动物，她家有两只小狗。
3. 如果你下个周末不忙，欢迎你来我家坐坐。
4. 你想喝点儿什么？我家有茶、可乐。

Part 2

1. 我会带点儿水果。
2. 在美国、人们常常带巧克力和花。
3. 二十一岁可以喝酒。
4. 我喜欢小动物、我们家有一只猫。
5. 我今年没有室友。

Part 3

大卫. 你好！

我觉得带茶、带 点儿吃的都很好、你不用太紧张。对了、带点儿水果也很不错。祝你在朋友家玩儿得高兴！

天明

LESSON 20

Warm up

1. 他们去了一个公园。
2. 他们看到公园里有很多花、也听了一个音乐会。
3. “我”很喜欢住在张文家、“我”以后还想去，因为可以吃不同的菜和水果。

Exercise

Part 1

1. 他只有黑色的衣服、没有别的颜色的衣服。
2. 上中学的时候、父母不让我找男朋友。
3. 他说中文说得很清楚、不过有点儿慢。
4. 不好意思、我因为明天还有考试、所以不跟你们去玩儿了。

Part 2

1. 我的同屋不喜欢说话。
2. 我自己住。
3. 我想去国外找工作。
4. 我喜欢黑色、不喜欢红色。
5. 可以带水果。

Part 3

1. 两个星期以前。
2. 我跟朋友一起去的。
3. 我带了一瓶酒。我的朋友很喜欢。
4. 我们一起跳舞、唱歌。

REVIEW EXERCISES (LESSON 16–20)

Part 1

1. **nǎlǐ** where	6. **liáotiān** chat
2. **róngyì** easy	7. **fángjiān** room
3. **zhòngyào** important	8. **háizi** children
4. **wénhuà** culture	9. **yīnyuè** music
5. **xiūxi** rest	10. **shuǐguǒ** fruit

Part 2

1. 开始	2. 认识	3. 节日	4. 考试	5. 电脑
6. 决定	7. 意思	8. 礼物	9. 欢迎	10. 因为

Part 3

1. 我觉得中文很有意思。
2. 我每天上网一个小时。
3. 我喜欢跟老师聊天。
4. 上次去朋友家做客是去年冬天。

Part 4

1. 大中的中文老师。
2. 大中常常学中文，可是他觉得中文很难。
3. 他想请张老师帮他学中文。
4. 今天下午和明天早上都可以

English-Chinese Index

clothes 衣 yī 92; 服 fú, 衣服 yīfu 93
cloudy; overcast; yin (i.e., yin and yang) 阴 yīn 194
coffee color 咖啡色 kāfēisè 182
coffee shop 咖啡店 kāfēidiàn 117
cola (often slang for the Coca-Cola brand) 可乐 kělè 77
cold 冷 lěng 126
cold dish 凉菜 liáng cài 126
cold drinks 冷饮 lěngyǐn 126
cold herbal tea 凉茶 liáng chá 126
colleague 同事 tóngshì 136
college 学院 xuéyuàn 176
College Entrance Examination (China) 高考 Gāokǎo 154
college student 大学生 dàxuésheng 44
color 颜 yán, 颜色 yánsè 181; 色 sè 182
come 来 lái 134
come again 再来 zài lái 61
come from 来自 láizì 184
come over 过来 guòlai 134
comfortable 舒 shū, 舒服 shūfu 130
comment; opinion; recommendation 意见 yìjiàn 136
common 平 píng 65; 常见 chángjiàn 66
common sense 常识 chángshi 147
comparatively; to compare 比较 bǐjiào 127
compare 比 bǐ 127
competition; game 比赛 bǐsài 127
complexion 容颜 róngyán 181
computer 电脑 diànnǎo 164
computer science 电脑科学 diànnǎo kēxué 164
conference 会议 huìyì 147
congratulations 恭喜 gōngxǐ 66
consider; think over 考虑 kǎolǜ 154
consider important 重视 zhòngshì 68
content 内容 nèiróng 149
convenience store 便利店 biànlìdiàn 86
convenient 便 biàn, 方便 fāngbiàn 86
conversation; dialogue 会话 huìhuà 155
cook 做饭 zuòfàn 49
calm down; relax 冷静 lěngjìng 126
cool 凉 liáng 126
correct; across; facing 对 duì 108
country 国家 guójiā 34
courtyard 院 yuàn 176
cross a street 过马路 guò mǎlù, 过街 guòjiē 110
culture 文 wén, 文化 wénhuà 145
cup; glass 杯子 bēizi 92
curriculum vitae 简历 jiǎnlì 157
cute 可爱 kě'ài 77
cycle 周 zhōu 74

D
(daily) rhythm 作息 zuòxī 167
daughter 女儿 nǚ'ér 52
dawn 天亮 tiānliàng 58
day 天 tiān 58; 日 rì 59
daytime 白天 báitiān 182
decade of a century 年代 niándài 59
develop 开发 kāifā 118
diary 日记 rìjì 59
dictation 听写 tīngxiě 148
dictionary (of characters) 字典 zìdiǎn 26
did not see 没看见 méi kànjiàn 61
differentiate 认出 rènchū 147
difficult; hard 难 nán 149
diligent 用功 yònggōng 156
direction 方 fāng, 方向 fāngxiàng 76
discuss; consult 商量 shāngliang 116
distance 远近 yuǎnjìn 113
divide 分 fēn 103
do; make 做 zuò 49
do business 做生意 zuò shēngyì 49; 做买卖 zuò mǎimài 117
do homework 做作业 zuò zuòyè 49
do not 不要 búyào 94
do not want to 不想 bù xiǎng 74
do temporary work 打工 dǎgōng 49
do what 做什么 zuò shénme 49
doctor 医生 yīsheng 52; (things relating to medicine) 医 yī 52
dog 狗 gǒu 173
dog food 狗粮 gǒuliáng 173
don't know how 不会 bú huì 33
don't want 不要 bú yào 94
door 门 mén 119
dot 点 diǎn 93
double bed 双人床 shuāngrén chuáng 90
downtown 市中心 shìzhōngxīn 101
dress 裙 qún 91
dress (*verb*) 穿衣服 chuān yīfu 95
drift 漂流 piāoliú 121
drink 喝 hē 174
drink alcoholic beverage 喝酒 hē jiǔ 174
drink tea 喝茶 hē chá 174
drink water 喝水 hē shuǐ 174
drive 开 kāi, 开车 kāichē 118
dusk 黄昏 huánghūn 182

E
earlier 早点儿 zǎo diǎnr 77
early 早 zǎo 77
early summer 初夏 chūxià 129
east 东 dōng 69; 东边 dōngbian 69
Easter 复活节 Fùhuójié 155
easy 易 yì, 容易 róngyì 149
eat 吃 chī 75; 吃饭 chīfàn 75
eat breakfast 吃早饭 chī zǎofàn 75
eat something 吃东西 chī dōngxi 75
edge 边 biān 112
eight 八 bā 18
eight hours 八个小时 bāge xiǎoshí 18
eight minutes 八分钟 bāfēn zhōng 18
eighteen years old 十八岁 shíbāsuì 43
elderly woman 大妈 dàmā 42
elective course 选修课 xuǎnxiūkè 158
electric 电 diàn 67
electricity bill 电费 diànfèi 67
electronic device 电器 diànqì 67
electronic dictionary 电子词典 diànzǐ cídiǎn 67
emails 电子邮件 diànzǐ yóujiàn 164
employ 用 yòng 156
end 末 mò 74
end of month 月末 yuèmò 74
end of term 期末 qīmò 60
end of year 年末 niánmò 74
energy 气 qì 105
England 英国 Yīngguó 35
English; British; brave 英 yīng 35
English language (usually written language) 英文 Yīngwén 35
entrance 入口 rùkǒu 41
enthusiastic; hospitable 热情 rèqíng 126
enthusiastically welcome or greet 迎接 yíngjiē 172
epic tale/poem 史诗 shǐshī 157
essay 作文 zuòwén 49
establishment 馆 guǎn 102; 院 yuàn 176
etiquette 礼 lǐ 172
even numbers 双号 shuānghào 90
evening; night 晚上 wǎnshang 77
every 每 měi 137
every day 每天 měitiān 137
every month 每个月 měige yuè 137
every time 每次 měicì 134
every week 每个星期 měige xīngqī 137
every year 每年 měinián 137
everyone 大家 dàjiā 44
everywhere 到处 dàochù 104
exactly 就是 jìushì, 到底 dàodǐ 104
exam 考试 kǎoshì 154
excuse me; may I ask 请问 qǐng wèn 31
exercise 运动 yùndòng 166
exit 出口 chūkǒu 41; 出 chū 194
expensive 贵 guì, (speaking of objects) 昂贵 ángguì 86
experience 历 lì, 经历 jīnglì 157
experienced and knowledgeable 见多识广 jiànduōshíguǎng 61
(expresses two simultaneous actions) 一边…一边… yìbiān... yìbiān... 112
extraordinarily 非常 fēicháng 66
eye 眼睛 yǎnjīng 194
eye-catching highlight 亮点 liàngdiǎn 121
eyesight 视力 shìlì 68

F
facial look 脸色 liǎnsè 182
factory 工厂 gōngchǎng 49
fair 公平 gōngpíng 65
fall 秋天 qiūtiān 130
fall asleep 睡着 shuìzháo 163
Fall semester 秋季学期 qiūjì xuéqī 130
family member 家人 jiārén 39
family name; be surnamed 姓 xìng 25
family name ; king 王 Wáng 27
family name; plum 李 Lǐ 27
famous 有名 yǒumíng 26; 闻 wén 166
famous for… 以…闻名 yǐ...wénmíng 166
famous painting 名画 mínghuà 26
far 远 yuǎn 113
farewell party 欢送会 huānsònghuì 66
fashionable 新潮 xīncháo 165
fast; quick 快 kuài 127
fast food 快餐 kuàicān 127
fate; destiny 命运 mìngyùn 166
father 爸 bà 41; 爸爸 bàba 41
father (formal) 父 fù 47; 父亲 fùqin 47
father (regional use) 阿爸 ābà 41
father-in-law (wife's father) 岳父 yuèfù 47
February 二月 èryuè 16
feel 觉 jué, 觉得 juéde 83
feeling 感觉 gǎnjué 83
female 女 nǚ 52
female student 女生 nǚshēng 52
festival 节 jié, 节庆 jiéqìng 158
few; less 少 shǎo, 很少 hěn shǎo 93
fifty *kuai* 五十块钱 wǔshíkuài qián 20
fifty minutes 五十分钟 wǔshífēn zhōng 104
fight 打架 dǎjià 68
file; document 文件 wénjiàn 145
film 电影 diànyǐng 68
film star 影星 yǐngxīng 60
final exam 期末考试 qīmòkǎoshì 74
find; found 找 zhǎo, 找到 zhǎodào 185
first; prior 先 xiān 156
fish 鱼 yú 196
five 五 wǔ 17
five (for animals such as cats and puppies) 五只 wǔzhī 17
five hundred *kuai* 五百块钱 wǔbǎikuài qián 20
five months 五个月 wǔge yuè 17
flat 平 píng 65
float 漂 piāo, 漂浮 piāofú 121
flour 面粉 miànfěn 183
flower 花 huā 117
(flower) yard 花园 huāyuán 112
follow 跟着 gēnzhe 158
food; meal 饭菜 fàncài 75
football (soccer) match 足球赛 zúqiúsài 69
for 为 wèi 181
(for bus route) 路 lù 111
for example 比方说 bǐfāngshuō 127
for the family 为了家人 wèile jiārén 181
for the sake of 为了 wèile 181
for the time being; tentatively 姑且 gūqiě 137
foreign guest 外宾 wàibīn 102
foreign language 外语 wàiyǔ 146
foreigner 外国人 wàiguó rén 34; 老外 lǎowài 50
founder 创始人 chuàngshǐ rén 145
four 四 sì 16
four (for papers or tables) 张四 sìzhāng 16
four hours 四个小时 sìge xiǎoshí 40
four o'clock 四点 sìdiǎn 16
freedom; free 自由 zìyóu 184
fresh 新鲜 xīnxiān 165
Friday 星期五 xīngqīwǔ 17
friend 朋 péng 36; 朋友 péngyou 36; 友 yǒu 36
friendly 友好 yǒuhǎo 36
friendship 友谊 yǒuyì 36
from 自 zì 184; 从 cóng 190
from now on 今后 jīnhòu 57
front 前面 qiánmiàn 120
front door; front gate 前门 qiánmén 119
fruit 水果 shuǐguǒ 175; 果 guǒ 184
fully; very 十分 shífēn 18

G
garden 园 yuán 112
gate 门口 ménkǒu 119
genes 基因 jīyīn 181
get off from work 下班 xiàbān 62
get up from bed 起床 qǐchuáng 109
gift 礼 lǐ 172; 礼物 lǐwù 173
girlfriend 女朋友 nǚpéngyou 36
give somebody a present 送礼 sònglǐ 172
give a try 试试 shìshì 95
globalization 全球化 quánqiúhuà 157
go 去 qù 134
go back home 回家 huíjiā 39
go for a walk 走走 zǒuzǒu 103
go now 先走了 xiān zǒule 103
go on the street 上街 shàngjiē 110
go out 外出 wàichū 136
go over there; in the past 过去 guòqu 110
go straight 往前 wǎng qián 102
go to bed 睡觉 shuìjiào 83
go to work 上班 shàngbān 62
godfather 干爸 gānbà 41
godmother 干妈 gānmā 42
gold 黄金 huángjīn 182
good 好 hǎo 26
good friend 好朋友 hǎo péngyou 36
good looking 好看 hǎokàn 26
"Good morning" 早 zǎo 77
"Good night" 晚安 wǎn'ān 77
good person 好人 hǎo rén 26
good to drink 好喝 hǎohē 174
goods 用品 yòngpǐn 156; 物品 wùpǐn 173
goodbye; see you again 再见 zàijiàn 61
grade 年级 niánjí 59
grades 分数 fēnshù 103
graduate school 研究所 yánjiūsuǒ 138
grammar 语法 yǔfǎ 146
green 绿色 lǜsè 182
green tea 绿茶 lǜchá 174
greet; greetings 问候 wènhou 32
guest 宾 bīn, 来宾 láibīn 102; 客 kè, 客人 kèren 105
guest of honor 贵宾 guìbīn 102
gym 体育馆 tǐyùguǎn 102

H
habit 习 xí, 习惯 xíguàn 155
had better 最好 zuìhǎo 154
half 半 bàn, 一半 yíbàn 163
half a month (2 weeks) 半个月 bàn'ge yuè 163
half a year 半年 bànnián 163
hall 厅 tīng 176
Han ethnic group 汉 hàn 146
handsome man 帅哥 shuàigē 42
hanger 衣架 yījià 92
happy 喜 xǐ, 欢 huan 66; 快乐 kuàilè 127
hardworking 认真 rènzhēn 147; 用功 yònggōng 156
have 有 yǒu 40
have a get-together 联欢 liánhuān 66
have a look 看看 kànkan 67
have a meeting 开会 kāihuì 118
have class 上课 shàngkè 62
have meals; eat 吃饭 chīfàn 75
have no electric power 没电了 méi diàn le 67
have no money 没有钱 méiyǒu qián 41
have no time 没有时间 méiyǒu shíjiān 41
have rain 有雨 yǒu yǔ 128
have something to do 有事 yǒu shì 163
have time 有时间 yǒu shíjiān 40
have what 有什么 yǒu shénme 25
he; him 他 tā 24
he has 他有 tā yǒu 24
he is at/in 他在 tā zài 24
he is not 他不是 tā bú shì 24
in one's face (of wind) 迎面 yíngmiàn 172
hear 听 tīng 148
hear it said that; hearsay 听说 tīngshuō 148
hear wrong 听错 tīngcuò 87
heating 暖气 nuǎnqì 127
heaven 天 tiān 58
hello; hi 你好 nǐ hǎo 26; 您好 nín hǎo 32
her 她的 tāde 24
here 这 zhè, 这儿 zhèr 83; 这里 zhèli 109
hero 英雄 yīngxióng 35
high-heeled shoes 高跟鞋 gāogēnxié 91
his 他的 tāde 24
his family name 他的姓 tāde xìng 25
history 历 lì, 史 shǐ, 历史 lìshǐ 157
historical material 史料 shǐliào 157
hold on a second; wait a moment 且慢 qiěmàn 137
holiday 节 jié, 节日 jiérì 158
home; family 家 jiā 39
(home) address 住址 zhùzhǐ 185
(home) tutor 家教 jiājiào 39
homework 作业 zuòyè 49
hope 希望 xīwàng 194
hospital 医院 yīyuàn 52
hospitalize 住院 zhùyuàn 176
hot 热 rè 126
hot dog 热狗 règǒu 173
hot water 热水 rè shuǐ 126
hotel 饭店 fàndiàn 75; 宾馆 bīnguǎn 102
hour 小时 xiǎoshí 86; 钟头 zhōngtóu 104
house 房 fáng, 房子 fángzi 175
housing 住房 zhùfáng 185
how 怎 zěn 84
how (much) [used in exclamations] 多么 duōme 25
how about 呢 ne 51; 怎么样 zěnmeyàng 84
How about you? 你呢? nǐ ne? 51
How about your family/home? 你家呢? nǐ jiā ne? 51
how far 多远 duō yuǎn 113
how long (time) 多久 duō jiǔ 146
how many 几 jǐ 40; 几个 jǐge 40
how many people 多少人 duōshǎo rén 44
how many people (in a family) 几口人 jǐkǒu rén 40
how much money 多少钱 duōshao qián 85
how much weight 多重 duō zhòng 44
how old (above ten) 多大 duō dà 44
how old (under ten) 几岁 jǐsuì 43
how tall/high 多高 duō gāo 44
how to 怎么 zěnme 84
how to say it 怎么说 zěnme shuō 84
how to write... 怎么写... zěnme xiě... 84
however 然而 rán'ér 137
howl; roar 吼叫 hǒujiào 24
hundred 百 bǎi 19
hurricane 飓风 jùfēng 129
husband 丈夫 zhàngfu 195; (intimate) 老公 lǎogōng 50

I
I; me 我 wǒ 23
I am... 我是... wǒ shì... 32
I am in/at 我在 wǒ zài 23
I have 我有 wǒ yǒu 23
I wish 但愿 dànyuàn 128
I wish you... 祝您 zhù nín 32
idea 想法 xiǎngfǎ 74
ignorant 无知 wúzhī 100
important news 要闻 yàowén 166
in advance 事先 shìxiān 156
in front of 前 qián, 前边 qiánbian 103
in person 亲自 qīnzì 184
in recent years 近年 jìnnián 113
in the beginning; to start 开始 kāishǐ 145
in the city 城里 chéngli 101
in the night 夜里 yèlǐ 138
in the vicinity 附近 fùjìn 113
inadvisable; not suitable 不宜 bùyí 87
indoor 室内 shìnèi 176
inform; notify; notice 通知 tōngzhī 100
information 息 xī/xi, 信息 xìnxī 167
inn 旅馆 lǚguǎn 102
inside 里 lǐ, 里边 lǐbiān 109
instant noodles 方便面 fāngbiànmiàn 86
instead; on the contrary 反而 fǎn'ér 137
internet 网 wǎng, 网路 wǎnglù 165
intersection 十字路口 shízìlùkǒu 18; 路口 lùkǒu 111
interesting 有趣 yǒuqù 40; 有意思 yǒu yìsi 40
introduce; introduction 介绍 jièshào 192
is/are what 是什么 shì shénme 25
it 它 tā 193

J
jam 果酱 guǒjiàng 184
Japan 日本 Rìběn 59
Japanese yen 日元 Rìyuán 20
jog; run 跑步 pǎobù 192
jogging 慢跑 mànpǎo 185
journey away from home 出远门 chūyuǎnmén 113
joyful event (usually a wedding) 喜事 xǐshì 66
juice 果汁 guǒzhī 184
July 七月 qīyuè 17
June 六月 liùyuè 17
junior male student 师弟 shīdì 50

K
kid 孩子 háizi 92
kilogram 公斤 gōngjīn 191
kilometer 公里 gōnglǐ 111
kin 亲 qīn 48
kindergarten 幼儿园 yòu'éryuán 112
king 国王 guówáng 27
know 知 zhī 100; 知道 zhīdao 101; 认 rèn, 识 shí, 认识 rènshi 147
know how to 会 huì 147
know oneself; intimate friends 知己 zhījǐ 184
knowledge 学问 xuéwèn 32; 识 shí, 知识 zhīshi 147

L
lamb 羊肉 yángròu 195
land 地 dì 76
landlord 房东 fángdōng 175
language 语言 yǔyán, (especially spoken) 语 yǔ 146; 话 huà 155
last month 上个月 shàngge yuè 59
last night 昨晚 zuówǎn 58; (full version of 昨晚) 昨天晚上 zuótiān wǎnshang 58
last time 上次 shàngcì 134
last week 上周 shàngzhōu 74
last year 去年 qùnián 134
late 晚 wǎn 77
later; afterwards 后来 hòulái 118
laugh heartily 欢笑 huānxiào 66
laundry detergent 洗衣粉 xǐyīfěn 183
laywer 律师 lǜshī 50
learn 学 xué 50; 学习 xuéxí 155
learning 学习 xuéxí 155
leather shoes 皮鞋 píxié 91
leave home; go out 出门 chūmén 119
left 左 zuǒ 119
left hand 左手 zuǒshǒu 119
left side 左边 zuǒbiān 119
letter (of alphabet) 字母 zìmǔ 26
level 水平 shuǐpíng 65; 等 děng 191
library 图书馆 túshūguǎn 102
life; live 生活 shēnghuó 51
light 亮光 liàngguāng 121
lightly; easily 轻易 qīngyì 149
like 喜欢 xǐhuan, 喜爱 xǐài 66
like that... 那么... nàme... 25
line; row 行 háng 110
listen; listening 听 tīng 148
listening, speaking, reading and writing 听说读写 tīng shuō dú xiě 165
listening proficiency 听力 tīnglì 148
literate 识字 shízì 147
literature 文学 wénxué 145
little 很少 hěn shǎo 93
live; reside; stop 住 zhù 185
living room 客厅 kètīng 176
long 很久 hěn jiǔ, (time ago) 久 jiǔ 146
long skirt 长裙 chángqún 91
"long time no see" 好久不见 hǎo jiǔ bú jiàn 146
look 看 kàn 67; 视 shì 68; 看起来 kànqǐlai 109; 容貌 róngmào 149
look for 找 zhǎo 185
look for whom 找谁 zhǎo shéi 185
look for work 找工作 zhǎo gōngzuò 185
looked; watched; read 看了 kànle 87
looked down on 看不起 kànbuqǐ 109

principal of a school 校长 xiàozhǎng 118
proceeding 前边 qiánbian 103
(progressive marker) 正在 zhèng zài 196
pronunciation 发音 fāyīn 183
public; metric 公 gōng 111
public bus 公共汽车 gōnggòng qìchē 111
purse; wallet 钱包 qiánbāo 85
put on 穿上 chuānshàng 95

Q
question 问题 wèntí 32
(question form) ...吗? ...ma? 60

R
rain 雨 yǔ, (*verb*) 下雨 xiàyǔ 128
rainy day 雨天 yǔtiān 128
read 读 dú 165
read again 再读 zài dú 61
reading 看书 kànshū 67; 阅读 yuèdú 165
reason 因 yīn, 原因 yuányīn 181
recent time 最近 zuìjìn 154
reception hall; lounge 大厅 dàtīng 176
recognize 认 rèn 147; 认出 rènchū 147
recognize words 认字 rènzì 26
regret 后悔 hòuhuǐ 118
relative 亲戚 qīnqi 48
rent (money) 房租 fángzū 175
repeat 复 fù, 重复 chóngfù 155
repeatly 重复 chóngfù 155
respond; reply 回复 huífù 155
restaurant 饭馆儿 fànguǎnr, 饭店 fàndiàn 75; 餐厅 cāntīng 176
rest 休 xiū, 息 xī/xi 167
restroom 厕所 cèsuǒ 138
retire 退休 tuìxiū 167
result 结果 jiéguǒ 184
return 复 fù 155
review 复习 fùxí 155
rice 米饭 mǐfàn 75
rich; to have money 有钱 yǒuqián 85
right 对吗? duìma 60; 右 yòu 120
right hand 右手 yòushǒu 120
right now 现 xiàn 120
rise 起 qǐ 109
road 道 dào 101; 路 lù, 马路 mǎlù 111
room 间 jiān, 房间 fángjiān 164; 房 fáng 175; 室 shì 176
roommate 室友 shìyou 36
round trip journey 来回 láihuí 134
rumor 传闻 chuánwén 166
run really fast 跑得真快 pǎode zhēn kuài 83

S
sad 难过 nánguò 149
same 相同 xiāngtóng 136
Saturday 星期六 xīngqīliù 17
save 节省 jiéshěng 158
say 说 shuō 148
say again; additionally 再说 zài shuō 61
say goodbye to someone 道别 dàobié 101
scenery 风景 fēngjǐng 129
school 校 xiào, 学校 xuéxiào 118; 学院 xuéyuàn 176
school bus 校车 xiàochē 118
school term 学期 xuéqī 60
school uniform 校服 xiàofú 93
science 科学 kēxué 50
seaside 海边 hǎibiān 112
see 看 kàn, 看见 kànjiàn 67
see a doctor 看医生 kàn yīsheng 67
see you tomorrow 明天见 míngtiān jiàn 61
seem 看起来 kànqǐlai 109
self 自 zì, 己 jǐ, 自己 zìjǐ 184
sell 卖 mài 117
sell to 卖给 mài gěi 117
senior in college 大四 dàsì 16
seniority among brothers and sisters 排行 páiháng 110
sense; reason 道理 dàolǐ 101
separate 分开 fēnkāi 103
September 九月 jiǔyuè 59
service 服 fú 93
seven 七 qī 17
seven days 七天 qītiān 17
seven years old 七岁 qīsuì 17
shadow; reflection; image 影 yǐng 68
share 分享 fēnxiǎng 103
she; her 她 tā 24
she has 她有 tā yǒu 24
she is 她是 tā shì 24
she is at/in 她在 tā zài 24
shoe 鞋 xié 91
short skirt 短裙 duǎnqún 91
shortcut 近路 jìnlù 113
shorts 短裤 duǎnkù 91
Sichuan (place name) 四川 Sìchuān 16
side 方 fang 76; 旁 páng, 边 biān 112
silver 银 yín 109
silver color 银色 yínsè 109
Sinology 汉学 Hànxué 146
sisters 姐妹 jiěmèi 43
sit; by (car/bus) 坐 zuò 174
sit at; on 坐在 zuò zài 111
six 六 liù 17
six (for chairs) 六把 liùbǎ 17
six hundred 六百 liùbǎi 19
six months 六个月 liùgeyuè 17
ski 滑雪 huáxuě 128
skilled; proficient 熟练 shúliàn 154
skirt 裙 qún, 裙子 qúnzi 91
sky 天 tiān 58
sleep 觉 jiào 83; 睡觉 shuìjiào 83; 睡眠 shuìmián 163; 睡 shuì 163
slippers 拖鞋 tuōxié 91
slow 慢 màn 185
slow-moving 缓慢 huǎnmàn 185
small; little 小 xiǎo 86
small change 零钱 língqián 19
small token of appreciation 小意思 xiǎo yìsi 136
smart 聪明 cōngming 58
snacks; small bites 小吃 xiǎochī 75
snow (*noun*) 雪 xuě 128
snowman 雪人 xuěrén 128
snowscape 雪景 xuějǐng 128
so 这么 zhème 25; 所以 suóyi 138; 然 rán 156
so-called 所谓 suǒwèi 138
so wonderful! 太好了! tài hǎo le! 85
soda 汽水 qìshuǐ 175
software 软件 ruǎnjiàn 92
solution 方法 fāngfǎ 76
sometimes 有时候 yǒu shíhou 78
son 儿子 érzi 33
sorry 对不起 duìbuqǐ 108
sound; musical note 音 yīn 183
south 南 nán, 南方 nánfāng 135
southeast 东南 dōngnán 135
Southeast Asia 东南亚 Dōngnányà 69
southwest 西南 xīnán 135
soybean 黄豆 huángdòu 182
(space) comfy 舒适 shūshì 130
space 空间 kōngjiān 164
speak 说 shuō 148
speak a bit more slowly 说慢一点儿 shuō màn yìdiǎnr 185
speak of 说到 shuō dào 148
speak well 说得好 shuōdehǎo 83
specialized shop 专卖店 zhuānmàidiàn 117
speech 话 huà 155
spend (money or time) 花 huā 117
spend money 花钱 huā qián 117
spend time 花时间 huā shíjiān 117
sports coach; trainer 教练 jiàoliàn 154
sports pants 运动裤 yùndòngkù 91
sports shoes 运动鞋 yùndòngxié 91
spread out 张 Zhāng 172
spring 春 chūn, 春天 chūntiān 129
spring break 春假 chūnjià 129
Spring Festival/Chinese New Year 春节 chūnjié 129
square 方 fang 76
standard 水平 shuǐpíng 65
star 星 xīng 60; 星星 xīngxing 60
stay warm 保暖 bǎonuǎn 127
still; or 还 hái 76
stir (the emotions) 动 dòng 166
store 店 diàn, 商店 shāngdiàn 117
store clerk 店员 diànyuán 117
story 故事 gùshì 163
street 街 jiē 110
strength 力气 lìqì 105
student 学生 xuésheng 50; 生 shēng 51
study 学 xué 50; 习 xí 155; 读 dú, 读书 dúshū 165
study (i.e., a room) 书房 shūfáng 67
studying 看书 kànshū 67; 读书 dúshū 165
style 样子 yàngzi 84
successful; have good prospects 有出息 yǒu chūxi 167
suddenly 突然 tūrán 156
suit pants 西裤 xīkù 91
summer 夏 xià, 夏天 xiàtiān 129
summer camp 夏令营 xiàlìngyíng 129
sunrise 日出 rìchū 59
supper; dinner 晚饭 wǎnfàn 77
surf the internet 上网 shàngwǎng 165
surface; face 面 miàn 120
(surname) 谢 Xiè 61; 夏 Xià 129; 舒 Shū 130; 史 Shǐ 157; 张 Zhāng 162; 颜 Yán 181
surnamed Li 姓李 xìng Lǐ 27
surnamed Wang 姓王 xìng Wáng 25
surnamed Wang 姓王 xìng Wáng 27
suspend schooling 休学 xiūxué 167
sweater 毛衣 máoyī 92

T
table; desk 桌子 zhuōzi 92
take a break; close 休息 xiūxi 167
take away 带走 dàizǒu 103; 拿去 náqu 134
talkative; verbose 多话 duōhuà 155
talking; talk 说话 shuōhuà 148
task 考验 kǎoyàn 154
tea 茶 chá 174
tea house 茶馆 cháguǎn 174
teacher 老师 lǎoshī 50; master 师 shī 50
teacher and student 老师和学生 lǎoshī hé xuésheng 48
television 电视 diànshì 68
tell a lie 说谎 shuōhuǎng 148
ten 十 shí 18
ten o'clock 十点 shídiǎn 18
tennis 网球 wǎngqiú 69
test 考 kǎo, 考试 kǎoshì, 考验 kǎoyàn 154
textbook 课本 kèběn 158
thank 感谢 gǎnxiè 61
thank you 谢谢您 xièxie nín 32; 谢谢 xièxie "Thank you" 61
thanks a lot 多谢 duō xiè 61
that 那 nà, 那个 nàge 84
that is 那是 nà shì 84
that's all right; no connection 没关系 méi guānxi 41
the best 最好 zuìhǎo 154
The Book of Changes 易经 Yìjīng 149
the day after tomorrow 后天 hòutiān 118
the day before yesterday 前天 qiántiān 103
the first time 第一次 dìyīcì 134
The Great Wall 长城 Chángchéng 101
the Han dynasty 汉朝 Hàncháo 146
the last 最后 zuìhòu 154
The Mid-Autumn Festival 中秋节 Zhōngqiūjié 130
the same 一样 yíyàng 84
the south; southern 南方 nánfāng 135
the year before last 前年 qiánnián 103
The Zhang family 张家 Zhāngjiā 172
their... 他们的... tāmende... 35
theme 题 tí 192
then 就 jiù 104; 然后 ránhòu 156
then 然后 ránhòu 156
then you'll have arrived 就到了 jiù dàole 104
there 那 nà, 那儿 nàr 84; 那里 nàli 109
these 这些 zhèxiē 83
they; them (male) 他们 tāmen 35; (female) 她们 tāmen 35
thing 东西 dōngxi 69; 事 shì, 事情 shìqing 163
think 想 xiǎng 74; 觉得 juéde 83; 认为 rènwéi 147
this 这 zhè, 这个 zhège 83
this is 这是 zhè shì 83
this piece of clothing 这件衣服 zhèjiàn yīfu 92
this time 这次 zhècì 134
this year 今年 jīnnián 57
those 那些 nàxiē 84
three 三 sān 16

U

V

W

Y

Z